CHURCHES SPEAK ON:

Sex and Family Life

Sources for Additional Research

For further information on the religious groups covered in this publication, consult J. Gordon Melton's *Encyclopedia of American Religions*, which contains information on approximately 1,600 churches, sects, cults, temples, societies, missions, and other North American religious organizations.

For additional information on the beliefs held by the religious groups covered in this publication, consult the *Encyclopedia of American Religions: Religious Creeds*, a companion volume to the *Encyclopedia of American Religions* that provides the creeds, confessions, statements of faith, and articles of religion of the groups covered.

To locate organizations concerned with the topics covered in this publication, consult the following terms in the Name and Keyword Index to Gale's *Encyclopedia of Associations*:

- Birth Control

- Contraception

- Divorce

- Families

- Family

- Marriage

- Remarried

- Sex

- Sex Addiction

- Sexual Abuse

- Sexual Freedom

- Sexual Health

- Sexuality

ISSN 1043-9609

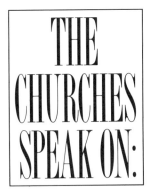

Sex and Family Life

Official Statements from Religious Bodies and Ecumenical Organizations

J. Gordon Melton
Nicholas Piediscalzi, Contributing Editor

 *Gale Research Inc.* • DETROIT • LONDON

Ielton

ntributing Editor

Gale Research Inc. Staff

Amy Lucas, *Senior Editor*

Bradley J. Morgan, *Project Coordinator*

Aided by: Donald B. Akers, Terri Kessler, Ruth E. Littmann

Donald G. Dillaman, *Programming Consultant*

Victoria B. Cariappa, *Research Manager*
Jack Radike, *Research Supervisor*
Phil Naud and Phyllis Sheperd, *Editorial Assistant*

Mary Beth Trimper, *Production Manager*
Marilyn Jackman, *External Production Associate*

Arthur Chartow, *Art Director*
C. J. Jonik, *Keyliner*

The paper used in this publication meets the minimum requirements
of American National Standard for Information Sciences—Permanence
Paper for Printed Library Materials, ANSI Z39.48-1984.

ISBN 0-8103-7649-0
ISSN 1043-9609

Printed in the United States of America

Published simultaneously in the United Kingdom
by Gale Research International Limited
(An affiliated company of Gale Research Inc.)

Contents

Statements

Roman Catholic Church

Statements in this section are arranged chronologically by issuing date.

Protestant and Eastern Orthodox Churches

This section is arranged alphabetically by individual church, religious body,
or ecumenical organization; the statements issued by each organization are
presented chronologically within that organization.

Jewish Groups

This section is arranged alphabetically by individual religious organization;
the statements issued by each organization are presented chronologically
within that organization.

Other Religious Bodies

This section is arranged alphabetically by individual church, religious body, or ecumenical organization; the statements issued by each organization are presented chronologically within that organization.

Preface

The Churches Speak is a quarterly series of monographs which systematically brings together the major official pronouncements of North American religious bodies and ecumenical organizations on the issues dominating today's headlines. Each monograph is devoted to a single topic and provides an overview of the topic itself, its historical background, and the full range of opinions found in the individual church statements. The statements themselves provide a unique and conveniently arranged survey of opinion on important contemporary issues, cutting across theological and denominational boundaries to influence the climate of social and political thought in our culture.

The formal statements issued by churches and other religious bodies are intended primarily to inform and guide their members, adherents, and supporters on the issue in question. These statements often attain additional importance, however, since they also exert influence on the actions of the religious agencies, clergy, and church administrators who initiate, direct, and regulate organizational programs. Church statements are also indirectly aimed at nonchurch members, in an attempt to alter public policy, mobilize public opinion, or advocate changes in legislation. And they can also become the focal point of intense controversy, functioning as the bulwark against which many people direct their dissent on a given issue. This controversy can become magnified within the issuing organization itself, when a significant minority of its members dissent from the positions taken by its hierarchies, judicatories, and boards of social concerns.

Focus is on Contemporary Topics From Major Religious Bodies

Each issue of *The Churches Speak* focuses on a single topic or a few closely related topics chosen for their high current public interest. Topics covered represent a wide range of vital social and political issues, such as AIDS, abortion, capital punishment, pornography, homosexuality, the ordination of women, and euthanasia. Statements of major North American churches and religious organizations are included for each topic, providing comprehensive representation of the full range of opinions held on each topic.

The documents included in *The Churches Speak* were obtained through a mailing to all of the religious bodies in North America with more than 100,000 members. On any given issue, additional churches and religious organizations (including some outside of North America), and even some secular organizations known to have a special interest in the topic under consideration, were also solicited for their statements. Other statements have been identified in the files of the Institute for the Study of American Religion in Santa Barbara, California.

While most large churches and religious bodies make formal statements on important issues, it should be noted that many of the more than 1,500 denominations and religious organizations located in North America will not formulate any official statement or speak out on such issues. A number of religious bodies, including some of the largest denominations, do not make such statements as a matter of principle. Rather, they choose to leave actions and beliefs concerning social issues strictly up to individual effort and opinion.

Authentic Texts Used for All Statements

The statements presented in this series are in their authentic form, although obvious typographical errors have been corrected. The original wording, grammar, and punctuation of each statement remains intact. No attempt has been made to introduce foreign material or explanatory notes into the body of the statements' text.

Arrangement and Content

Each issue of *The Churches Speak* begins with an introductory essay which provides an overview of the topic itself and traces its recent historical manifestations. This essay also summarizes, compares, and contrasts the opinions found in the individual statements, allowing the user to place each one in the appropriate context. Each essay concludes with bibliographic citations to sources for further reading on the topic.

The statements presented in each monograph are arranged into four main sections based on broad religious families or traditions: The Roman Catholic Church (which represents the single largest religious body in the United States); Protestant and Eastern Orthodox Churches; Jewish Groups; and Other Religious Bodies.

Within the Roman Catholic Church section, statements are arranged chronologically by issuing date. The remaining sections are subarranged alphabetically by individual churches, religious bodies, or ecumenical organizations; the statements issued by each organization are presented chronologically within that organization.

Each of the four religious family sections is preceded by a note which provides background information on the family and analysis of its perspective on the issue in question. Individual statements contain the following elements:

Issuing organization. The name of the religious body or ecumenical organization issuing the statement.

Statement name. The actual or formal title of the statement. When no formal title is given, a descriptive title has been assigned.

Text of statement. The text of the statement is presented in its original form.

Notes. These appear in italic type following the text of each statement. When applicable, these remarks provide background information on the issuing organization's membership size and geographic distribution, and details about the circumstances under which the statement was made—including when it was passed, why it was passed, and whether or not it is binding on church members.

Index to Organizations, Statements, and Subjects Provided

To facilitate access to the material presented, each issue of *The Churches Speak* contains an Index to Organizations, Statements, and Subjects included in that issue. The index lists, in a single alphabetical sequence, the full titles of all the statements, the names of all religious bodies and ecumenical organizations mentioned in the statements' texts and notes, and specific subjects covered within the statements. Statement titles and organization names are also listed by important keywords that appear in their titles/names. Citations in the index refer to page numbers; page numbers rendered in boldface after an organization name indicate the location of that organization's statement(s) within the main text.

Sources of Additional Information

Additional information on many of the religious bodies covered in *The Churches Speak* can be found in the *Encyclopedia of American Religions*. The *Encyclopedia* provides details on approximately 1600 religious and spiritual groups in the United States and Canada, and is divided into two parts. The first part contains an essay covering the development of American religion, an essay providing a historical survey of religion in Canada, and historical essays grouped by general religious family. The second part contains directory sections listing individual churches and groups constituting the religious families discussed in the historical essays.

A companion volume, the *Encyclopedia of American Religions: Religious Creeds,* provides a comprehensive compilation of 464 religious creeds, confessions, statements of faith, summaries of belief, and articles of religion currently acknowledged by many of the churches or religious groups described in the *Encyclopedia of American Religions.* It also includes extensive notes on the history and textual variations of creeds, reflecting changing social, political, and doctrinal climates throughout the centuries. The material is arranged by major religious families, following, with minor variations, the approach used in the *Encyclopedia.*

Institute for the Study of American Religion

The Institute for the Study of American Religion was founded in 1969 for the purpose of researching and disseminating information about the numerous religious groups in the United States. More recently, the Institute's scope has been expanded to include religious groups in Canada, making it the only research facility of its kind to cover so broad a range of activity. After being located for many years in Evanston, Illinois, the Institute moved to Santa Barbara, California, in 1985. At that time, its collection of more than 25,000 books and its extensive files covering individual religious groups were donated to the Special Collections department of the library of the University of California—Santa Barbara. *The Churches Speak* has been compiled in part from the Institute's collection.

Suggestions Are Welcome

Users with particular questions about a religious group, suggested topics for coverage in or changes to *The Churches Speak,* or other information are invited to write to the Institute in care of its Director:

> Dr. J. Gordon Melton
> Institute for the Study of American Religion
> Box 90709
> Santa Barbara, CA 93190-0709

Introductory Essay:

The Changing Vision of Sexuality and the Family
by Nicholas Piediscalzi

Social Changes Affecting Sexuality and the Family

Dramatic societal changes and technological innovations over the past 30 years have transformed the ways in which groups and individuals view sexuality and the family. Fifteen of these alterations are outlined below. Some pertain solely to sexuality, some only to marriage, while others concern both.

1) The introduction of the highly reliable birth control pill made it possible for individuals to engage in sexual intercourse without the fear of pregnancy, thereby removing one of the major inhibitors of coitus outside of marriage and, for some, within marriage.

2) The rise of the feminist movement paved the way for new understandings of female and male roles which eschew the double standard previously practiced in sexual ethics and empower women to make independent decisions about their sexual behavior. This movement also contributed significantly to the realignment of power relationships in marriage by calling for equal authority and shared power for both wife and husband.

3) The acceleration of the onset of puberty in both girls and boys, very early adolescent dating without chaperonage, and exposure to explicit sexual scenes in television programs, movies, and advertising have introduced young people to their sexuality and forced them to make decisions about actualizing their sexuality much earlier than adolescents of previous time periods.

4) The delay of marriage for educational, economic, and personal reasons has provided opportunity and incentive to engage in sexual activity outside of marriage.

5) A new emphasis on the contributions that sexual intercourse can make to the establishment and nurture of fulfilling personal relationships has led many to argue against those who insist that coitus must be reserved for marriage and those who claim that the only purpose of sex and marriage is procreation.

6) The inability of husbands to provide the financial resources necessary to maintain an adequate standard of living in developed and emerging nations has forced wives to take up employment outside the home, thereby changing the family pattern characteristic of the late nineteenth and early twentieth centuries in Western nations and the century-old traditional arrangements in emerging societies. According to the Anglican Consultative Council's report "Transforming Families and Communities" (see index), as the nations of the world industrialize and move toward establishing the contemporary nuclear family as normative, there is a "shift from the 'sacred family' with its more pragmatic, rational philosophy which encourages family members to adopt new goals for themselves and the community."

7) A growing divorce rate has produced an increasing number of single parent families, usually with the mother as the head. Also, it has added many individuals with prior sexual experiences to the growing number of single persons, many of whom feel the need to fulfill their emotional and sexual needs outside the bonds of marriage.

8) The growing tendency for couples to live together without committing themselves to marriage has changed attitudes towards tradtional family values and sexual mores.

9) Experiments in communal living in the 1960s and early 1970s encouraged alternative family arrangements.

10) A growing knowledge of the variety of family arrangements practiced throughout the world has forced people to recognize that the monogamous nuclear family is only one of many options available to human beings. As a result, some groups, including the Anglican Consultative Council (see index), have defined the family as "permanent or temporary, nuclear or extended, married or not, but it will include households of both sexes, and in the majority of cases it will be a place where children live and grow and develop."

ll) Historical-critical studies of the Bible have revealed that the Bible sanctioned different forms of family life, thereby challenging (for some) the claim that God wills the monogamous nuclear family.

12) Historical-critical studies have also revealed that the Christian community, under the influence of Hellenistic categories, adopted a dualistic interpretation of human nature that pits an evil body against a good soul. Sexuality, being solely identified with the body in this tradition, was declared evil and to be avoided. This view contradicted the Hebrew roots of Christianity, which asserted that sexuality was good and not to be avoided.

13) The industrialization and urbanization of the world, accompanied by economic and geographic mobility for many individuals and families, has weakened traditional family and communal ties and the traditional authority exercised by these institutions over family patterns and sexual morality.

14) A growing emphasis upon individual freedom, especially in the personal realm, has challenged the authority families, communities, and religious institutions have exercised in the area of sexual morality. Individuals now claim the right and prerogative to make such decisions according to the dictates of their own consciences rather than to those of an institutional authority.

15) The publication of the Kinsey report, which revealed that many individuals did not adhere to the sexual mores of their primary institutions, led many to conclude that society needed a new sexual morality which reflected common practice. Others argued, and continue to argue, that the behavior of the majority is neither an adequate nor proper foundation for morality.

Range of Religious Positions

These 15 changes have forced religious bodies to reexamine their teachings on sexuality and the family. Some have restated their position without change but with added vigor. Others have issued new statements with minor modifications. Still others appointed commissions to study the areas of sexuality and the family and to issue reports for discussion and action. Many of these reports recommend radical changes in their institutions' theologies and moral teachings on sexuality and the family. While most of these reports have been accepted, they have not been officially adopted. Instead they have been remanded to official bodies and/or local congregations for further study and discussion. In some instances, these reports have stimulated minority reports and the formation of organizations to prevent the parent organization from adopting the reports or incorporating their ideas and suggestions into the groups' theologies and moral teachings.

The positions taken by religious bodies tend to fall fairly consistently along the conservative/liberal lines established for other topics. For example, a Christian church that is conservative in its theology (i.e., promotes a literal interpretation of the Bible) has likely taken conservative positions on other personal and social moral issues and will almost certainly teach that sexual intercourse is reserved solely for marriage, that patriarchal, nuclear families are biblically mandated, and that adultery is the only admissable cause for divorce. Some of these groups also hold that an individual who is awarded a divorce on the grounds of adultery may not remarry, while others allow the person to enter a new marriage.

A Christian church with a liberal theology (i.e., promotes a more contextual, metaphoric, or allegorical interpretation of the Bible) has likely taken liberal positions on other personal and moral issues and will tend to adopt a more flexible stance on sexuality, the family, divorce, and the remarriage of divorced prople. However, most, if not all, continue to uphold in their official statements the primacy of the monogamous marriage relationship and tend to discourage the practice of sexual intercourse outside of marriage.

Conservative Christians who claim to interpret the Bible literally tend to project a late nineteenth and early twentieth century view of sexuality and the family onto the Bible and overlook the fact that the Hebrew Bible, while prohibiting adultery, does not proscribe premarital sexual intercourse.[1] The same is true for the New Testament, with the exception of several epistles which reserve sexual intercourse for the marriage relationship.

Liberal Christians recognize that the Bible records various and different patterns of family life and sexual morality. Therefore, they claim, it is impossible to derive a single pattern for the family or a single sexual morality from the Bible. On the other hand, they tend to teach that the Bible provides the norms of covenant, love, and fidelity to define or redefine family patterns and sexual moralities according to the needs of individuals and groups in any given period.

Whether Roman Catholic or Protestant, conservative or liberal, most contemporary Christian groups, following the creation accounts in the book of Genesis, reject all negative evaluations of sexuality and declare that it is a good gift from God for human enjoyment. At the same time, they contend that, because human beings are sinful creatures who live in an imperfect world, they often misuse or abuse their sexuality and prevent themselves from experiencing the full potential and joy of sexual life.

Most of these groups, utilizing insights gained from the human sciences, also call for a wide definition of sexuality. The Church of the Brethren's 1983 "Annual Conference Statement on Human Sexuality from a Christian Perspective" (see index) states that sexuality is one of humanity's foundational dimensions: "It encompasses all that we are when we say 'I am female' or 'I am male.' Physical attributes, including genitals, are an integral part of our sexual identity;'however, sexuality is not just physical. It includes all thinking, feeling, acting and interacting that is derived from our maleness and femaleness."

This vision of an all encompassing sexuality places emphasis on its relational power rather than on genital acts and calls for a morality which gives greater attention to the intention and quality of concrete relations and less to simple, abstract rules about when to or not to engage in coitus. The individuals who hold this view also assert that the biblical concepts of covenant, love, fidelity, and justice support their claim. They also believe that an affirmative and all encompassing view of sexuality will help the church overcome its counterproductive preoccupation with genital sex and enable the church to help individuals affirm their multidimensional sexuality and thereby enrich and expand their lives.

Those who hold a wide view of sexuality, and a few who do not, also claim that the purposes of marriage are companionship, personal and social fulfillment, and procreation. Many within this group also teach that marriage reflects the dynamic interaction and unity of the "male" and "female" dimensions of the diety. For these individuals, sexual intercourse within marriage serves functions that are as equally important, if not more so, than procreation. Therefore, sexual ethics for married couples should include sanctions for the practice of birth control.

Christians following the New Testament also claim that fidelity in marriage reflects the faithful relationship Jesus the Christ maintains with the church, thereby enhancing the religious dimensions of marriage.

With a few exceptions, religious groups and individuals who ascribe personal, social, and religious purposes to sexuality insist that these goals may only be achieved within a monogamous relationship. Only a faithful and trusting relationship can provide the atmosphere and conditions conducive to the successful fulfillment of these purposes.

Christian groups and a few others are also making concerted efforts to gain recognition for the validity and significance of the single life. Marriage should not be elevated to a superior position which leads those in the single life to feel that they are defective or inferior. Furthermore, they recommend that religious bodies give more attention to the needs of these individuals than they have in the past.

With very few exceptions, religious groups now recognize the prevalence of divorce and the pain and problems it causes for many of their members and their children. Therefore, they call for establishing a communal spirit of empathy and acceptance and special programs for divorced individuals and their children.

Most religious groups also are turning their attention to the relationship of sexuality and the family to public policy and social structures. They recognize, according to the authors of the United Church of Christ's "Human Sexuality: A Preliminary Study" (see index), that "human sexuality is part of our experience, with significant implications for many arenas of life. Sexual awareness plays a role in decisions we make about politics, economics, law, medicine, and a large number of other institutions."[2] Likewise, social structures influence how individuals view and experience sexuality and how they relate to each other in family settings. For example, the use of sexual allure by the advertising industry creates false expectations that can never be met and that lead many to experience sexual frustration. Structural racism supports inequalities in the realms of employment and housing that mitigate against the fulfillment of family life. These issues and many more like them lead many church groups to study and take stands on policy issues and societal structures which have a direct bearing on sexuality and the family. Examples of this trend can be seen in Cardinal John O'Connor's statement "Addressing the Issues of Work and the Family" (see index), in statements from the Southern Baptist Convention (see index), and in statements from Jewish organizations.

Finally, many of the religious bodies in the second and third groupings are seeking to redress the unequal treatment of women in society at large and within their own ranks. Some are only making token gestures while others are taking radical measures. Some observers believe that the question of complete equality for women presents Christian communities with a challenge as serious and momentous as the one faced by the early church when it was forced to decide whether to require gentile converts to fulfill all of the ritual practices and cultural customs of Judaism.

This summary of how religious groups are responding to the revising of attitudes toward sexuality and the family in the closing years of the twentieth century provides a background and context for the specific and detailed discussion of the views, policies, and practices of the selected religious bodies discussed below.

Approaches of the Major Traditions: Roman Catholic

John T. Noonan, Jr., in his monumental and definitive *Contraception: A History of Its Treatment by the Catholic Theologians and Canonists,* asserts that the Roman Catholic Church over the centuries has defined the nature and purpose of sexuality and the family by combining unique "appeals to divine instruction, natural laws, and psychological and social consequences."[3] Some words from Pope Paul VI's encyclical *Humanae Vitae* (see index) illustrate this claim: "Such questions [about procreation] required from the teaching authority of the Church a new and deeper reflection upon the principles of the moral teaching on marriage: a teaching founded on the natural law, illuminated and enriched by divine revelation." He adds that the natural law, like the law of the Gospel, "is also an expression of the will of God, the faithful fulfillment of which is equally necessary for salvation."

Early Catholic theologians turned to natural law philosophies and moralities on sexuality because the Bible, especially the New Testament, gives little attention to the many different issues and problems individuals confront in their sexual lives. Noonan points out that basic Roman Catholic natural law teaching on sexuality is derived from Stoic philosophy that, unlike the Hebrew Bible, distrusted pleasure and insisted that every human act must serve a rational purpose. Musonius Rufus, an influential Stoic teacher in first century A.D. Rome "taught that marital intercourse was morally right only if its purpose were procreative; intercourse for pleasure within the limits of marriage was reprehensible."[4] Because the Stoics distrusted affection and all forms of dependence, they were unable to derive the purpose of sexuality and marriage from humanity's psychological, emotional, and spiritual dimensions. Rather, they located it in the biological. "The supreme norm for them was not love, but nature."[5]

This limited view of marriage and sexuality continued in the Roman Catholic Church until the twentieth century. The Second Vatican Council (1962-1965) introduced a new dimension to this teaching when it proclaimed in its 1965 Pastoral Constitution, *Gaudium et Spes* (see index), that sexuality and marriage were designed by God not only for procreation but also for the personal growth of the marriage partners. This innovation, according to a study on human sexuality commisioned by the Catholic Theological Society of America, enlarged the natural law argument to include the psychological, emotional, and spiritual dimensions of sexuality. *Gaudium et Spes* asserts that, because the human person is responsible for integrating her or his various dimensions, personal and interpersonal norms must be used in defining human sexuality. *Gaudium et Spes* "calls attention to the human quality of expressions of sexuality and how they must contribute to the growth and development of the person."[6] It also asks the church to recognize "the social and communal dimensions of human sexuality" while grounding all three dimensions (person-al, social, and communal) in God—"the source and summit of human sexuality sanctified in a special way in the sacramental union that is marriage. . . ."[7]

The society's study claims that this new "personalist" approach was applied to every area of human sexuality by the Sacred Congregation for the Doctrine of the Faith's 1975 document, "Declaration on Certain Questions Concerning Sexual Ethics" (see index). It places sexuality at the center of human development:

> The human person is so profoundly affected by sexuality that it must be considered as one of the factors which give to each individual's life the principal traits that distinguish it. In fact it is from sex that the human person receives the characteristics which on the biological, psychological and spiritual levels, make that person a man

or a woman, and thereby largely condition his or her progress towards maturity and insertion into society.

This new emphasis, which has been reiterated in subsequent official Catholic statements, "prepares the way," states the society's study, "for a far more positive and wholistic approach to sexual questions."[8] However, the Vatican continues to impede the development and application of this new personalist norm by holding fast to *Humanae Vitae*'s teaching that "each and every marriage act must remain open to the transmission of life" and the Curia's attempt to silence theologians who question this emphasis. As a result, serious disagreement exists between the Vatican and some bishops, clergy, and laity. For example, Father Andrew M. Greeley argues that, according to the findings of contemporary biological and social sciences,

> frequent and passionate sex between the male and the female of the human species is "natural" because it reinforces the quasi pair bonding, and to abstain from sex is to some extent "unnatural" because it weakens the quasi pair bonding. It would appear, therefore, that the Catholic attempt to minimize marital sexuality in the name of the natural law in fact betrays that law. The refusal of Church leaders and Church theologians to take seriously what the human sciences teach us about the nature of human nature is a violation of the tradition which in the great natural-law thinkers like Thomas Aquinas was always empirical, seeking to learn by investigation instead of deriving propositions on *a priori* grounds about the nature of human nature.[9]

Greeley's outspoken views reflect those of many other Catholic clergy and laity, which led Cardinal Joseph Bernardin of Chicago (see index) to assert at the 1980 International Synod of Bishops that "a significant gap [exists] between . . . [the church's] teaching on sexual morality and the ideas and attitudes on the same subject held by many of the laity and clergy. . . . This constitutes a serious crisis for the church, intellectually, spiritually and organizationally."

Many bishops and clergy seek to alleviate some of the tension between the church and the laity on the issue of birth control by referring their parishioners to the section in *Gaudium et Spes* on the primacy of individual conscience where it is stated that, in the last analysis, all moral decisions are to be made by the individual conscience in communion with God. In light of this teaching, these bishops and clergy neither condemn nor refuse to administer the sacraments to those individuals in their flocks who in good conscience choose to practice birth control.

The debate between the Vatican and its bishops, clergy, and laity on how to apply *Gaudium et Spes* "personalist" norm to every area of sexual and marital morality will continue for years to come.

Approaches of the Major Traditions: Protestant and Eastern Orthodox

The Protestant and Eastern Orthodox groups represented in this volume, with the exception of one or two, trace their roots to one of three traditions: Lutheran, Reformed, or Anabaptist. At the time of their origins, all three denied that marriage is a sacrament and rejected the Roman Catholic elevation of celibacy to a special status above marriage. For these groups, marriage is one of God's holy ordinances which symbolizes the spiritual unity of Christ with his bride the church.

Lutheran and Reformed Christians recommended monogamous marriage. The Anabaptists were divided. Some encouraged monogamous marriage but counselled couples to engage in sexual intercourse only for procreation. They held that the establishment and maintenance of strong affectional and sexual ties would impede faithful and loyal service to God, who calls each person to be a missionary. Others practiced experimental forms of group marriage. They believed that they were establishing eschatological communities. Others followed Paul's admonition to remain single and celibate, if possible, because Christ's Second Coming was imminent.

According to William G. Cole, neither Luther nor Calvin viewed "sex as a means of expressing conjugal love, of symbolizing physically a union of two personalities. Procreation remained for them as for Augustine and Aquinas, the only really positive purpose of sex."[10] However, neither one believed that sex in and of itself was sinful. Rather, because of the universality of sin, sex, like all other human acts, is tainted by sin.

Luther viewed marriage and the family as schools in character and virtue for husband and wife and parents and children. Luther taught that the home is "where the Christian virtues find their readiest exemplification, and, whereas in Catholicism monasticism is the sphere for the cultivation of the counsels of perfection, in Protestantism the home is as it were a functional substitute."[11]

While Calvin believed that the only purpose of sex was procreation, he taught that marriage was instituted by God to enable men and women to establish mutual societies in which they help each other come to completion. Calvin elevated women to a new status for his times. "The principal purpose of the female is not sexual but social. She is to be a companion to the man primarily and only secondarily the agent of generation."[12]

The late Roland Bainton claimed that Calvin's followers, especially English Puritans, developed a new concept of marriage from his teaching on "companionability."[13] However, they also held that while the "delights" and companionship of marriage should be enjoyed, they always must be kept subordinate to loyalty to and service of God:

> In consequence, marriage becomes under God a joint enterprise. The Puritan concept . . . altered not only the concept of marriage but of relations of the sexes in general, and that camaraderie which Continentals remark as peculiarly British is the fruit of Puritanism, which by putting God first has enabled men and women to labor together without consciousness of their biological differences.[14]

As mentioned, practically all Protestant groups represented in this volume trace their roots to one of the three main groups. As such, they tend to respond to the revising of attitudes towards sexuality and the family in the latter part of the twentieth century in one of three ways. The first group, as exemplified by the Evangelical Mennonite Church, teaches that monogamous marriage is a divinely ordained institution. Divorce is allowed only on the grounds of adultery. Those who divorce for other reasons and remarry live in adultery. The home is ordained to be the most important instrument for nurturing children in the Christian faith. The husband is the head of the family but must serve his wife and children according to Christ's law of love. The statements issued by the religious organizations in this group do not discuss the nature of sexuality—they tend to assume that its purpose is for procreation and therefore should be reserved solely for marriage. These organizations claim that their teachings are based on a literal interpretation of the Bible.

A second group, as exemplified by the 1984 statement from the Evangelical Lutheran Church in America (see index), views sexuality as a gift from God to be enjoyed within the monogamous marriage relationship. Marriage is an institution designed by God for the mutual fulfillment of individuals and propagation. Divorce is permitted for reasons other than adultery, and remarriage of divorced individuals, while neither officially condoned nor prohibited, is recognized for limited reasons and under guarded conditions.

Sexual differences, according to this Lutheran statement, were designed by God to provide the opportunity for men and women to enrich and fulfill their individual lives. Because they are created in God's image, men and women can express and receive a love that reflects

God's considerate, self-giving, and fulfilling love. Because sexual intercourse expresses a unique commitment to another individual, thereby constituting a marriage, it is not to be indulged outside of marriage. While sexual harmony is an important factor in any marriage, it should not be a goal of marriage. Rather, it should be an expression of the love and unity individuals establish in their faithful living together.

Recognizing the problems presented by the acceleration of puberty and the delay of marriage for economic, social, and personal reasons, the Church of the Brethren (see index), another denomination within this second group, advises teenagers to refrain from sexual intercourse for maturational reasons and encourages older single people and divorced and widowed individuals to do the same in order to experience "the benefits of self-discipline and the positive aspects of a life of commitment and fidelity." However, the Church of the Brethren recognizes that such counsel presents problems for individuals living in the contemporary world where the single life often is a matter of "circumstances rather than choice." It also admits that this situation did not exist in biblical times to the extent that it does in the world today and concludes that it is incumbent upon the church to recognize and explore ways to resolve these problems.

The Church of the Brethren, like other religious groups in this category, also holds that fidelity in marriage does not exclude marriage partners from having meaningful relationships with members of the opposite sex. These are necessary for emotional and personal fulfillment. However, they should not be allowed to move into the realm of romantic involvement. If they show any signs of doing this, they should be terminated.

The church also points out that fidelity in marriage includes more than genital fidelity. It also embraces emotional and spiritual fidelity which strive to meet the needs of one's partner and serve her or his well-being.

The churches included in this second group use the Bible in a less rigid manner than those in the first category. They admit that the Bible offers several patterns of family life, and that both the Hebrew Bible and New Testament offer very little specific guidance on premarital intercourse. However, they maintain that the biblical norms of covenant, love, and justice provide adequate guidelines for meeting the challenges presented to Christians by the revising of sexuality and family in the latter half of the twentieth century.

The Protestant and Eastern Orthodox organizations in the third category, as exemplified by the study group and task force reports contained in this volume, are similar to those in the second—especially in their use of the Bible, their all encompassing definitions of sexuality and the family, their celebration of the pleasurable functions of sexuality, and their sympathetic use of knowledge and insights from the human sciences. However, they differ from the second group in their willingness to offer radical solutions to some of the problems confronting their churches in the areas of sexuality and family life. They claim that alternative forms of family life, couples living together before marriage, and coitus for single, divorced, and widowed individuals in certain circumstances may be morally good and permissible.

They justify their approach by claiming that Jesus calls people to live in an immediate relationship with God's reconciling love and to make free, responsible, reconciling decisions about their own sexuality and family life. This approach sanctions neither casual liaisons nor promiscuity. Individuals still are called to make their decisions according to the biblical norms of covenant, love, and justice. However, the emphasis is upon following the spirit rather than the letter of these norms. The task force report from the Presbyterian Church (U.S.A.) (see index) states:

We regard as contrary to the covenant all those actions which destroy community and cause persons to lose hope, to erode their practical confidence in the providence of God, and to lose respect for their own integrity as persons. . . .

By the same token, those sexual expressions which build up communion between persons, establish a hopeful outlook on the future, minister in a healing way to the fears, hurts and anxieties of persons and confirm to them the fact that they are truly loved, are actions which can confirm the covenant Jesus announced.

Although these groups suggest alternatives which are often contrary to the teachings of the Christian tradition, they do not deny that the monogamous family and faithful, covenanted sexual relationships serve important purposes within God's plan for humanity. According to a task force of the Episcopal Church's (see index) Diocese of Newark, New Jersey,

The Church must continue to sustain persons in the fulfillment of traditional marriage relationships both for the well-being of the marriage partners and because such marriage provides the most stable institution that we have known for the nurturing and protection of children.

Approaches of the Major Traditions: Jewish

In *Choosing a Sex Ethic: A Jewish Inquiry,* Eugene B. Borowitz provides a summary of how interpretations of sexuality and the family in the Hebrew Bible, *Mishnah*, and *Talmud* provide the foundation for contemporary Jewish views on these topics. All three celebrate sex, marriage, and procreation as gifts from God. It is a religious duty for Jews to marry because it is the institution established by God for the continuation of humanity. Moreover, sexuality, because it is a gift from God, is good and should be enjoyed. Traditional Judaism views human beings as psychosomatic unities and does not pit an evil body against a good soul. Each human being is a unity with freedom to use the gifts given by God for either good or evil purposes. Human beings display a propensity to misuse the gift of sexuality. This tendency is not caused by an evil body; rather, it is the result of choosing to act against God's law. Because the frequent misuse of sexuality is widespread, and because it disrupts the social order at several levels, the Bible not only castigates sexual misconduct but uses it as a symbol for human rebellion against God. It also employs fidelity in marriage as a metaphor of humanity's ideal relationship to God. Thus the Bible presents "a delicate balance in the attitude toward sexuality. On the one hand, it is natural, created, commanded, and joyful. On the other, it is the most common symbol of the broader human problems of temptation and the transgression of God's law."[15]

Paradoxically, while the Bible, *Mishnah*, and *Talmud* view marriage and fidelity as divine commands, they contain no prohibitions against premarital sexual relations. Instead, there are laws which forbid "adultery, incest, selling one's daughter into prostitution, and the rape or seduction of a betrothed maiden."[16] There appear to be three reasons for this: First, the Hebrew Bible treats the premarital sexual status of daughters as property rights of the father. Young women were traditionally viewed as the property of their fathers until they were either married or passed the required marriageable age (12½ years). Those who were married were viewed as the property of their husbands. Their sexuality was included as part of the property of their fathers and then of their husbands. For this reason, the Bible treats the spoiling of virginity and adultery as offenses against the property rights of the father, male betrothed, or husband and not the female betrothed or wife.

Second, women who passed the time period alloted for contracting marriages became "mature ones." They were considered legally competent to act for themselves in sexual, marital, and other matters.[17] They were free to decide whether to engage in sexual intercourse outside of marriage. However, they were not granted any legal protection against those who might take sexual advantage of them. On the other hand, no man who married a single woman over 12½ could make a legal claim against her for not being a virgin.

Finally, because property rights were paramount in marriage relationships, and because these rights were not extended to unmarried women beyond the age of 12½, the authors of the Hebrew Bible, *Mishnah*, and *Talmud* were preoccupied with the sexual sins most disruptive of basic family relations—adultery and prostitution.

Borowitz traces a trend beginning in the first centuries C.E. to limit sexual intercourse to the marriage relationship. It received significant support in the twelfth century when Maimonides included "a flat, full-scale legal prohibition against premarital intercourse" in his *Mishneh Torah*.[18] Eventually his interpretation of the law became normative for the Jewish community.

The Bible, *Mishnah*, *Talmud*, and contemporary Jewish interpretations of the law permit divorce and remarriage.

In summary, the Hebrew Bible, *Mishnah*, and *Talmud* teach that sexuality and marriage are gifts and commands of God. Both are good, as is procreation. Sexual fulfillment in marriage completes each partner and enables each. Husband "and wife are the model of integrated humanity."[19]

The Orthodox, Reform, and Conservative traditions within Judaism all use the Bible, *Mishnah*, and *Talmud* as foundation stones for their understandings of sexuality and the family. The Orthodox and Conservative groups accept all three as divinely given and take their laws as eternal commands from God. The Reform movement approaches them with more flexibility. According to Borowitz, a Reform rabbi and professor, "time not only brings changed social circumstances in which traditional practices can no longer operate effectively, but it can also bring new insights into what man is or what society can be or what God requires of them. The law changes to reflect both."[20] Despite this different approach to the law, official Reform statements read very similar to those issued by the Conservative and Orthodox groups. Like the liberal Protestant denominations, the official bodies of the Reform movement maintain traditional stances on sexuality and the family.

In recent years Jewish groups have devoted a great deal of attention to the problems of intermarriage. Having been accepted into the mainstream of American life, Jews now face the challenge of assimilation. Many of their young people are marrying gentiles and are no longer maintaining their Jewish traditions. Because peoplehood is central to Judaism, assimilation and these marriages threaten its very identity and existence. This is why most statements on marriage issued recently by Jewish groups center on the problems of intermarriage.

Approaches of the Major Traditions: Other Religious Bodies

Islam, like Judaism, teaches that sexuality and marriage are gifts and commands of Allah. The purpose of both is twofold: procreation and the completion and fulfillment of each marriage partner. Sexuality is viewed as a good but very strong drive which needs disciplined restraint in order to insure the completion of each individual in marriage and to protect the integrity of the family, a foundational institution. Hence premarital chastity is demanded of each individual and adultery is forbidden. Within marriage sexual pleasures are to be enjoyed to their fullest.

Fidelity in marriage is not limited to monogamy in Islam. Muslim men may take as many as four wives. They may do so only if they can support each wife in equal style and with equal love. Divorce is permitted primarily for men. However, there are some circumstances which allow women to sue for divorce.

Muslim teachings on sexuality, marriage, and the family are derived from the *Quran, Hadith,* and *Shariah.* They are interpreted according to the various legal schools and different traditions within Islam. Being a world religion, Muslim sexual mores and marriage practices vary according to the cultures in which they are practiced. They tend to be conservative and interpreted literally except in those societies which have adopted Western European customs.

The remaining religious groups represented in this volume reflect a variety of traditions and approaches. The Church of Jesus Christ of Latter-day Saints (see index) continues to hold a traditionally conservative view of sexuality and marriage. Marriage, a sacred institution, is divinely ordained by God who commands men and women to reserve sexual intercourse for monogamous marriage relationships. Marriages consecrated in Latter-day Saints' temples are believed to be not only for this life, but for all eternity. The Church of Jesus Christ of Latter-day Saints forbids polygamy, a practice originally permitted by its founders.

The New Vrindaban Community (see index) holds that sexual intercourse deprives one of energy which could be used to experience higher forms of knowledge and religious fulfillment. Abstinence from sexual intercourse and sublimation of sexual energy are viewed as the best means to acquiring superior knowledge and intelligence.

"The Humanist Manifesto I and II" (see index) teaches a "responsible" sexual ethic which promotes individual fulfillment and mature interpersonal relationships based on the free choice of adult individuals who treat each other as ends and not as means.

The Unification Church (see index) founded in the latter half of the twentieth century in Korea, now has a worldwide membership. According to the *Divine Principle,* the Fall of Adam and Eve disrupted God's original plan to establish his kingdom on earth through families. Jesus, whose task was to rectify the disruptive consequences of the Fall, did not accomplish his mission of salvation because he was crucified before he could marry and establish a saving family for humanity. The Reverend Sun Myung Moon, founder of the Holy Spirit Association for the Unification of World Christianity, teaches that he and his wife and all of his followers who marry within the Unification Church are in the process of establishing the new divine family which will bring God's new kingdom to earth.

The Future

In all probability, religious groups will continue for the foreseeable future to respond to the revising of sexuality and the family according to the three types of responses outlined above: 1) restatements of previously adopted teachings and moral codes without change, 2) moderate reformulations of teachings and moral codes, and 3) recognition of proposed radical changes in teachings and moral codes but refusal to adopt them as official policy. In the second and third groups, tension between conservatives and liberals will continue and the gap between official teachings and actual behavior will remain and may increase. There is no sign that those who are calling for radical modifications have sufficient numbers to win the day. In some quarters, conservatives appear to be gaining strength.

Endnotes

[1] Borowitz, p. 31: "[N]either the *Torah,* the rest of the Bible, the *Mishna,* nor the *Talmud* contains a law prohibiting premarital sexual relations."

[2] New York: United Church Press, 1977, p. 142.

[3] Noonan, p. xiv.

[4] Ibid., p. 67.

[5] Ibid., p. 68.

[6] Kosnik, et al., p. 50.

[7] Ibid.

[8] Ibid., p. 51.

[9] Greeley, p. 365.

[10] Cole, p. 131.

[11] Bainton, p. 79.

[12] Cole, p. 20. He adds, "Calvin obviously displayed a greater appreciation of woman than any previous theologian, emancipating her from her enforced role as a mere baby factory or safety valve for male libido."

[13] Bainton, p. 91.

[14] Ibid., p. 95.

[15] Borowitz, p. 34.

[16] Ibid., p. 31.

[17] Ibid., p. 36.

[18] Ibid., p. 41.

[19] Ibid., p. 33.

[20] Ibid., p. 49.

Selected Sources

Bainton, Roland H. *What Christianity Says about Sex, Love, and Marriage.* New York: Association Press, 1957.

Borowitz, Eugene B. *Choosing a Sex Ethic: A Jewish Inquiry.* New York: Schocken Books, 1969.

Cole, William G. *Sex in Christianity and Psychoanalysis.* New York: Oxford University Press, 1955.

Greeley, Andrew M. *Confessions of a Parish Priest: An Autobiography.* New York: Pocket Books, 1986.

Kosnik, Anthony, et al. *Human Sexuality: New Directions in American Catholic Thought.* New York: Paulist Press, 1977.

Noonan, John T., Jr. *Contraception: A History of Its Treatment by the Catholic Theologians and Canonists.* New York: The New American Library, 1967.

Sex and
Family Life

Roman Catholic Church

The Roman Catholic Church, which is the largest Christian church in the world, is headquartered in Vatican City. With more than 50,000,000 members in the United States, it is also the single largest religious body in North America. Its self-definition, namely the divinely appointed guardian and interpreter of divine and natural laws, and its immense size, influence, and resources have both required and enabled it to issue normative statements on the meaning, purpose, and function of human sexuality and the family. Its highly centralized, hierarchical structure has allowed these statements to be particularly powerful in their ability to speak on behalf of the whole church. In the United States, the National Conference of Catholic Bishops and the U.S. Catholic Conference are the policy-setting bodies, following the guidelines set by the Pope and other officials in the Vatican. Authoritative statements may come from the U.S. Catholic bishops as a whole, from a committee, or from individual officials such as Cardinal Joseph Bernardin and Cardinal John O'Connor.

For many centuries the Catholic Church taught that sexuality and marriage served one function—procreation. The Second Vatican Council (1962-1965) introduced a new "personalist" dimension to this teaching—sexuality and marriage were designed by God not only for procreative purposes and pleasure but also for the personal and social fulfillment of the marriage partners. While this theme has been included in all official statements since the publication of the council's Pastoral Constitution Gaudium et Spes *in 1965, the hierarchy of the church continues to promulgate teachings that either inhibit or reject conclusions and recommendations derived from* Gaudium et Spes *by individuals and officially appointed study and advisory groups (for example, Pope Paul VI's rejection of some of the major recommendations of the special Papal Commission for the Study of Population, The Family and Birth).*

In late 1990, the National Conference of Catholic Bishops approved a 188-page comprehensive statement entitled Human Sexuality: A Catholic Perspective for Education and Lifelong Learning. *This document was reported to reiterate recent traditional Catholic teachings on sexuality that sex should be reserved for the monogamous marriage relationship and that its purpose is twofold: 1) the expression and deepening of a loving and fulfilling relationship; and 2) procreation. All forms of artificial birth control are forbidden, and homosexuality is viewed as a sinful, disordered orientation, although the bishops did not extend their censure to include individuals who are homosexual.*

According to several reports, there was a division of opinion on the statement. Some conservative bishops complained that the document forced school-sponsored sex education on all Catholic families whether they wanted it or not. A group of liberal bishops criticized the document for not taking into consideration the views of those Catholics who are displeased with the church's ban on artificial birth control devices and its condemnation of homosexuality. *Some Bishops from both groups wanted the document remanded to committee for major revisions.*

Like other recent Catholic documents, this one asserts that all moral decisions about sexuality within or outside of marriage ultimately must be made by each individual according to her or his own discernment of God's will. Studies reveal that U.S. Catholic clergy allow individuals to use this teaching to decide to practice artificial birth control without moral condemnation.

ROMAN CATHOLIC CHURCH—VATICAN COUNCIL II

EXCERPT FROM "GAUDIUM ET SPES" (1965)

Part II

Some Problems of Special Urgency

Preface

46. This council has set forth the dignity of the human person and the work which men have been destined to undertake throughout the world both as individuals and as members of society. There are a number of particularly urgent needs characterizing the present age, needs which go to the roots of the human race. To a consideration of these in the light of the gospel and of human experience, the Council would now direct the attention of all.

    Of the many subjects arousing universal concern today, it may be helpful to concentrate on these: marriage and the family, human culture, life in its economic, social, and political dimensions, the bonds between the family of nations, and peace. On each of these may there shine the radiant ideals proclaimed by Christ. By these ideals may Christians be led, and all mankind enlightened, as they search for answers to questions of such complexity.

Chapter I: Fostering the Nobility of Marriage and the Family

Marriage and Family in the Modern World

47. The well-being of the individual person and of human and Christian society is intimately linked with the healthy condition of that community produced by marriage and family. Hence Christians and all men who hold this community in high esteem sincerely rejoice in the various ways by which men today find help in fostering this community of love and perfecting its life, and by which spouses and parents are assisted in their lofty calling. Those who rejoice in such aids look for additional benefits from them and labor to bring them about.

    Yet the excellence of this institution is not everywhere reflected with equal brilliance. For polygamy, the plague of divorce, so-called free love, and other disfigurements have an obscuring effect. In addition, married love is too often profaned by excessive self-love, the worship of pleasure, and illicit practices against human generation. Moreover, serious disturbances are caused in families by modern economic conditions, by influences at once social and psychological, and by the demands of civil society. Finally, in certain parts of the world problems resulting from population growth are generating concern.

    All these situations have produced anxious consciences. Yet, the power and strength of the institution of marriage and family can also be seen in the fact that time and again, despite the difficulties produced, the profound changes in modern society reveal the true character of this institution in one way or another.

Therefore, by presenting certain key points of Church doctrine in a clearer light, this council wishes to offer guidance and support to those Christians and other men who are trying to keep sacred and to foster the natural dignity of the married state and its superlative value.

The Sanctity of Marriage and the Family

48. The intimate partnership of married life and love has been established by the Creator and qualified by His laws. It is rooted in the conjugal covenant of irrevocable personal consent. Hence, by that human act whereby spouses mutually bestow and accept each other, a relationship arises which by divine will and in the eyes of society too is a lasting one. For the good of the spouses and their offspring as well as of society, the existence of this sacred bond no longer depends on human decisions alone.

For God Himself is the author of matrimony, endowed as it is with various benefits and purposes. All of these have a very decisive bearing on the continuation of the human race, on the personal development and eternal destiny of the individual members of a family, and on the dignity, stability, peace, and prosperity of the family itself and of human society as a whole. By their very nature, the institution of matrimony itself and conjugal love are ordained for the procreation and education of children, and find in them their ultimate crown.

Thus a man and a woman, who by the marriage covenant of conjugal love "are no longer two, but one flesh" (Mt. 19:6), render mutual help and service to each other through an intimate union of their persons and of their actions. Through this union they experience the meaning of their oneness and attain to it with growing perfection day by day. As a mutual gift of two persons, this intimate union, as well as the good of the children, imposes total fidelity on the spouses and argues for an unbreakable oneness between them.

Christ the Lord abundantly blessed this many-faceted love, welling up as it does from the fountain of divine love and structured as it is on the model of His union with the Church. For as God of old made Himself present to His people through a covenant of love and fidelity, so now the Savior of men and the Spouse of the Church comes into the lives of married Christians through the sacrament of matrimony. He abides with them thereafter so that, just as He loved the Church and handed Himself over on her behalf, the spouses may love each other with perpetual fidelity through mutual self-bestowal.

Authentic married love is caught up into divine love and is governed and enriched by Christ's redeeming power and the saving activity of the Church. Thus this love can lead the spouses to God with powerful effect and can aid and strengthen them in the sublime office of being a father or a mother.

For this reason, Christian spouses have a special sacrament by which they are fortified and receive a kind of consecration in the duties and dignity of their state. By virtue of this sacrament, as spouses fulfill their conjugal and family obligations, they are penetrated with the spirit of Christ. This spirit suffuses their whole lives with faith, hope and charity. Thus they increasingly advance their own perfection, as well as their mutual sanctification, and hence contribute jointly to the glory of God.

As a result, with their parents leading the way by example and family prayer, children and indeed everyone gathered around the family hearth will find a readier path to human maturity, salvation, and holiness. Graced with the dignity and office of fatherhood and motherhood, parents will energetically acquit themselves of a duty which devolves primarily on them, namely education, and especially religious education.

As living members of the family, children contribute in their own way to making their parents holy. For they will respond to the kindness of their parents with sentiments of gratitude, with love and trust. They will stand by them as children should when hardships overtake their parents and old age brings its loneliness. Widowhood, accepted bravely as a continuation of the marriage vocation, will be esteemed by all. Families will share their spiritual riches generously with other families too. Thus the Christian family, which springs from marriage as a reflection of the loving covenant uniting Christ with the Church, as a participation in that covenant, will manifest to all men the Savior's living presence in the world, and the genuine nature of the Church. This the family will do by the mutual love of the spouses, by their generous fruitfulness, their solidarity and faithfulness, and by the loving way in which all members of the family work together.

Conjugal Love

49. The biblical Word of God several times urges the betrothal and the married to nourish and develop their wedlock by pure conjugal love and undivided affection. Many men of our own age also highly regard true love between husband and wife as it manifests itself in a variety of ways depending on the worthy customs of various peoples and times.

This love is an eminently human one since it is directed from one person to another through an affection of the will. It involves the good of the whole person. Therefore it can enrich the expressions of body and mind with a unique dignity, ennobling these expressions as special ingredients and signs of the friendship distinctive of marriage. This love the Lord has judged worthy of special gifts, healing, perfecting, and exalting gifts of grace and of charity.

Such love, merging the human with the divine, leads the spouses to a free and mutual gift of themselves, a gift proving itself by gentle affection and by deed. Such love pervades the whole of their lives. Indeed, by its generous activity it grows better and grows greater. Therefore it far excels mere erotic inclination, which, selfishly pursued, soon enough fades wretchedly away.

This love is uniquely expressed and perfected through the marital act. The actions within marriage by which the couple are united intimately and chastely are noble and worthy ones. Expressed in a manner which is truly human, these actions signify and promote that mutual self-giving by which spouses enrich each other with a joyful and a thankful will.

Sealed by mutual faithfulness and hallowed above all by Christ's sacrament, this love remains steadfastly true in body and in mind, in bright days or dark. It will never be profaned by adultery or divorce. Firmly established by the Lord, the unity of marriage will radiate from the equal personal dignity of wife and husband, a dignity acknowledged by mutual and total love.

The steady fulfillment of the duties of this Christian vocation demands notable virtue. For this reason, strengthened by grace for holiness of life, the couple will painstakingly cultivate and pray for constancy of love, largeheartedness, and the spirit of sacrifice.

Authentic conjugal love will be more highly prized, and wholesome public opinion created regarding it, if Christian couples give outstanding witness to faithfulness and harmony in that same love, and to their concern for educating their children, also, if they do their part in bringing about the needed cultural, psychological, and social renewal on behalf of marriage and the family.

Especially in the heart of their own families, young people should be aptly and seasonably instructed about the dignity, duty, and expression of married love. Trained thus in the cultivation of chastity, they will be able at a suitable age to enter a marriage of their own after an honorable courtship.

The Fruitfulness of Marriage

50. Marriage and conjugal love are by their nature ordained toward the begetting and educating of children. Children are really the supreme gift of marriage and contribute very substantially to the welfare of their parents. The God Himself who said, "It is not good for man to be alone" (Gen. 2:18) and "who made man from the beginning male and female" (Mt. 19:4), wished to share with man a certain special participation in His own creative work. Thus He blessed male and female, saying: "Increase and multiply" (Gen. 1:28).

Hence, while not making the other purposes of matrimony of less account, the true practice of conjugal love, and the whole meaning of the family life which results from it, have this aim: that the couple by ready with stout hearts to cooperate with the love of the Creator and the Savior, who through them will enlarge and enrich His own family day by day.

Parents should regard as their proper mission the task of transmitting human life and educating those to whom it has been transmitted. They should realize that they are thereby cooperators with the love of God the Creator, and are, so to speak, the interpreters of that love. Thus they will fulfill their task with human and Christian responsibility. With docile reverence toward God, they will come to the right decision by common counsel and effort.

They will thoughtfully take into account both their own welfare and that of their children, those already born and those which may be foreseen. For this accounting they will reckon with both the material and the spiritual conditions of the times as well as of their state in life. Finally, they will consult the interests of the family group, of temporal society, and of the Church herself.

The parents themselves should ultimately make this judgment, in the sight of God. But in their manner of acting, spouses should be aware that they cannot proceed arbitrarily. They must always be governed according to a conscience dutifully conformed to the divine law itself, and should be submissive toward the Church's teaching office, which authentically interprets the law in the light of the gospel. That divine law reveals and protects the integral meaning of conjugal love, and impels it toward a truly human fulfillment.

Thus trusting in divine Providence and refining the spirit of sacrifice, married Christians glorify the Creator and strive toward fulfillment in Christ when, with a generous human and Christian sense of responsibility, they acquit themselves of the duty to procreate. Among the couples who fulfill their God-given task in this way, those merit special mention who with wise and common deliberation, and with a gallant heart, undertake to bring up suitably even a relatively large family.

Marriage to be sure is not instituted solely for procreation. Rather, its very nature as an unbreakable compact between persons, and the welfare of the children, both demand that the mutual love of the spouses, too, be embodied in a rightly ordered manner, that it grow and ripen. Therefore, marriage persists as a whole manner and communion of life, and maintains its value and indissolubility, even when offspring are lacking— despite, rather often, the very intense desire of the couple.

Harmonizing Conjugal Love with Respect for Human Life

51. This Council realizes that certain modern conditions often keep couples from arranging their married lives harmoniously, and that they find themselves in circumstances where at least temporarily the size of their family should not be increased. As a result, the faithful exercise of love and the full intimacy of married life is broken off, it is not safe for its faithfulness to be imperiled and its quality of fruitfulness ruined. For then the upbringing of the children and courage to accept new ones are both endangered.

To these problems there are those who presume to offer dishonorable solutions. Indeed, they do not recoil from the taking of life. But the Church issues the reminder that a true contradiction cannot exist between the divine laws pertaining to the transmission of life and those pertaining to the fostering of authentic conjugal love.

For God, the Lord of life, has conferred on men the surpassing ministry of safeguarding life—a ministry which must be fulfilled in a manner which is worthy of man. Therefore from the moment of its conception life must be guarded with the greatest care, while abortion and infanticide are unspeakable crimes. The sexual characteristics of man and the human faculty of reproduction wonderfully exceed the dispositions of lower forms of life. Hence the acts themselves which are proper to conjugal love and which are exercised in accord with genuine human dignity must be honored with great reverence.

Therefore when there is question of harmonizing conjugal love with the responsible transmission of life, the moral aspect of any procedure does not depend solely on sincere intentions or on an evaluation of motives. It must be determined by objective standards. These, based on the nature of the human person and his acts, preserve the full sense of mutual self-giving and human procreation in the context of true love. Such a goal cannot be achieved unless the virtue of conjugal chastity is sincerely practiced. Relying on these principles, sons of the Church may not undertake methods of regulating procreation which are found blameworthy by the teaching authority of the Church in its unfolding of the divine law.

Everyone should be persuaded that human life and the task of transmitting it are not realities bound up with this world alone. Hence they cannot be measured or perceived only in terms of it, but always have a bearing on the eternal destiny of men.

All Must Promote the Good Estate of Marriage and the Family

52. The family is a kind of school of deeper humanity. But if it is to achieve the full flowering of its life and mission, it needs the kindly communion of minds and the joint deliberation of spouses, as well as the painstaking cooperation of parents in the education of their children. The active presence of the father is highly beneficial to their formation. The children, especially the younger among them, need the care of their mother at home. This domestic role of hers must be safely preserved, though the legitimate social progress of women should not be underrated on that account.

Children should be so educated that as adults they can, with a mature sense of responsibility, follow their vocation, including a religious one, and choose their state of life. If they marry, they can thereby establish their family in favorable moral, social, and economic conditions. Parents or guardians should by prudent advice provide guidance to their young with respect to founding a family, and the young ought to listen gladly. At the same time no pressure, direct or indirect, should be put on the young to make them enter marriage or choose a specific partner.

Thus the family is the foundation of society. In it the various generations come together and help one another to grow wiser and to harmonize personal rights with the other requirements of social life. All those, therefore, who exercise influence over communities and social groups should work efficiently for the welfare of marriage and the family.

Public authority should regard it as a sacred duty to recognize, protect, and promote their authentic nature, to shield public morality, and to favor the prosperity of domestic life. The right of parents to beget and educate their children in the bosom of the family must be safeguarded. Children, too, who unhappily lack the blessing of a family should be protected by prudent legislation and various undertakings, and provided with the help they need.

Redeeming the present time, and distinguishing eternal realities from their hanging expressions, Christians should actively promote the values of marriage and the family, both by the example of their own lives and by cooperation with other men of good will. Thus when difficulties arise, Christians will provide, on behalf of family life, those necessities and helps which are suitably modern. To this end, the Christian instincts of the faithful, the upright moral consciences of men, and the wisdom and experience of persons versed in the sacred sciences will have much to contribute.

Those, too, who are skilled in other sciences, notably the medical, biological, social, and psychological, can considerably advance the welfare of marriage and the family, along with peace of conscience, if by pooling their efforts they labor to explain more thoroughly the various conditions favoring a proper regulation of births.

It devolves on priests duly trained about family matters to nurture the vocation of spouses by a variety of pastoral means, by preaching God's Word, by liturgical worship, and by other spiritual aids to conjugal and family life; to sustain them sympathetically and patiently in difficulties, and to make them courageous through love. Thus families which are truly noble will be formed.

Various organizations, especially family associations, should try by their programs of instruction and action to strengthen young people and spouses themselves, particularly those recently wed, and to train them for family, social, and apostolic life.

Finally, let the spouses themselves, made to the image of the living God and enjoying the authentic dignity of persons, be joined to one another in equal affection, harmony of mind, and the work of mutual sanctification. Thus they will follow Christ who is the principle of life. Thus, too, by the joys and sacrifices of their vocation and through their faithful love, married people will become witnesses of the mystery of that love which the Lord revealed to the world by His dying and His rising up to life again.

Notes: Gaudium et Spes, *by extending the purpose of marriage to include the personal and social fulfillment of the individual partners, introduced a new "personalist" element to Roman Catholic teachings on marriage and sexuality which, prior to the Second Vatican Council, held that marriage only had one purpose—procreation. Subsequent Roman Catholic documents repeat this innovation and seek either to extend or limit its range of influence.*

ROMAN CATHOLIC CHURCH—POPE PAUL VI

EXCERPT FROM "HUMANAE VITAE" (1968)

The most serious duty of transmitting human life, for which married persons are the free and responsible collaborators of God the Creator, has always been a source of great joys to them, even if sometimes accompanied by not a few difficulties and by distress.

At all times the fulfillment of this duty has posed grave problems to the conscience of married persons, but, with the recent evolution of society, changes have taken place that give rise to new questions which the Church could not ignore, having to do with a matter which so closely touches upon the life and happiness of men.

2. The changes which have taken place are in fact noteworthy and of varied kinds. In the first place, there is the rapid demographic development. Fear is shown by many that world population is growing more rapidly than the available resources, with growing distress to many families and developing countries, so that the temptation for authorities to counter this danger with radical measures is great. Moreover, working and lodging conditions, as well as increased exigencies both in the economic field and in that of education, often make the proper education of a larger number of children difficult today. A change is also seen both in the manner of considering the person of

woman and her place in society, and in the value to be attributed to conjugal love in marriage, and also in the appreciation to be made of the meaning of conjugal acts in relation to that love.

Finally and above all, man has made stupendous progress in the domination and rational organization of the forces of nature, such that he tends to extend this domination to his own total being: to the body, to psychical life, to social life and even to the laws which regulate the transmission of life.

3. This new state of things gives rise to new questions. Granted the conditions of life today, and granted the meaning which conjugal relations have with respect to the harmony between husband and wife and to their mutual fidelity, would not a revision of the ethical norms, in force up to now, seem to be advisable, especially when it is considered that they cannot be observed without sacrifices, sometimes heroic sacrifices?

    And again: by extending to this field the application of the so-called "principal of totality," could it not be admitted that the intention of a less abundant but more rationalized fecundity might transform a materially sterilizing intervention into a licit and wise control of birth? Could it not be admitted, that is, that the finality of procreation pertains to the ensembled of conjugal life, rather than to its single acts? It is also asked whether, in view of the increased sense of responsibility of modern man, the moment has not come for him to entrust to his reason and his will, rather than to the biological rhythms of his organism, the task of regulating birth.

4. Such questions required from the teaching authority of the Church a new and deeper reflection upon the principles of the moral teaching on marriage: a teaching founded on the natural law, illuminated and enriched by divine revelation.

    No believer will wish to deny that the teaching authority of the Church is competent to interpret even the natural moral law. It is, in fact, indisputable, as our predecessors have many times declared, [1] that Jesus Christ, when communicating to Peter and to the Apostles His divine authority and sending them to teach all nations His commandments, [2] constituted them as guardians and authentic interpreters of all the moral law, not only, that is, of the law of the Gospel, but also of the natural law, which is also an expression of the will of God, the faithful fulfillment of which is equally necessary for salvation. [3]

    Conformably to this mission of hers, the Church has always provided—and even more amply in recent times—a coherent teaching concerning both the nature of marriage and the correct use of conjugal rights and the duties of husband and wife. [4]

5. The consciousness of that same mission induced us to confirm and enlarge the study commission which our predecessor Pope John XXIII of happy memory had instituted in March, 1963. That commission which included, besides several experts in the various pertinent disciplines also married couples, had as its scope the gathering of opinions on the new questions regarding conjugal life, and in particular on the regulation of births, and of furnishing opportune elements of information so that the magisterium could give an adequate reply to the expectation not only of the faithful, but also of world opinion. [5]

    The work of these experts, as well as the successive judgments and counsels spontaneously forwarded by or expressly requested from a good number of our brothers in the episcopage, have permitted us to measure more exactly all the aspects of this complex matter. Hence with all our heart we express to each of them our lively gratitude.

6. The conclusions at which the commission arrived could not, nevertheless, be considered by us as definitive, nor dispense us from a personal examination of this serious question; and this also because, within the commission itself, no full concordance of

judgments concerning the moral norms to be proposed had been reached, and above all because certain criteria of solutions had emerged which departed from the moral teaching on marriage proposed with constant firmness by the teaching authority of the Church.

Therefore, having attentively sifted the documentation laid before us, after mature reflection and assiduous prayers, we now intend, by virtue of the mandate entrusted to us by Christ, to give our reply to these grave questions.

7. The problem of birth, like every other problem regarding human life, is to be considered, beyond partial perspectives—whether of the biological or psychological demographic or sociological orders—in the light of an integral vision of man and of his vocation, not only his natural and earthly, but also his supernatural and eternal vocation. And since, in the attempt to justify artificial methods of birth control, many have appealed to the demands both of conjugal love and of ''responsible parenthood,'' it is good to state very precisely the true concept of these two great realities of married life, referring principally to what was recently set forth in this regard, and in a highly authoritative form, by the Second Vatican Council in its pastoral constitution *Gaudium et Spes*.

8. Conjugal love reveals its true nature and nobility when it is considered in its supreme origin, God, who is love,[6] ''the Father, from whom every family in heaven and on earth is named.''[7]

   Marriage is not, then, the effect of chance or the product of evolution of unconscious natural forces; it is the wise institution of the Creator to realize in mankind His design of love. By means of the reciprocal personal gift of self, proper and exclusive to them, husband and wife tend towards the communion of their beings in view of mutual personal perfection, to collaborate with God in the generation and education of new lives.

   For baptized persons, moreover, marriage invests the dignity of a sacramental sign of grace, inasmuch as it represents the union of Christ and of the Church.

9. Under this light, there clearly appear the characteristic marks and demands of conjugal love, and it is of supreme importance to have an exact idea of these.

   This love is first of all fully *human*, that is to say, of the senses and of the spirit at the same time. It is not, then, a simple transport of instinct and sentiment, but also, and principally, an act of the free will, intended to endure and to grow by means of the joys and sorrows of daily life, in such a way that husband and wife become one only heart and one only soul, and together attain their human perfection.

   Then, this love is *total*, that is to say, it is a very special form of personal friendship, in which husband and wife generously share everything, without undue reservations or selfish calculations. Whoever truly loves his marriage partner loves not only for what he receives, but for the partner's self, rejoicing that he can enrich his partner with the gift of himself.

   Again, this love is *faithful* and *exclusive* until death. Thus in fact do bride and groom conceive it to be on the day when they freely and in full awareness assume the duty of the marriage bond. A fidelity, this, which can sometimes be difficult, but is always possible, always noble and meritorious, as no one can deny. The example of so many married persons down through the centuries shows, not only that fidelity is according to the nature of marriage, but also that it is a source of profound and lasting happiness.

   And finally this love is *fecund* for it is not exhausted by the communion between husband and wife, but is destined to continue, raising up new lives. ''Marriage and conjugal love are by their nature ordained toward the begetting and educating of children. Children are really the supreme gift of marriage and contribute very substantially to the welfare of their parents.''[8]

10. Hence conjugal love requires in husband and wife an awareness of their mission of "responsible parenthood," which today is rightly much insisted upon, and which also must be exactly understood. Consequently it is to be considered under different aspects which are legitimate and connected with one another.

    In relation to the biological processes, responsible parenthood means the knowledge and respect of their functions; human intellect discovers in the power of giving life biological laws which are part of the human person.[9]

    In relation to the tendencies of instinct or passion, responsible parenthood means that necessary dominion which reason and will must exercise over them.

    In relation to physical, economic, psychological and social conditions, responsible parenthood is exercised, either by the deliberate and generous decision to raise a numerous family, or by the decision, made for grave motives and with due respect for the moral law, to avoid for the time being, or even for an indeterminate period, a new birth.

    Responsible parenthood also and above all implies a more profound relationship to the objective moral order established by God, of which a right conscience is the faithful interpreter. The responsible exercise of parenthood implies, therefore, that husband and wife recognize fully their own duties towards God, towards themselves, towards the family and towards society, in a correct hierarchy of values.

    In the task of transmitting life, therefore, they are not free to proceed completely at will, as if they could determine in a wholly autonomous way the honest path to follow; but they must conform their activity to the creative intention of God, expressed in the very nature of marriage and of its acts, and manifested by the constant teaching of the Church.[10]

11. These acts, by which husband and wife are united in chaste intimacy, and by means of which human life is transmitted, are as the Council recalled, "noble and worthy,"[11] and they do not cease to be lawful if, for causes independent of the will of husband and wife, they are foreseen to be infecund, since they always remain ordained towards expressing and consolidating their union. In fact, as experience bears witness, not every conjugal act is followed by a new life. God has wisely disposed natural laws and rhythms of fecundity which, of themselves, cause a separation in the succession of births. Nonetheless the Church, calling men back to the observance of the norms of the natural law, as interpreted by their constant doctrine, teaches that each and every marriage act (*quilibet matrimonii usus*) must remain open to the transmission of life.[12] . . .

17. Upright men can even better convince themselves of the solid grounds on which the teaching of the Church in this field is based, if they care to reflect upon the consequences of methods of artificial birth control. Let them consider, first of all, how wide and easy a road would thus be opened up towards conjugal infidelity and the general lowering of morality. Not much experience is needed in order to know human weakness, and to understand that men—especially the young, who are so vulnerable on this point—have need of encouragement to be faithful to the moral law, so that they must not be offered some easy means of eluding its observance. It is also to be feared that the man, growing used to the employment of anti-conceptive practices, may finally lose respect for the woman and, no longer caring for her physical and psychological equilibrium, may come to the point of considering her as a mere instrument of selfish enjoyment, and no longer as his respected and beloved companion.

    Let it be considered also that a dangerous weapon would thus be placed in the hands of those public authorities who take no heed of moral exigencies. Who could blame a government for applying to the solution of the problems of the community those means acknowledged to be licit for married couples in the solution of a family problem? Who will stop rulers from favoring, from even imposing upon their peoples, if they were to consider it necessary, the method of contraception which they judge to be most efficacious? In such a way men, wishing to avoid individual, family, or social difficulties encountered in the observance of the divine law, would reach the point of placing at the mercy of the intervention of public authorities the most personal and most reserved sector of conjugal intimacy.

Consequently, if the mission of generating life is not to be exposed to the arbitrary will of men, one must necessarily recognize insurmountable limits to the possibility of man's domination over his own body and its functions; limits which no man, whether a private individual or one invested with authority, may licitly surpass. And such limits cannot be determined otherwise than by the respect due to the integrity of the human organism and its functions, according to the principles recalled earlier, and also according to the correct understanding of the "principle of totality" illustrated by our predecessor Pope Pius XII.[21]

18. It can be foreseen that this teaching will perhaps not be easily received by all: Too numerous are those voices—amplified by the modern means of propaganda—which are contrary to the voice of the Church. To tell the truth, the Church is not surprised to be made, like her divine Founder, a "sign of contradiction",[22] yet she does not because of this cease to proclaim with humble firmness the entire moral law, both natural and evangelical. Of such laws the Church was not the author, nor consequently can she be their arbiter; she is only their depositary and their interpreter, without ever being able to declare to be licit that which is not so by reason of its intimate and unchangeable opposition to the true good of man.

    In defending conjugal morals in their integral wholeness, the Church knows that she contributes towards the establishment of a truly human civilization; she engages man not to abdicate from his own responsibility in order to rely on technical means; by that very fact she defends the dignity of man and wife. Faithful to both the teaching and the example of the Saviour, she shows herself to be the sincere and disinterested friend of men, whom she wishes to help, even during their earthly sojourn, "to share as sons in the life of the living God, the Father of all men."[23]

19. Our words would not be an adequate expression of the thought and solicitude of the Church, Mother and Teacher of all peoples, if, after having recalled men to the observance and respect of the divine law regarding matrimony, we did not strengthen them in the path of honest regulation of birth, even amid the difficult conditions which today afflict families and peoples. The Church, in fact, cannot have a different conduct towards men than of the Redeemer: She knows their weaknesses, has compassion on the crowd, receives sinners; but she cannot renounce the teaching of the law which is, in reality, that law proper to a human life restored to its original truth and conducted by the spirit of God.[24]

20. The teaching of the Church on the regulation of birth, which promulgates the divine law, will easily appear to many to be difficult or even impossible of actuation. And indeed, like all great beneficent realities, it demands serious engagement and much effort, individual, family and social effort. More than that, it would not be practicable without the help of God, who upholds and strengthens the good will of men. Yet, to anyone who reflects well, it cannot but be clear that such efforts ennoble man and are beneficial to the human community.

21. The honest practice of regulation of birth demands first of all that husband and wife acquire and possess solid convictions concerning the true values of life and of the family, and that they tend towards securing perfect self-mastery. To dominate instinct by means of one's reason and free will undoubtedly requires ascetical practices, so that the affective manifestations of conjugal life may observe the correct order, in particular

with regard to the observance of periodic continence. Yet this discipline which is proper to the purity of married couples, far from harming conjugal love, rather confers on it a higher human value. It demands continual effort yet, thanks to its beneficent influence, husband and wife fully develop their personalities, being enriched with spiritual values. Such discipline bestows upon family life fruits of serenity and peace, and facilitates the solution of other problems; it favors attention for one's partner, helps both parties to drive out selfishness, the enemy of true love; and deepens their sense of responsibility. By its means, parents acquire the capacity of having a deeper and more efficacious influence in the education of their offspring; little children and youths grow up with a just appraisal of human values, and in the serene and harmonious development of their spiritual and sensitive faculties.

22. On this occasion, we wish to draw the attention of educators, and of all who perform duties of responsibility in regard to the common good of human society, to the need of creating an atmosphere favorable to education in chastity, that is, to the triumph of healthy liberty over license by means of respect for the moral order.

Everything in the modern media of social communications which leads to sense excitation and unbridled customs, as well as every form of pornography and licentious performances, must arouse the frank and unanimous reaction of all those who are solicitous for the progress of civilization and the defense of the common good of the human spirit. Vainly would one seek to justify such depravation with the pretext of artistic or scientific exigencies,[25] or to deduce an argument from the freedom allowed in this sector by the public authorities.

23. To Rulers, who are those principally responsible for the common good, and who can do so much to safeguard moral customs, we say: Do not allow the morality of your peoples to be degraded; do not permit that by legal means practices contrary to the natural and divine law be introduced into that fundamental cell, the family. Quite other is the way in which public authorities can and must contribute to the solution of the demographic problem: namely, the way of a provident policy for the family, of a wise education of peoples in respect of moral law and the liberty of citizens.

We are well aware of the serious difficulties experienced by public authorities in this regard, especially in the developing countries. To their legitimate preoccupations we devoted our encyclical letter *Populorum Progressio*. But with our predecessor Pope John XXIII, we repeat: no solution to these difficulties is acceptable "which does violence to man's essential dignity" and is based only on an utterly materialistic conception of man himself and of his life. The only possible solution to this question is one which envisages the social and economic progress both of individuals and of the whole of human society, and which respects and promotes true human values.[26] Neither can one, without grave injustice, consider divine providence to be responsible for what depends, instead, on a lack of wisdom in government, on an insufficient sense of social justice, on selfish monopolization, or again on blameworthy indolence in confronting the efforts and the sacrifices necessary to ensure the raising of living standards of a people and of all its sons.[27]

May all responsible public authorities—as some are already doing so laudably—generously revive their efforts. And may mutual aid between all the members of the great human family never cease to grow: This is an almost limitless field which thus opens up to the activity of the great international organizations.

24. We wish not to express our encouragement to men of science, who "can considerably advance the welfare of marriage and the family, along with peace of conscience, if by pooling their efforts they labor to explain more thoroughly the various conditions favoring a proper regulation of births."[28] It is particularly desirable that, according to the wish already expressed by Pope Pius XII, medical science succeed in providing a sufficiently secure basis for a regulation of birth, founded on the observance of natural

rhythms.[29] In this way, scientists and especially Catholic scientists will contribute to demonstrate in actual fact that, as the Church teaches, "a true contradiction cannot exist between the divine laws pertaining to the transmission of life and those pertaining to the fostering of authentic conjugal love."[30]

25. And now our words more directly address our own children, particularly those whom God calls to serve Him in marriage. The Church, while teaching imprescriptible demands of the divine law, announces the tidings of salvation, and by means of the sacraments opens up the paths of grace, which makes man a new creature, capable of corresponding with love and true freedom to the design of his Creator and Saviour, and of finding the yoke of Christ to be sweet.[31]

Christian married couples, then, docile to her voice, must remember that their Christian vocation, which began at baptism, is further specified and reinforced by the sacrament of matrimony. By it husband and wife are strengthened and as it were consecrated for the faithful accomplishment of their proper duties, for the carrying out of their proper vocation even to perfection, and the Christian witness which is proper to them before the whole world.[32] To them the Lord entrusts the task of making visible to men the holiness and sweetness of the law which unites the mutual love of husband and wife with their cooperation with the love of God the author of human life.

We do not all intend to hide the sometimes serious difficulties inherent in the life of Christian married persons; for them as for everyone else, "the gate is narrow and the way is hard, that leads to life."[33] But the hope of that life must illuminate their way, as with courage they strive to live with wisdom, justice and piety in this present time,[34] knowing that the figure of this world passes away.[35]

Let married couples, then, face up to the efforts needed, supported by the faith and hope which "do not disappoint . . . because God's love has been poured into our hearts through the Holy Spirit, who has been given to us,"[36] let them implore divine assistance by persevering prayer, above all, let them draw from the source of grace and charity in the Eucharist. And if sin should still keep its hold over them, let them not be discouraged, but rather have recourse with humble perseverance to the mercy of God, which is poured forth in the sacrament of Penance. In this way they will be enabled to achieve the fullness of conjugal life described by the Apostle: "husbands, love your wives, as Christ loved the Church . . . husbands should love their wives as their own bodies. He who loves his wife loves himself. For no man ever hates his own flesh, but nourishes and cherishes it, as Christ does the Church . . . this is a great mystery, and I mean in reference to Christ and the Church. However, let each one of you love his wife as himself, and let the wife see that she respects her husband."[37]

26. Among the fruits which ripen forth from a generous effort of fidelity to the divine law, one of the most precious is that married couples themselves not infrequently feel the desire to communicate their experience to others. Thus there comes to be included in the vast pattern of the vocation of the laity a new and most noteworthy form of the apostolate of like to like; it is married couples themselves who become apostles and guides to other married couples. This is assuredly, among so many forms of apostolate, one of those which seem most opportune today.[38]

27. We hold those physicians and medical personnel in the highest esteem who, in the exercise of their profession, value above every human interest the superior demands of their Christian vocation. Let them persevere, therefore, in promoting on every occasion the discovery of solutions inspired by faith and right reason, let them strive to arouse this conviction and this respect in their associates. Let them also consider as their proper professional duty the task of acquiring all the knowledge needed in this delicate sector, so as to be able to give to those married persons who consult them wise counsel and healthy direction, such as they have a right to expect.

28. Beloved priest sons, by vocation you are the counselors and spiritual guides of individual persons and of families. We now turn to you with confidence. Your first task—especially in the case of those who teach moral theology—is to expound the Church's teaching on marriage without ambiguity. Be the first to give, in the exercise of your ministry, the example of loyal internal and external obedience to the teaching authority of the Church. That obedience, as you know well, obliges not only because of the reasons adduced, but rather because of the light of the Holy Spirit, which is given in a particular way to the pastors of the Church in order that they may illustrate the truth.[39] You know, too, that it is of the utmost importance, for peace of consciences and for the unity of the Christian people, that in the field of morals as well as in that of dogma, all should attend to the magisterium of the Church, and all should speak the same language. Hence, with all our heart we renew to you the heartfelt plea of the great Apostle Paul: "I appeal to you, brethren, by the name of Our Lord Jesus Christ, that all of you agree and that there be no dissensions among you, but that you be united in the same mind and the same judgment."[40]

29. To diminish in no way the saving teaching of Christ constitutes an eminent form of charity for souls. But this must ever be accompanied by patience and goodness, such as the Lord himself gave example of in dealing with men. Having come not to condemn but to save,[41] he was indeed intransigent with evil, but merciful towards individuals.

    In their difficulties, may married couples always find, in the words and in the heart of a priest, the echo of the voice and the love of the Redeemer.

    And then speak with confidence, beloved sons, fully convinced that the spirit of God, while He assists the magisterium in proposing doctrine, illumines internally the hearts of the faithful inviting them to give their assent. Teach married couples that indispensable way of prayer; prepare them to have recourse often and with faith to the sacraments of the Eucharist and of Penance, without ever allowing themselves to be discouraged by their own weakness.

30. Beloved and venerable brothers in the episcopate, with whom we most intimately share the solicitude of the spiritual good of the People of God, at the conclusion of this encyclical our reverent and affectionate thoughts turn to you. To all of you we extend an urgent invitation. At the head of the priests, your collaborators, and of your faithful, work ardently and incessantly for the safeguarding and the holiness of marriage, so that it may always be lived in its entire human and Christian fullness. Consider this mission as one of your most urgent responsibilities at the present time. As you know, it implies concerted pastoral action in all the fields of human activity, economic, cultural and social; for, in fact, only a simultaneous improvement in these various sectors will make it possible to render the life of parents and of children within their families not only tolerable, but easier and more joyous, to render the living together in human society more fraternal and peaceful, in faithfulness to God's design for the world.

31. Venerable brothers, most beloved sons, and all men of good will, great indeed is the work of education, of progress and of love to which we call you, upon the foundation of the Church's teaching, of which the successor of Peter is, together with his brothers in the episcopate, the depositary and interpreter. Truly a great work, as we are deeply convinced, both for the world and for the Church, since man cannot find true happiness—towards which he aspires with all his being—other than in respect of the laws written by God in his very nature, laws which he must observe with intelligence and love. Upon this work, and upon all of you, and especially upon married couples, we invoke the abundant graces of the God of holiness and mercy, and in pledge thereof we impart to you all our apostolic blessing.

    Given at Rome, from St. Peter's, this 25th day of July, feast of St. James the Apostle, in the year 1968, the sixth of our pontificate.

14

Endnotes

[1] Cf. Pius IX, encyclical *Qui Pluribus,* Nov. 9, 1846; in PII IX P. M. Acta, I, pp. 9-10; St. Pius X, encyc. *Singulari Quadam,* Sept. 24, 1912; in AAS IV (1912), p. 658; Pius XI encyc. *Casti Connubii,* Dec. 31, 1930; in AAS XXII (1930), pp. 579-581; Pius XII, allocution *Magnificate Dominum* to the episcopate of the Catholic world, Nov. 2, 1954; in AAS XLVI (19540, pp. 671-672; John XXIII, ency. *Mater et Magistra,* May 19, 1961; in AAS LIII (1961), p. 457.

[2] Cf. Matt. 28:18-19.

[3] Cf. Matt. 7:21.

[4] Cf. *Catechismus Romanus Concilii Tridentini,* part II, ch. VIII; Leo XIII, encyc. *Arcanum,* Feb. 19, 1880; in *Acta Leonis* XIII, II (1881), pp. 26-29; Pius XI, encyc. *Divini Illius Magistri,* Dec. 31, 1929, in AAS XXII (1930), pp. 58-61; encyc. *Casti Connubii,* in AAS XXII (1930), pp. 545-546; Pius XII, alloc. to the Italian medico-biological union of St. Luke, Nov. 12, 1944, in *Discorsi e Radiomessaggi,* VI, pp. 191-192; to the Italian Catholic union of midwives, Oct. 29, 1951, in AAS XLIII (1951), pp. 857-859; to the seventh Congress of the International Society of Haematology, Sept. 12, 1958, in AAS L (1958), pp. 734-735; John XXIII, encyc. *Mater et Magistra,* in AAS LIII (1961), pp. 446-447; *Codex Iuris Canonici,* Canon 1067; Can. 1968, S 1, Can. 1066 S 1-2; Second Vatican Council, Pastoral constitution *Gaudium et Spes,* nos. 47-52.

[5] Cf. Paul VI, allocution to the Sacred College, June 23, 1964, in AAS LVI (1964), p. 588; to the Commission for Study of Problems of Population, Family and Birth, March 27, 1965, in AAS LVII (1965), p. 388, to the National Congress of the Italian Society of Obstetrics and Gynaecology, Oct. 29, 1966, in AAS LVIII (1966), p. 1168.

[6] Cf. I John 4:8.

[7] Cf. Eph. 3:15.

[8] Cf. II Vat. Council, Pastoral const. *Gaudium et Spes,* No. 50

[9] Cf. St. Thomas, *Summa Theologica,* I-II, q. 94, art. 2.

[10] Cf. Pastoral Const. *Gaudium et Spes,* nos. 50, 51.

[11] *Ibid.,* no. 49.

[12] Cf. Pius XI, encyc. *Casti Connubii,* in AAS XXII (1930), p. 560; Pius XII, in AAS XLIII (1951), p. 843. . . .

[21] Cf. AAS XLV (1953), pp. 674-675; AAS XLVIII (1956), pp. 461-462.

[22] Cf. Luke 2:34.

[23] Cf. Paul VI, encyc. *Populorum Progressio,* March 26, 1967, No. 21.

[24] Cf. Rom. 8.

[25] Cf. II Vatican Council, decree *Inter Mirifica,* On the Media of Social Communication, nos. 6-7.

[26] Cf. encyc. *Mater et Magistra,* in AAS LIII (1961), p. 447.

[27] Cf. encyc. *Populorum Progressio,* nos. 48-55.

[28] Cf. Pastoral Const. *Gaudium et Spes,* n. 52.

[29] Cf. AAS XLIII (1951), p. 859.

[30] Cf. Pastoral Const. *Gaudium et Spes,* no. 51.

[31] Cf. Matt. 11:30.

[32] Cf. Pastoral Const. *Gaudium et Spes,* no. 48; II Vatican Council, Dogmatic Const. *Lumen Gentium,* no. 35.

[33] Matt. 7:14; cf. Heb. 11:12.

[34] Cf. Tit. 2:12.

[35] Cf. 1 Cor. 7:31.

[36] Cf. Rom. 5:5.

[37] Eph. 5:25, 28-29, 32-33.

[38] Cf. Dogmatic Const. *Lumen Gentium*, nos. 35 and 41; Pastoral Const. *Gaudium et Spes*, nos. 48-49; II Vatican Council, Decree *Apostolicam Actuositatem*, no. 11.

[39] Cf. Dogmatic Const. *Lumen Gentium*, no. 25.

[40] Cf. 1 Cor. 1:10.

[41] Cf. John 3:17.

Notes: *This excerpt from* Humanae Vitae *(meaning "human life") was Pope Paul IV's reaffirmation of the church's long-standing bans on the use of artificial means of contraception and abortion. Because* Gaudium et Spes *states that marriage has two purposes—procreation and the personal and social fulfillment of each partner—and because the Second Vatican Council (which issued* Gaudium et Spes*) was conducted in a liberal atmosphere, many Roman Catholics anticipated a more flexible statement on birth control. It was not, however, and since then the American Roman Catholic Church in particular has encountered heavy opposition to the Pope's stance, especially since he rejected many of the more liberal recommendations of the special Papal Commission for the Study of Population, the Family and Birth. Pope John Paul II upholds* Humanae Vitae *and shows no signs of changing his conservative stance. The opposition to his views continues.*

ROMAN CATHOLIC CHURCH—SACRED CONGREGATION FOR THE DOCTRINE OF THE FAITH

EXCERPT FROM "DECLARATION ON CERTAIN MORAL QUESTIONS CONCERNING SEXUAL ETHICS" (1975)

1. According to contemporary scientific research, the human person is so profoundly affected by sexuality that it must be considered as one of the factors which give to each individual's life the principal traits that distinguish it. In fact it is from sex that the human person receives the characteristics which, on the biological, psychological and spiritual levels, make that person a man or a woman, and thereby largely condition his or her progress towards maturity and insertion into society. Hence sexual matters, as is obvious to everyone, today constitute a theme frequently and openly dealt with in books, reviews, magazines and other means of social communication. . . .

   In . . . [the] domain of sexual ethics there exist principles and norms which the Church has always unhesitatingly transmitted as part of her teaching, however much the opinions and morals of the world may have been opposed to them. These principles and norms in no way owe their origin to a certain type of culture, but rather to knowledge of the divine law and of human nature. They therefore cannot be considered as having become out of date or doubtful under the pretext that a new cultural situation has arisen.

It is these principles which inspired the exhortations and directives given by the Second Vatican Council for an education and an organization of social life taking account of the equal dignity of man and woman while respecting their difference.[8]

Speaking of "the sexual nature of man and the human faculty of procreation," the Council noted that they "wonderfully exceed the dispositions of lower forms of life."[9] It then took particular care to expound the principles and criteria which concern human sexuality in marriage, and which are based upon the finality of the specific function of sexuality.

In this regard the Council declares that the moral goodness of the acts proper to conjugal life, acts which are ordered according to true human dignity, ''does not depend solely on sincere intentions or on an evaluation of motives. It must be determined by objective standards. These, based on the nature of the human person and his acts, preserve the full sense of mutual self-giving and human procreation in the context of true love.''[10]

These final words briefly sum up the Council's teaching—more fully expounded in an earlier part of the same Constitution[11]—on the finality of the sexual act and on the principal criterion of its morality: it is respect for its finality that ensures the moral goodness of this act.

This same principle, which the Church holds from divine Revelation and from her authentic interpretation of the natural law, is also the basis of her traditional doctrine, which states that the use of the sexual function has its true meaning and moral rectitude only in true marriage.[12] . . .

7.   Today there are many who vindicate the right to sexual union before marriage, at least in those cases where a firm intention to marry and an affection which is already in some way conjugal in the psychology of the subjects require this completion, which they judge to be connatural. This is especially the case when the celebration of the marriage is impeded by circumstances or when this intimate relationship seems necessary in order for love to be preserved.

This opinion is contrary to Christian doctrine, which states that every genital act must be within the framework of marriage. However firm the intention of those who practice such premature sexual relations may be, the fact remains that these relations cannot ensure, in sincerity and fidelity, the interpersonal relationship between a man and a woman, nor especially can they protect this relationship from whims and caprices. Now it is a stable union that Jesus willed, and he restored its original requirement, beginning with the sexual difference. ''Have you not read that the creator from the beginning made them male and female and that he said: This is why a man must leave father and mother, and cling to his wife, and the two become one body? They are no longer two, therefore, but one body. So then, what God has united, man must not divide.''[13] Saint Paul will be even more explicit when he shows that if unmarried people or widows cannot live chastely they have no other alternative than the stable union of marriage: ''. . . it is better to marry than to be aflame with passion.''[14] Through marriage, in fact, the love of married people is taken up into that love which Christ irrevocably has for the Church,[15] while dissolute sexual union[16] defiles the temple of the Holy Spirit which the Christian has become. Sexual union therefore is only legitimate if a definitive community of life has been established between the man and the woman. . . .

Experience teaches us that love must find its safeguard in the stability of marriage, if sexual intercourse is truly to respond to the requirements of its own finality and to those of human dignity. These requirements call for a conjugal contract sanctioned and guaranteed by society—a contract which establishes a state of life of capital importance both for the exclusive union of the man and the woman and for the good of their family and of the human community. Most often, in fact, premarital relations exclude the possibility of children. What is represented to be conjugal love is not able, as it absolutely should be, to develop into paternal and maternal love. Or, if it does happen to do so, this will be to the detriment of the children, who will be deprived of the stable environment in which they ought to develop in order to find in it the way and the means of their insertion into society as a whole.

10.   The observance of the moral law in the field of sexuality and the practice of chastity have been considerably endangered, especially among less fervent Christians, by the current tendency to minimize as far as possible, when not denying outright, the reality of grave sin, at least in people's actual lives.

There are those who go as far as to affirm that mortal sin, which causes separation from God, only exists in the formal refusal directly opposed to God's call, or in that selfishness which completely and deliberately closes itself to the love of neighbor. They say that it is only then that there comes into play the fundamental option, that is to say the decision which totally commits the person and which is necessary if mortal sin is to exist; by this option the person, from the depths of the personality, takes up or ratifies a fundamental attitude towards God or people. On the contrary, so-called "peripheral" actions (which, it is said, usually do not involve decisive choice), do not go so far as to change the fundamental option, the less so since they often come, as is observed, from habit. Thus such actions can weaken the fundamental option, but not to such a degree as to change it completely. Now according to these authors, a change of the fundamental option towards God less easily comes about in the field of sexual activity, where a person generally does not transgress the moral order in a fully deliberate and responsible manner but rather under the influence of passion, weakness, immaturity, sometimes even through the illusion of thus showing love for someone else. To these causes there is often added the pressure of the social environment.

In reality, it is precisely the fundamental option which in the last resort defines a person's moral disposition. But it can be completely changed by particular acts, especially when, as often happens, these have been prepared for by previous more superficial acts. Whatever the case, it is wrong to say that particular acts are not enough to constitute mortal sin.

According to the Church's teaching, mortal sin, which is opposed to God, does not consist only in formal and direct resistance to the commandment of charity. It is equally to be found in this opposition to authentic love which is included in every deliberate transgression, in serious matter, of each of the moral laws. . . .

11. As has been said above, the purpose of this Declaration is to draw the attention of the faithful in present-day circumstances to certain errors and modes of behavior which they must guard against. The virtue of chastity, however, is in no way confined solely to avoiding the faults already listed. It is aimed at attaining higher and more positive goals. It is a virtue which concerns the whole personality, as regards both interior and outward behavior.

Individuals should be endowed with this virtue according to their state in life: for some it will mean virginity or celibacy consecrated to God, which is an eminent way of giving oneself more easily to God alone with an undivided heart.[27] For others it will take the form determined by the moral law, according to whether they are married or single. But whatever the state of life, chastity is not simply an external state; it must make a person's heart pure in accordance with Christ's words: "You have learned how it was said: You must not commit adultery. But I say this to you: if a man looks at a woman lustfully, he has already committed adultery with her in his heart."[28]

Chastity is included in that continence which Saint Paul numbers among the gifts of the Holy Spirit, while he condemns sensuality as a vice particularly unworthy of the Christian and one which precludes entry into the kingdom of heaven.[29] "What God wants is for all to be holy. He wants you to keep away from fornication, and each one of you to know how to use the body that belongs to him in a way that is holy and honorable, not giving way to selfish lust like the pagans who do not know God. He wants nobody at all ever to sin by taking advantage of a brother in these matters. . . . We have been called by God to be holy, not to be immoral. In other words, anyone who objects is not objecting to a human authority, but to God, who gives you his Holy Spirit."[30] "Among you there must not be even a mention of fornication or impurity in any of its forms, or promiscuity: this would hardly become the saints! For you can be quite certain that nobody who actually indulges in fornication or impurity or promiscuity—which is worshipping a false god—can inherit anything of the kingdom of God. Do not let anyone deceive you with empty arguments: it is for this loose living that God's anger comes down on those who rebel against him. Make sure that you are not included with them. You were darkness once, but now you are light in the Lord; be like children of light, for the effects of the light are seen in complete goodness and right living and truth."[31]

In addition, the Apostle points out the specifically Christian motive for practicing chastity when he condemns the sin of fornication not only in the measure that this action is injurious to one's neighbor or to the social order but because the fornicator offends against Christ who has redeemed him with his blood and of whom he is a member, and against the Holy Spirit of whom he is the temple. "You know, surely, that your bodies are members making up the body of Christ. . . . All the other sins are committed outside the body; but to fornicate is to sin against your own body. Your body, you know, is the temple of the Holy Spirit, who is in you since you received him from God. You are not your own property; you have been bought and paid for. That is why you should use your body for the glory of God."[32]

The more the faithful appreciate the value of chastity and its necessary role in their lives as men and women, the better they will understand, by a kind of spiritual instinct, its moral requirements and counsels. In the same way they will know better how to accept and carry out, in a spirit of docility to the Church's teaching, what an upright conscience dictates in concrete cases. . . .

At the audience granted on November 7, 1975 to the undersigned Prefect of the Sacred Congregation for the Doctrine of the Faith, the Sovereign Pontiff by divine providence Pope Paul VI approved this Declaration "On certain questions concerning sexual ethics," confirmed it and ordered its publication.

Given in Rome, at the Sacred Congregation for the Doctrine of the Faith, on December 29, 1975.

FRANJO Card. SEPER
Prefect
fr. JÉRÔME HAMER, O.P.
Titular Archbishop of Lorium
Secretary

Footnotes

[8] Cf. Second Vatican Ecumenical Council, Declaration *Gravissimum Educationis,* 1, 8: *AAS* 58 (1966), pp. 729-730; 734-736. *Gaudium et Spes,* 29, 60, 67: *AAS* 58 (1966), pp. 1048-1049, 1080-1081, 1088-1089.

[9] *Gaudium et Spes,* 51: *AAS* 58 (1966), p. 1072.

[10] *Ibid.;* cf. also 49: *loc. cit.,* pp. 1069-1070.

[11] *Ibid.,* 49, 50: *loc. cit.,* pp. 1069-1072.

[12] The present Declaration does not go into further detail regarding the norms of sexual life within marriage; these norms have been clearly taught in the Encyclical Letters *Casti Connubii* and *Humanae Vitae.*

[13] Cf. Mt 19:4-6.

[14] 1 Cor 7:9.

[15] Cf. Eph 5:25-32. . . .

[16] Sexual intercourse outside marriage is formally condemned: 1 Cor 5:1; 6:9; 7:2; 10:8; Eph 5:5; 1 Tim 1:10; Heb 13:4; and with explicit reasons: 1 Cor 6:12-20.

[27] [C]f. 1 Cor 7:7, 34; Council of Trent, Session XXIV, can. 10: *DS* 1810; Second Vatican Council, Constitution *Lumen Gentium,* 42, 43, 44: *AAS* 57 (1965), pp. 47-51; Synod of Bishops, *De Sacerdotio Ministeriali,* part II, 4, b: *AAS* 63 (1971), pp. 915-916.

[28] Mt 5:28.

[29] Cf. Gal 5:19-23; 1 Cor 6:9-11.

[30] 1 Thess 4:3-8; cf. Col 3:5-7; 1 Tim 1:10.

[31] Eph 5:3-8; cf. 4:18-19.

[32] 1 Cor 6:15, 18-20.

Notes: This statement extends the "personalist" ideas expressed in Gaudium et Spes *on sexuality and marriage to every area of human sexuality. It places sexuality at the center of human nature and human development. This extension is reflected in several subsequent Roman Catholic documents and lays the foundation for a positive and holistic approach to sexuality.*

ROMAN CATHOLIC CHURCH—NATIONAL CONFERENCE OF CATHOLIC BISHOPS

EXCERPT FROM "TO LIVE IN CHRIST JESUS: A PASTORAL REFLECTION ON THE MORAL LIFE" (1976)

II. Moral Life in the Family, the Nation, and the Community of Nations

30. We turn now to three social clusters, three concentric communities, which provide the setting for human life and fulfillment in Christ: the family, the nation, and the community of nations.

    In speaking of matters which bear upon these three communities today, we treat them as moral issues in light of the values given us by Jesus Christ and His Church, in whose name we proclaim them. We cannot here discuss every important issue. Moreover, we admit that in some cases the complexity of the problems does not permit ready, concrete solutions. Nevertheless, as teachers of morality we insist that even such complex problems must be resolved ultimately in terms of objective principles if the solutions are to be valid.[44]

31. Our point of focus is the human person. "The progress of the human person and the advance of society itself hinge on each other."[45] Every human being is of priceless value: made in God's image, redeemed by Christ, and called to an eternal destiny. That is why we are to recognize all human beings as our neighbors and love them with the love of Christ.

32. This love of neighbor, inseparably linked to love of God and indeed an expression and measure of it, is summoned forth first in regard to those closest to us—the members of our own families.

The Family

33. Every human being has a need and right to be loved, to have a home where he or she can put down roots and grow. The family is the first and indispensable community in which this need is met. Today, when productivity, prestige, or even physical attractiveness are regarded as the gauge of personal worth, the family has a special vocation to be a place where people are loved not for what they do or what they have but simply because they are.

34. A family begins when a man and woman publicly proclaim before the community their mutual commitment so that it is possible to speak of them as one body.[46] Christ teaches that God wills the union of man and woman in marriage to be lifelong, a sharing of life for the length of life itself.

35. The Old Testament takes the love between husband and wife as one of the most powerful symbols of God's love for His people: "I will espouse you to Me forever: I will espouse you in right and in justice, in love and in mercy: I will espouse you in

fidelity, and you shall know the Lord."[47] So husband and wife espouse themselves, joined in a holy and loving covenant.

36. The New Testament continues this imagery: only now the union between husband and wife rises to the likeness of the union between Christ and His Church.[48] Jesus teaches that in marriage men and women are to pledge steadfast unconditional faithfulness which mirrors the faithfulness of the Son of God. Their marriages make His fidelity and love visible to the world. Christ raised marriage in the Lord to the level of a sacrament, whereby this union symbolizes and effects God's special love for the couple in their total domestic and social situation.

37. Jesus tells us that the Father can and will grant people the greatness of heart to keep such pledges of loving faithfulness.[49] The Church has always believed that in making and keeping noble promises of this sort people can through the grace of God grow beyond themselves—grow to the point of being able to love beyond their merely human capacity. Yet contemporary culture makes it difficult for many people to accept this view of marriage. Even some who admire it as an ideal doubt whether it is possible and consider it too risky to attempt. They believe it better to promise less at the start and so be able to escape from marital tragedy in order to promise once again.

38. But this outlook itself has increased marital tragedy. Only men and women bold enough to make promises for life, believing that with God's help they can be true to their word as He is to His, have the love and strength to surmount the inevitable challenges of marriage. Such unselfish love, rooted in faith, is ready to forgive when need arises and to make the sacrifices demanded if something as precious and holy as marriage is to be preserved. For the family to be a place where human beings can grow with security, the love pledged by husband and wife must have as its model the selfless and enduring love of Christ for the Church. "Husbands, love your wives, as Christ loved the Church. He gave Himself up for her."[50]

39. Some say even sacramental marriages can deteriorate to such an extent that the marital union dies and the spouses are no longer obliged to keep their promise of lifelong fidelity. Some would even urge the Church to acknowledge such dissolution and allow the parties to enter new, more promising unions. We reject this view.[51] In reality it amounts to a proposal to forgo Christian marriage at the outset and substitute something entirely different. It would weaken marriage further, while paying too little heed to Jesus' call to identify ourselves with His redeeming love, which endures all things. Its fundamental difficulty is that it cannot be reconciled with the Church's mission to be faithful to the word entrusted to it. The covenant between a man and a woman joined in Christian marriage is as indissoluble and irrevocable as God's love for His people and Christ's love for His Church.

40. Since the following of Christ calls for so much dedication and sacrifice in the face of strong, contrary social pressures, Christ's Church has a serious obligation to help His followers live up to the challenge. In worship, pastoral care, education, and counseling we must assist husbands and wives who are striving to realize the ideal of Christ's love in their lives together and with their children. Young people and engaged couples must be taught the meaning of Christian marriage. Married couples must have the support and encouragement of the Christian community in their efforts to honor their commitments.

41. It remains a tragic fact that some marriages fail. We must approach those who suffer this agonizing experience with the compassion of Jesus Himself. In some cases romanticism or immaturity may have prevented them from entering into real Christian marriages.

42. But often enough "broken marriages" are sacramental, indissoluble unions. In this sensitive area the pastoral response of the Church is especially needed and especially difficult to formulate. We must seek ways by which the Church can mediate Christ's

compassion to those who have suffered marital tragedy, but at the same time we may do nothing to undermine His teaching concerning the beauty and meaning of marriage and in particular His prophetic demands concerning the indissolubility of the unions of those who marry in the Lord. The Church must ever be faithful to the command to serve the truth in love.[52]

Children

43. The love of husband and wife finds its ideal fulfillment in their children, with whom they share their life and love. Children are really the supreme gift of marriage who in turn substantially enrich the lives of their parents.[53]

44. Openness to children is vitally linked to growth in marital and family love. Couples have a right to determine responsibly, in accord with God's law, how many children they should have, and they may also have valid reasons for not seeking children immediately. But in marrying with the intention of postponing children indefinitely, some appear simply to wish to enjoy one another's company without distraction or to achieve an arbitrary level of material comfort. This can mark a selfish entry into what should be an experience of generous giving. Even worse, children may come to be regarded as an intrusion and a burden instead of a gift. This may lead to a rejection of the children, particularly those who are disadvantaged, either before or after birth.

45. In order to reflect seriously upon the value they assign children, couples should begin by reflecting upon their understanding of marriage itself. Do they believe God is with them in this adventure to which they have committed themselves? If so, their love will reach confidently toward the future and provide a setting in which new life can be generously accepted, take root and grow. Openness to new life, founded on faith, in turn will strengthen their love. They will come to see how the love-giving and life-giving meanings of their love are joined in loving acts of marital intercourse, linked by a necessary relationship which exists not only on the biological level but on all levels of personality.

46. One need not always act to realize both of these values, but one may never deliberately suppress either of them. The love-giving and life-giving meanings of marital intercourse are real human values and aspects of human personhood. Because they are, it is wrong to act deliberately against either. In contraceptive intercourse the procreative or life-giving meaning of intercourse is deliberately separated from its love-giving meaning and rejected; the wrongness of such an act lies in the rejection of this value.[54]

47. Some distinguish between a so-called contraceptive mentality—a deep-seated attitude of selfish refusal to communicate life and love to a future generation—and particular contraceptive acts during a marriage otherwise generally open to the transmission of life. Though there is a difference, even in the latter case an act of contraceptive intercourse is wrong because it severs the link between the meanings of marital intercourse and rejects one of them.

48. We ask Catholics to reflect on the value at stake here. The Church is not engaged in a mere quibble over means of birth regulation; it is proclaiming the value of the life-giving meaning of marital intercourse, a value attacked, though in different ways, by both the ideology of contraception and by contraceptive acts.

49. Pastoral sensitivity requires that we be understanding toward those who find it hard to accept this teaching, but it does not permit us to change or suppress it. We recognize that couples face increasing pressure in family planning. Contraceptive birth control results not only from selfishness and improperly formed conscience but also from conflicts and pressures which can mitigate moral culpability. Therefore, we ask our people not to lose heart or turn away from the community of faith when they find themselves caught in these conflicts. We urge them to seek appropriate and under-

standing pastoral counsel, to make use of God's help in constant prayer and recourse to the sacraments, and to investigate honestly such legitimate methods of birth limitation as natural family planning.[55] At the same time we urge those who dissent from this teaching of the Church to a prayerful and studied reconsideration of their position.

50. Our Christian tradition holds the sexual union between husband and wife in high honor, regarding it as a special expression of their covenanted love which mirrors God's love for His people and Christ's love for the Church. But like many things human, sex is ambivalent. It can be either creative or destructive. Sexual intercourse is a moral and human good only within marriage; outside marriage it is wrong.[56]

51. Our society gives considerable encouragement to premarital and extramarital sexual relations as long as, it is said "no one gets hurt." Such relations are not worthy of beings created in God's image and made God's adopted children nor are they according to God's will.[57] The unconditional love of Christian marriage is absent, for such relations are hedged around with many conditions. Though tenderness and concern may sometimes be present, there is an underlying tendency toward exploitation and self-deception. Such relations trivialize sexuality and can erode the possibility of making deep, lifelong commitments.

52. Some persons find themselves through no fault of their own to have a homosexual orientation. Homosexuals, like everyone else, should not suffer from prejudice against their basic human rights. They have a right to respect, friendship, and justice. They should have an active role in the Christian community. Homosexual activity, however, as distinguished from homosexual orientation, is morally wrong. Like heterosexual persons, homosexuals are called to give witness to chastity, avoiding, with God's grace, behavior which is wrong for them, just as nonmarital sexual relations are wrong for heterosexuals. Nonetheless, because heterosexuals can usually look forward to marriage, and homosexuals, while their orientation continues, might not, the Christian community should provide them a special degree of pastoral understanding and care.

53. Though most people have two families, the one in which they are born and the one they help bring into being, the single and celibate have only the first. But from this experience they, too, know family values. Love and sacrifice, generosity and service have a real place in their lives. They are as much tempted as the married—sometimes more—to selfishness. They have as great a need for understanding and consolation. Family values may be expressed in different terms in their lives, but they are expressed.

The Aged

54. The adventure of marriage and family is a continuing one in which elderly people have important lessons to teach and learn. Contemporary American society tends to separate the aging from their families, isolating kin in ways that are more than physical, with the result that the wisdom of experience is often neither sought, imparted, nor further developed.[58]

55. Families should see the story of loving reciprocity through life's closing chapters. Where possible, the elderly should be welcomed into their own families. Moreover, children have an obligation of human and Christian justice and love to keep closely in touch with aging parents and to do what lies in their power to care for them in their old age. "If anyone does not provide for his own relatives and especially for members of his immediate family, he has denied the faith; he is worse than an unbeliever."[59] The community should provide for those who lack families and, in doing so, attend to all their needs, not just physical ones. Here the Church has played and continues to play a special role. The elderly must be cherished, not merely tolerated, and the Church community, through parishes and other agencies, should seek to mediate to them the loving concern of Jesus and the Father.

56. Euthanasia or mercy killing is much discussed and increasingly advocated today, though the discussion is often confused by ambiguous use of the slogan "death with dignity." Whatever the word or term, it is a grave moral evil deliberately to kill persons who are terminally ill or deeply impaired. Such killing is incompatible with respect for human dignity and reverence for the sacredness of life.

57. Something different is involved, however, when the question is whether hopelessly ill and painfully afflicted people must be kept alive at all costs and with the use of every available medical technique.

58. Some seem to make no distinction between respecting the dying process and engaging in direct killing of the innocent. Morally there is all the difference in the world. While euthanasia or direct killing is gravely wrong, it does not follow that there is an obligation to prolong the life of a dying person by extraordinary means. At times the effort to do so is of no help to the dying and may even be contrary to the compassion due them. People have a right to refuse treatment which offers no reasonable hope of recovery and imposes excessive burdens on them and perhaps also their families. At times it may even be morally imperative to discontinue particular medical treatments in order to give the dying the personal care and attention they really need as life ebbs. Since life is a gift of God we treat it with awesome respect. Since death is part and parcel of human life, indeed the gateway to eternal life and the return to the Father, it, too, we treat with awesome respect.

The Family and Society

59. Marriage and the family are deeply affected by social patterns and cultural values. How we structure society, its approach to education and work, the roles of men and women, public policy toward health care and care of the young and old, the tone and cast of our literature, arts, and media—all these affect the family. The test of how we value the family is whether we are willing to foster, in government and business, in urban planning and farm policy, in education and health care, in the arts and sciences, in our total social and cultural environment, moral values which nourish the primary relationships of husbands, wives, and children, and make authentic family life possible.

Endnotes

[44] Many of the matters treated here have been discussed in detail in papal and conciliar documents, documents of the Holy See and the Synods of Bishops, and statements of national episcopal conferences. The references which follow note a few of the sources.

[45] Vatican Council II. *The Church in the Modern World,* 25.

[46] Cf., Gn 2:24.

[47] Hos 2:21-22.

[48] Cf., Eph 5:25-32.

[49] Cf., Mt 19:10-12.

[50] Eph 5:25.

[51] Cf., Vatican Council II. *The Church in the Modern World.* 48.

[52] Eph 4:15.

[53] Vatican Council II. *The Church in the Modern World,* 50.

[54] Cf., Humanae Vitae 12, 13.

[55] Cf., Vatican Council II. *The Church in the Modern World,* 52; Humanae Vitae, 24.

[56] Cf., Sacred Congregation for the Doctrine of the Faith, *Declaration on Certain Questions Concerning Sexual Ethics,* December 29, 1975.

[57] Cf., 1 Cor 6:9-10, 18.

[58] Cf., United States Catholic Conference, *Society and the Aged: Toward Reconciliation,* May 5, 1976.

[59] 1 Tim 5:8.

Notes: *This statement reasserts the main theses put forth by* Gaudium et Spes *and the Sacred Congregation for the Doctrine of Faith's ''Declaration on Certain Moral Questions Concerning Sexual Ethics'' and underscores the importance of a sensitive pastoral approach to those Roman Catholics who find it difficult to accept the Roman church's teaching on birth control. The bishops, in making this point, seek to find ways to maintain a dialogue with these individuals and to keep them within the fold of the Roman Catholic Church.*

ROMAN CATHOLIC CHURCH—NATIONAL CONFERENCE OF CATHOLIC BISHOPS

CHANGING ROLES OF WOMEN AND MEN (1980)

I. Overview of World Situation

Despite 2,000 years of Christianity, every culture throughout the world has elements which deny human beings the opportunity to develop their personal talents as God wants. Every culture has traditions which impose wrongful expectations and restrictions on men and women, thus violating their human rights. In many places there still exists a severe separation between the sexes which can be seen in sex-determined social roles.

In many cultures women are discriminated against in one way or another and left in a subservient position. Men, on the other hand, are also often forced to assume dominant and competitive roles. Also, in other cultures, a dominant matriarchal society thwarts male development.

II. Influences and Signs of Change

Recently, in many countries there are increasingly visible signs of a change in the roles of men and women. Strong influences are bringing about these changes:

A. The spread of technology, allowing both men and women to do the same kind of work;

B. The growth of cities, breaking down traditional cultural patterns and offering anonymity;

C. The penetrating influence of mass media, notably television, presenting new models of behavior and new expectations for both sexes;

D. The pressure of consumerism, demanding that both men and women work to earn more money.

At the same time, under the influence of the Holy Spirit, people around the world are becoming more and more sensitive to the dignity of each person, regardless of sex, creed and race, recognizing the person's innate right to respect and freedom from unjust oppression. All of these movements and forces have affected and will continue to affect in a deeper way the traditional roles assigned to men and women in the family and in society. To mention but a few changes taking place in the United States:

1. Within the family unit men and women are learning to help one another according to their gifts and talents rather than limiting themselves to traditional roles of father and mother. Both are willing to cook, clean, earn money and care for the children. In broader society also both men and women are developing new skills and confidences in a variety

25

of roles that were once the exclusive domain of the other sex. Now both men and women can be doctors and nurses, politicians and scientists, workers and managers.

2. More and more women see themselves as gifted, fully autonomous persons, able to define themselves in ways other than in relation to men. Their self-concept has been enlarged.

3. There is a growing demand, mostly initiated by women, that there be a more equitable sharing of the duties of family life and recognition by society of the importance of equal opportunity for meaningful work outside the home.

4. Women are stronger in their refusal to accept low pay, low status, poor working conditions and blocked access to executive-level jobs. They resent the expectation that they share in the financial support of the family while carrying alone the full burden of child care.

5. There is a marked change in the pattern of interpersonal relationships between men and women. Women are no longer content to be passive.

6. Work place and schedule are being altered: flexible hours in the work place; part-time work with benefits; parental leave with pay so that both fathers and mothers can leave their work temporarily to care for their infants; flexible work arrangements so that they can work at home, etc.

7. There is an increased sensitivity to ''sexist'' language in all areas of society, secular and religious.

8. The personal God-given qualities of man and woman are often repressed out of fear of being considered ''chauvinist'' or ''sexist.''

All these changes are altering the structure of marriage and family life, social consciousness, legal systems and other major institutions of society. In the face of these changes, where both good and evil are being experienced, the church—and notably this synod on the family—cannot remain a passive observer.

Our pastoral and prophetic roles demand that together with our people we discern these changes in the light of the Gospel. What does the Lord want us to encourage and support? Where must we take the lead and motivate? In what areas must we denounce the evil of injustice and oppression?

III. Criteria for Discernment

The creation narratives of Genesis reveal the equality of man and woman. God created male and female in his image (Gn. 1:27).

Jesus Christ called both men and women to be his friends and followers. Men and women are mentioned in Acts as fellow laborers of the apostles in building the new Christian communities.

Catholic teaching through the ages has defended the intrinsic equality and dignity of men and women, affirming their mutual partnership. Their mission is to complete one another, not only in the task of procreation, but in the whole of human life.

Many of the documents of Vatican II articulate this principle of equality. *Gaudium et Spes,* for example, refers to ''new social relationships between men and women'' (No. 3) and notes that ''since women now engage in almost all spheres of activity . . . it is incumbent upon all to acknowledge and favor the proper and necessary participation of women in cultural life'' (No. 60). And it sees married life and love as ''an intimate partnership'' (No. 48).

Since Vatican II there has been a growing body of papal statements which clearly set forth the equality of men and women. Some speak implicitly to the issue within the context of the dignity and freedom of all human persons (*Pacem in Terris, Populorum Progressio*). Others speak directly of the evolution of roles.

Pope John Paul II has frequently referred to the absolute equality between the sexes as ontological and theological. In his Wednesday general audience of Nov. 14, 1979, he reflected on the unity of masculinity and femininity as imaging the communion of divine persons.

In point of fact, there is no reputable theologian today who would deny that the equality of man and woman is constituted by God and confirmed by Christian teaching.

IV. Prophetic and Pastoral Implications

To be both prophets and pastors we must face the inevitable tensions which all these changes engender. Even more important, we must use these very tensions to help the people grow in maturity as Christians. As prophets, we share in the prophetic mission of Christ to set people free in truth and love by using every opportunity we have to proclaim that:

A. Co-equality, interdependence and complementary of men and women in marriage and in the institutions of society are the will of God. It is a fact that major tasks in society—government, medicine, education, religion, child rearing—can be best accomplished by men and women in co-equal and complementary cooperation and partnership. The world in fact needs the benefits of this total creative energy in all areas. The Holy Father affirms and encourages this when in his exhortations he has asked women to transpose the exercise of their qualities from the private sphere to the public one . . . and when he has asked men to allow the nurturing sides of their personalities to enrich their family life and child care.

B. Those changes in the roles of sexes which reflect gospel values and the teaching of the church are legitimate and respond to the inspiration of the Holy Spirit. As parents discover that certain values traditionally deemed "feminine" or "masculine" can be reappraised and adopted by both men and women on behalf of the family, children will develop a broader and deeper range of mental and emotional reactions to functions they may later have to perform. They will also be in a better position to critically evaluate the meaning of personal qualities as opposed to "sex-determined" functions. In this way both church and civil society will be enriched by a proper appreciation and use of God's gifts.

C. The importance of work in Christian life must be adequately understood, and women must be given free access to meaningful work and equal pay. Work must be seen not only as a means of earning one's living, but also as a means for persons to develop their own creative capacities and skills, to take part in the process of building up a more just society as a link whereby people can experience and develop solidarity with others, an opportunity for broader dialogue and self-fulfillment. This way the private and social aspects of people's lives will be linked.

As pastors, assisted by our people, we must seek ways to serve the church and wider society by:

A. Counteracting the oppressive evil of depersonalizing situations, of consumerism, of dominance and exploitation by either sex.

B. Encouraging local ministries to assist families in shaping new, more Christian patterns of work and family life, so that both the family and society at large can benefit from the partnership of men and women.

C. Urging educational institutions to study and correct as needed any structures or attitudes which tend to stifle or ignore the rightful and complete development of boys and girls as total persons.

D. Supporting movements which strengthen love and interpersonal communications in individual families through sharing the experiences and concerns of other families.

E. Promoting in our own pastoral exhortations and actions whatever will reduce the stereotyping of the roles and functions of the sexes.

The church, particularly during and after the Second Vatican Council, has spoken clearly about the rights, the dignity and the role of women and their basic equality with men. While this synod paper focuses on the role of women and men in the family, we do recognize the need to study, in the light of the doctrine of the faith, the role of women in the church itself.

Notes: *This statement was prepared by the National Conference of Catholic Bishops for presentation at the 1980 World Synod of Bishops. It acknowledges the emerging equality of men and women in the contemporary world and claims that this equality is grounded in values found in both the book of Genesis and the New Testament. It concludes by stating that the Roman Catholic Church needs to turn its attention to the question of equality for women within the church, a problem usually ignored by the hierarchy.*

ROMAN CATHOLIC CHURCH— CARDINAL JOSEPH BERNARDIN

SEXUALITY AND CHURCH TEACHING (1980)

At least in many parts of the world, the church today faces an enormous problem: the existence of a significant gap between its teaching on sexual morality and the ideas and attitudes on the same subject held by many of the laity and even many priests.

Reputable surveys in the United States, for example, have documented this reality. We have also learned in the last 10 to 15 years that simply restating our position has minimal effect. This constitutes a serious crisis for the church, intellectually, spiritually and organizationally.

Not only is this a problem as far as teaching about sexual morality is concerned, but undermining the church's credibility on this important issue will lead—indeed, already has—to undermining its credibility in many other areas. What can be done to reverse this situation?

Two needs must be addressed. The first concerns our manner of conceptualizing and presenting our teaching on sexuality and the ethical and moral norms which flow from that teaching. The second has to do more with motivation—with helping people not only to understand the teaching more fully but to respond to it in an affirmative way. Let us consider the teaching first.

The church's moral teaching on sexuality has perennial validity. A more positive theology of sexuality is needed, not to replace this moral teaching with a substantively different one, but to help people see more clearly why the tradition takes the positions it does. Few people today accept moral teaching solely on the basis of authority. Generally, they accept it only if they perceive it as reasonable and persuasive, and only if they can relate it in a positive way to their own experience.

A brief paper such as this cannot fully develop a theology of sexuality. Nor can the synod. But it is useful and important to highlight some elements which might be part of a more positive theology of sexuality, as a basis for further study and development. It is in this light that I offer the following ideas.

1. Sexuality is a gift from God. Therefore, it is good in itself and, used as God intends, enriching and ennobling. This point must be stressed so as to counteract dualistic thinking of the past and also of the present which denigrates the body and sexuality.

2. Sexuality is a relational power. It is not merely a capacity for performing specific acts. It is part of our God-given natural power or capacity for relating to others. It colors the qualities of sensitivity, warmth, openness and mutual respect in our interpersonal relationships.

   In this connection, it is important to note that human sexuality also has a social dimension. As a constituent part of our nature, it influences our societal relationships and well-being, as well as our personal relationships with other individuals.

3. Understood in this way, sexuality cannot be equated with genitality, which is a narrower concept referring to the physical expressions of sexuality leading to genital union. The special context of marriage is needed for the supreme physical expression of sexuality to serve human love and life generously and without the deception that premarital and extramarital relations contain.

4. It cannot be taken for granted that people understand and accept a natural-law ethic, or that citing natural-law principles and formulas, as found in our traditional manuals, will be persuasive or even comprehensible to people unaccustomed to thinking in these categories. This does not mean that the natural-law tradition should be abandoned. It should not. But this tradition needs to be expanded, enriched.

   One way to do this is to work toward a more holistic approach to sexuality and conjugal love within the context of natural law. In such an approach, the body is understood not only in relation to the physically identifiable purposes of its parts (e.g., genitals for reproduction) but also as an expression of what it means to be made in God's image.

   The complementarity of sexuality (male and female) and its urgent inner dynamism toward union are seen as reflecting in human terms the dynamic unity within the triune God. Thus the difference between the sexes clearly is good, willed by God from the beginning as an integral part of his self-revelation; and light is shed on the need for both physical and psychic integrity in the act of sexual union through which spouses express and accomplish self-giving.

   Pope John Paul seems to be taking this approach in his weekly audience talks on the first three chapters of Genesis, where he has developed what he calls the "nuptial meaning of the body." The following passages reflect his thinking in this regard.

   "Man became the 'image and likeness' of God not only through his own humanity, but also through the communion of persons which man and woman form right from the beginning. . . . Man becomes the image of God not so much in the moment of solitude as in the moment of communion. He is, in fact, right 'from the beginning' not only an image in which there is reflected the solitude of a person who rules the world, but also, and essentially, an image of an inscrutable, divine communication of persons . . ."[1]

   "Precisely the function of sex, which is in a sense a constituent part of the person (not just 'an attribute of the person'), proves how deeply man, with all his spiritual solitude, with the uniqueness, never to be repeated, of his person, is constituted by the body as 'he' or 'she.' The presence of the female element, alongside the male element and together with it, signifies an enrichment for man in the whole perspective of his history, including the history of salvation."[2]

   "Man and woman constitute . . . two different ways of the human 'being a body' in the unity of that image (of God)."[3]

   "The human body, with its sex, and its masculinity and femininity, seen in the very mystery of creation, is not only a source of fruitfulness and procreation . . . but includes right 'from the beginning' the 'nuptial' attribute, that is, the capacity of expressing love: that love precisely in which the man-person becomes a gift and—by means of this gift—fulfills the very meaning of his being and existence."[4]

   "The awareness of the meaning of the body (from Genesis)—in particular its 'nuptial' meaning—is the fundamental element of human existence in the world. . . . The body has a 'nuptial' meaning because the man-person, as the (Second Vatican) Council says, is a creature that God willed for its own sake, and that, at the same time, can fully discover its true self only in the sincere giving of itself.''[5]

5. As the development of a more positive theology of sexuality proceeds upon such lines as these, it should become both more urgent and more simple to situate within it our traditional teaching on such issues as premarital sex, homosexuality and contraception. This can be done by linking the ''nuptial meaning of the body'' with the human procreative potential (in the marriage context).

Then, in this context, the high value placed on the child as an expression of the parents' love and generosity can be emphasized. Pope John Paul expressed this beautifully and forcefully in his homily at the Washington Mall last October:

''In the sacrament of marriage, a man and woman—who at baptism became members of Christ and hence have the duty of manifesting Christ's attitudes in their lives—are assured of the help they need to develop their love in a faithful and indissoluble union and to respond with generosity to the gift of parenthood. . . . In order that Christian marriage may favor the total good and development of the married couple, it must be inspired by the Gospel, and thus be open to new life—new life to be given and accepted generously.''

The approach outlined here also brings into clearer focus the incompleteness, and therefore the basic disorder, of masturbation, premarital sex and homosexual acts. It provides a much more credible foundation for our teaching. Moreover, if a theology of the body and of sexuality is developed along these lines, it will go a long way toward disabusing people of the notion that the church has nothing to offer relative to marriage other than prohibitions—e.g., against divorce and contraception—and making it clear why the prohibitions themselves are essential safeguards of positive values.

6. While the fullest realization of the ''nuptial meaning of the body'' is the procreation of children in the marriage context, as noted above, it is also realized—admittedly in a different way—in those who are single or celibate for the sake of the kingdom. A single or celibate person must also be generative, life-giving and life-producing, not in a genital, physical sense but in a genuinely personal sense through a wide range of loving relationships. Too frequently we have tended to define celibacy in negative terms (one who is not married in order to. . .). It would be much more productive for the church if we could look upon celibacy in a more positive, enriching way. This would be more in line with our understanding of sexuality as a relational power which is the basis of intimacy and can be made fruitful in many different ways.

7. Finally, an integral theology of sexuality must also take into account the reality of original sin and its concomitant, concupiscence, without however slipping into a Jansenistic mentality. Whatever aspect of original sin one chooses to emphasize, it is a limitation and deficiency. It results in a tendency toward defective relationships both with God and with our fellow human beings.

This is because original sin, as well as actual sin, causes an inner disintegration of the elements of our personhood. Theologically, we use the term concupiscence to describe this disintegration or fragmentation. (And concupiscence is thus not synonymous with sensuality or sexual desire).

When sexuality, which is so expressive of the person, contributes to the integration of our inner selves—in a way consonant with God's plan and vision for the individual and society—it is healing and good. When, however, sexuality is expressed in a way that runs counter to the God-given orientation of the human person, it contributes to disintegration; it becomes destructive.

We now turn to the question of motivation. Most institutions in recent years have suffered from a credibility problem. People no longer accept at face value the pronouncements of institutions or the rationales which they give for their policies or programs.

People have become much more independent in their thinking. They want reasons for adopting a position, and they reserve the right to decide for themselves whether or not they will accept the reasons and embrace the position.

As noted, the church faces a similar situation in the area of doctrine. We believe that one of the church's most important responsibilities is teaching. And we hold that the teaching authority of the church, as exercised in an official way by the Holy Father and the bishops in union with him, receives special guidance from the Holy Spirit so that God's message will be preserved in every era.

It is that teaching which forms the core of religious education's doctrinal content. Today, however, much of the church's teaching is challenged and even contradicted. This is especially true in the area of morality. The church's teaching concerning human sexuality, marriage and social justice, for example, simply does not have the impact it should on many people.

Let us reflect for a moment on one aspect of this difficulty and then offer a suggestion. Too many people look on our moral teaching as a laundry list of dos and don'ts based more on historical accident or institutional concern than a gospel mandate. So they pick and choose what they want and reject the rest.

In confronting this problem a greater evangelistic effort is needed. Without minimizing the intellectual dimension—the necessity of well-reasoned arguments—we must recognize that this alone is not sufficient.

Before people can fully live by the values Jesus taught us, they must experience conversion. They must come to know and love the Lord. They must experience him in their lives; his love, mercy, understanding and compassion must be real to them. Only then will they be willing to commit themselves to him and accept the demands that he makes. Only then will they be ready to make that surrender which is expected of every Christian.

It is true that one cannot precisely "motivate" people to undergo conversion, but it is possible to motivate them so to dispose themselves as to be open to the grace of conversion.

Persons who have experienced conversion begin to understand that we are called to a totally new way of life involving new personal and societal responsibilities—a way of life, furthermore, which runs counter to many of the values of our contemporary culture. They also find that the demands of the Gospel, which humanly speaking are impossible, are not only possible but can indeed by accepted willingly and joyfully in consequence of God's grace and the strength which it confers.

Even when, because of human weakness, one does not live up to the Lord's expectations, one does not despair. One asks for forgiveness and starts over again.

Seen in the context of our living, personal relationship with Christ, doctrine takes on a deeper, richer meaning. Learning more about his message can then become a very exciting adventure, for one grasps the fact that fidelity to Christ's teaching is an important measure of personal fidelity to him, while infidelity or indifference to what he teaches calls into question the authenticity of our commitment to him.

Footnotes

[1] L'Osservatore Romano, Nov. 19, 1979, 3.

[2] L'Osservatore Romano, Nov. 26, 1979, 1.

[3] L'Osservatore Romano, Jan. 7, 1980, 2.

[4] L'Osservatore Romano, Jan. 21, 1980, 1D.

[5] L'Osservatore Romano, Jan. 21, 1980, 5.

Notes: *In this statement prepared for delivery at the 1980 World Synod of Bishops, Cardinal Joseph Bernardin calls to the attention of his fellow bishops the serious gap that exists between the official Roman Catholic teaching on sexual morality and the ideas and attitudes on this topic held by a large number of parish priests and lay people. This division, according to Bernardin, presents a serious threat to the overall credibility of the church on all moral issues, not just sexual ones.*

ROMAN CATHOLIC CHURCH— ARCHBISHOP GABRIEL ZUBEIR

MARRIAGE IN THE AFRICAN ENVIRONMENT (1980)

In the Sudan, the average rate of church marriages is three per diocese per year. The provisions of Canon 1098 (that when a priest is not available for an extended period, a couple may marry before two witnesses) and the use of *sanatio in radice* have produced scanty results. Even longstanding "traditional" marriages resist so-called "normalization" with a church rite. There are several reasons for this. I wish, however, to touch only one of them: the church rite of marriage.

The church law requiring *forma canonica* (mutual consent expressed before a priest and two witnesses) vies with other teachings of the church on marriage. Among them we can note:

—"Christ did not institute a new rite, but made marriage itself a sacrament for baptized people" (Synod Working Paper, n. 32).

—The couple are the ministers of the sacrament.

—Canon 1098, which in the Sudan at least, should become the rule by reason of great distances and the shortage of priests.

—The sacramentality of Christian marriage does not stem from a rite but from the sanctifying presence of Christ at work through the faith and the interpersonal relationship of mutual self-giving of the spouses.

—The new rite of marriage has given bishops' conferences the faculty of adapting marriage rites to local usages (Introduction to Rite of Marriage, nn. 17-18).

To do this latter successfully, our conference must bridge the gap between the church rites and the customary rites. No church marriage in the Sudan is stable unless it is first valid and stable according to tribal norms. This inevitably leads to a dichotomy in marriage celebrations and reduces the church celebration to a mere and often formalistic blessing.

We would have to take church marriage out of its isolation and put it in touch with the people's lives. Our preparation for marriage is practically limited to proximate preparation for its celebration in church.

According to our people's customs, the marriage "contract" takes place within a series of rites leading to the accompaniment of the bride to the bridegroom's house. Education for marriage begins in childhood, is intensified during initiation rites, reaches its culmination in the immediate preparations for and the celebration of marriage, and continues into the early part of the couple's married life. The community, in particular the extended family, assumes the task of this education and integrates it into the life of the community. In this way, marriage becomes an integral part of the community's life.

The church rite must fit into this chain, make the education for marriage an integral part of the Christian formation of the faithful, and place greater emphasis on the role of the community both in the formation to and the celebration of marriage, as well as in helping the couple after the marriage. We would have to shift the emphasis from the priest to the community elders. In the customary marriage, these are the people who ratify and bless marriages, and they still bless them before the church celebration. Their judgment before the community affects also marriages contracted in church.

We would not achieve much, however, if we took only the rite of marriage as the object of revision. A meaningful adaptation should be based on an organized pastoral action and formation, centered on the family and strengthened by a caring community of faith. We would have to develop to greater depth the meaning of marriage as a sacrament for the Christians, and as a covenant between persons and their God. These two ideas are very much in keeping with the ideas of our people on marriage.

Notes: *In this paper presented at the 1980 World Synod of Bishops, Archbishop Zubeir calls upon the Roman Catholic Church to take cognizance of African marriage customs and practices and to allow African Catholic leaders to integrate them into the church's marriage rituals.*

ROMAN CATHOLIC CHURCH—WORLD SYNOD OF BISHOPS

EXCERPT FROM "MESSAGE TO CHRISTIAN FAMILIES" (1980)

I. Introduction

1. We have come to the end of the synod. For the past month we bishops from all over the world have met here in Rome in union with the Holy Father and under his leadership. Before returning to our own countries, we wish to address these few words to you. It is not our intention to give answers to all the complex questions raised in our day about marriage and the family. We only want to share with you the love, confidence and hope which we feel. As your bishops and pastors, who are also your brothers in the faith, we have been united with you during these weeks; nor have we forgotten that we too grew up in families with all their joys and sorrows. To you and to our own families we are deeply grateful.

II. The Situation of Families Today

2. In our discussions of family life today we have found joys and consolations, sorrows and difficulties. We must look first for the good things and seek to build on them and make them perfect, confident always that God is present everywhere in his creatures and that we can discern his will in the signs of our times. We are encouraged by the many good and positive things that we see. We rejoice that so many families, even in the face of great pressure to do otherwise, gladly fulfill the God-given mission entrusted to them. Their goodness and fidelity in responding to God's grace and shaping their lives by his teaching gave us a great hope.

    The number of families who consciously want to live the life of the Gospel, giving witness to the fruits of the Spirit, continues to grow in all our lands.

3. During this past month we have learned much about the many and varied cultural conditions in which Christian families live. The church must accept and foster this rich diversity, while at the same time encouraging Christian families to give effective witness to God's plan within their own cultures. But all cultural elements must be evaluated in light of the Gospel, to ensure that they are consistent with the divine plan for marriage and the family. This duty—of acceptance and evaluation—is part of the same task of discernment.

4. A more serious problem than that of culture is the condition of those families who live in need in a world of such great wealth. In many parts of the globe, as well as within individual countries, poverty is increasing as a result of social, economic and political structures which foster injustice, oppression and dependence. Conditions in many places are such as to prevent many young men and women from exercising their right to marry and lead decent lives. In the more developed countries, on the other hand, one finds another kind of deprivation: a spiritual emptiness in the midst of abundance, a misery of mind and spirit which makes it difficult for people to understand God's will for human life and causes them to be anxious about the present and fearful of the future. Many find it difficult to enter into and live up to the permanent commitment of marriage. Their hands are full, but their wounded hearts are waiting for a Good Samaritan who will bind up their wounds, pouring on them the wine and oil of health and gladness.

5. Often certain governments and some international organizations do violence to families. The integrity of the home is violated. Family rights in regard to religious liberty, responsible parenthood and education are not respected. Families regard themselves as wards and victims rather than as human beings responsible for their own affairs. Families are compelled—and this we oppose vehemently—to use such immoral means for the solution of social, economic and demographic problems as contraception or, even worse, sterilization, abortion and euthanasia. The synod therefore strongly urges a charter of family rights to safeguard these rights everywhere.

6. Underlying many of the problems confronting families and indeed the world at large is the fact that many people seem to reject their fundamental vocation to participate in God's life and love. They are obsessed with the desire to possess, the will for power, the quest for pleasure. Instead of looking upon their fellow human beings as brothers and sisters, members of the human family, they regard them as obstacles and adversaries. Where people lose their sense of God, the heavenly Father, they also lose their sense of the human family. How can human beings see one another as brothers and sisters if they have lost their consciousness of having a common Father? The fatherhood of God is the only basis for the unity of the human family.

III. God's Plan for Marriage and the Family

7. God's eternal plan (cf. Eph. 1:3ff) is that all men and women should participate and share in the divine life and being (cf. 1 Jn. 1:3; 2 Pt. 1:4). The Father summons people to realize this plan in union with their fellow human beings, thus forming the people of God (cf. *Lumen Gentium*, 9).

8. In a special way the family is called to carry out this divine plan. It is, as it were, the first cell of the church, helping its members to become agents of the history of salvation and living signs of God's loving plan for the world.

    God created us in his own image (cf. Gn. 1:26), and he gave us the mission to increase and multiply, to fill the earth and subdue it (cf. Gn. 1:28). To carry out this plan man and woman are joined in an intimate union of love for the service of life. God calls spouses to participate in his creative power by handing on the gift of life.

    In the fullness of time, the Son of man born of woman (Gal. 4:4) enriched marriage with his saving grace, elevating it to the level of a sacrament and causing it to share in the covenant of his redemptive love sealed with his blood. Christ's love and gift to the church and those of the church to Christ become the model of the mutual love and self-giving of man and woman (cf. Eph. 5:22-32). The sacramental grace of matrimony is a source of joy and strength to the spouses. As ministers of this sacrament, they truly act in the person of Christ himself and bring about their mutual sanctification. Spouses must be conscious of this grace and of the presence of the Holy Spirit. Each day, dear brothers and sisters, you must hear Christ saying to you: "If only you recognized God's gift" (cf. Jn. 4:10).

9. This divine plan shows us why the church believes and teaches that the covenant of love and self-giving between two people joined in sacramental marriage must be both permanent and indissoluble. It is a covenant of love and life. The transmission of life is inseparable from the conjugal union. The conjugal act itself, as the encyclical *Humanae Vitae* tells us, must be fully human, total, exclusive and open to new life (*Humanae Vitae,* 9 and 11).

10. God's plan for marriage and the family can only be fully understood, accepted and lived by persons who have experienced conversion of heart, that radical turning of the self to God by which one puts off the "old" self and puts on the "new." All are called to conversion and sanctity. We must all come to the knowledge and love of the Lord and experience him in our lives, rejoicing in his love and mercy, his patience, compassion and forgiveness, and loving one another as he loves us. Husbands and wives, parents and children, are instruments and ministers of Christ's fidelity and love in their mutual relationships. It is this which makes Christian marriage and family life authentic signs of God's love for us and of Christ's love for the church.

11. But the pain of the cross, as well as the joy of the resurrection, is part of the life of one who seeks as a pilgrim to follow Christ. Only those who are fully open to the paschal mystery can accept the difficult but loving demands which Jesus Christ makes of us. If because of human weakness, one does not live up to these demands, there is no reason for discouragement. "Let them not be discouraged, but rather have recourse with humble perseverance to the mercy of God" (*Humanae Vitae,* 25).

IV. The Family's Response to God's Plan

12. Just as we are doing, you also are seeking to learn what your duties are in today's world. In looking at the world, we see facing you certain important tasks of education. You have the tasks of forming free persons with a keen moral sense and a discerning conscience, together with a perception of their duty to work for the betterment of the human condition and the sanctification of the world. Another task for the family is to form persons in love and also to practice love in all its relationships, so that it does not live closed in on itself but remains open to the community, moved by a sense of justice and concern for others as well as by a consciousness of its responsibility toward the whole of society. It is your duty to form persons in the faith—that is, in knowledge and love of God and eagerness to do his will in all things. It is also your task to hand on sound human and Christian values and to form persons in such a way that they can integrate new values into their lives. The more Christian the family becomes, the more human it becomes.

13. In fulfilling these tasks the family will be, as it were, a "domestic church," a community of faith living in hope and love, serving God and the entire human family. Shared prayer and the liturgy are sources of grace for families. In fulfilling its tasks the family must nourish itself on God's word and participate in the life of the sacraments, especially reconciliation and the eucharist. Traditional and contemporary devotions, particularly those associated with the Blessed Virgin, are rich sources of growth in piety and grace.

14. Evangelization and catechesis begin in the family. Formation in faith, chastity and the other Christian virtues, as well as education in human sexuality, must start in the home. Yet the outlook of the Christian family should not be narrow and confined only to the parish; it should embrace the whole human family. Within the larger community it has a duty to give witness to Christian values. It should foster social justice and relief of the poor and oppressed. Family organizations should be encouraged to protect their rights by opposing unjust social structures and public and private policies which harm the

family. Such organizations should also exercise a healthy influence on the communications media and build up social solidarity. Special praise is due those family organizations whose purpose is to help other married couples and families appreciate God's plan and live by it. This like-to-like ministry should be encouraged as part of comprehensive family ministry.

15. Out of a sense of fidelity to the Gospel, the family should be prepared to welcome new life, to share its goods and resources with the poor, to be open and hospitable to others. Today the family is sometimes obliged to choose a way of life that goes contrary to modern culture in such matters as sexuality, individual autonomy and material wealth. In the face of sin and failure, it gives witness to an authentically Christian spirit, sensitive in its life and in the lives of others there to the values of penance and forgiveness, reconciliation and hope. It gives evidence of the fruits of the Holy Spirit and the Beatitudes. It practices a simple style of life and pursues a truly evangelical apostolate toward others.

V. The Church and the Family

16. During the synod we have grown in awareness of the church's duty to encourage and support couples and families. We have deepened our commitment in this regard.

17. Family ministry is of very special interest to the church. By this we mean efforts made by the whole people of God through local communities, especially through the help of pastors and lay people devoted to pastoral work for families. They work with individuals, couples and families to help them live out their conjugal vocation as fully as possible. This ministry includes preparation for marriage; help given to married couples at all stages of married life; catechetical and liturgical programs directed to the family; help given to childless couples, single-parent families, the widowed, the separated and divorced, and, in particular, to families and couples laboring under burdens like poverty, emotional and psychological tensions, physical and mental handicaps, alcohol and drug abuse, and the problems associated with migration and other circumstances which strain family stability.

18. The priest has a special place in family ministry. It is his duty to bring the nourishment and consolation of the word of God, the sacraments, and other spiritual aids to the family, encouraging it and in a human and patient way, strengthening it in charity so that families which are truly outstanding can be formed (cf. *Gaudium et Spes,* 52). One precious fruit of this ministry, along with others, ought to be the flourishing of priestly and religious vocations.

19. In speaking of God's plan, the church has many things to say to men and women about the essential equality and complementarity of the sexes, as well as about the different charisms and duties of spouses within marriage. Husband and wife are certainly different, but they are also equal. The difference should be respected but never used to justify the domination of one by the other. In collaboration with society, the church must effectively affirm and defend the dignity and rights of women.

VI. Conclusion

20. As we reach the end of our message, we wish to say to you, brothers and sisters, that we are fully aware of the frailty of our common human condition. In no way do we ignore the very difficult and trying situation of the many Christian couples who, although they sincerely want to observe the moral norms taught by the church, find themselves unequal to the task because of weakness in the face of difficulties. All of us need to grow in appreciation of the importance of Christ's teachings and his grace and to live by them. Accompanied and assisted by the whole church, those couples continue along the difficult way toward a more complete fidelity to the commands of the Lord.

"The journey of married couples, like the whole journey of human life, meets with delays and difficult and burdensome times. But it must be clearly stated that anxiety or fear should never be found in the souls of people of good will. For is not the Gospel also good news for family life? For all the demands it makes, is it not a profoundly liberating message? The awareness that one has not achieved his full interior liberty and is still at the mercy of his tendencies and finds himself unable to obey the moral law in an area so basic causes deep distress. But this is the moment in which the Christian, rather than giving way to sterile and destructive panic, humbly opens up his soul before God as a sinner before the saving love of Christ'' (Pope Paul VI, ''Address to the Equipes de Notre Dame,'' May 4, 1970).

21. Everything we have said about marriage and the family can be summed up in two words: love and life. As we come to the end of this synod, we pray that you, our brothers and sisters, may grow in the love and life of God. In turn we humbly and gratefully beg your prayers that we may do the same. We make St. Paul's words to the Colossians our final words to you: ''Over all these virtues put on love, which binds the rest together and makes them perfect. Christ's peace must reign in your hearts, since as members of the one body you have been called to that peace. Dedicate yourselves to thankfulness'' (Col. 3:14-15).

Notes: *Like the previous Roman Catholic documents in this volume, this message reasserts the basic themes found in* Gaudium et Spes *and* Humanae Vitae: *the purposes of marriage are procreation and the personal and social fulfillment of the marriage partners. However, this ''personalist'' approach does not include permission to practice artificial means of birth control. The bishops forwarded this public statement and a list of confidential propositions to Pope John Paul II. The latter were not made public but were seen by a National Catholic News Service reporter who claimed that the propositions affirm traditional doctrine while calling for greater sensitivity on the part of the hierarchy for the needs of practicing Catholics who find it difficult to follow the church's teachings on birth control.*

ROMAN CATHOLIC CHURCH—CARDINAL JOHN O'CONNOR

ADDRESSING THE ISSUES OF WORK AND THE FAMILY (1986)

This Labor Day provides an opportunity to reflect on the rapid changes in work and family life in our nation. The moral vision embodied in Catholic social teaching provides a framework for analyzing some of the public policies needed to address the important issues of work and family. The responsibility of the church to address the new problems of families on many levels is clear: upholding moral standards and helping to shape individual moral conduct through teaching and pastoral care as well as providing services to families in crisis. It is imperative as well to recognize the church's role in working for social and economic policies in support of families. What follows here is offered within the context of such a role. A much more comprehensive treatment is provided in the third draft of the proposed pastoral letter of the bishops of the United States, ''Economic Justice for All.''

Dramatic Changes in Family and Work

The past 25 years have radically altered many basic assumptions about work and family. Men and women can no longer assume they will have stable employment and family lives. In 1961 couples generally could anticipate lifelong marriages in which husbands assumed most economic responsibility and wives handled most family duties. Those arrangements were supported by public policies and employer practices and an economic structure that provided relatively steady employment for men in a growing economy. Despite the fact that throughout our history many mothers have had to support families, divorce and labor laws, pensions, Social Security, the income tax and alimony awards were all predicated on the assumption that fathers would be the sole providers.

By the 1970s the United States was exporting more jobs and less manufactured goods. As a result, many well-paid unionized jobs in heavy industry were lost forever. Between 1979 and 1984, more than 11 million workers lost employment due to plant closings and relocation. Wildly fluctuating energy prices first brought depression-level unemployment rates to the Rust Belt and, more recently, to the Sun Belt. Now the Farm Belt faces similar dislocation as economic forces displace families from their farms and force workers in related jobs onto the unemployment rolls. In short, many providers are facing greater job insecurity in today's economy.

While many men face continuing cycles of unemployment, many women have been caught up in comparable crises. Married mothers, faced with the uncertainty of their husbands' jobs and lower living standards, have more than doubled their labor-force participation. In the wake of "no-fault" divorce laws and rising rates of divorce and out-of-wedlock births, millions of women find themselves supporting children on inadequate earnings, no alimony and little or no child support. By the 1980s, less than 10 percent of American families had both a male breadwinner and a mother at home tending full time to the family. Now many children are thrust into a variety of fragmented day-care arrangements of uncertain quality; many are unsupervised for hours each day.

While as individuals we may be aware of these dramatic changes, our social institutions have barely begun to respond. To a great extent our public policies and employment practices still reflect an earlier time when fathers were the sole providers in stable families. With one in two new marriages expected to end in divorce, with continuing cycles of unemployment and with growing poverty among women and children, society has an urgent responsibility to cushion the shock to the victims and to deal with the root causes of the problems themselves.

Welfare Policy

One of the major items on the public-policy agenda is the coming consideration of welfare reform. The question of work and family must be at the center of this discussion. Too often the issue is phrased in terms of how best to get welfare mothers out of the home and into the work place. Little attention is paid to the impact of mothers' full-time employment on very young children growing up in single-parent families with few resources. Some proposals would even compel mothers to leave their young children in day care while participating in so-called "workfare" programs that provide neither the dignity nor the remuneration of real jobs.

While the ideal is certainly that children should be cared for in their own homes by their own mothers, public policy offers little support of that option for those at the bottom of the economic scale. What do we say to low-income mothers trying to provide for their children's economic and emotional security? Unmarried mothers who are poor are offered two choices. They can go on welfare and give their young children their full attention but with a standard of living less than three-fourths of the official poverty line (even with welfare and food stamps combined). Or they can leave the children in child care and take a minimum-wage, poverty-level job that offers only a slightly better net income and some hope for advancement. That so many mothers choose to work under such conditions indicates their strong determination to work for the sake of giving their children a better life.

What about married mothers? In only half the states can a family receive welfare aid if the father is present in the home and unemployed. In no state can the family get help if the father is present in the home and working, however low the wages. The system virtually pushes low-income married as well as single mothers away from their children and into the labor force.

True welfare reform must meet at least five criteria if it is to protect human dignity:

promotion of family stability, adequate levels of assistance, opportunity for healthy child development, support for eventual self-sufficiency and humane administration. The current welfare system meets none of these criteria adequately. Surely the sole test for eligibility should be valid need. Families should certainly not be denied aid because the parents are married and living together or when the income of a working father is inadequate. Parents who want to work should have access to job training and placement and subsidized work when appropriate. Job training should equip parents to support their children above the poverty level. Working parents should have access to high-quality and affordable child care and health programs so that working does not deprive their children of these essentials. Mothers should not have to leave their children to take jobs or training unless the family would be better off as a result. Pregnant women should receive special consideration, with additional welfare assistance to meet their needs for appropriate clothing, food and rest. Benefit levels should be increased across the board and brought to at least a decent minimum federal level. Most current welfare levels are scandalously low. Moreover the administration of welfare programs all too frequently has been marked by humiliation of and perceived indifference to applicants and recipients. Arbitrary decisions, long delays, invasions of privacy and terminations of aid without careful review or prompt reconsideration have been among the problems crying out for reform.

Other Family Policy Issues

Further up the income scale, the options are not much better. While these families may have their basic needs met, mothers must take jobs for other important goals to be within reach: buying a home, tuition and books in non-public schools, higher education for the children. Despite the fact that so many mothers are working, the real income of average families has actually fallen. The economic data confirm the experience of many families—that even with both parents working, their standard of living is below that achieved by their own parents on just a father's income.

According to the U.S. Department of Labor, three-fifths of mothers of children under 5 have jobs. Most of that group have hurried back to work within weeks of giving birth, partly because their families depend so heavily on their earnings and partly because, even if they can afford to take a few months off without pay, they are in danger of losing their jobs. Losing a job and health insurance and pension benefits seems foolhardy to many in times of economic insecurity.

Some employers have developed innovative programs that support women employees in their roles as mothers, such as subsidized child care at the work place, generous paid and unpaid pregnancy and family leave, and flexible and part-time hours. Such policies have been successful in retaining highly qualified workers and improving efficiency. But many women workers are not represented by unions, and few have such specialized skills that on their own they can negotiate adequate maternity leave or part-time work. Most working parents get no help from employers in trying to balance the competing demands of work and family.

In the absence of voluntary action by employers, what should be the role of government in safeguarding the well-being of young children and supporting family life? This country has a long history of labor legislation designed to protect working people and their families in situations where the record of employers was weak. Child-labor and minimum-wage laws are just two examples of the acknowledged need for government action when private employers and the forces of the marketplace fail to protect basic rights and human dignity.

Catholic teaching on the role of government in such areas is a rich resource that we should not forget. For almost a century papal encyclicals have defended the rights of workers and assigned to government a positive and active role in protecting human dignity and basic human rights. In recent years Pope John Paul II in ''On Human Work'' and ''On the Family'' has eloquently reaffirmed the role of government in this arena.

"In the conviction that the good of the family is an indispensable and essential value of the civil community, the public authorities must do everything possible to ensure that families have all those aids—economic, social, educational, political and cultural assistance—that they need in order to face all their responsibilities in a human way" ("On the Family," 45).

Our Holy Father has spoken many times in support of the idea that incomes should be adjusted for family size and in order to accommodate mothers staying home to care for young children. In an American context, this goal could be accomplished in several ways: paid maternity leave and children's allowances, as in most other developed nations, and a system of special tax treatment to offset lost wages of mothers at home. Certainly public policy should support the decision of mothers to stay home when their children are very young. Government can also support that decision by ensuring that mothers do not subsequently pay a high price for devoting their full energies to child care. A fair allocation of pension and Social Security benefits and property for widows and divorced women and more vigorous enforcement of just maintenance and child-support payments can help to protect mothers from poverty later, when their years of child care mean lower earnings and less retirement income.

It is important to point out, however, that such a policy should not be accompanied by penalties for mothers who, for whatever reason, are in the work force. The Holy Father also warns against discrimination against women in employment and reminds us of the shared responsibility of government, employers and the rest of society to see that affordable, high-quality child care is available for the children of working mothers. John Paul II has said that in order for the evolution of society and culture to be fully human, women must have opportunities to "harmoniously combine" their private and public, family and occupational roles ("On the Family," 23).

In the future, society, including government, will also have to increase its support for families caring for frail elderly relatives. This has traditionally been a female role; but with two-thirds of the women now in the work force full time, some accommodation will have to be made for greater sharing of that role. Public and private support will also have to be provided for workers who must take responsibility for such care.

Too often proposals for special protection for mothers and families have been resisted on the grounds that such special consideration constitutes discrimination against others. Yet the ultimate goal of pro-family policies is the good of the whole society. The health of the whole society is heavily dependent on healthy families which can provide care and support for the very young and the very old. Thus, the concept of the common good should not be lost amid conflicting claims for individual or group interests.

In the next several years our state and national governments will be making critical choices about public and private roles in the areas of work and family. Our long tradition of Catholic social teaching in defense of workers and families can bring to the debate a focus on the moral dimension of those choices. We offer that tradition to all, with deepest sincerity, on this Labor Day of 1986.

Notes: *Bishop John O'Connors' 1986 Labor Day Message reflects many of the themes found in the third draft of the National Conference of Catholic Bishops' pastoral letter on Catholic Social Teaching and the U.S. economy and illustrates how church leaders find it necessary today to give serious consideration to the social, cultural, and economic context of human life when they speak about the nature and purpose of the family.*

Protestant and Eastern Orthodox Churches

Over half of the religiously affiliated individuals in North America identify with one of the many Protestant or Eastern Orthodox denominations. Within these bodies there exists widely divergent Christian theologies and opinions on sexuality. However, all hold that the Bible is normative in defining sexual morality and the family. And the great majority hold that the family unit is the normative social unit. Most, if not all, continue to state in their official documents that sexual activity should be limited to heterosexual relations between couples in a monogamous marriage.

Challenged in the 1960s and 1970s to reconsider their traditional approaches to sexuality and the family, several church bodies conducted a variety of seminars and other activities to address those issues. In addition to educating a generation of church leaders on the complex problems of sexuality and the family in the contemporary world, these activities produced preliminary studies and reports with highly controversial recommendations. While these recommendations have not been officially adopted, they have been accepted and remanded to congregations and/or official bodies for further study. On the other hand, these recommendations have also stimulated the formation of minority movements that seek to prevent the integration of new approaches to sexuality and the family into the belief and moral systems of their churches.

Statements from a diverse group of religious organizations are included. When appropriate, a number of different statements from the same group or from minority units within that group are included to illustrate the continuing interest in the issue and to show how a community may deal differently with the issue at different times.

Lengthy portions of some of the most recent studies and reports are included to illustrate how the leaders and members of some religious bodies struggle to remain true to their traditions while recognizing new knowledge from the natural and social sciences and seeking to respond responsibly to dramatic and at times cataclysmic changes in society.

AMERICAN BAPTIST CHURCHES IN THE U.S.A.

EXCERPT FROM "POLICY STATEMENT ON FAMILY LIFE" (1984)

Biblical-Theological Base

The Bible approaches family life with great honesty and with serious idealism. The rivalry of brothers (Genesis 4:1-16; 25:21-34; 27; 37), the duplicities and infidelities of spouses

(Genesis 27; 30:1-25; Judges 14; 2 Samuel 11), the tensions of parent and child (Genesis 26:34-35; 37:5-10; 2 Samuel 14-18; Luke 2:41-51) are vividly portrayed. Equally vivid are stories of great love (Genesis 25:19-21; 29; 37:3; Hosea 1-3), examples of faithfulness and loyalty (Genesis 39; 45:4-5; Ruth; 1 Samuel 18-20), moments of reconciliation (Genesis 33; 45). In the Old Testament, family relationships are taken again and again as metaphors for the relationship of God and Israel (e.g. Deuteronomy 32:11, 12, 18; Isaiah 46:3-4; 49:14-16; Jeremiah 3:1-5; Ezekiel 16; Hosea 2:19-20). In the parables and sayings of Jesus, images of marriage and family life are used frequently to express the nature and reality of God's rule (e.g. Matthew 21:28-32; 22:1-14; Matthew 25:1-13; Luke 11:11-13; Luke 15:11-32; John 3:3-6).

Baptists read the Old Testament from the perspective of the New and especially in the light of Jesus' teachings. As a result, three Old Testament themes are highly valued.

1. A vision of marriage as monogamous, life-long one-flesh union is affirmed by Jesus as God's intention for marriage "from the beginning" (Genesis 1:27; 2:24; Matthew 19:3-6; Mark 10:2-9).

2. A vision of the parent-child relationship as one of tender care, mutual responsibility, and mutual benefit (Exodus 20:12; Deuteronomy 6:6-7; Proverbs 1:8-9; 6:20-22) is reinforced by Jesus' special attention to children (Matthew 18:1-6; Mark 10:13-16), his assumptions about the depth of parental care (Matthew 7:9-11) and his insistence in word and deed that adult children fulfill their responsibilities to dependent parents (Matthew 15:1-9; John 19:26-27).

3. A recognition that God creates new family bonds where none existed before (Deuteronomy 26:5-11; Ruth) is proclaimed by the Church as the New Covenant in Christ through which the brokenness and partiality of human kinship is transcended and healed (Matthew 3:9; 1 Peter 2:9-10). The New Testament church became the new family of God for those whose acceptance of Christ cut them off from their biological families (John 9) and for those in special need, such as widows, for whom the church became a family (Acts 6:1-6; 1 Timothy 5:1-16).

Jesus assumed marriage and family relationships as givens. Even though the gospels include stories of conflict between Jesus and his family (Mark 3:20-21, 31-35; Luke 2:41-51; John 7:5), he saw in marital and parent-child relationships images of the divine-human bond. Jesus blessed a wedding at Cana, enjoyed the warmth of family gatherings in the homes of Peter, and of Mary and Martha, responded with compassion to the parents of sick and dying children, and thereby affirmed the rich possibilities of family life. His teachings of humility, mutual service, forgiveness, and the primacy of persons over property and tradition form the bedrock of any Christian approach to questions of family life in any culture or historical era.

At the same time Jesus put the highest priority on the Kingdom of God and recognized the potential for conflicts between family loyalties and commitment to God's will and rule (Matthew 10:21, 35-37; Mark 10:29-30). For Jesus, *no* institution, neither Temple, nor Law, nor Sabbath, nor Family can claim ultimate allegiance. Only participation in God's will and acknowledgement of God's rule can claim our ultimate concern. Jesus' own singleness and celibacy (Matthew 19:10-12) accents the priority of the Kingdom in his own life.

Salvation history begins with the call to Abraham and Sarah to leave father's house and kin and land and venture to a new place and through divine covenant to found a new family by which all the families of the earth may find blessing. Salvation history culminates in the Son of Abraham (Matthew 1:1) and the Son of God who founded a more inclusive, spiritual family in which the blessings of family relationship are made available to all regardless of race, or sex, or life condition.

Finally, the New Testament both refers to a wide variety of familial households (e.g. Mark 1:29; Mark 6:1-3; Luke 1:5-25, 39-44, 57-66; Luke 10:38-41; John 11:1-44, 13:1-11;

Acts 9:36-42; Acts 10; Acts 16:1-2; Acts 18:1-19) and includes specific attempts to guide Christians in family living. The common touchstone of these teachings is mutuality of responsibility and service to one another in Christ (Ephesians 5:21-6:9). There is in the New Testament, and we affirm, a vision of Christian family living in which Christ is the head of the household and all members are mutually responsible to one another and to Christ. With this vision, with a sense of serious idealism and biblical honesty we seek to articulate an American Baptist policy on family life today.

Situation Analysis

Americans are at a turning point in our collective understanding of the significance, the needs, and the potential of family life for the health of the whole society. The aspirations of Americans for satisfying family relationships, as reported in national polls, are very high. New methods for family education are available along with new knowledge of the dynamics of family systems and a new appreciation for the impact of public policies on families. This is an opportune moment to define American Baptist policy toward the family. Two significant developments require our response. The diversity of family patterns [which] is normative for America . . . [and] the liberation movements among minorities, youth, the aged, the handicapped, and women that emerged in new ways during the 1960's that challenged the assumption that there either was or should be a prescribed pattern for family. . . .

New Knowledge About Family Life is Available

Since 1960, new knowledge about family life has been emerging almost in parallel with the growing diversity of family life patterns.

- Behavioral scientists have learned to look at families as biological-psychological-social systems, in which each member is affected by every other. Understanding what makes a healthy family system has grown, as well as understanding how family systems transmit persistent patterns of relating, learning, and coping from generation to generation.

- Professional educators have rediscovered the educative role and function of families. New understandings have been gained of how families mediate the influence of television, school, church, and other community institutions.

- Sociologists, political scientists, and ecologists have begun to perceive and measure the impact of governmental policy, corporate practices, and the quality of the environment on families. In spite of our highly individualistic culture, a new appreciation is emerging for the familial connections all persons carry.

Policy

American Baptists, with our heritage of respect for the Word of God and for the individual conscience, have a contribution to make to the public discussion of family life today.

1. A basic theological conviction underlying American Baptist policy toward families is that God calls each Christian to discipleship in every area of life. Believers make life-shaping decisions in response to God's call. We affirm that for Christian disciples choices about singleness, marriage, parenthood, and living in covenantal, intentional family arrangements are to be made soberly, with prayer, and as integral parts of the Christian's response to God's call in Jesus Christ. We affirm the competence of the individual soul to determine God's will in such matters through the reading and interpreting of Scripture, through dialogue with God, by considering the teaching and counsel of the Christian community, and by seeking and testing the wisdom of sisters and brothers in Christ.

2. We affirm that God intends marriage to be a monogamous, life-long, one flesh union of a woman and a man, who in response to God's call leave father and mother and cleave to one another. We affirm God's blessing and active presence in marriage relationships so entered in response to God's call.

43

We affirm the full implications of this understanding of marriage, especially that God calls partners to work at personal growth, to deepen skills in communication and decision making, and to invest both their time and energy in the development of their marriage.

We affirm that the grace and forgiveness of God are sufficient to sustain, heal, and renew our lives when our marriages are ended by death or separation or divorce.

We affirm that in God's grace remarriage for divorced Christians is appropriate where the issues which ended an earlier marriage have been addressed and the new marriage shows promise of fulfilling God's intention for the marriage relationship.

3. We affirm that children are a gift from God, entrusted to parents for love, care, and nurture. We affirm parents as the first teachers and spiritual guides of their children; we believe parents are responsible for involving their children in the life of the Christian community. We affirm the reciprocal responsibility of grown children for the well-being of aging parents.

4. We affirm Christian families as agents through which the Good News is proclaimed, received, and lived out so that persons might fulfill God's redemptive purpose in history.

5. We affirm the Church as the inclusive family of God in which

   - persons living alone find intimacy and support with sisters and brothers in Christ;

   - youth are challenged to become autonomous disciples of Jesus Christ and are helped in their journey by committed peer and adult friends;

   - aging persons are enabled to share the wisdom of years through intergenerational fellowship;

   - divorced persons and single-parent families are strengthened by the presence and involvement of caring Christian friends in their lives;

   - family groups experiencing conflict within marriages or between generations are supported, reminded of God's grace, and helped to find resources for healing;

   - individuals and family units will experience God's love and come to know and accept Jesus Christ;

   - individuals and family units are equipped and inspired to build a social order of respect and care for every person, all family groups, and ethnic communities.

6. We are committed to providing programs of education and support

   - To guide and nurture persons making choices about singleness, marriage, divorce, remarriage, and parenthood;

   - to enrich couples seeking to fulfill God's intention in their marriage;

   - to empower parents striving to raise children according to Christian principles; to enable parents in their roles as teachers, managers, and advocates; and to sustain parents when young adult children struggle with sexual orientation, divorce, job loss, or death;

   - to strengthen family units of all kinds, including single-parent and blended families, foster/adoption families, those living in group homes and other covenantal family-like groups;

   - to equip family members and family units with skills and vision for witness to God's grace and participation in God's work of making peace and justice in the lives of individuals and society.

7. We are committed to working with others for public policies and practices which

enhance the status of families and empower them to do their unique work of nurturing succeeding generations of citizens.

8. We are committed to advocating for the rights of all families, and especially those with dependent children and aging members, to the necessities of life: shelter, safety, nutrition, medical care, and education.

9. We are committed to advocacy on behalf of families with special needs including

- those where parents are separated by illness, military service, or work;
- those caring for a family member with disabilities or the infirmities of age;
- those whose breadwinners are unemployed.

10. We are committed to modeling in our congregations and denominational life a vision of an inclusive, intergenerational community, a family of God, in which the variety of family forms, the richness of ethnic traditions, and the gifts of all persons from newborns to the very old, are respected, enjoyed, and celebrated.

Notes: *This statement was adopted by the General Board of the American Baptist Church in June of 1984 with 140 affirmative, 24 negative votes and 4 abstentions. It reflects a mainline Protestant church's attempt to reformulate its teachings on the family in light of changing conditions while remaining true to its own biblical tradition.*

ANGLICAN CONSULTATIVE COUNCIL

EXCERPT FROM "TRANSFORMING FAMILIES AND COMMUNITIES"(1987)

Foreword

Family issues are no longer soft options for the Church. They have become the leading edge of social reality.

For families live in communities, and these affect and are affected by political, economic and social pressures from outside, and by relationship difficulties and traumas within.

How a family functions, whether it survives or not, is not a microcosm of how the whole world is going.

That is why it has been entirely appropriate to have "family and community" as a major theme for the 1988 Lambeth Conference of Anglican Bishops. In order to provide information and advice both on what is happening to families and communities in the world today, and how the Church might respond, the Anglican Consultative Council set up an International Project on Family and Community. . . .

In this program six consultancies were held in different parts of the world: Hong Kong, Kenya, Philippines, Canada, New Zealand and Australia. Special Papers were written on the situation of families in Latin America, Nigeria, Southern Africa and England. Occasional Papers were commissioned on the Future of the Family, Media and Families, and Women's Issues. National contributions were made from the Middle East and other Provinces. All of this, together with stories shared when the Family Network met in Singapore in April 1987, and supported by a computerised literature search, have gone into producing this report. It has been a complex operation of which this report is the culmination. It is the hope of the Project Team that it will provide significant input to the Lambeth Conference together with some preliminary suggestions for pastoral ministry strategy.

The reader may ask: what can any international study of the family teach us? My country is unique! To which the answer must be: maybe we can learn from one another; maybe developing churches can teach the West a few things; maybe as a universal consumer culture consumes the whole world, we can learn to cling together and minister in similar ways!

There is a note of hope in this report—both about the future of the family, and about the opportunity local congregations have of creating communities of welcome which embrace and include the poor and the powerless, as our Lord did.

There is also a strong note of reality in this report, as the Church at local and diocesan level grapples with the external political and economic pressures and the social injustices which affect the families and communities they are seeking to minister to. This is where the "peace and justice" and "family and community" agendas intersect.

It is our hope that this report, with its many stories of ministries around the Anglican Communion, will inform the Lambeth Conference and the whole Church, and will help us all to focus on how we may more effectively minister the Gospel of Christ to families and communities where we are situated.

3. Families in Transformation

> *"Traditional Chinese extended family culture is rapidly changing towards Western style nuclear living arrangements, although the Chinese family generally remains emotionally close."* (Hong Kong Consultancy Report)

> *"Economic, medical and educational influences are probably going to have much greater effects on the future of the family in society than religious influences. The old structure of the extended family in Nigeria is already breaking down."* (Nigerian Occasional Paper)

> *"In spite of its stubbornness, the Asian family has given way to certain significant changes which are now actually taking place. Foremost among these changes which have produced other changes, is the shift from the 'sacred family' which is centered around moral and religious values, to the 'secular family' with its more pragmatic, rational philosophy which encourages family members to adopt new goals for themselves and for the community."* (Christian Conference of Asia)

"Family" is a universal idea, but it has been expressed throughout the centuries in a great variety of relationships, households and networks. What is now clear is that the variety is diminishing, as Western cultural forms and expectations spread across the world. In one sense, the whole world is moving towards nuclear families, and this brings with it a host of problems which can be identified from the experience of large cities in Western countries, and from which we should be able to draw lessons to use in pastoral ministry in other places.

First, it will be helpful to identify the variety of family formation and structure which the Family Project has discovered in the process of its consultancies from Province to Province of the Anglican Communion.

In Hong Kong, we came across traditional "klongs" (villages) which in the few remaining rural parts of Hong Kong and the New Territories continued to provide amazingly strong social support for the smaller family units and households living within it. Then there is the traditional extended Chinese family, which often has grandmother living with parents and grandchildren, in very tight accommodation in small flats in Kowloon or other parts of Hong Kong. It is these extended units which are being broken up by the Government policy, which has a lot of popular support, of moving the nuclear family—just parents and their children—into new high rise apartments in Tai Po in the New Territories. So the patterns are very rapidly changing, as over one million people have already been moved from one form of housing and community to another.

In Kenya, the traditional tribal family in the rural areas is of an extended form, with a lot of social and personal supports built in. But as in most countries in Africa this is being dramatically changed by the drift to the large cities to find work. Either the whole family moves to the city and very often finds itself in very poor slum conditions; or the father with the aim of holding onto the land, moves to the city to find work and before long has two homes—his original family back home where basically the mother has child rearing obligations, and the home in the city where he lives with another woman and may even form another family. Loyalties become very divided and both family units are under strain. In the process, individuals, including children, break away from one home or the other, become socially isolated, and are forced to prostitute themselves in the streets. Around these large cities, there are also the more middle class urban nuclear families, rather on the Western pattern. And as those marriages come under strain, as they do in all Western societies, commonly the woman finishes up with the children and forms a single parent family which may last for a considerable time. There is no social security in a country like Kenya which can act as a ''safety net'' for such single parents, whether urban or rural.

In the Philippines, our consultancy found local communities which are really collections of families based around ''atos'', which are groups of young people living together in gender-segregated long houses. In these rural communities, the whole community makes the decisions and works together, and only couples with young children live by themselves in separate households. This system is breaking down as the ''cash economy'' is introduced and individuals must compete against one another for jobs. Community structures are being replaced by alien political and legal bureaucracies. A consequence is social isolation of families, without a social history to enable them to function adequately. The search for work in distant places also further fragments these families, whether they go to the cities of the Philippines for work or whether they become part of the ''export labour'' working in Hong Kong, Singapore, or the Middle East.

In New Zealand, minority groups of Maori or Samoan origin are expressing their sense of alienation from white society around them. They are doing this in the context of their own extended family of a traditional kind breaking down under the pressure of suburban or urban living and under the temptations of consumerism. Those highly conscious of their ethnic origin want to retain their identity against what they see as unreasonable pressure to conform to the white consumerist society, and this makes them politically active.

Many Australian Aborigines leave economically depressed rural areas and drift into the cities in search of work. Because of the many new pressures in the cities, however, tribal marriages break up, adult relationships become short-term and confused, and women often find themselves in shelters or refuges, receiving emergency care from white social workers. They become classic cases of ''anomie''—alienation and dislocation from society around them. This sense of anomie is well illustrated by graffiti written on a fence in New Zealand about the concept of the Anglican Diocese of Aotearoa: ''The Land of the Wrong White Crowd'' (Note: New Zealand has traditionally referred to itself as ''The Land of the Long White Cloud'').

In Canada, as in other developed nations, the more common Western pattern of suburban nuclear families comes under increasing pressure because of violence within the home, inadequate relationships and community breakdown. The result is a vast number of single parent families headed by women, some of them homeless and most of them very poor. There is an increasing proportion of households without children—young couples, young singles and elderly living alone. Informal and communal ''collectives'' are also growing up around the cities. So even the traditional Western nuclear family pattern is changing dramatically.

Historically the nuclear family model is a relatively modern phenomenon. In economic and geographical terms it is still a minority model. It has had a significant part to play in modern capitalism in that it has enabled a split between the domestic and public spheres for the organisation of labour and consumption. Many of its proponents emphasise the positive aspects of family: privacy, competitiveness, emotional space, achievements and fulfillment. The negative aspects must also be considered.

Women have had to carry the greater burden in fostering and maintaining family life. For the mothers, themselves, this has resulted in long periods of social isolation, an under-development of skills that will enable active participation in other spheres of community life and the subsequent need to define their identity wholly in terms of their children and of their spouses's interests. For the male spouse, this has meant an emotional retreat from the responsibilities of family life and too ready an identification of the public sphere as the domain of the masculine gender.

These sex roles have been an implicit part of much of the Western world's social organisation throughout this century and are relevant to an understanding of such problems as domestic violence, family breakdown and the associated concerns of family law and property distribution, and the feminisation of poverty. The increasing participation of women in fields of paid employment should not be seen as a return to the "symmetrical family" and therefore a resolution of the domestic-public dichotomy in the organisation of labour. Rather it may simply be an indication of a trend towards increasing individuation. The fostering and maintenance of kinship values and structures therefore requires a transformation in attitudes of males as well as females. Moreover, it requires greater recognition by the community at large of the kinds of impacts that our political and economic structures have on social structures.

The ideology of the "nuclear" family is still pervasive in our society at the cost of the more just, inclusive and equitable family and community structures. As dealt with elsewhere, not only is this middle class, Western ideal promoted in advertising and television programs but it is still implicit in many government, social, political and private markets such as in the type of housing and community services provided.

The institutional and structural effects of this underlying ideology are discriminatory towards minorities, mentally and physically disable people, women and children in general, and those who choose to live in non-nuclear family households.

Nuclear families are becoming the central institution in the private realm of existence. Cut off from the public sphere and the workplace nuclear families are characterised by female symbols of endurance, emotional expression, and commitment. By contrast masculine identity is conceived to involve a facility for impersonality, rationality, coping with tension and the representation of the family in the public world. The woman as homemaker and man as breadwinner are not only roles assigned by a division of labour but are now associated with gender identities and two separate spheres of social existence. These two separate spheres, the public and the private with their associated gender characteristics each presuppose the other.

The power of our thoughts about the nuclear family stems from the fact that in the public world of capitalism the real needs of people can never be met. Nurturance, support, security, commitment are symbolically located in the family groupings that increasingly cannot supply them. Women are denied freedom to participate in public life. Men are excluded from the activities of care and emotional support.

It is not assumed that everything in the traditional extended family setting was good or perfect and that everything to do with the nuclear family presents difficulties. There are obviously strong and weak aspects in both types. What is important is to understand that communities cannot recreate an extended family form that has its ideal in the past. Rather, some of the difficulties associated with nuclear family groupings must be dealt with especially the dichotomy between the public and private spheres mentioned above. Recognition of the way government policies—national, State or provincial, and local—affect family life must be considered in any pastoral ministry.

The role of the State is important in that it can reinforce the inadequacies of the nuclear family or assist in fostering kin relations and social stability. The question is no longer whether or not State intervention occurs, but how. Awareness of the direct effects of policies relating to social security, taxation, housing, health, education and family law is needed.

For example, tax transfer systems in industrial and post-industrial nation states often redistribute resources in favour of the male or the breadwinner, rather than women and children. Even when women work, tax allowances strongly favour men's activities and responsibilities rather than women's. Dependent spouse rebates, family allowances (for dependent children), superannuation allowances, insurance, and housing allowances tend to enhance the man's position.

The social stigma attached to lone-parent families in some countries affects the level of social security payments and allowances to mothers and their dependent children.

In Canada, government housing policies splits families in a dramatic way. For example, for a supporting parent, when the last child reaches 18 years old, a mother is no longer eligible for public housing despite the fact that she may have two, three or four older children living with her. A family of four people, for example, are each forced to find private accommodation. The result is often that the woman is forced to live in a single room on a public housing estate and the children likewise on different estates.

One of the worrying things about how national family policy is determined by governments, particularly in the Western world, is how the so called New Right Movement has taken a "pro-family" stance, and has sometimes seemed to corner the market of family policy. This is often a mistake in people's perception, because the New Right Movement on the whole supports tax concessions for the middle class, and expresses little concern for the lower income families or the unemployed or the socially isolated. Moreover, it actively promotes the illusion that families are independent of other social and economic structures. At the same time the New Right Movement advocates the removal of many of these social and economic supports that are necessary to the healthy functioning of families.

It is important that churches consider very carefully any pro-family public statements by political parties, to make sure that they really have a preference for the poor and are not just bolstering the economic position of individuals already quite well off in the middle economic streams of national life.

Homeless Families

One of the key indicators of poverty in any nation is accommodation. Either it is too expensive to rent, or access is denied for some racist or sexist reason. It provides the continuing worry for sole parents with dependent children. In all Western countries the increasing rate of marriage breakdown has resulted in women sole parents adding to the waiting lists for public housing.

Our Canadian consultancy showed that even on a stringent budget 26% of family income goes on shelter, a percentage considered acceptable by housing and income authorities. But it leaves very little for necessities, and some items like entertainment can never be afforded.

The Canadian consultancy shows that the vacancy rate of affordable housing in Ottawa is 0.3%. The waiting list in May 1986 for family accommodation was 1460 families listed in government agencies and another 368 families in one of the non-profit housing organisations. Such high demand is a direct result of a decision by the Ontario Housing Ministry to stop increasing the stock of public housing available to families. No public housing has been constructed in the Ottawa area since 1974.

One result has been that public housing is limited to families with children under 18 years of age and still in school, or at the other end of the life cycle it is available to low income people over 60 years of age. So a woman of 45 years who has two or three children over the age of 18 living with her is not eligible for public housing until she reaches 60 years of age. She is supposed to find employment, and her chances of doing this are slim. This forces the break-up of the family.

Partly to counteract this, self-help groups have developed co-operative housing arrangements, using government-provided low interest housing loans, sometimes as low as 2%. But these arrangements have never kept up with demand, and the result is long waiting lists. Housing remains then one of the most important issues in the debates on poverty in Canada.

In the New Zealand consultancy, carried out by United Nations Development Officer Faga Matalavea of Samoa, homelessness closely correlated with unemployment. Without adequate incomes families can no longer afford housing, and high levels of homelessness have concentrated in the urban areas of Auckland, Wellington and Christchurch. It is currently estimated by community workers nationally that there are 20,000 homeless families in New Zealand.

Strangely, as unemployment accelerated in the early 1980s, as the current recession grew so the government subsidised housing program contracted. Some estate housing stock was sold off to tenants, but there was no accompanying building or acquisition program to offset the effects of this policy. The consequence was an increasing number of unemployed, benefit-dependent families and low-wage earning people with no homes.

The consultancy reported: "Families therefore double and treble up with other families in two or three bedroom homes. The detrimental effects of over-crowding and instability are seen in the children as they move from school to school and have no security of belonging. It can also be seen in the relationships of family members which have been placed under great strain. Other families stay in tents, caravans, motor cars, sheds and other makeshift shelter." In particular welfare programs, a pattern emerges where Maori and Pacific Island families are in proportion in the greatest need of housing. At this point, it is obvious that racism operates to exclude them from the housing market, the consultancy found.

In Perth, Australia homelessness could be compared between Aboriginal and white communities. "For Aboriginal people, the loss of relationship with their land involves a disintegration of their law and identity. Aboriginal people are now homeless in this sense. The dislocation of extended family elements and a result of the pressures of being a minority discriminated against in a Western culture has further dismantled a sense of relationship for Aboriginal people", the consultancy found.

By contrast, in the European/Australian community, homelessness is about a lack of quality relationships within families and communities. Young people dislocated from their families and placed in an Anglican welfare housing program seek to develop relationships and to have a home. "It is the dysfunction of relationships within the family and the lack of other extended family and social support which cause homelessness among this group", the consultancy found.

These stories can be repeated in cities all over the world. Either because of relationship breakdown, or poverty caused by unemployment, people individually or in family groups seek accommodation. Some communities and welfare groups provide emergency accommodation, but the long term housing shortage remains in most communities. Governments make better or worse attempts at solving this problem, depending on resources and the priority they give to it. Increasingly, the Church around the world is becoming concerned about this and either providing emergency shelters, or taking up the cause of the homeless as part of the whole spectrum of poverty and disadvantage.

Pastoral Principles

Because in most countries traditional extended family and kin systems are breaking down into small nuclear units without much social support,

and because the family is a basic set of relationships in which Christian faith must make a significant difference,

and because in Nigeria, New Zealand and other places the Church is developing ministries relevant to public policies on family, could your church adopt as a principle for pastoral ministry the following?—

FAMILIES SHOULD NOT BE UNDERSTOOD OR MINISTERED TO IN ISOLATION. RATHER, PASTORAL MINISTRY SHOULD RESPOND TO FAMILIES IN THEIR WIDER CONTEXT AND SEEK AND DEVELOP SOCIAL SYSTEMS OF SUPPORT.

4. Women and Men: Love and Alienation

As the community faith, the Church around the world is seeing it as its responsibility to name the dominance of men over women throughout our societies and our histories as the sin of sexism.

They are looking at the different ways women and men are treated, and are identifying the injustices which have been perpetrated by men against women. We have a responsibility to recognise this domination and submission along gender lines, and to see it as similar to humankind's domination over nature; to that of race against race; that of masters over slaves; and that of oppressors over the oppressed.

Relations between the sexes are fundamental to the social construction of reality in all societies. In themselves, sex roles and identities vary greatly across time and between cultures. We do not believe they are fixed by nature or by divine decree.

In particular, the Church is coming to believe that women's lives are not conditioned by the biological reality of their capacity to bear children, nor do people believe that their function is simply to provide the stability of continuity within the domestic sphere or household.

The Church has been slow to acknowledge the different household arrangements of different cultures and periods. But it is now clear that modern technological societies, both capitalist and socialist, have dramatically altered and reshaped gender relations and the status of women. The fairly recent advent of the nuclear child-centered family and urban migration have weakened traditional women's cultures and isolated them from supports. As the social value of their culture declined, they became disempowered. It is critical for the Church's survival, and for its credibility in the next generation, that we address these issues which affect women. . . .

Clergy Families

A particular concern for pastoral care for the Church is the breakdown of clergy marriages and the disintegration of clergy families.

In the United States, Christine Folwell is undertaking a study of clergy marriages for the Episcopal Family Network. It is already showing up a divorce rate not dissimilar from the national average.

In Canada, pressures on clergy families are recognised in at least one area by ''networking'' set up by Mary Parke-Taylor which provides a support system for clergy wives and which utilises the professional skills of other clergy wives—counselling, business, etc.—over a wide geographical distance. Confidentiality is guaranteed. Mary has also developed a policy for surviving or deserted spouses of clergy in Toronto. The policy covers use of the rectory, stipend and benefits, legal advice, funeral benefits and survivor's benefits.

In the Philippines, clergy and clergy families experience conflicting role expectations by the Church and the local community, enforced family separation due to low remuneration, geographical isolation and regular shifts in work location. All of these factors contribute to significant clergy family stress.

Pastoral Principles

Because women face horrendous problems in most societies when they are single, poor or have suffered violence,

and because women are more than half the worshippers in most Anglican congregations, and because the Bible calls on us to treat all women and men as equal,

could an appropriate pastoral principle for your church be?—

PASTORAL CARE FOR WOMEN MUST FACE THEIR ACTUAL SOCIAL CIRCUM-STANCES, ADDRESS THE INJUSTICES INFLICTED AGAINST THEM IN SOCIETY, AND AFFIRM THE PLACE OF WOMEN IN THE CHURCH BY TRANSFORMING THE CHURCH'S OWN STRUCTURES TO REMOVE ANY OPPRESSION OR ALIENATION OF WOMEN TO GIVE THEM OPPORTUNITIES FOR SERVICE.

FURTHER, THE ANGLICAN CHURCH MUST DEVELOP ADEQUATE PASTORAL CARE AND SUPPORT FOR CLERGY FAMILIES.

6. What We Affirm

Traditionally Anglican Theology on family starts with sex and marriage. Here the order is deliberately reversed, to emphasise the impact of national and community factors on family life. These affirmations are preliminary reflections on the information emerging from the Family Project. They are not intended in any way to be definitive, but a starting point for discussion.

National

Just as the Church has always proclaimed that the whole world belongs as one family to God, only in this century have we witnessed an emerging understanding that we belong together as one world. The Family Project is already demonstrating that what is happening to families and communities in one part of the world is directly related to what is happening in the rest of the world.

Every nation and its rulers are accountable to God for the way in which human beings are treated within it. This is especially so because many nation states are politically formed in ways unrelated to communities which have a natural unity. This is often how human rights are ignored or abused. The test of accountability to God is commonly with how "minorities" are treated, especially with regard to traditional ownership of land, maintenance of kinship and cultural patterns, and freedom of choice.

Governments have a responsibility to recognise the family (of whatever local cultural types) as a basic unit of society, the laboratory of human development, and a place where God can be known and loved. Does the nation have a national family policy reflecting a commitment to maintain the family/extended family networks? Is social legislation reviewed for its possible impact on these families? How do civil marriage and Christian marriage integrate? How does a government by its policies uphold the sanctity and validity of marriage, and how does it provide for marriage breakdown? Are social justice principles applied to what happens to women and children after marriage breakdown?

Development

Both nation and Church have a role in improving the quality of life of those who are victims of unjust political or economic structures.

For the nation, this requires health, education, welfare and social planning policies which distribute resources from the rich to the poor and creates a basic minimum of standard of living which enables people to participate in work and community.

The Church has traditionally provided a range of community based services, particularly in health and education, and supported by missionary societies and aid agencies. The Church in under-developed countries needs to augment its fight against poverty, illiteracy and disease.

From the Christian point of view, a theology of development needs to be articulated to provide a holistic ministry involving mental, physical, spiritual and social development of individuals and communities. This is all the more urgent in places of rapid social change or social disintegration.

Community and Culture

How does the Church in a place like Kenya develop the potential to develop a theology of the community which will combine some of the strengths of traditional African life with the tenets of Christian living?

Given the rapid changes to family life and obligations, kinship loyalties and affiliations, is there an opportunity for the congregation to become the natural basis of the Christian community, within which people open their homes to each other, eat together and give mutual support?

The breakdown of communities and families are often interwoven because of external factors. This will be complicated if Christian and traditional belief systems are in conflict, and both are disintegrating, as in the Philippines.

Where destructive elements in a local community, such as racism, separate and divide people from one another, the prevailing culture must be challenged and redeemed. We must not tolerate what God opposes.

Any development of the community needs to be rooted in the community, and not imposed from outside. For this, large helping institutions need to be ''debureaucratised'' as much as possible, and somehow made applicable locally.

The Church at the local level can provide substitute family and community experiences for communities in the process of breakdown. This may include childcare, protection on the streets, education and supportive networks.

Family

Throughout the entire period of biblical history, the family played an important role in the structuring of society. There was however no one biblical model of the family for its size, structure and nature varied greatly during the different periods of history. Culture, economics and religious values all exerted an influence in determining the shape of family life at various times.

Today also there is no one model of family life which could, or should be made mandatory for all Christians. Variations in culture, economics and religious values will again result in variations in family life, and it is not without significance that Jesus did not seek to develop, even in theory, a model of family life which could be transported from one culture to another. Though we may learn from one another, the healing of the family which we seek in Jesus Christ will take place within our respective cultures.

So ''the family'' may be permanent or temporary, nuclear or extended, married or not, but it will include households of both sexes, and in the majority of cases it will be a place where children live and grow and develop. Someone has said: ''The family is—when you go there, they have to take you in.'' So it is a set of relationships based on a household and based on acceptance. It is also a set of networks which are inter-generational and extend beyond blood kin.

One of our theological tasks is to define the quality of relationships which either do or ought to apply within families. Any definition of the family can disenfranchise individuals, or become instruments of social policy which exclude some people. A household of single adults living together may feel themselves to be ''a family''. A single adult may still belong to a family of a previous generation—that is, their brothers and sisters and aging parents.

The Church in its theology may be able to develop what is the essence of family. Is it in functioning, nurturing, caring, development of family members? An essential aspect of ''family'' is that it is based on mutual support and recognition of the rights and responsibilities of all members.

The Church is the ultimate family/household to which we are called, and yet in practice it often denies or suppresses aspects of humanity.

Marriage

We affirm the institution of marriage as a vocation of fundamental importance, but not of necessity for personal development. Marriage is part of God's creation, but like all other relationships, it needs redeeming. The ingredients of Christian marriage are fidelity, trust, acceptance, commitment, an intention of permanence, mutual service and empowerment. It is unreasonable and unrealistic to expect marriage to meet all individual emotional needs. Disappointment at this point may lead to breakdown.

Marriage assumes equality between the sexes and mutuality. Is the traditional affirmation of life-long marriage unrealistic in the present times, given how long people live; economic changes and pressures; higher expectations from marriage? How do we deal with the tension between the Christian ideal and the reality of marriage breakdown?

Fidelity within marriage is important not only for its implications about the relationship between the two people, but also with the family network, friends and others.

How does the Christian ideal of monogamous marriage relate to someone already in a polygamous set of relationships? Here, the will of God is not so easy to discern as shown by our discussion above in Section 4.

Sexuality

We affirm the complementarity of the sexes in the image of God, and affirm the broad definition of sexuality as to be much wider than genital sex. We recognise that all people are sexual beings and need to be affirmed in their being as whole human beings irrespective of age, gender, disability, orientation and experience. We recognise that sexuality is as much socially constructed as it is biologically determined.

Marriage is not the only unit for loving personal relationships. There are rich and deep friendships between people of the same sex and different sexes, which are very meaningful in our personal human development.

While affirming the equality of men and women in God's sight, this is not the same as identity. Men and women bring different qualities and perspectives to every friendship and relationship. But all relationships are affected by sin to some extent, and so we have the capacity even within our deepest relationships to oppress, alienate and hurt each other.

The question of sexual orientations is a complex one which the Church is still grappling with: many Provinces have traditionally maintained that homosexuality is a sin whilst others are responding differently to the issue. As sexuality is an aspect of life which goes to the very heart of human identity and sociality it is a pastorally sensitive issue which requires further study and reflection by the Church leadership. Promiscuity in any relationships, whether hetero-or homosexual, adds further complications, and in recent times carries with it serious health risks.

Medical and technical advances have increased the complexity of ethical issues surrounding sexuality, in particular means of contraception which have allowed sexual relationships without the fear of pregnancy. At the very least, abortion (the ultimate contraception) is seen by Christians as a dangerous cheapening of a reverence for human life. Many believe that each embryo is already part of God's creative plan, and thereafter abortion is the equivalent of infanticide. Traditionally, Anglicans have supported a form of therapeutic abortion in extreme cases, when the mother's life is threatened.

When the God-given human mind has been able to devise contraceptive means by which procreation can be controlled, this should be seen as a way of enhancing sexuality, family life and human life more generally. Indeed, contraception provides the possibility of responsible parenthood in a world where the distribution of food is inequitable.

Pastoral Principles

Because our Christian idealism must be tempered by our constant failure as humans to achieve the ideal,

and because people desperately need a fresh start,

and because marriage is more than sexuality and sexuality is more than a matter of the flesh,

could it be appropriate for your church to develop a pastoral ministry along this line?—

IN DEVELOPING CHRISTIAN AFFIRMATIONS ON FAMILY, THE CHURCH MUST ENSURE THAT ITS OWN LAWS, GUIDELINES OR PASTORAL PRACTICES LIBERATE AND FACILITATE THE TRANSFORMATION OF PEOPLE WHEN THEIR MARRIAGE, FAMILY OR COMMUNITY HAS FOR SOME REASON BROKEN DOWN.

Recommendations for Guidelines for Pastoral Ministry to Families

1. Because political motives and government actions on the macro scale directly affect how families and communities hold together, and because the theology of God's sovereignty forces us to regard governments as under his control, and because the Church in Kenya and Australia and other places has become directly and positively involved in the national political process, could this pastoral principle be appropriate in your church—

   Pastoral ministry should be based on the political and economic realities which either support or hinder effective family functioning.

   To do this effectively, such a strategy would need to be based on available data on international trade and the economic order, must include an objective assessment of the local political situation, and should build on the skills and resources which the Church has among its people as it builds its place in national life.

2. Wherever racist attitudes in a nation result in discrimination or oppression, because the Gospel teaches that all people are equal and must be treated fairly, could this be an appropriate pastoral principle for your church—

   No pastoral ministry to families can be effective in communities unless the Church directly tackles racism as degrading and nonchristian.

   For this to be effective, the Church will need to develop a theology of social justice as an expression of the Gospel which allows it to participate in debates about attitudes such as racism. But if it does, it will begin to identify with minorities who have not always looked to the Church for support.

3. Because technology can bring great advances, but also brings many disadvantages to developed and developing countries, and because consumer-oriented media have the effect of undermining cultural values, could it be appropriate for your church to adopt as principles for pastoral ministry—

   The Church at the local level should identify and support aid and development projects which use technology appropriate to the needs and goals of local communities as identified by them;

   To do this, the Church will at its national level need to develop a clear set of ethical values about family life, and therefore attitudes to such issues as pornography, prostitution, abortion, family planning, violence, sexism and other attitudes which are commonly portrayed in the media as "normal" behaviour.

4. Because in most countries, traditional extended family and kin systems are breaking down into small nuclear units without much social support, and because the family is a basic set of relationships in which the Christian faith must make a significant difference, and because in Nigeria, New Zealand and other places, the Church is developing ministries relevant to public policies on families, could your church adopt as a principle for pastoral ministry the following—

Families should not be understood or ministered to in isolation. Rather, pastoral ministry should respond to families in their wider context and seek and develop social systems of support.

To accomplish this, the Church will need to call on professional and experienced resources among its membership in order to understand the way in which local communities are operating, how social systems are disintegrating, and how they may be replaced with effective alternative socialising mechanisms which can be both supportive to individuals and family groups, and also thoroughly Christian.

5. Because women face horrendous problems in most societies when they are single, poor or have suffered violence, and because women are more than half the worshippers in most Anglican congregations, and because the Bible calls on us to treat all women and men as equal, could an appropriate pastoral principle for your church be—

Pastoral care for women must face their actual social circumstances, address the injustices inflicted against them in society, and affirm the place of women in the Church by transforming the Church's own structures to remove any oppression or alienation of women, and to give them opportunities for service.

Further, the Anglican Church must develop adequate pastoral care and support for clergy families.

To accomplish better ministry with women, the Church in most countries will need to do a lot more homework on their political, economic and social circumstances, as well as examine honestly the structures and legislation within the Church to make sure there is an adequate place for women to make their contribution and exercise their gifts.

6. Because our theology must come out of our practice, we suggest this principle for pastoral ministry—

That the Church must develop its theology on marriage, family and community by reflecting honestly on ministries dealing directly with the hard social realities of life for families. In particular, our theology must be able to handle brokenness in human relationships, and the possibility of a new start in Christ.

For this to happen, there must be more dialogue within national Churches between theologians, those engaged in ethical debates on behalf of the Church, pastors of local congregations, and counsellors and others directly engaged in reconciliation and healing ministries. Only as these people come together, will our theology emerge from our practice, and will we be able to match our ideals with the realities.

7. Because our Christian idealism must be tempered by our constant failure as humans to achieve the ideal, and because people desperately need a fresh start, and because marriage is more than sexuality and sexuality is more than a matter of the flesh, could it be appropriate for your church to develop a pastoral ministry along this line—

In developing Christian affirmations on family, the Church must ensure that its own laws, guidelines and pastoral practices liberate and facilitate the transformation of people when their marriage, family or community has for some reason broken down.

At this point, our words and actions must coincide. Any verbal affirmations in marriage, family or community must be matched now by pastoral ministries, welfare programs and community development. Otherwise, the Church will become less and less credible when it says things. The world is now looking at what the Church does, more than what it says.

No general model for pastoral ministry can be laid down at an international level which would be applicable to all parts of the Church. Each Province or Diocese must do the planning for themselves. But the renewed Partners in Mission Program provides the Anglican Communion with an ongoing way for Partners from other Churches to make a positive contribution to reviewing pastoral priorities. And we hope that this report on

Family and Community will also make a contribution to that review. But, in the end, each national Church must decide these things for themselves.

Let the African Church have the last word, quoting Bishop Gitari from the report of our Kenyan Consultancy: "Liberating the Church means freeing the Christians to be a community of believers that serves as a agent for the Kingdom of God. As the Church becomes a community in the New Testament sense, it is able to create community and to enhance existing community not only among Christians but in society at large. With so many fractured and lonely families in the cities and so many people living alone, the Church should see itself as an extended family where every believer finds a home, not just figuratively but literally. The Church must work to build strong homes, exploring extended family models, so that each home truly is a church and the Church truly a family."

Notes: *The Anglican Consultative Council is the central council for the worldwide Anglican Communion. Established in 1969, its membership includes bishops, priests, and lay people. The council has no legislative powers; instead it fills a liason role, consulting, recommending, and at times representing the Anglican Communion. This statement grew out of an International Project on Family and Community set up by the Anglican Consultative Council. It seeks to take into consideration the diverse cultural settings in which Anglican churches conduct their ministries as well as dramatic changes in social and economic structures throughout the world. It affirms a holistic approach to sexuality and marriage and calls for equality for women.*

BIBLE MISSIONARY CHURCH

EXCERPT FROM "MANUAL OF THE BIBLE MISSIONARY CHURCH, INC." (1983)

I. Marriage and Divorce

32. 1. Marriage. We believe that the holy estate of matrimony was ordained and instituted by God in the time of man's innocency and is, according to apostolic authority, "honorable in all"; that it is the mutual union of one man and one woman for helpfulness, fellowship, and the orderly propagation of the race. Our people should cherish this sacred estate as becomes Christians, and should enter it only after earnest prayer for divine direction, and when assured that the contemplated union is in accordance with scriptural requirements. Marriage of Christians to unconverted persons should be discouraged (Gen. 6:1-3; Amos 3:3; 2 Cor. 6:14; 1 Cor. 7:39). It is evident that in most cases such have thereby placed obstacles in their own way and have been hindered in serving the Lord. Yea, some have even turned back to the world and Satan. The marriage covenant is morally binding so long as both shall live and, therefore, may not be dissolved at will.

    2. Divorce. We believe that there is no other ground for divorce except that specified in the word of God, namely fornication or adultery; that persons otherwise divorced by civil law, and who subsequently remarry, live in adultery and are therefore unworthy of membership in The Bible Missionary Church. A pastor need not violate his conscience by receiving anyone into the church whom he does not feel to be worthy of membership.

    3. All ministers of The Bible Missionary Church are positively forbidden to perform the marriage ceremonies of persons not having the Bible right to marry (Matt. 5:31-32; 19:1-9; Mark 10:11-12).

    No minister of The Bible Missionary Church shall perform a wedding ceremony in which a ring is used.

57

4. Should any member seek divorce on any but scriptural grounds (Matt. 5:32; 19:7-9), and that well proven, he or she shall be brought to trial, and if proven guilty of such offense, his or her membership in The Bible Missionary Church shall cease.

5. Should any minister of The Bible Missionary Church, knowingly or unknowingly, receive any person who is unscripturally divorced and remarried into membership, such membership shall not be valid.

6. No minister who has been divorced and remarried shall be licensed or ordained while his or her former companion is living, except upon ¾ majority vote of the District Board of Orders and Relations, the District Conference and the unanimous vote of the Board of General Moderators.

Notes: *The Bible Missionary Church has a tradition of strict adherence to literal fulfillment of the Bible's commandments. As a result, its statement reiterates biblical teachings without taking into consideration the conditions under which Christians live in the modern world. Christians are expected to be in, but not of, the world.*

CHURCH OF THE BRETHREN

EXCERPT FROM "ANNUAL CONFERENCE STATEMENT ON HUMAN SEXUALITY FROM A CHRISTIAN PERSPECTIVE" (1983)

I. Position of the Church

Sexuality is elemental in human beings. It encompasses all that we are when we say "I am female" or "I am male." Physical attributes, including genitals, are an integral part of our sexual identity; however, sexuality is not just physical. It includes all thinking, feeling, acting and interacting that is derived from our maleness and femaleness.

This sexuality enriches human relationships in ways that are basic to God's own nature (Gen. 1:27). Furthermore, it offers human beings partnership with God in holy creation and re-creation (Gen. 1:28).

In their enjoyment of these privileges concomitant with sexuality, God's people are to be responsible. The church identifies love and covenant as two guidelines for sexual responsibility. Furthermore, the church holds to the teaching that sexual intercourse, which can be the most intimate expression of sexuality and the most bonding of human relationships, belongs within heterosexual marriage.

The church maintains an attitude of openness and willingness to evaluate specific issues related to sexuality. Moreover, the church recognizes that highly personal issues are best resolved in the confidentiality of a private setting with pastor, counselor, or family rather than in the open debate of conferences and council meetings. Seeking the guidance of Scripture, the Holy Spirit, and responsible contemporary research, the church continues to study and search for the mind of Christ in dealing with the complexities of responsible sexuality.

II. Biblical Perspective

The significance of sexuality is evident in scripture. In the Genesis 1 account of creation, sexuality is one of the first human attributes to be identified: Male and female God created them (Gen. 1:27). Other distinguishing characteristics—race, stature, intelligence—are omitted. The lifting up of sexuality in this concise account of human origin suggests how basic sexuality identity is.

In Genesis 2, sexuality is associated with companionship and completeness. The first reference to humans in this chapter is neither masculine nor feminine. The Hebrew word *adham* (verse 7), translated "man" in English, is a collective noun, undifferentiated by gender. In this state, *adham* was lonely. Then another type of human was made from *adham*. Only then is one human called *ish*, a masculine noun meaning "man," and the other is called *ishshah*, a feminine noun meaning "woman." *Adham's* problem of loneliness was remedied by the separation of humankind into two sexes and by the intimacy they experienced together. This creation of *ish* and *ishshah* and the ensuing companionship culminates the Genesis 2 account of creation.

As revealed in Genesis 3, this dual sexuality can exacerbate the discordant, testing, rebellious nature of man and woman. Adam and Eve allowed themselves to be seduced by the serpent and its offer of forbidden fruit. The freedom they exerted in choosing evil rather than good resulted in their separation from each other and from God. Immediately they "knew" they were naked and they were ashamed. They were thrust into a world of conflict with all of creation, even with each other (Gen. 3:6-24).

Human experience substantiates and vitalizes these biblical revelations about sexuality. We rejoice in God's creation of two sexes, *ish* and *ishshah*. Despite "the fall" and the conflict we experience, we do not prefer an absence of sexuality. Brokenness can be healed. By God's grace we discover anew that femaleness and maleness enrich and complete our personhood.

Yet while sexuality is an important component of our being, it is not paramount. Paul urged his readers to keep perspective. His emphasis was on the new life in Christ, not on sexuality. He wrote: ". . . there is neither male nor female, for you are all one in Christ Jesus" (Gal. 3:28). Our oneness in Christ supersedes the old human distinctions and inequalities including race, economic status, and sex. Paul gave enough attention elsewhere to sexuality to make it clear that he did not ignore this subject. Yet, sexuality was not his foremost concern.

Likewise, sexuality was not central for Jesus. Although Jesus briefly addressed a few issues related to sexuality—adultery, marriage, divorce, and celibacy—these were not the emphases in his teaching. When asked to identify the greatest commandment, he named two: "Love God and love neighbor" (Mark 12:28-30). For Jesus, love was primary in all human relationships; sexuality was secondary.

Our society is preoccupied with sexuality. The repression of sex in earlier generations has been replaced now by an obsession with sex. One result is that increasing numbers of people expect too much of sexual intercourse. Performance is stressed over relationship, resulting in personal frustration and interpersonal strain. Christian values are ignored. Sex rather than God becomes the center of life.

Even the church loses perspective, although in a different way. To prepare and to consider a denominational statement on human sexuality creates anxiety. Such statements are called "monumental" by some and "the most controversial issues the church has faced in a generation" by others. If these appraisals are true, the church has overreacted. Alarmists fail to remember that generations come and generations go, but the Lord remains forever (Psa. 90:1-2). Sexual misuses and abuses are serious sins; however, they are not the only sins. There is no reason to become tense and condemnatory about sexual abuses out of proportion with numerous other sins that are equally serious. For the sake of the world, for the unity of the church, and for the benefit of our personal health, this is a timely moment in history to keep sexuality in perspective.

III. Biblical Guidelines for Sexual Morality

In order for sexual experiences to be complete and appropriate in God's sight, persons need to make choices based upon the counsel of the Scriptures and also of the church. Two key biblical words relating to the morality of sexual experiences are love and covenant.

A. Love

The English word love has two antecedents in the Greek language, *eros* and *agapé*, which are crucial to the understanding of sexual morality.[1,2] *Eros* is the love that grows out of one's own need to love and to be loved. It is the love that fulfills one's dreams and desires. It is the impulse toward life, union, creativity, and productivity. It is the self-actualizing drive affirmed in Genesis 1 where God created male and female and told them to be fruitful and multiply. It is the satisfying union affirmed in Genesis 2: "The two shall become one flesh."

Sexual attraction is a dynamic of *eros*, but *eros* is more than the mere sensation of physical pleasure. A preoccupation with techniques in our society strips *eros* of its tenderness and delight. The human body—its sensations, its beauty, its capability—is not to be disparaged. The whole body is a marvelously designed gift from God. It is to be enjoyed and utilized. But the body is not to be separated from the soul. Lovemaking is most fulfilling when it is a comfort to the body and the soul. This blending of physical pleasure and spiritual intimacy is *eros* at its best.

The Song of Songs affirms romantic love emphatically and delightfully. It is the unashamed, sensual, joyful poetry of two youthful lovers. The poem romantically describes the lips, eyes, and hair of the lovers. The man tells the woman he loves her because her love is sweet (4:10-11). He desires her because he finds her beauty attractive. She loves him because his body and his speech are desirable (5:11-16). They love each other because each brings to the other a gladness and a fullness of life. Very early, the book was viewed as an allegory by the Jews as Yahweh's love for Israel, and by the Christians as Christ's love for the church. This interpretation influenced the book's acceptance into the canon and has inspired Christian thought through the centuries. Still, the book itself contains no clue that it is meant to be understood allegorically. We must also be ready to read it as it stands: an appropriate celebration of the *eros* that leads to and finds its consummation within marriage. The Song of Songs affirms the *eros* that is a valued aspect of the human nature God created.

Agapé is an equally significant dimension of love. *Agapé* is unrestrained compassion for another. It is selfless giving. It is a generous responsiveness to another's needs beyond any gain for oneself. It is the love of 1 Corinthians 13 that is patient and kind, not jealous or boastful, nor arrogant or rude, does not insist on its own way, is not irritable or resentful, does not rejoice in the wrong but rejoices in the right (13:4-6). The ultimate expression of *agapé* is to lay down one's life for the sake of another (John 15:13). The prototype of *agapé* is Jesus' giving his life on the cross.

Eros is of the order of creation, a God-given gift to our human nature. *Agapé,* on the other hand, is of the order of redeeming grace, the gift of the covenanting God to covenanting people. Even so, *eros* and *agapé* are gifts of God and part of his plan for humanity. Neither is to be despised. Indeed, it is only when romantic love is constituted of both that it can be said, "Lo, it is very good."

B. Covenant

Christians need more than love to guide them in decision-making. Love is nebulous. Moreover, we are susceptible to self-deception, particularly in moments of sexual excitement and desire. At such times the claim of love is to be tested by actual commitment that gives content to the declaration of love. Such commitment disciplines, protects, and nurtures love relationships. Christians need covenant as well as love to guide them.

Covenants abound in biblical history, shaping relationships and undergirding community. These covenants take many forms. Some are written; many are spoken. Some are unilateral promises without obligations upon the recipient; others are conditional with specified terms. Some covenants are between equals; others are between a superior and a subordinate.

Since no single model exists, it is difficult to describe biblical covenants precisely. Characteristics present in some are absent in others, but despite these variations, several elements of biblical covenants can be identified.

Biblical covenants were generally *public*. They were not private agreements isolated from community. Even God's covenants with Noah, Abraham, and Moses were not merely individualistic. They were major covenants affecting and including the whole community for many generations. To acknowledge these communal ties, the covenants were generally confirmed by formal acts—a sign, a ritual, a recognizable verbal formula—visible or audible to the community. The rainbow was a sign of God's covenant with Noah (Gen. 9:12). Circumcision was a sign of God's promise to Abraham (Gen. 17). The "blood of the covenant," splashed over the alter and over the people, signified God's covenant with Moses (Exod. 24:5-8). In the New Testament, the bread and the cup symbolize the new covenant (1 Cor. 11:23-26). These tokens and rituals are continuing witnesses to the community of the covenants that are the foundation of the people's life together.

Biblical covenants are *pious*, reflecting Israel's sense that covenants are grounded in God. Sometimes God initiates the covenant as a primary participant. Other times God is only indirectly involved. For example, people make covenants between themselves but seal them with an oath. The oath implies religious sanction. Thus, being faithful to God implies being faithful to the covenant.

Biblical covenants are *permanent*. Sometimes this expectation of permanence is challenged by changing circumstances and bitter disappointments, yet the promise is not withdrawn. For example, the Davidic covenant that the throne of Israel would remain forever in the line of David's descent did not collapse with the Exile (586-538 B.C.). Instead there emerged new hope for a future king who would be the son of David. Furthermore, when terms of the covenant are violated, broken relationships and misery result. In such circumstances the old covenant may be dissolved by God and a new beginning offered (Jer. 31:31-34). Despite these vicissitudes in covenantal relationships, the common understanding is that covenants last forever.[3]

Finally, biblical covenants often presuppose *pilgrimage*. Abraham, Moses, and David were adventurers. God's covenants with these men pointed beyond their present realms of living to a destination—to a nation, a land, and a kingdom not yet fully reached. Jesus and his disciples were travelers. Initially, Jesus beckoned them to a journey, "Follow me. . . ." Later, he commissioned them to another journey, "Go into all the world. . . ." He promised them, ". . . I am with you always . . ." (Mark 1:17, Matt. 28:19-20). His promise was a covenant: He said he would be with them in their journeys. Such covenants have unfolding qualities. They foster adventure, newness, and surprise.

Pilgrims accept a code of conduct for their journey. Sometimes the code is specific and direct about behavioral expectations (the Holiness Code in Leviticus 17-26, the Deuteronomic Code, or Zacchaeus' promise to Jesus in Luke 19:8). Covenants set limits. Yet the spirit of the covenant is to nourish relationships, not regiment them. Covenants, unlike contracts, offer fidelity that exceeds specification: "You will be my people; I will be your God" (Jer. 31:3b, Hosea 2:23).

The influence of covenants upon sexual behavior and relationships within Israel is evident. Unlike much contemporary, popular literature, the Bible is not primarily a story about lovers and their disconnected affairs. Rather, it is an account of families and marriages and continuing loyalties. To be sure, there are many lapses in covenantal faithfulness. This reality does not diminish the significance of covenant in the life of Israelites; rather it underscores their need for a new covenant that incorporates not only law and judgment but also grace and renewal.

C. The Church's Guidance

In contemporary life we are often hesitant to make covenants. There are many reasons for that hesitancy. We make hasty, unwise commitments and find ourselves entangled in painful relationships. We say, "Never again." We are motivated by self-interest, convenience, and momentary pleasure at the expense of long-range rewards. We resist the responsibility of long-term commitment. We want to be autonomous, with little obligation to the community. For all these reasons we may resist making covenants, choosing instead agreements that are tentative.

The result is that in contemporary life we lack the sense of belonging and the covenantal structure that helps a relationship endure through periods when emotion is not a sufficient bond. We lack a sense of being part of a purpose and a people that extends far beyond our individual lives. It is time for the church to speak assertively of covenant, of belonging and loyalty.

To apply biblical covenant to sexuality in the modern world does not require the church to formulate a comprehensive code to cover all eventualities and contingencies. Ours is a complex and changing world. Differing family patterns, changing male and female roles, effective contraceptives, overpopulation, and the science dealing with human sexual behavior are among the phenomena that represent new dilemmas and choices profoundly affecting sexual relationships.

In addressing these realities the church must avoid undercutting individual discretion, eliminating personal responsibility for growth, and stifling the work of the Spirit among us. Yet within the covenant community, there is need for general guidelines, Bible study, and frank conversation.

In a society in which people are purported to "have sex more but enjoy it less," the time has come to reconsider the importance of both love and covenant. There are no easy answers about how to apply love and covenant to some of the real-life situations in which people find themselves. Is the church willing to struggle with these issues even when answers are not always clear? The struggle will be unsettling and difficult, but the outcome may enhance morality, not diminish it, and contribute to a fuller, more human life for all persons.

IV. Implications for Human Sexuality

Much research on the subject of human sexuality is being done by physical and social scientists. For the church, however, scriptural guidance and biblical scholarship must be brought to bear upon that scientific information in order to come to an adequate understanding of the implications of human sexuality for our day.

Some specific concerns related to human sexuality have been dealt with in recent Annual Conferences: birth control,[4] pornography,[5] male and female roles,[6] abortion,[7] marriage,[8] artificial insemination,[9] and divorce.[10] It would be repetitious to dwell again on these issues.

Major issues that have not been dealt with by recent Annual Conferences include (1) sexuality for single persons, (2) homosexuality, and (3) marital fidelity. Sexuality for single persons is an area of rapidly changing mores in our society. Homosexuality is discussed now more openly than ever before in modern history. The difficulties of maintaining marital fidelity are compounded by current social stresses and continuing silence within the church on sexuality.

A. *Single Persons and Sexuality*

More than one-third of the adults in our society are single—unmarried, divorced, or widowed. Our biblical faith affirms singleness as a meaningful lifestyle. The lifestyles and teachings of both Jesus and Paul are models of singleness. Jesus placed singleness on a par with marriage (Matt. 19:12). Paul felt that in terms of an undivided allegiance to Christ, being single had some advantages (1 Cor. 7:1-9, 24-40).

Fullness of life for single persons depends upon certain conditions. Family is important but may exist in different forms in different times and places. However, the endurance of the family reflects the need of people, whether married or unmarried, for a primary relationship in which personhood is fostered, loneliness is diminished, and closeness and belonging are experienced. Jesus cherished his family of faith as much as his biological family (Matt.

10:35-37, 12:49). His example should spur the church toward being a spiritual family to one another in the fellowship.

Furthermore, every adult needs significant friends of the opposite sex. Jesus had female friends. His friendship with Mary, sister of Martha and Lazarus, was especially close. It was a friendship not just of chores, convenience, and function, but also of warm conversation and closeness (Luke 10:38-42). Priscilla (Acts 18:2, 18; 1 Cor. 16:19; Rom. 16:3) and Phoebe (Rom. 16:1-2) were especially important to Paul in his work. St. Francis of Assisi had a very close female companion, Sister Clara, whose friendship was invaluable especially in his later years. These all are helpful models of a nurturing friendship between persons of opposite sex, a friendship not involving sexual union. Such intimacy is an affirmation of maleness and femaleness and addresses basic human needs for wholeness of personhood among single people.

1. Biblical Insights
Although the Scriptures do not deal extensively with the sexual behavior of single persons, some boundaries are established. In the Old Testament, certain types of premarital sexual activity are punishable (Deut. 22:13-21, 23-29). In the New Testament, Paul teaches that union with a prostitute is immoral because that act inseparably joins two persons (1 Cor. 6:12-20). Paul also specifically addresses the unmarried and the widowed who find it difficult to control sexual passion (1 Cor. 7:2, 9, 36-38). Paul advocates marriage for such persons, implying that sexual intercourse is to be practiced within marriage.

2. The Church's Response
The requirement of celibacy for singles is a thorny issue that the church faces. Our current social circumstances heighten the difficulties. Physical maturation has accelerated three years in one generation. A girl now reaches puberty at 11 or 12 years of age and a boy at 13 or 14 years. Moreover, the median age at first marriage is later than ever before: 23 years for men and 21 years for women. The 10-year span between sexual maturity and marriage creates a difficult situation in which to preserve chastity, a situation different from the biblical era.

Premarital sexual relationships, especially among teenagers, are creating many problems in our society. Sexually active adolescents experience conflict in determining their values. Emotional and psychological development is impaired, at times irreversibly. Suicide is sometimes a factor. Teenage pregnancy, venereal disease, and permanent sterilization are occurring in epidemic proportions. Often these problems are the inevitable result of a society that is seductive and permissive, and promotes freedom and pleasure above responsibility and long-term satisfactions. This society and all too often a negligent church have failed to provide moral support to those many youth who do have values and seek to live by them.

The teen years should be used to mature socially and emotionally, to learn the skills of communication and problem-solving, and to express sexual identity in nongenital ways. These experiences contribute to the maturity that is necessary in order to learn what love really is, to find a compatible partner, and to establish a covenant that is sound and lasting. The church believes that these principles are still valid in our time.

The engagement period should be a time for the couple to share about families, dreams, goals, habits, likes, dislikes, past experiences. It is the time to develop common interests and good communication patterns. Christian persons in dating relationships should resist the strong desire for full sexual expression and the pressures of the media and culture for sexual exploitation.

Also in contemporary society there are rapidly increasing numbers of previously married single adults. A higher divorce rate, an extended life expectancy, and the preponderance of women over men in the middle and upper age brackets are among the factors leading to this increase. Many of these persons have experienced sexual intercourse within marriage, but such experience is no longer available to them. Some of the problems that exist in our contemporary world when singleness is a matter of circumstances rather than choice did not exist in such proportions in the biblical world. It is incumbent on our society and the church to acknowledge these problems and to seek solutions.

The church counteracts the cultural emphasis on sexual self-indulgence by teaching the benefits of self-discipline and the positive aspects of a life of commitment and fidelity. In a time of casual love making and pleasure seeking, covenants provide structure that sustains us in the fluctuating joys and pains of authentic relationships. Ongoing loyalties give continuity to our lives. The marks of covenant include mutual respect, public vows, lifetime accountability, and religious sanction. The church teaches that sexual intercourse belongs within the bonds of such love and covenant.

The church as a covenant community encourages single people, as well as married people, to speak of their needs and concerns including sexuality. In the continuing interchange of ideas and feelings, the church seeks to be more evangelical and caring than condemnatory. . . .

C. Married Persons and Sexuality

The Christian faith affirms that heterosexual marriage is the intended culmination of sexuality. Sexual intercourse, the most intimate of human relationships, belongs within heterosexual marriage. Within the covenant of lifelong fidelity, married couples learn to enjoy this full-bodied, full-spirited union. Furthermore, it is this loyal, loving partnership that is most conducive to the responsible conception of children.

Marriage fidelity is a matter of spirit and emotion as well as body (Matt. 5:28). Our sexuality, a sacred trust from our Creator, is too powerful and too elemental a force to be treated lightly or casually. Sexual activity that embraces spirit, emotion, and body is just as valid when engaged in for pleasure as for procreation. Such pleasure will be found as much in receiving as in giving. The need to care in consistent ways about the well-being of one's spouse is essential. The desires and needs of each must be paramount in a mutual relationship. Demands and satisfactions designed to meet the needs of one partner to the exclusion of the satisfactions and needs of the other will only erode the act of intercourse and cause mutual trust and respect to disintegrate. True mutuality exists when the spiritual, emotional, and physical hungers of both persons are satisfied. Each has a responsibility for such mutual fulfillment.

Sexual intercourse between two persons who are bound by love and covenant can foster the most intimate and intense kinds of communication. At that moment—unlike any other—those two do truly become as one. Unfortunately, even within the context of marriage this is not always so. Sexual relationships, of every expression, become destructive of the Creator's design when used in self-centered ways. Sexual activity within the context of marriage can sometimes be as exploitative and selfish and destructive as sexual activity outside of marriage. This happens when sexual relationships are:

—used only to gratify personal desires,

—used as a weapon,

—withheld as punishment,

—proffered as reward,

—demanded unilaterally, or

—used as a cover-up for personal inadequacies.

In any such case, marital sexual activity is just as immoral as the misuse of sex outside of marriage. Sexual relationships ought to be a wholly fulfilling link between two affectionate people from which they emerge unanxious and satisfied.

When genuine communication exists between spouses, they will be able to tell each other about their needs and what brings them pleasure and satisfaction, without inhibition or embarrassment. It is destructive to a marriage relationship (at every level but especially in regard to sexual matters) to assume that one should instinctively know what the needs and desires and satisfactions of the other are. The risk is that expectations will not be met and one or both of the parties will feel rejected and unloved. Once those seeds of rejection take root they produce grudges, resentments, and hostility. Demanding that your mate automatically understand and fulfill your needs is a most unreasonable expectation. It is important to communicate those needs, desires, and satisfactions both verbally and non-verbally without embarrassment.

Compassion is also an essential component of satisfying sexual relationships. "Making love" is a term often used for sexual intercourse even though sometimes "love" is the missing ingredient. Intercourse without expressed feeling and caring is empty or worse. It is exploitative and selfish. Love that is communicated through the intimacies of sexual intercourse is a love that goes beyond words; indeed, is often verbally inexpressible and is, therefore, expressed through the act itself.

The importance of sexual fidelity is not to be underestimated (1 Thess. 4:2-8, Heb. 13:4). Unlike less easily recognized aspects of fidelity, sexual faithfulness is identifiable. Marriage partners know when they are sexually faithful, at least as far as overt behavior is concerned. Being loyal in this overt way may help couples learn to be faithful in other aspects of their lives together.

The covenant of faithfulness does not preclude meaningful relationships with persons other than the marriage partner. Indeed, such friendships are to be cherished. However, if these ties move beyond friendship and become amorous, the intimate relationship outside of marriage will need to be terminated. Adultery is one of the most serious temptations faced by married persons.

1. Biblical Insights
The old covenant forbids adultery. The seventh commandment in the Decalogue (Exod. 20:14 and Deut. 5:18) is concise: "You shall not commit adultery." The exact nature of adultery, however, is somewhat obscure in the old covenant. For men, adultery was often narrowly defined as sexual intercourse with the wife of a fellow Israelite (Lev. 18:20; 20:10; Deut. 5:21, 22:22, Exod. 20:17). Polygamy, concubinage and perhaps secular harlotry were allowed the married male but not the married female (Gen. 16:1-4, 30:1-13; 38; 2 Sam. 5:13). The double standard was evident. The rights of the male were paramount and the restraints against his sexual relationships were primarily to protect the rights of other Israelite men: the father, the betrothed, the husband.

In the new covenant, this double standard for adultery disappears. When a group of men caught a woman in adultery and inquired whether she should be stoned to death, Jesus appealed to the conscience of the men regarding their own sins (John 8:1-11). Jesus applied the prohibition of adultery to husbands and wives on an equal basis (Mark 10:10-12). Marriage, as understood by Jesus, was intended by God from the beginning of creation to be the indissoluble union by two persons (Mark 10:8-9).

Moreover, for Jesus, adultery was a matter of attitude as well as action (Matt. 5:28). He taught in the Sermon on the Mount that lust is adultery. Lust is not a passing fantasy but an untamed craving. Unless *eros* is infused and counterbalanced with *agapé*, attitudes become adulterous.

Paul taught that sexual relationships are not just physical acts but deeply interpersonal experiences. It was Paul's view that even a sexual relationship that was intended to be highly casual involved a mystical union (1 Cor. 6:16).

Although adultery is a sin, neither Jesus nor Paul suggests that it is unforgivable. Jesus did not condemn the adulteress, though he told her, "Go, sin no more" (John 8:11). Paul wrote about believers whose former immorality had been washed away (1 Cor. 6:11). Quite clearly, adultery is perceived to be a violation of the marital union. But by God's grace, sexuality though defiled, can become again what it was intended to be.

2. The Church's Response

Amidst changing values and relaxed morality, the church should continue to speak out against adultery as well as other threats to the marriage covenant. Casual acceptance of sexual relationships outside of marriage is a part of our society and is reflected to us by our media. The church, however, should continue to hold up in its teachings the image of marriage as the permanent, spiritual, physical, and emotional bonding between a man and a woman, modeled upon God's everlasting covenant with his people (Gen. 12) and Christ's eternal union with the church (Eph. 5).

D. Family Life Education

Quality education is needed to attain an understanding of sexuality and a competence in family relationships. This education begins in the home where parents teach their children not only by word but also by conduct and expression of feeling. This is the proper forum for teaching morality. The importance of confining sexual intercourse to marriage takes root in daily contact with nurturing, caring adults who teach and model this behavior.

However, given the severe stresses and strains of the family in our society, parents need the church's support and assistance in conveying Christian attitudes on sexual morality. The church should provide biblical and theological guidance on sexuality.

Education for family life is appropriate also within the public school. It is needed to supplement instruction in the home and church. Public school instruction should include information about the body, sex organs, and the reproductive system, but the emphasis should be on values and relationships. Teachers who are responsible for this task should be well trained and themselves be worthy models of mature and responsible sexuality. The church supports responsible family-life education in the public school as long as the religious commitment of all students and residents of the community is respected.

Parents should keep themselves informed about the content of family-life education courses in which their children are influenced, and use that educational experience to foster open discussion of the topic of sexuality with their children. Parents should also be acquainted with the content of such courses for the purposes of continuing dialogue with school officials. In such dialogue parents should clarify their Christian principles to insure that their own ethical values are not undermined.

Family-life education will not solve all sex, marriage, and family problems. The task requires the coordinated efforts of home, church, and school.

V. Conclusion

Sexuality is God's good gift. It is a spoilable gift. Who among us does not regularly need God's grace to restore this gift that we have abused so that it again beautifies and deepens human relationships? These problems that arise for ourselves and our generation are to be faced and confessed, but this need not turn our attitude toward sexuality into a tangle of negatives. God's grace is real. Sexuality remains for us, as it was for *adham*, God's antidote for human loneliness and the answer to the human need to have a counterpart, to be one with someone, and to be in love.

Action of 1983 Annual Conference: *The delegate body of the 1983 Annual Conference in a ⅔ majority vote adopted the paper on HUMAN SEXUALITY FROM A CHRISTIAN PERSPECTIVE as a position paper with one amendment which is incorporated in the preceding wording of the paper.*

Human Sexuality Study Committee:
Guy Wampler, chair
Doris Cline Egge
James F. Myer
Mary Sue Rosenberger
Clyde R. Shallenberger

Background of the Paper

As part of the 1977 Annual Conference Statement on Marriage and Divorce, a recommendation urged the General Board to appoint a committee to address "in a comprehensive way" the basic issues of human sexuality from a Christian perspective.

In follow-up, a five-member committee named by the General Board conducted a hearing at the 1978 Annual Conference as background for a draft statement. In 1979 the General Board requested an extension until 1981 for its report to Annual Conference, and appointed a new committee of General Board members. Named to the committee were Guy Wampler, Jr., chair, Doris Cline Egge, James F. Myer, Mary Sue Rosenberger, and Clyde R. Shallenberger.

This board committee brought a paper to Annual Conference in 1981. The Standing Committee recommendation, which Annual Conference adopted, was to distribute the paper as a study document to the church at large, to solicit the response of the church, and to prepare a paper for consideration in 1983. A Leader's Guide and response sheets were circulated with the paper. By the end of 1982, a total of 2,639 responses were received from 153 congregations in 22 districts.

In addition to compiling the responses by mail, study committee members met with 36 groups for study and interpretation of the paper in process. Additional hearings were conducted at Annual Conference in 1981, 1982, and 1983.

In March 1983, a revised paper was presented to the General Board which approved the paper for presentation to the 1983 Annual Conference. With one amendment, Annual Conference voted approval of the paper.

Endnotes

1. Barclay, William, *Letters to Galatians and Ephesians*. Philadelphia: Westminster Press, 1954; p. 54. In addition to *eros* and *agapé*, there are two additional Greek words for love: *philia* which refers to the warm but nonromantic love we feel for those close to us and *storge* which refers especially to the love between parents and children.

2. Nygren, Anders, *Agapé and Eros*. Philadelphia: Westminster Press, 1953. The separation between the words *eros* and *agapé*, *eros* having to do with love involving the needs of self and *agapé* having to do with love involving the needs of other persons, has been in vogue since the publication of this book. It is not clear that this neat, sharp distinction can in fact be sustained either in the New Testament or in Hellenistic literature. However, the perspective commonly called *eros* is definitely in the biblical tradition even if the word is not.

3. Roop, Eugene, "Two Become One Become Two," *Brethren Life and Thought*, Vol. XXI, No. 3, Summer 1976; pp. 133-137. An analysis of the expectation of permanence with covenants and yet the possibility of new covenants.

4. *Minutes of the Annual Conference, 1955-64*, "Family Planning and Population Growth," (1964), p. 328.

5. *Minutes of the Annual Conference, 1965-69*, "Theological Basis of Personal Ethics," (1966), p. 118.

6. *Minutes of the Annual Conference, 1975-79*, "Equality for Women in the Church of the Brethren," (1977), p. 340.

7. *Minutes of the Annual Conference, 1970-74,* "Abortion," (1972), p. 227.

8. *Minutes of the Annual Conference, 1955-64,* "Divorce and Remarriage," (1964), p. 320, and *Minutes of the Annual Conference, 1975-79,* "Marriage and Divorce," (1977), p. 300.

9. *Minutes of the Annual Conference, 1955-64,* "Family Planning and Population Growth," (1964), p. 328.

10. *Minutes of the Annual Conference, 1955-64,* "Divorce and Remarriage," (1964), p. 320 and *Minutes of the Annual Conference, 1975-1979,* "Marriage and Divorce," (1977), p. 298.

Notes: *This statement from the Church of the Brethren demonstrates how a fairly conservative Protestant group takes the unique needs of its members seriously in a rapidly changing world. It seeks to remain true to the spirit of the New Testament while recognizing these dramatic changes and their effects upon individuals. Empathetic and compassionate application of New Testament norms of "covenant" and "love" are stressed, as well as recognition of the validity and significance of the single life.*

CHURCH OF THE BRETHREN

EXPLODING THE FAMILY MYTH (1983)

These days everyone from preachers to President Reagan is extolling the benefits of strong families. The home is regarded as the source of such various virtues as honesty, industry, sobriety, patriotism and religious devotion. In the popular mind the family ranks right up there with apple pie as a symbol of all that is right and good about life.

Rhetoric about the importance of the family and the aura of sanctity that has surrounded it have become profound sources of both hypocrisy and guilt in our psyche.

Ever since the basis for selection of a marriage partner came to be that of romantic love, the family has suffered from the intense pressure of high expectations. In previous generations, when the family was seen primarily as an economic unit and when marriages were arranged by parents, the situation was far different. Father, mother and children clearly understood what was expected of them by their kinfolk, the church and the community. Little opportunity existed to do anything else. Expectations were realistic.

Not so today. As I talk with couples who come to me for premarital counseling, I find their expectation lists are lengthy indeed. At the top of their list, of course, is love. But they want lots more as well companionship, financial security, social contacts, a home of their own, shared responsibility for housework, children who will arrive in the exact numbers and at the precise time they are desired. None of this is wrong. But it does mean the pressure is on, right from the start.

Society wants everyone in families to feel happy, at least most of the time. Society expects people to get along harmoniously at home, because that's the way it ought to *be,* for heaven's sake. This attitude prevails even though personalities sometimes clash in any family. The only way to avoid conflict is to bottle up frustrations. But when *that* happens, hardly any meaningful communication is possible.

What results then is a view of the family that is a hopeless jumble of contradictions. The dream of a happy, sharing, communicating, cooperative, fulfilling family life is just that: a dream. It's something only saints could pull off. The trouble is that not many people are pure saints. They're just people with strengths and weaknesses and quirks in their personalities. Sometimes, for all their good intentions, people nearly drive each other crazy.

Earlier the words *hypocrisy* and *guilt* were used. Hypocrisy, because while society gives lip service to what a wonderful thing the family is, experience proves otherwise. But, of course, people couldn't admit that. So they go on with the big pretense. To do so inevitably leads to guilt when people realize that life within the family does not measure up to society's high standards. As a result, family life bears the additional burden of disappointment and frustration as it fails to meet expectations.

The truth is that society's image of what the family ought to be has become oppressive. Especially so when it has been linked with religion.

What exactly is "the Christian family"? Is it a family in which each member is a committed follower of Jesus Christ? Not exactly. Is it a family that attends church on a more or less regular basis? Perhaps. "The Christian family" is one of those phrases the church has blithely tossed around for years without having a good idea of what it actually means. Someone recently wrote that, strictly speaking, there is no such thing as a Christian family. Christians may live in families, but the idea of a Christian family finds no support in Scripture or Christian theology. This fact hasn't prevented Sunday school teachers and television preachers from waxing eloquent about the wonderfulness of the Christian family.

What does the Bible reveal about family life? Two familiar commandments deal with adultery and the honoring of parents. But the Old Testament offers something far removed from a glowing picture of family life. Within the families of the heroes of the faith, all kinds of problems existed: childless marriages, polygamy with quarreling among the wives, disobedient children, sibling rivalries. The very first family was torn apart by one brother murdering another. The prophet Hosea was married to a woman who kept leaving him for her former trade as a prostitute. It is hardly an encouraging picture.

In the New Testament, the apostle Paul frequently included in his letters instructions about family life. But Paul thought it best that Christians not marry at all. That isn't exactly a vote of confidence for the family. Paul would certainly be amazed that his words about love, as recorded in 1 Corinthians 13, are today read as part of so many church weddings. Paul didn't write those lovely words about marriage. He was talking about relationships within the church.

The Bible takes a far more realistic approach to life in the family than we do in the 20th century. The Bible doesn't contain the gushy sentimentalizing about the delights of family togetherness. Writers of Scripture recognized the undeniable presence of sin in the human heart, and they knew that the family was not exempt from the effects of it.

The words of Jesus in Matthew's Gospel are especially important: "He who loves father or mother more than me is not worthy of me; and he who loves son or daughter more than me is not worthy of me . . ."

Nearly parallel to these words is an incident recorded in Mark where Jesus' mother and brothers came to visit him. Standing outside, they sent word in to the house that they had arrived. When the message reached him, Jesus said, "Who are my mother and brothers?" Then he looked around at the people with him and said, "Here are my mother and brothers! Whoever does the will of God is my brother, and sister, and mother."

What did Jesus mean? From other references he made to marriage and family we know that he was not calling for the dissolution of the family. But Jesus was saying that the family can never be the salvation of humanity.

Jesus announces that something transcends family relationships, namely, the kingdom of God. That idea strikes the ear with a discordant sound. Society brings us up on the ideal of morality which equates "the good family man" with the best there is. But this too is hypocrisy. On the one hand our society praises the family, but the world of education, jobs and careers puts pressures on the family that virtually guarantee its destruction. Jesus cuts through this hypocrisy by telling Christians that unless following him into the kingdom of God is their top priority, they are doomed to failure.

Where does all this leave Christians? It leaves them, one would hope, with the resolve to take a more honest, realistic look at family life. It ought to reinforce their determination to value people for themselves and not, for example, to make those who are unmarried feel like second-class Christians. It ought to challenge them to have realistic expectations of each other as family members. It ought to help them get rid of the guilt they carry because home life is sometimes irksome, sometimes frustrating, sometimes boring, occasionally even unbearable. It ought to help them celebrate the times of joy and beauty in families when hurts are shared in a redemptive way, when children make parents proud, when husband and wife are drawn together in genuine communion in their lovemaking, when any member of the family shows caring by a willingness to listen rather than by insisting on his or her own way.

All this is what I mean when I say, "Down with the family." Christians need to bring family life down from the pedestal. They need to bring the family down to earth, where God intended it to be.

When they have done that, then they can recognize that, at its best, life within the family is very good indeed. Family life can offer kindness, generosity, zest for life, intimacy, compassion and commitment. That last one is a big one. The essence of family life is commitment, to be in relationship with others as fully and honestly as possible, recognizing that we will fail but asking God to help us fulfill our promises. The words of the traditional vows are still valid: "for better, for worse; for richer, for poorer; in sickness and in health." That's what commitment means. Only people committed to each other as husbands and wives, as parents and children, can have any hope of succeeding as a family in the pressure cooker of contemporary life.

"Down with the family" is not a call for its demise, only a recognition that the family is not, nor ought to be, the kingdom of God on earth. What it *can* be is a foretaste, however limited, of that kingdom. It is so only by the grace of God, who created us all to live in *his* family.

Notes: *Kenneth L. Gibble is promotion director for* Messenger, *the official publication of the Church of the Brethren. In this article he points out a major discrepancy between what the Bible defines as "ideal" family life and what most contemporary Christians believe this ideal to be. Those individuals who follow the latter "ideal" create highly frustrating problems for themselves.*

CHURCH OF THE NAZARENE

EXCERPT FROM "MANUAL" (1985)

Marriage and Divorce and/or Dissolution of Marriage

[The meaning of divorce in this rule shall include "dissolution of marriage" when it is used as a legal substitute for divorce.]

34.   The Christian family, knit together in a common bond through Jesus Christ, is a circle of love, fellowship, and worship to be earnestly cultivated in a society in which family ties are easily dissolved. We urge upon the ministry and congregations of our church such teachings and practices as will strengthen and develop family ties.

The institution of marriage was ordained of God in the time of man's innocency and is, according to apostolic authority, "honourable in all"; it is the mutual union of one man and one woman for fellowship, helpfulness, and the propagation of the race. Our people should cherish this sacred estate as becomes Christians, and should enter it only after earnest prayer for divine direction, and when assured that the contemplated union is in accordance with scriptural requirements. They should seek earnestly the blessings which God has ordained in connection with the wedded state, namely, holy companionship, parenthood, and mutual love—the elements of home building. The marriage covenant is morally binding so long as both shall live, and therefore may not be dissolved at will [Genesis 1:26-28, 31; 2:21-24; Malachi 2:13-16; Matthew 19:3-9; John 2:1-11; Ephesians 5:21—6:4; 1 Thessalonians 4:3-8; Hebrews 13:4].

34.1. Ministers of the Church of the Nazarene are instructed to give due care to matters relating to solemnizing marriages. They shall seek, in every manner possible, to convey to their congregations the sacredness of Christian marriage. They shall provide premarital counseling in every instance possible before performing a marriage ceremony. They shall only solemnize marriages of persons having the scriptural right to marry. [107-7.1, 411.14]

34.2. Members of the Church of the Nazarene are to seek prayerfully a redemptive course of action when involved in marital unhappiness, in full harmony with their vows and the clear teachings of the Scripture, their aim being to save the home and safeguard the good name of both Christ and His Church. Couples having serious marital problems are urged to seek counsel and guidance of their pastor. Failure to comply with this procedure in good faith and with sincere endeavor to seek a Christian solution, and subsequent obtainment of an unscriptural divorce and remarriage, makes one or both parties subject to discipline as prescribed in 501.

34.3. Though there may exist such other causes and conditions as may justify a divorce under the civil law, only adultery is a scriptural ground for divorce, and only adultery will supply such ground as may justify the innocent party in remarrying [Matthew 5:31-32; 19:3-9].

34.4. Through ignorance, sin, and human frailties, many in our society fall short of the divine ideal. We believe that Christ can redeem these persons even as He did the woman at Samaria's well. Where the scriptural ground for divorce did not exist and remarriage followed, the marriage partners, upon genuine repentance for their sin, are enjoined to seek the forgiving grace of God and His redemptive help in their marriage relation. Such persons may be received into the membership of the church at such time as they have given evidence of their regeneration and an awareness of their understanding of the sanctity of Christian marriage. [26, 107.1]

Notes: *This statement from the Church of the Nazarene (approximately 544,000 members) presents a conservative interpretation of marriage and divorce derived from a strict literal reading of the Bible.*

EPISCOPAL CHURCH

EXCERPT FROM THE "REPORT OF THE TASK FORCE ON CHANGING PATTERNS OF SEXUALITY AND FAMILY LIFE" (1987)

Introduction

Following the mandate of the Diocesan Convention on January, 1985, the Task Force on Changing Patterns of Sexuality and Family Life has been meeting for study and discussion, focusing its attention on three groups of persons representative of some of the changing patterns of sexuality and family life: 1) young people who choose to live together without being married; 2) older persons who choose not to marry or who may be divorced or widowed; 3) homosexual couples. All three kinds of relationships are widely represented in the Diocese Newark, and it has been recognized that the Church's understanding of and ministry among the people involved has not been adequate.

The aim of the Task Force has not been original social scientific research. Members of the Task Force have engaged in Biblical, theological, historical, sociological and psychological study, and in extensive discussion of the issues raised. The intent of the Task Force has been two-fold: to prepare a document that would help the clergy and laity of the diocese to think about the issues, and to suggest broad guidelines for the Church's pastoral response to persons in the three groups and to those not in those groups but who are concerned about the issues raised. . . .

We understand the Church to be a community in search, not a community in perfection. As a community in search, the Church must recognize the needs among its members, among all Christians, indeed among all persons, for loving support, for mutual trust, and for growth through learning from each other. As one contemporary writer has put it ". . . as such a *community* the Church is of prime significance in making love a reality in human life— incarnating the Incarnate Love. . . . These images affirm not only intimacy and mutuality but also inclusiveness; there are implications for a diversity of sexual patterns within a congregation. Different sexual lifestyles being lived out with integrity and in Christianly humanizing ways need not simply be tolerated—they can be positively supported. The 'family of God' can ill afford to make the nuclear family its sole model." (James Nelson, *Embodiment.* Minneapolis: Augsberg Publishing House, 1978, p. 260.)

This report crystallizes the Task Force's perspective on these issues. It does not summarize each discussion, nor does it present all the research and data that informed these discussions. The report is offered to the Diocese of Newark to stimulate our corporate thinking and discussion. The Task Force's major recommendation is that discussion continue on an intentional, Diocese-wide basis. This and other recommendations are offered in the final section.

I. The Cultural Situation

The social and cultural changes that have occurred in American society over the past half-century are increasingly being reflected in the changing attitudes of members of the Anglican communion regarding some of the basic moral values and assumptions which have long been taken for granted. Profound changes have occurred in our understanding and practices in areas involving sexuality and family life. Traditionally, the Church has provided, virtually unchallenged, direction and guidance on these matters that deeply affect the individual, the family unit and the community at large. Today, the Church is no longer the single arbiter in these matters, which were once thought to be within its sacred province. Some of the factors that have led to the diminution of this status are:

1. Secularization of American society as it moved from a predominately rural background at the turn of the century to today's predominately urban setting. This has produced new and competing centers of values and morality.

2. Social, economic and geographical mobility that has individually and collectively loosened structures traditionally provided by the community, church and family. These structures tended to channel and constrict values, choices, and behavior in the areas involving sexuality, marriage and family life.

3. Advances of technology, which have provided means of disease control and birth control, which have effectively separated the act of sexual intercourse from procreation.

4. Reduction of the age at which puberty begins. This confronts children with issues of sexuality earlier than in the past.

5. Adolescent dating without chaperonage. This removes a powerful external structure of control of sexual behavior.

6. Many in contemporary culture begin and establish a career at a later age than formerly. Marriage also tends to occur later. These two developments combined with convenient methods of birth control, the earlier onset of puberty and the absence of chaperonage,

significantly lengthens the period when sexuality will be expressed outside of marriage.

7. The gradual, but perceptible changes in attitude regarding what constitutes a "complete" human being: the human body and sex are no longer considered something to be ashamed of, and these physical realities as well as intellect and spirituality constitute essential elements in the development of a complete human being.

8. The decline of exclusive male economic hegemony, which has resulted in a realignment of the male/female relationships in society.

9. The existence of a better educated society, which does not depend upon authorities to determine "what is right" on issues such as nuclear war or power plants, abortion, birth control, poverty, environment, etc.

10. The intensifying clash between the claims of traditional authority as demanded by the family, church and society and the aims of twentieth century men and women to seek their own fulfillment in ways that were not necessarily acceptable in the past. This is, of course, an ancient tension; it gains its particular contemporary character in American society from the dissolution of the degree of ethical consensus as the society has become increasingly pluralistic.

The Church needs to think clearly about these social, cultural, and ethical realities. It must order its teachings and corporate life so as to guide and sustain all persons whose lives are touched by these realities. The challenges that these realities pose to our beliefs and practices must be examined and responded to.

As indicated in the introduction, this report is intended to contribute to the Church's understanding of these issues, and to offer perspective on and suggestions for the Church's response.

II. Biblical and Theological Considerations

A. Tradition and Interpretation

The Judeo-Christian tradition is a tradition precisely because, in every historical and social circumstance, the thinking faithful have brought to bear their best interpretation of the current realities in correlation with their interpretation of the tradition as they have inherited it. Thus, truth in the Judeo-Christian tradition is a dynamic process to be discerned and formulated rather than a static structure to be received.

The Bible is misunderstood and misused when approached as a book of moral prescriptions directly applicable to all moral dilemmas. Rather, the Bible is the record of the response to the word of God addressed to Israel and to the Church throughout centuries of changing social, historical, and cultural conditions. The Faithful responded within the realities of their particular situation, guided by the direction of previous revelation, but not captive to it.

The text must always be understood in context: first in the historical context of the particular Biblical situation and then in our own particular social and historical context. The word of God addresses us through scripture. It is not freeze-dried in prepackaged moral prescriptions, but is actively calling for faithful response within the realities of our particular time. Any particular prescription in scripture, any teaching of the law, must be evaluated according to the overarching direction of the Bible's witness to God, culminating in the grace of Christ.

B. The Centrality of Christ and the Realm of God

The central point of reference for the thinking Christian is the life, ministry, death, and resurrection of Jesus Christ. The history of interpretations of the meaning of that event begins in scripture itself and continues into our immediate present. The central fact about Jesus's life and teaching is that he manifested in his relationships, acts, and words, the imminent and future Kingdom of God, which will be referred to as the Realm of God.

73

The Realm of God as presented by Jesus in his relationships and in his parables is characterized by loving action on behalf of all men and women including especially the poor, the sick, the weak, the oppressed and the despised, the outcast, and those on the margins of life. The Realm of God presents us with both the fulfillment and the transcendence of the inherited law. The Realm of God presents us with an overturning— even a reversal—of the structures by which humans attempt to establish their own righteousness, which inevitably oppresses or exploits, or marginalizes others.

The challenge to the Church to respond creatively to changing patterns of sexuality and family life in America must be seen as an instance of the Holy Spirit leading us to respond to the blessing and claim of the Realm of God foreshadowed and made continually present by the life of Christ Jesus. In his death Jesus exemplifies sacrificial love that is faithful to his vision of the Realm of God. In the resurrection we know God's ultimate faithfulness and sovereignty.

It is in response to this central example and teaching of Jesus regarding the Realm of God that we attempt to discern what should be the Church's response to changing patterns of sexuality and family life. We discover in the actions and parables of Jesus that the Realm of God manifests grace unfettered by legalistic obligation to tradition and "the law". When the choice is between observance of the law or active, inclusive love, Jesus embodies and teaches love. It is in the light of this fundamental principle of God's active reconciling love that any religious law or dogma, social or economic arrangement is to be assessed.

C. The Realm of God and Human Social Structures

The specific instances of changing patterns of sexuality and family life that this Task Force addresses do not occur in a cultural vacuum but in the cultural turmoil marked by the ten developments noted in the opening section of this document. Not one of these developments is morally unambiguous. All of them are marked—as has been every development of social history—by the human propensity for self-deception and self-aggrandizement at the expense of others, which Christians call "sin".

Jesus's radical claim is that in his person the Realm of God confronts us, in every age, with our bondage to sin. Included in sin's manifestations are the social norms and arrangements by which we conventionally order our lives. In parable after parable Jesus presents us with the need to see historical relativity, the need to examine the arbitrariness and the maintenance of power by traditional structures. The Church itself and the authority of its traditional teachings is subject to judgement by the ongoing activity of the Realm of God.

Judged by the grace of God starkly presented by the parables, Jesus's preaching and his actions show us that response to the Realm of God requires us to be ready to perceive and modify those structures in our society that hurt and alienate others rather than heal and extend love to those in circumstances different from our own.

With this consciousness we hear the challenges to our conventional attitudes and practices regarding sexuality and the family and try to discern how these challenges should influence our understanding of our traditional values and our response to new realities. We engage in this process knowing (and discovering anew) that all our thoughts are laced with our desire for self-justification, our need for self-aggrandizement, and the willingness to hurt those whom we see as opposing us. Sin is our human condition; it permeates all our institutions, all our traditions, and all our relationships, so it has always been for humankind; so it has always been in the Church.

D. Historical Relativity

Recalling our sinful condition causes us to look critically both at the Church's conventions and at the demands for change put forward by various groups in our culture. The relativizing impact of the Realm of God enables us to see more clearly what Biblical and historical research discloses: that beliefs and practices surrounding marriage and sexuality have varied according to time, culture and necessity. We tend to sacralize the familiar and project into the past our current practices and beliefs and the rationales supporting them.

Such is the case with our assumptions about marriage. We tend to project into early Biblical times a twentieth century model of monogamous self-chosen marriage when clearly, at various periods in the Old Testament records, polygamy was assumed (at least for the wealthy). Even into the Middle Ages a marriage was an economic event, perhaps an alliance, between two families or clans.

Marriage was not given the status of a sacrament by the Church until 1439. And not until 1563 did the Church require the presence of a priest at the event. And even then marriage functioned to solemnize an agreement which had been entered into more for reasons of procreation, the channeling of sexuality, and economic benefit to the families than as a means for preexisting love between the two persons to develop and flourish, as we expect of present-day marriage.

In the Bible and in our own Western heritage, sexuality outside of marriage has been proscribed for women—not men. When women were found adulterous, the violation was of property rights rather than of sexual morality as we tend to conceive it, because women were viewed as property of fathers, and then of their husbands.

Homosexual behavior was condemned because it was part of pagan religious practices from which Israel sought always to differentiate itself. Biblical scholarship maintains that in the story of Sodom and Gomorrah, Lot's concern was not with the homosexual nature of the implied rape of his guests, but with such behavior as a violation of rules of hospitality. Homosexuality as a fundamental human orientation is not addressed in scripture; and Jesus himself was entirely silent on the subject.

E. Revised Understanding of the Person

A major change in perspective is occurring in religious thinking regarding sexuality and the body. Greek philosophical and agnostic thought had great influence on the early development of Christianity. Since that time the Church has tended to teach that the body is a dangerous vessel, subject to temptation and sin which temporarily houses the superior soul or spirit. Whereas the Greeks regarded the mind or spirit as able to reach its triumph only by freeing itself from the corrupting captivity of the physical body, the Hebrews knew no such separation. In Hebraic thought one does not *have* a body, one *is* a body. What we today refer to as body, mind, and spirit were—in Hebraic thought—dimensions of an indivisible unity.

The contemporary more Hebraic understanding of the person runs counter to the traditional dualistic teaching of the Church, which has tended either to try to ignore the fact that humans are embodied selves, or has looked at the physical, sexual body as the root of sin. The contemporary attitude views sexuality as more than genital sex having as its purpose procreation, physical pleasure and release of tension. Sexuality includes sex, but it is a more comprehensive concept.

Sexuality is not simply a matter of behavior. Our sexuality goes to the heart of our identity as persons. Our self-understanding, our experience of ourselves as male or female, our ways of experiencing and relating to others, are all reflective of our being as sexual persons.

We do not have *bodies,* we *are* bodies, and the doctrine of the Incarnation reminds us that God comes to us and we know God in the flesh. We come to know God through our experience of other embodied selves. Thus our sexual identity and behavior are means for our experience and knowledge of God. This theological perspective means that issues of homosexuality, divorce, and sexual relations between unmarried persons involve not only matters of ethics but have to do with how persons know and experience God.

It is our conclusion that by suppressing our sexuality and by condemning all sex which occurs outside of traditional marriage, the Church has thereby obstructed a vitally important means for persons to know and celebrate their relatedness to God. The teachings of the Church have tended to make us embarrassed about rather than grateful for our bodies. As means of communion with other persons our bodies sacramentally become means of communion with God.

III. Ethical Essentials

From the perspective of Jesus's teaching regarding the Realm of God, all heterosexual and homosexual relationships are subject to the same criteria of ethical assessment—the degree to which the persons and relationships reflect mutuality, love and justice. The Task Force does not in any way advocate or condone promiscuous behavior which by its very definition exploits the other for one's own aggrandizement. The commitment to mutuality, love and justice which marks our ideal picture of heterosexual unions is also the ideal for homosexuals unions. Those who would say homosexuality by its very nature precludes such commitment must face the fact that such unions do in fact occur, have occurred and will continue to occur. The Church must decide how to respond to such unions.

It is becoming clear that many persons—single, divorced, or widowed—may not seek long-term unions, while some commit themselves to such unions without being formally married. The overriding issue is not the formality of the social/legal arrangement, or even a scriptural formula, but the quality of the relationship in terms of our understanding of the ethical and moral direction pointed to by Jesus in the symbol of the Realm of God.

The challenge to the Church is to discern and support the marks of the Realm of God in all these relationships. The Church should be that community above all which is marked by its inclusion of persons who are seeking to grow in their capacity for love and justice in their relationships and in their relation to their world-neighbors. The Church should actively work against those social and economic arrangements which militate against the establishment of such relationships.

IV. Marriage and Alternate Forms of Relationship

Our nation has been described as a "highly nuptial" civilization. This means that for whatever reasons many Americans see marriage as a vehicle for happiness and satisfaction. Life-long marriage offers the possibility of profound intimacy, mutuality, personal development, and self-fulfillment throughout the years of the life cycle. On the other hand, of course, a marriage can be marked with the sin of self-centeredness and exploitation of the other, and by the estrangements of male from female, weaker from stronger.

Ideally, marriage can be a context in which children can develop their identities by drawing on both male and female ways of being a person. It can therefore provide a uniquely rich context for the formation of children into adults who cherish and intend the qualities of the Realm of God—love and justice—in the context of ongoing relationships marked by sacrifice, forgiveness, joy, and reconciliation. It can also give to parents the opportunity to mature and develop their own capacities for caring generativity.

The Church must continue to sustain persons in the fulfillment of traditional marriage relationships both for the well-being of the marriage partners and because such marriage provides the most stable institution that we have known for the nurturing and protection of children. But the Church must also recognize that fully intended marriage vows are fraught with risks. Belief that deeper knowledge each of each in marriage will enable the original intentions of love and devotion is not always fulfilled. Persons living through the dissolution of marriage need especially at that time the support of an understanding and inclusive community. Such is true obviously also for divorced persons, whether living singly or in new relationships.

One of the Church's present deficiencies is its exclusionary posture toward those who have "failed" in the conventional arrangement of marriage and family and the conventional understanding (and avoidance) of sexuality has blinded us to present reality. The Church needs actively to include separating and divorced individuals and single parents.

The Church must take seriously that Jesus's teaching and manifesting of the Realm of God were concerned not with the formal arrangements of our lives but with our responsiveness to the vision of the Realm of God. Admittedly, this confronts all of us with a relativization of all personal, social and economic arrangements by which we live. We cannot live without structure in our relationships; but these structures are subject to continual correction by the image of the Realm of God. If the Church is to err it must err on the side of inclusiveness rather than exclusiveness.

Marriage has served as a stabilizing force in American society, channeling sexuality in socially acceptable directions, providing a structure for the procreation and nurturing of children, and enabling enduring companionship between a man and a woman by defining the legal and spiritual responsibilities of the married couple. Although marriage has taken many forms in human society, it has been a central, constant building block of human society in all cultures. The power of sexuality both to attract persons, and satisfy persons, and to disrupt the social order has been recognized in the practices, mythologies, and laws of all cultures.

Marriage has bound the family, clan, and tribe to customs and traditions which insure survival and identification of a people as a people. The church must consider the consequences of calling into question institutional relationships which have permitted the Church to flourish and survive. However, our contemporary consciousness of racial, sexual, and economic domination and exploitation has raised our culture's consciousness about some of the oppressive, repressive and exploitative dimensions of marriage and family arrangements. This heightened sensitivity, combined with a cultural ethos that favors self-fulfillment over the dutiful but self-abnegating adherence to conventional marriage and family arrangements has caused many to deny that life-long monogamous, heterosexual marriage is the sole legitimate structure for the satisfaction of our human need for sexuality and intimacy.

There are those who think that even though the forms have been enormously diverse, the pervasive human tendency to union with an individual of the opposite sex in a committed relationship and the universal presence of family structure in some form evidences something fundamental about the nature of the created human order itself. Biologically, this has been the only option for the perpetuation of the human race as we know it. While other arrangements may be appropriate to the given nature of particular individuals, monogamous, life-long marriage and family organization ought not to be thereby relativized as simply one option among others.

Given the Church's traditional view of the exclusive primacy of marriage and the nuclear family and the (relative) opprobrium with which the Church has viewed other options, the Church must learn how to continue to affirm the conventional without denigrating alternative sexual and family arrangements. Again, the criteria are the quality of the relationships and their potential for developing persons responsive to the Realm of God. The Church must find ways genuinely to affirm persons as they faithfully and responsibly choose and live out other modes of relationship.

We live after the Fall. The metaphor of the Realm Of God reinforces the realization of brokenness and finitude in all our human arrangements and relationships. We sin daily in our self-deception, self-centeredness, self-justification, and readiness to exploit and oppress others for our own material and emotional self-aggrandizement. And this is clearly seen in our readiness to interpret scripture and tradition to reinforce what we perceive as our own best interests so that we appear righteous and those who differ from us appear unrighteous.

The dynamic process of God's incarnational truth has brought us to a time in history when the critical consciousness made possible by modern forms of knowledge - including

Biblical scholarship - enables us to see the Realm of God as a present reality relativizing all human knowledge and social arrangements. We are therefore suspicious of the invocation of tradition even while we believe that in God's ongoing creation not all relational arrangements are equally aligned with a caring God's purposes for humankind.

Those who believe that the heterosexual family unit headed by monogamous heterosexual partners offers the best possibility for the development of children who will become confident, loving, compassionate and creative adults must acknowledge the historical fallibility of the family in accomplishing such results. All sexual and family arrangements must be judged by the same criteria suggested by the metaphor of the Realm of God.

Ultimately, do couples (of whatever orientation) and families of (whatever constitution) exist for the sake of their own self-fulfillment? The Gospel does not support such an individualistic possibility. Nor does it support promiscuous behavior, which by its very nature uses the other person simply for one's self-aggrandizement, whether mere sexual release, as compensation for feelings of inadequacy or to express hostility. Theologically, patterns of sexual and family arrangements are to be judged according to the degree to which they reflect and contribute to the realization of the Realm of God. Since this is a dynamic not a static reality, continual diversity, exploration, experimentation, and discernment will mark the life of the faithful Church.

In the absence of set rules, great demands are thus placed on clergy and others who counsel persons regarding these issues. We believe that at the level of congregational life, the Church ought not focus its concern on this or that particular pattern. The Church's focus ought to be on persons as they seek to understand and order their lives and relationships. All relationships and arrangements are to be assessed in terms of their capacity to manifest marks of the Realm of God: healing, reconciliation, compassion, mutuality, concern for others both within and beyond one's immediate circle of intimacy.

V. Considerations Regarding the Three Alternate Patterns

As indicated in the Introduction, the Task Force decided to address specifically the Church's response to young adults who choose to live together unmarried, adults who never married or who are "post-marriage", due to divorce or the death of their spouse, and homosexual couples. We do not address the subject of adolescent sexuality, although we agree on the need for more thorough-going education of adolescents within the Church regarding sexuality and relationships.

We believe that certain questions of context are appropriate whenever persons consider beginning a sexual relationship: a) Will the relationship strengthen the pair for greater discipleship in the wider context? Will they be better enabled to love others? Will their relationship be a beneficial influence on those around them? b) Will the needs and values of others in the larger context be recognized and respected, especially the needs of their own children (if any), their parents, and their parish community? Since an ongoing sexual relationship between two persons occurs within a network of relationships to parents, children (perhaps adult children), colleagues, and fellow parishioners, such a relationship needs to be conducted with sensitivity to the possible emotional and relational effects on these other persons. c) What is the couple's intention regarding the procreation and/or raising of children?

Regarding the relationship itself, the following considerations are appropriate: a) The relationship should be life-enhancing for both partners and exploitative of neither. b) The relationship should be grounded in sexual fidelity and not involve promiscuity. c) The relationship should be founded on love and valued for the strengthening, joy, support and benefit of the couple and those to whom they are related.

A. Young Adults

One of the issues facing the Church in our time comes under the broad category of what used to be called "pre-marital sex". The issue for the Church to which attention is given in the following discussion is specifically defined as that of young adults of the opposite sex living together and in a sexual relationship without ecclesiastical or civil ceremony. (Of course, many young adults, for economic and social reasons share housing without having a sexual relationship. We do not address these relationships in what follows.)

From an historical perspective, such relationships are not unfamiliar to our culture. For many years common-law marriage had legal validity for purposes of property and inheritance settlements. Attitudes concerning careers, emotional and sexual commitments and intimacy, marital economics, and experiences (either through observation or background) all contribute to decisions concerning the form of relationship a man and a woman choose. In the contemporary world, young adults may live together to deepen their relationships, as a trial period prior to a commitment to marriage, or as a temporary or a permanent alternative to marriage.

In order to maintain the sacredness of the marital relationship in the sacrament of Holy Matrimony, The Church has generally been opposed to the actions of couples choosing to live together without ecclesiastical or civil ceremony. Opposition has been and is expressed both in direct statement and by silent tolerance. The effect of the opposition has been to separate those couples from the ministry of the Church, to the detriment of the quality of their relationship, of the spiritual growth of the individuals, of their involvement in the mutual ministry of the Church, of their contribution to the building up of the Christian community. Current research documents that persons living under these circumstances are less likely to profess an affiliation with an established religion or to attend church. And yet these persons might well benefit from a church affiliation.

To minister to or engage in ministry with those who choose to live together without marriage does not denigrate the institution of marriage and life-long commitments. Rather it is an effort to recognize and support those who choose, by virtue of the circumstances of their lives, not to marry but to live in alternative relationships enabling growth and love.

In a community in search, all benefit from mutual support and concern. Although living among persons of differing lifestyles can be threatening, it can provide those who have committed themselves to a lifelong relationship in marriage the opportunity to renew, to reform, to recreate their loyalties and vows in an atmosphere of alternative possibilities.

We emphasize that the Church's focus should be on persons as they seek to understand and order their lives and relationships. All relationships are to be assessed in terms of their capacity to manifest marks of the Realm of God: healing, reconciliation, compassion, mutuality, concern for others both within and beyond one's immediate circle of intimacy. Extending the image of the Church as a community of persons in search raises pastoral implications. A community in search seeks wisdom, understanding and truth in the experience and hopes of each of its members and from those (too often ignored) who choose not to participate in that community

Both at the diocesan and congregational levels, the Church can actively engage in education and discussion on all issues of sexuality. Members of the congregation, persons from specific disciplines in the secular world, and persons who have in their own lives wrestled with pertinent issues can all be asked to participate in such efforts. Congregations should encourage open, caring conversation, leading to trust and mutual, supportive acceptance. This makes more credible the Church's claim to faithfulness to the Realm of God.

Persons who have been ignored or rejected by the Church's ministry, or who have assumed such rejection, can only be reached and loved by a community that witnesses in *deed* to its faith that God calls all people to new hopes, to new possibilities, by a community that knows it does not have all the answers and in which each member contributes to its growth and future wholeness in the Realm of God.

B. "Post-Married" Adults

Some mature persons, by life-long choice or because of divorce or the death of a spouse find themselves unmarried but desiring an intimate relationship. We affirm that there can be life-enhancing meaning and value for some adult single persons in sexual relationships other than marriage. Economic realities may militate against traditional marriage arrangements. For example Social Security payments are reduced for two individuals who marry; channeling inheritances for children can become legally expensive and complicated where re-marriage occurs; maintaining a one-person household is for many persons prohibitively costly.

The choice of celibacy or estrangement from the Church for such persons who choose not to marry is not consonant with the Church's hope of wholeness for all persons in the Realm of God. Our understanding of the Church is one of inclusiveness. As we struggle to understand what the Church is called to in our time, one of our goals is inclusion in the Christian body of persons who have thoughtfully chosen lifestyles different from that of the mainstream.

Because we are whole human beings, and not, in the last analysis, separate compartments of body and soul, therefore the spiritual, mental, emotional, physical, and sexual aspects of our personalities are all to be nurtured and expressed in responsible ways if we are to continue to grow towards wholeness in our mature years. We are created sexual beings, and our spiritual health, no less than any other aspect of health, is therefore linked to sexuality. When therefore, mature single adults choose to celebrate their love and live their lives together outside of marriage, provided that they have considered and responded sensitively to the public and personal issues involved, we believe that their decision will indeed be blessed by God and can be affirmed as morally acceptable and responsible by the Church.

C. Homosexual Couples

Changing patterns of sexuality and family life confront pastors and congregations with new challenges and opportunities for understanding and for ministry. Rather than arguing about these issues we need first to listen to the experience of those who are most directly involved. Where homosexuality is concerned, fear, rejection, and avoidance by the heterosexual community is common and entrenched; we believe that pastors and congregations must meet members of the homosexual community person to person. The first step toward understanding and ministry is listening.

We need as much as is possible to bracket our judgements and listen to persons as they are. The Church needs to acknowledge that its historic tendency to view homosexual persons as homosexual rather than as persons has intensified the suffering of this 5%-10% of our population. A congregation's willingness to listen is a first step toward redeeming our homophobic past.

Listening is also a first step toward acknowledging that our own understanding needs ministry. Those of us fearful and angry regarding homosexuality need liberation, and this can only come through person to person communication. So the Church's response includes permitting itself to be ministered to by the homosexual community.

This process will help the Church recognize that whatever our historical experience, we encounter each other as we are with all our many limitations and potentialities. What we may become is a function of our open meeting of each other and of the reconciling, empowering spirit of God active in such open meeting.

Such person to person meeting, by means of open forums, small group discussions, and one to one conversations needs to be accompanied by the study of Biblical, historical, theological, and social scientific perspectives. Accurate information and informed opinion are important counterbalances to the fear and distortion, which have so often inhibited the Church's ability to respond appropriately.

Listening opens the door of hospitality, which has so long been firmly shut. Such words as

80

ministry and hospitality, however, still suggest a relationship of inequality, we and they. As such they perpetuate the image of the Church as separate from the homosexual community. In fact, however, we believe that the Church should be as inclusive of homosexual persons as it is of heterosexual persons. In this light, all the normal avenues of inclusion should be available to homosexual persons.

Criteria for membership, for participation in church committees, choirs, education, vestries, etc. and for ordination should be no different for any given group. Some persons express fear that including homosexual persons in the full round of church life will influence others - especially children - to become homosexual. In fact, we know of no evidence or experience to confirm that such association can bring about a homosexual orientation.

Ideally, homosexual couples would find within the community of the congregation the same recognition and affirmation which nurtures and sustains heterosexual couples in their relationship, including, where appropriate, liturgies which recognize and bless such relationships. . . .

Notes: *This statement was issued by the Episcopal Diocese of Newark, New Jersey, which is a member of the Protestant Episcopal Church, popularly called the Episcopal Church. This denomination was founded in 1789 and represents the Anglican tradition in the United States. This statement received by the 113th Convention of the Diocese of New Jersey received a great deal of attention in the press and produced tensions in the Diocese because it sanctions pre- and post-marital sexual intercourse and recognizes homosexual relationships. Because of its radical nature, it should not be construed to represent the views of all members of the New Jersey Diocese or all members of the Episcopal Church. In fact, it is rejected by many. Because of the controversy surrounding the document, many of its positive dimensions, e.g., its holistic approach to sexuality, go unnoticed.*

EPISCOPAL CHURCH

REPORT TO THE 114TH CONVENTION OF THE DIOCESE OF NEWARK OF THE TASK FORCE ON HUMAN SEXUALITY AND FAMILY LIFE (1988)

The 113th Convention of the Diocese of Newark received the Report of the Task Force on Changing Patterns of Sexuality and Family Life and called for a year of study and discussion within the Diocese to be monitored and reported on by the Task Force at the 114th Convention. At the instruction of the Convention, a study guide was prepared reflecting a broad range of perspectives and resources on the issues, and circulated to each congregation. Included as part of the study guide was a form requesting a report from each congregation which studied the issues. Since this congregational report form was not utilized, this Task Force Report depends upon the observation of the Task Force members, who led studies in their own and other congregations and who have talked with diocesan personnel, clergy and laypersons throughout the diocese. The response to the Report has been as varied as the Diocese of Newark itself.

Not all congregations have formally discussed the Report. Some clergy and congregations consider the issues as having no urgency; others have felt that the Report merely spelled out and affirmed the basic beliefs, attitudes, and practices of the clergy and congregation. Still others will be studying the Report during the coming year.

However, more than one-half of the parishes in the Diocese undertook some form of study of the Report on Changing Patterns of Sexuality and Family Life. Given the historical reluctance of congregations to deal with these issues publicly, the Task Force regards this widespread open discussion as a major diocesan accomplishment. Persons with widely divergent views expressed themselves and were heard.

The structure of the discussions varied from congregation to congregation. The most common was the adult education forum of Sunday morning. Study of the document and the issues took various forms according to the judgement of the clergy and lay leadership. In some cases, study of the Report was part of a series dealing with various aspects of sexuality and family life. Several congregations called in resource persons with medical, social service, and academic training. Attendance varied from four to over one hundred. Throughout the diocese clergy have addressed the issues raised by the Report in sermons, congregational newsletters, and other means.

The Task Force Report was a pastoral document intended to occasion discussion by providing a biblically and theologically based perspective on sexuality. In addition, the Report advocated supportive, compassionate and inclusive openness toward persons within and outside of the church who are attempting to create and sustain committed, faithful, loving and life-enhancing relationships within and outside traditional marriage and family structures. The media attention surrounding the issuance of the Report focused on those recommendations which seemed most at variance with the Church's traditional positions on these issues. In many discussions this distracted attention from the deeper issues raised by the Report regarding the more fundamental meanings of human sexuality itself. The Task Force believes that polarized debate around specific recommendations too often supplanted serious engagement with the more profound meanings of human sexuality itself.

In the congregational discussions, there has been vigorous resentment toward the Task Force advocacy of change in the Church's traditional stance on these issues. But there has also been - often less outspoken - relief and gratitude that the Church may at last be willing to recognize the need for reconsideration. Many in the congregations have felt that the Church has left them unsupported as they have had to deal with the sexual dimension of their own personhood, with the changing realities of the relationship between men and women, and with the instruction and guidance of their children regarding the complex and often frightening issues of human sexuality.

The Report and the discussions which it occasioned, the debates of Bishops Spong and Wantland, the media attention, and the discussion within the House of Bishops have generated for many in this diocese itself and its environs the hope that the Church will continue to provide educational and pastoral leadership in this complex and highly charged domain of life. The Task Force continues to believe that a deeper understanding of the issues of sexuality and family life is essential for our own wholeness as persons and as members of the Body of Christ.

The year's study and discussion has not created unanimity in our diocese. There has been the conflict which attends every serious reappraisal of issues fundamental to individual human lives and to human community. But many serious, ethical, committed persons inside and outside the Church, who have assumed that the Church is either irrelevant to or ignorant and intolerant of their pattern of sexuality and family life or to their understanding of what the Church's stance ought to be now look to this diocese and to this Convention with hope for leadership, support, understanding, compassion, and inclusion. The Task Force takes this expectancy, generated by this year of study, debate, and discussion as its mandate for the following recommendations and resolutions.

1. RESOLVED, that the 114th Annual Convention of the Diocese of Newark shall establish an ongoing committee under the auspices of the Faith Development Commission to be called the Committee on Human Sexuality to be comprised of persons from various professions, clergy, and lay persons. This Committee shall develop a parish based program and be trained to train leaders within parishes to conduct the program to instruct, nurture, and strengthen church people in their understanding of human sexuality and the problems and possibilities it presents for the wholeness of persons in the image of God.

Supporting Information: It has become apparent to the Task Force that the conflict around issues of divorce, pre- or post-marital sexual relationships, and homosexuality reflects deeper uncertainity and confusion about human sexuality itself. As suggested in the Report, the discussions of the past year have revealed how inadequate has been the Church's ministry to its own people in the area of sexuality. While the Task Force believes that the Church must open itself to persons in non-traditional patterns of sexuality and family life, it must at the same time nurture, guide and educate its people in the fundamental issues and problematics of the full range of human sexuality.

2. RESOLVED, that this Convention affirms those pastors and congregations who minister to and seek to include persons living out alternate patterns of sexuality and family life; and be it further

RESOLVED, that this Diocese supports them as they receive, encourage, and affirm such persons in responsible and faithful commitment to Christ, to each other, their families and to the Gospel.

Supporting Information: The Task Force believes that pastors and congregations engaged in such an inclusive ministry deserve and would be strengthened by the public, official support of the diocese as they minister in this controversial and conflict-laden sphere of human life.

Task Force on Human Sexuality and Family Life

The Rev. Dr. Nelson S.T. Thayer, Chair
The Rev. Cynthia Black
Ms. Ella DuBose
The Rev. Abigail Hamilton
Ms. Diane Holland
Mr. Thomas Kebba
Mr. Townsend Lucas
Dr. Teresa Marciano
The Rev. Gerard Pisani
The Rev. Gerald Riley

Results

Resolution 1:   Passed

Resolution 2:   Clergy Order: 115 for, 35 against
                       Lay Order: 234 for, 128 against
                       Passed in both orders.

I certify the above results are correct.

Christine M. Barney
Secretary of Convention

Notes: *This report to the 114th Convention of the Newark, New Jersey Diocese of the Episcopal Church traces the reactions and responses to and conflicts surrounding the Task Force on Human Sexuality and Family Life Report that the 113th Convention of the Diocese received and sent to its parishes for a year-long study. The document's sanctioning of pre- and post-marital sexual intercourse and homosexual relationships as well as other radical revisions of the church's teachings on sexuality, marriage and the family sparked the controversy.*

EVANGELICAL CHURCH OF NORTH AMERICA

EXCERPT FROM "THE DISCIPLINE OF THE EVANGELICAL CHURCH" (1982)

6. Marriage

216. Marriage is an institution of divine appointment, upon the proper establishment of which are conditioned human happiness and well-being, and the maintenance of the most important factor of civilization, the Christian home. Virtue and morality in society, stability and permanence of free government can be had only as the Christian home is maintained in its integrity. In view of the gravity of the interests involved in marriage, the church admonishes all persons as follows:

   1. To cherish only worthy and ennobling thoughts on the subject of courtship and marriage.

   2. To avoid undue haste, and practice intelligent deliberation in every step pertaining to this matter.

   3. To enter into marriage only after a favorable personal acquaintanceship sufficient to insure compatibility and the blessings of a Christian home, and to do so only when it can be "in the Lord" (1 Corinthians 7:39), and thus avoid being "unequally yoked together with unbelievers" (11 Corinthians 6:14) in life's most intimate relationship.

   Ministers of the church shall not solemnize any marriage without first counseling earnestly with the couple, presenting the claims of the Gospel and the Biblical teaching on the Christian home. (Hebrews 13:4).

7. Divorce

217. Since marriage is of divine appointment and the union of one man and one woman entered into mutually, it is sacred and morally binding so long as both shall live and ought not be dissolved at will. When human failure results in placing the marriage in jeopardy, the church strongly urges the persons involved to seek counsel with their minister in order to effect reconciliation so that the marriage may be preserved. The church does not sanction nor condone divorce except on the ground of adultery. (Mark 10:4-12; Romans 7:1-3; 1 Cor. 7:10-16). Whenever divorced persons seek marriage through the church, ministers may solemnize such marriages only after having ascertained the circumstances through counsel with the persons involved, presenting the claims of the Gospel and the Biblical teaching on the Christian home. Ministers may, if it seems desirable, consult with fellow ministers and/or local church officials.

Notes: *The Evangelical Church of North America was formed in 1968 by members of the Evangelical United Brethren who did not wish to proceed into the merger with The Methodist Church. Both the Evangelical Church of North America and that of Canada follow the tradition of Methodism as developed within the Evangelical United Brethren. It includes a special emphasis on entire sanctification. This statement reflects the church's conservative stance on marriage and divorce based on a literal reading of the Bible.*

EVANGELICAL CONGREGATIONAL CHURCH

EXCERPT FROM "THE CREED, RITUAL AND DISCIPLINE OF THE EVANGELICAL CONGREGATIONAL CHURCH" (1983)

143.1.2 Human Sexuality

God created mankind male and female (Genesis 1:27). Each is to complete the other in the marriage bond (Genesis 2:24). A man and a woman who seal the bond of mutual love through Christian marriage are to live for each other as set forth in Holy Scripture (Ephesians 5:21-23). Within this marriage relationship, and only within it, is human sexuality to be expressed in sexual union.

143.1.2.1 Marriage

143.1.2.1.1 The Biblical Ideal

The Bible conceives of marriage as a life-long, monogamous commitment between a man and a woman. The institution of marriage, ordained of God (Genesis 2:24), has been reaffirmed by Jesus (Matthew 19:5) and Paul (Ephesians 5:31). Our Lord Jesus further declared this union to be indissoluble when he said, "What God has joined together, let man not separate" (Matthew 19:6). This marriage covenant is morally binding so long as both shall live (Romans 7:2; 1 Corinthians 7:39), and may not be dissolved at will.

Since the strength of any society is based upon a firm family foundation, and a strong family is based upon total commitment of husband and wife, we strongly urge that:

—appropriate instruction by precept and example in the sacredness of marriage be given to our children from the earliest ages, both at home and in the church;

—our pastors seek, by every means possible, to convey to their congregations the sacredness of Christian marriage;

—our pastors insist on adequate pre-marital counseling prior to solemnizing any marriage;

—every effort be made to insure that persons entering into marriage harbor no reservations with regard to life-long commitment;

—this step be taken only when it can be done in the Lord (1 Corinthians 7:39) and thus avoid being "yoked together with unbelievers" (2 Corinthians 6:14) in life's most intimate relationship.

143.1.2.1.2 Family Planning

143.1.2.1.2.1 Procreation

In the beginning God breathed life into the man He created (Genesis 2:27). Since that day, all human life owes its existence to the breath of God. But God has given to man, His creation, the privilege of being a partner in the life-giving process. Hence He told our progenitors to "be fruitful and increase in number" (Genesis 1:28).

143.1.2.1.2.2 Responsible Parenthood

Children are a blessing from the Lord (Psalms 127:3-5), and every new life has a right to be loved and wanted. Therefore, we encourage responsible parenting, including the spacing of children. We must recognize, however, that God may overrule our carefully laid plans. In such an event, the child has a full right to life, acceptance and love.

143.1.2.1.2.3 Adoption

Adoption is a means by which unwanted and homeless children can live in homes of love, and share in the joys of family life. Therefore we support all proper means for the adoption of children and recognize this, rather than abortion, as a suitable solution to difficulties arising from unwanted pregnancies.

143.1.2.1.3 Divorce

Divorce is an admission of failure in human relationships which negates the Biblical ideal of marriage. Jesus indicated that Moses permitted divorce only because of hardness of heart, and that it was not intended in the beginning. (Matthew 19:8).

When serious difficulties occur in a marriage, the couple involved should seek the counsel and guidance of the pastor or other respected persons within the Christian fellowship. If the distressed couple fails to seek help, loving, discreet biblical counsel and exhortation should nevertheless be offered in a spirit of helpfulness and humility (Galatians 6:1) in an effort to restore harmony. Counsel which would make dissolution of the marriage bond an easy solution even to difficult problems should be rejected. If actual separation takes place, every possible effort should be continued to resolve difficulties and effect lasting reconciliation.

When failures do occur in this less-than-perfect world, we encourage compassion and concern for all persons involved. God's love extends to all, even to those who have failed to live up to His standards. Therefore every separated or divorced person has a right to be loved in Christ Jesus. Like any other penitent sinner, he or she should be granted the privilege of Church membership and full participation in the life of the Church.

Extreme caution must be exercised by our pastors in solemnizing a marriage in which either party has been divorced. Clear evidence of biblical grounds shall be present (Matthew 5:32; 19:9; 1 Corinthians 7:39), and adequate counseling shall be given to guard against the recurrence of a broken relationship. As long as reconciliation with the previous spouse is a viable option, marriage to another person should not be considered.

143.1.2.1.4 Adultery

Marriage is a life-long commitment to a mate of the opposite sex "so long as . . . both shall live". The two have become one flesh (Genesis 2:24), and therefore intimate sharing of the body is reserved exclusively for the marriage partner (1 Corinthians 7:3-4). Attempts to justify adulterous acts by explaining them as occasional lapses, temporary flings, or as "the leading of the Lord" are only thinly disguised rationalizations which elevate subjective feeling above the clear teaching of Scripture.

143.1.2.2 Pre-Marital Sex

We oppose all forms of sexual activity outside of the Biblical understanding of life-long monogamous marriage. The pre-marital performance of the sex act at any time is to engage in fornication, and can be looked at only as sin (Galantians 5:19).

143.1.2.3 Homosexuality

Homosexuality was the sin of Sodom for which that city was destroyed (Genesis 19), and is uniformly seen as a perversion of sex in the New Testament (Romans 1:26-27); Colossians 3:5). Therefore a homosexual relationship is not acceptable as an alternative life-style, and any homosexual act, even between consenting adults is a violation of the Biblical ethic.

143.1.2.4 Temptation

Temptation is the common lot of mankind (1 Corinthians 10:13) and even our Lord was tempted (Matthew 4:1-10). Therefore temptation to sin does not itself involve transgression of the law of God. However, realizing the power of the tempter (1 Peter 5:8) and recalling Jesus' warnings against murder and adultery in the heart (Matthew 5:22,28), we should seek to avoid situations which entice us to inner feelings of lust or outward acts of homosexuality, fornication or adultery. While such attitudes and acts are sinful, we recognize our

86

obligation to extend the love of Christ to persons caught in such circumstances and affirm our duty to minister to them as redeemable human beings.

143.1.2.5 Abortion

The moral issue of abortion is more than a question of the freedom of a woman to control the reproductive functions of her own body. It is a question of those circumstances under which a human being may be permitted to take the life of another.

Since life is a gift of God, neither the life of an unborn child nor the mother may be lightly taken. The value of life prior to birth is seen throughout the Scriptures (Psalms 139:13-16; 51:5; Jeremiah 1:5; Luke 1:41-44). Divine blessing is conferred upon an unborn infant (Luke 1:42, "Blessed is the child you will bear!"). The strife-filled lives of Jacob and Esau are shown already in process prior to birth (Genesis 25:22-23).

It is neither right nor proper to terminate a pregnancy solely on the basis of personal convenience or sociological considerations. Abortion on demand for social adjustment or to solve economic problems is morally wrong. On those rare occasions when abortion may seem morally justified the decision should be made only after there has been thorough and sensitive medical, psychological and religious consultation and counseling.

143.1.3 The Single Life

We affirm the dignity and acceptability of the single life. While the married state is good, and family life necessary for the continuation of human life, not all persons may be led into this shared relationship. Our Lord himself did not enter the married relationship, and Paul wrote, "Now to the unmarried and the widows I say: It is good for them to stay unmarried, as I am" (1 Corinthians 7:8). Paul also suggests that for those who are able, the unmarried state might allow one to serve God better (1 Corinthians 7:37-38; 7:32-36).

Notes: *The Evangelical Congregational Church was formed in 1922 by members of the United Evangelical Church who opposed reuniting with the Evangelical Association.*

EVANGELICAL FREE CHURCH OF AMERICA

RESOLUTION ON THE CHURCH, FAMILY LIFE AND SEXUALITY (1977)

The following resolutions represent the core conviction that the family is a biblically defined sub-unit in any society which must be nurtured and protected. The weight of stress which our society brings upon the family and the ordered relationships which preserve its integrity are duly recognized even sympathetically so.

The biblical imperatives remain, nevertheless. By seeking to respect the biblical ordering of human sexual relations, by protecting the family unit and manifesting regard for the human person from conception to old age, these resolutions call the Christian to faithfulness in its own relationships and in its witness to the larger society. . . .

Singleness, Marriage and the Family

In light of the millions of single adults in our society, we affirm singleness as a valid biblical lifestyle (1 Cor. 7:8). Therefore, we encourage our churches to develop meaningful ministries to single persons and to see their essential role in the fellowship and ministry of the Body.

In light of the fact that one and one half million unmarried couples are living together in America, we affirm marriage as consistent with the biblical norm.

In light of the million divorces occurring in the United States each year, we affirm the biblical ideal of marriage as being an indissoluble relationship and we regret the rising trend of divorce; and where it affects people within or without our churches we urge that our churches extend compassion and ministry to the affected.

In light of the widespread breakdown of the family in our society, we likewise affirm the importance of the family unit and its importance to the nurture and development of human life and the health of society.

Recognizing the pressures in our society that have contributed to the breakdown of marriage and the family, such as, the changing value systems, the high mobility of society and the impact of television; we urge the following:

1. The complexities of our modern industrial society have reduced the amount of time a family spends together. Therefore, it becomes increasingly important that the family compensate by carving out time to be together.

2. That the local church structure its program so as to allow sufficient time for family units to have time together.

3. That the local church help its families to develop meaningful family activities.

4. That parents take the initiative in relating more effectively to their children and to each other.

5. That parents use discretionary judgment not only in the selection of television programs, but also in the amount of time that television is in use in the home.

6. That parents give serious consideration to the implications of uprooting the family for the sake of personal advancement.

7. That parents use biblical family patterns and principles in the development of their family.

Notes: *The Evangelical Free Church of America was formed in 1950 by the merger of the Swedish Evangelical Free Church and the Norwegian-Danish Evangelical Free Church Association. In this statement, the church reaffirms a conservative morality while recognizing the changes occurring in family life and sexuality.*

EVANGELICAL FRIENDS CHURCH, EASTERN DIVISION

EXCERPT FROM "FAITH AND PRACTICE: THE BOOK OF DISCIPLINE" (1981)

Testimonies With Regard to the Christian Family

A. The Family

85. The family is the basic unit of human relationship, and as such is also the foundation unit of society and of the church. The many Biblical references to the family assure us of its divine origin and of God's concern for the family and the home.

B. Marriage

86. Marriage is the union of a man and woman into a oneness which no other human relationship can provide. Made before God and men, the marriage vow unites a couple so fully that they "become one flesh." Marriage also, even more importantly, involves mental, emotional, and spiritual union. Friends should therefore enter into marriage under the full persuasion that it is a life-long commitment and union.

87. A union so solemn is to be entered into only after much forethought, planning and prayer, and "in the fear of the Lord." Friends should seek earnestly the will of our

Lord concerning their choice of a mate, remembering the apostolic injunction, ''Do not be unequally yoked together with unbelievers.'' (II Cor. 6:14a)

88. Parents should use watchful care to help their children find mates of Christian character and commitment.

C. Divorce

89. Since the only clear Biblical allowance for divorce is adultery, Friends discourage seeking a divorce on any other grounds (Mark 10:2-9). The sanctity of the marriage vows requires Friends to seek earnestly to prevent serious marital discord, perhaps through counseling, and to make every effort toward a happy, harmonious, and holy marriage.

90. The break-up of many marriages in our day lays great responsibility upon the congregation to be sensitive to the needs of those becoming involved in such crises and to be quick in loving concern for them.

91. Friends ought not to marry divorced persons, except where divorce was granted on grounds of adultery. We ask our ministers to consider the circumstances carefully, perhaps in consultation with the leaders of their congregations, before deciding whether to perform the ceremony.

Notes: *Prior to 1971, the Evangelical Friends Church, Eastern Division was known as the Ohio Yearly Meeting of Friends, that branch of the Friends most influenced by the holiness movement. It has become a haven for conservative congregations who have withdrawn from the Friends United Meeting in both the United States and Canada. Like other conservative groups, the Evangelical Friends approach questions of sexual morality, marriage, and divorce from a literal interpretation of the Bible.*

EVANGELICAL LUTHERAN CHURCH IN AMERICA

TEACHINGS AND PRACTICE ON MARRIAGE, DIVORCE AND REMARRIAGE (1984)

I. Marriage

A. Basic Understanding of Marriage

1. Marriage is a structure of human life built into the creation by the Creator. It builds upon our creation as male and female (Gen. 1:27). Sexual differences are of God's good design, intended to bring joy and enrichment to human life as well as to provide for procreation. The essence of marriage is that in the act and relationships of marriage two persons become one flesh (Gen. 2:24). In this complementary nature of the two sexes as God created them lies the basis for marriage and each new family.

2. Marriage exists within a world characterized by our alienation from God and from each other; it therefore is affected by human sinfulness. Nevertheless, being part of God's creative and sustaining order, marriage continues to exist under God's goodness and protection. It is a means by which God places us into an intimate relationship with another, signifying that we were not meant to be alone. Marriage ceremonies serve as symbols of public acceptance of responsibility of husband and wife to one another. Marriage provides the framework within which children can be nurtured and trained for living with others. Laws, regulations, and customs which order and control marriage are a social and moral necessity, and, when rightly drawn and administered, they serve God's good purposes.

3. Christian people recognize their marital union as belonging to God's created order; it is not merely a contract between two individuals, the essential elements of which can be arbitrarily altered. Christian people seek also the fulfillment of their marital union in Christ as they grow in loving one another even as Christ has loved them, as they learn to forgive one another in the spirit of Christ, and as they draw upon the resources which the Lord of the church makes available to his people. The faith of Christian people affects, often decisively, every aspect of their marriage.

4. Marriage is not an estate in which all persons should be expected to exercise their calling as Christians. For some, the single estate may be that in which they can best serve the purposes of God and the needs of their neighbors. Whether married or single, a Christian's affirmation of God's calling within God's kingdom liberates one from the need to conform to the pressures of society.

B. The Unity of Marriage

5. The devotion to one another and the unity named in Gen. 2:24 are of the essence of marriage. Husband and wife ought to become a harmony of personalities, a couple belonging together, "no longer two but one" (Mark 10:7, 8; Eph. 5:31). They become a paired unity—in sexual expression, in values and goals, and often in parenthood.

6. The unity which God intends for marriage requires a lifelong commitment of husband and wife to each other. Such commitment provides the foundation for real freedom and growth. The oneness of husband and wife, marked by unwavering lifetime fidelity, is compared in Scripture to the oneness of Christ and his church. Just as love, faithfulness, and service mark the relationship of Christ and the church, so also they should characterize the relationship of husbands and wives. Both husband and wife are to be subject to one another out of reverence for Christ (Eph. 5:21). Husband and wife yield to each other full devotion and unselfish consideration. It is on this exalted level that conjugal rights and obligations are granted and accepted. Neither lords it over the other nor insists selfishly on rights or duties. Together husband and wife become one in love, serving on another within marriage. (See Gal. 5:22, 23; Eph. 5:21-25; Col. 3:18, 19; 1 Peter 3:1-7)

7. Every person has been created by God with gifts that make him or her a unique personality. The strength and unity of marriage come from mutual recognition and sharing of each other's needs and gifts. This unity recognizes the freedoms of husband and wife to express their own interests as well as their duty to share in those relationships where sharing is essential to the success of the marriage. The unique gifts of husband and wife should be utilized, within the harmony of marriage, toward the meaningful goals and purposes of human life assigned by God.

C. Love in Marriage

8. As God is love, so has God given to male and female, created in God's image, the capacity to express love. Marriage can be a prime opportunity through which we can reflect the divine relationship of love. That love which reflects divine love is mature, kind, considerate, self-giving, dedicated to the well-being and the fulfillment of the other as of oneself, and faithful to the beloved until death. Its characteristics are described in 1 Cor. 13:4-7. It seeks to give rather than to get. Such love is the goal and gift of marriage, the quality in which the marriage partners ought to grow and mature, even though our capacity for such love is warped by human selfishness.

9. Sexual intercourse is expressive of the unique union established between a husband and wife in marriage. It provides a unique knowing of the other person which can be realized in no other way. By its very nature sexual intercourse expresses a commitment to another person which constitutes marriage. It is for this reason that the biblical witness condemns sexual intercourse outside marriage as contrary to God's intention. Sexual intercourse should be an expression of love, but love is both richer and more

inclusive than the sex act. Sexual harmony, truly one of the joys of marriage, nevertheless is not so much the goal of marriage as it is a reflection of the total unity and love of the married pair. The sexual relationship has often been exploited as an instrument of power and aggression, or falsely portrayed as a magic panacea, leading many couples to be disappointed with sex as they experience it. Major marital problems may stem from or be reflected in such unwholesome experience with sex.

10. Married Christians seek to fulfill God's intentions for marriage. Even the marriage of Christians, however, daily falls short of the Christian ideal. Hence the Christian husband and wife daily need God's forgiveness for their sins of omission and commission, followed by a readiness to be forgiving toward one another. In gratitude to God they daily rededicate themselves to God and to one another, realizing that their marital unity is never completed but is always in the process of becoming.

D. Preserving the Marriage

11. Problems are inevitable in marriage. Conflicts and problems can be used constructively to further communication and understanding upon which marriage thrives, or they may become destructive of the relationship of love between husband and wife. When people become involved in marital difficulties, it should be a concern of pastors, relatives, and friends to provide help and understanding in overcoming the conflicts, thereby strengthening and preserving the marriage. The total costs of disruption of a marriage are high, not only for the husband and wife but also for any children involved. Broken marriages are destructive of family, congregational, and community strength. Therefore couples having difficulties with their marriage should be helped to find competent counsel before the marriage itself is threatened.

II. Divorce

A. The Nature of Divorce

12. Divorce is never God's intention for our marriages. The breakdown of a marriage relationship is the consequence of human sinfulness, leading to a process of alienation from which there seems to be no other way out. Divorce needs to be seen realistically as the breaking of an order of God, the public and legal recognition of an already broken marriage, the culmination of a process of alienation.

13. Divorce, according to the teaching of Jesus, is a concession to the fact and reality of sin in a fallen world. Being the friend of sinners, Jesus did not condemn or drive away a divorced person. Neither did he excuse divorce. Rather, he declared, ''What therefore God has joined together, let no man put asunder'' (Mark 10:9). He spoke no word by which a man or a woman might rationalize divorce into a righteous act. Jesus did, however, explain divorce as resulting from the hardness of human hearts (Matt. 19:8; Mark 10:5). Divorce arises from self-centeredness or other obstacles the couple cannot or will not overcome.

B. Appraising Reasons for Divorce

14. Divorce is a consequence of human sinfulness. Christians contemplating divorce do so with a sense of the seriousness of their decision, and often with a sense of anguish. Christian spouses will do everything in their power to restore their marriage. Certainly before they decide on divorce they will give themselves time and opportunity to evaluate the total costs of the possible termination of their marriage, for themselves as well as for their families and others involved. They will seek the counsel of their pastor or other competent counsel. If after careful consideration the marriage relationship is deemed beyond repair, and the effects of continuing the marriage to be more destructive of the welfare of persons than divorce, the decision for divorce may be recognized as a responsible choice, the lesser of several evils in a fallen world.

Recognizing that each party generally bears some responsibility for the failure of the marriage, a decision for divorce may be made in reliance upon God's grace.

C. Ministering to the Divorced

15. The church must seek to deal in an evangelical rather than a legalistic manner with the problems of divorce and divorced persons. Divorced persons will be fully included in the life of the Christian church, which expresses God's spirit of love and forgiveness. These persons should not become the victims of gossip, ostracism, or undue attention. They need rather to be brought to feel anew the bonds of human fellowship and the sense of God's continuing presence, so that their divorce, unfortunate though it may be, may lead toward a more mature Christian life. They continue to be part of the Christian community of Word and Sacraments.

III. Remarriage

16. Remarriage of divorced persons is neither forbidden nor automatically endorsed by the American Lutheran Church. The second marriage of divorced persons may result in a new union which faithfully witnesses to God's purpose for marriage. Such remarriages will more likely result, however, if persons carefully consider the dynamics which led to the dissolution of a previous marriage. There should be a willingness to acknowledge one's own failures in a spirit of forgiveness toward all involved, and to work at correcting whatever personal characteristics may be detrimental to a marital relationship. Legitimate obligations to any children and to the former spouse must be fulfilled. When such is the case, the church can add its blessing to the remarriage of divorced Christians.

17. The remarriage of a person whose previous marriage was terminated by death normally can be commended as a sound decision, renewing the blessings of companionship which a good marriage brings. This is as true for persons in the years of retirement as for those in young adulthood or in middle years.

IV. Recommended Practice

18. Because it regards marriage in such high esteem, the Christian congregation is concerned about the character and quality of marriages, both among its members and in the larger society. Because persons encounter difficulties in marriage and family life, the church needs to give special attention to this aspect of its total ministry. While all members of the congregation share this concern, and each has a part in the total ministry of the congregation, pastors are called to carry a unique responsibility.

19. In light of current trends and pressures, positive Christian education and preparation for marriage and family life belong in every congregation's ministry. The pastor should be alert to opportunities in the pulpit, home, church schools, confirmation classes, and auxiliaries for influencing commitment to Christian standards in the choice of a marriage partner and in patterns for marriage and family living. In counseling sessions, persons can be led to see the implications of their Christian commitment for the marriage and family relationships they are experiencing. Programs for marital and family enrichment can be developed. Pastors should encourage members of congregations to assume a constructive attitude toward the preservation and strengthening of marriage.

20. When officiating at any marriage the pastor acts both as an agent of the state and as a servant of Christ. Therefore the pastor should be satisfied that both the man and woman desiring to be married know what is required in marriage and earnestly intend by the help of God to live up to its obligations. Normally the couple should be expected to participate in a program of premarital education. In the case of remarriage of divorced persons, pastors should discuss with the divorced person whether he or she has come to an understanding of the failure of the former marriage. If the pastor, in clear conscience before God, is convinced that a particular couple is not ready to enter upon a

responsible marriage, that pastor should be supported by the congregation in refusing to perform the desired marriage.

21. Requests to officiate at the marriage of a man and a woman markedly different in such characteristics as religion, race, age, and cultural backgrounds should receive special attention. Such differences should not be understood as constituting fundamental impediments to marriage. However, such a marriage may present complex problems. The couple should examine carefully the effects of their marriage for themselves, their children, their families, their congregations, and their community. If the pastor is convinced that the two are not sufficiently strong and mature, both spiritually and emotionally, to overcome the hazards to a sound marriage which their marked differences in background, experience, and outlook may impose, he or she should not officiate at the desired marriage.

22. In situations where young or immature persons, under pressure of pregnancy, seek to be married, the pastor may counsel strongly against marriage, which is an estate for adults able to accept its obligations. The pastor may point out that to marry may be to compound an already difficult situation. Adults ought not to insist that the youth be married, whether "to give the baby a name" or for other face-saving reasons. When marriage of the couple is not desirable the pastor should work in consultation with an appropriate social agency to see that the needs of the couple are adequately met and the interests of the child are protected.

23. Each pastor should become informed on the marriage and divorce laws of the state in which he or she ministers. Pastors also should take an informed interest in any family life education programs which may be conducted in the public schools, as well as in the work of agencies supporting family life in the community. All pastors, as well as other church members, should support sound legislation both to foster high standards for marriage and the family and to correct the evils and abuses which much divorce legislation now condones.

24. The pastor's ministry to persons contemplating marriage, divorce, or remarriage should proclaim and demonstrate both God's law and his gracious gospel. The pastor will proclaim and demonstrate God's law by holding up God's intention for marriage. The pastor will proclaim and demonstrate God's gracious gospel by pointing to the resources of grace and forgiveness. In this way, the pastor's ministry and practice in relation to marriage, divorce, and remarriage will be consistent with the total ministry of Christ's church.

Notes: *The Evangelical Lutheran Church in America was formed in April, 1987 when the American Lutheran Church merged with the Lutheran Church in America and the Association of Evangelical Lutheran Churches. The teachings, statements and policies of each of the merging bodies are considered valid and in force until the new church formulates and adopts new ones. This statement was adopted by the Eleventh General Convention of the American Lutheran Church to replace the statement "Teachings and Practice on Marriage and Divorce" adopted by the Second General Convention.*

GREEK ORTHODOX ARCHDIOCESE OF NORTH AND SOUTH AMERICA

EXCERPT FROM "ECUMENICAL AND PASTORAL DIRECTIVES ON CHRISTIAN MARRIAGE: 'THE MEANING OF MARRIAGE IN ORTHODOX CHRISTIANITY'" (UNDATED)

For Orthodox Christianity, Marriage is a Sacrament, one of the seven commonly designated Sacraments of the Church. This means that from the point of view of the Orthodox Christian community, it is directly and immediately related to the experience of being God's people and with the mystical experience of membership in the Church. It is crucial to the understanding of the Orthodox Christian practices and views regarding marriage to emphasize that marriage as a Sacrament begins with the presupposition that the partners entering the marital union are already members of the Body of Christ, share in its liturgical and worship life and "belong" to it.

Generally speaking, that identity of the partners with the Church is emphasized and experienced in the Divine Liturgy. Attendance and frequent reception of Holy Communion by all Orthodox Christians is the most important dimension and sign of the Orthodox Christian's membership in the Church. It is from this fact that we understand the basic impetus of the Orthodox understanding of marriage. Though today, the Orthodox marriage ceremony is a complex, yet most beautiful service usually not conducted in conjunction with the Divine Liturgy, it is significant that originally, Orthodox Christians entered into marriage by attending the Divine Liturgy together, receiving Holy Communion together and being blessed by the Bishop with a simple prayer in which God was asked to unite the couple.

Naturally, what is presupposed is that the couple has freely consented to unite their lives as husband and wife in love and faithfulness. However, it is not their free consent alone which makes Marriage a Sacrament. It is the presenting of themselves as a couple to the gathered body of the Church, the sharing as a couple in the Eucharist and the whole experience of the Divine Liturgy, as well as the blessing of the Bishop or Priest in the presence of the Church that make it a Sacrament. It is precisely in the fact that *this* marriage, unlike civil marriages, is incorporated in the very life of the Church, and is sanctified, blessed and hallowed by the grace of God that gives it its special significance. The key words in the Orthodox Christian Marriage Service are those uttered by the Priest as he joins the hands of the couple: he prays to God saying, . . . "and extend *Thy* hand from *Thy* Holy dwelling place and join this *Thy* servant (groom's name) unto this *Thy* servant (bride's name) for *by Thee* are husband and wife united . . ." The hands of the bride, the groom and the priest are joined momentarily at that point in the service, signifying that the couple becomes one in the presence of the Church and through the sanctifying action and grace of God. The early connection of the Sacrament of Matrimony with the Eucharist is still maintained in the Orthodox Church through the world-spread practice according to which the engaged couple receive Holy Communion together on the Sunday preceding their marriage.

Thus, for Eastern Orthodoxy, marriage is not simply an agreement of a man and woman to share their lives together; nor is it a mere legal sanction. It is not "performed" by the couple themselves with the clergyman and the congregation as witnesses to their decision. Their union-based on their freely-willed decision to join their lives together as husband and wife becomes sacramental because they are joined together as Orthodox Christians who are members of the Eucharistic Community sharing together the Body and Blood of Christ and receiving the grace of God for their union through the ministrations of the whole Church in the person of Bishop or priest and in the presence of the gathered people of God.

This explains why the Church cannot comfortably and easily accept the marriage of an Orthodox Christian with a non-Orthodox Christian and finds it impossible to "unite in Christ" an Orthodox Christian and a non-Christian. Just as participation in the Sacrament of Holy Communion, the Eucharist is reserved only to the Orthodox Christian, so in like manner, the Sacrament of Holy Matrimony retains its full meaning when both husband and wife are practicing Orthodox Christians.

It is for the same kind of reason that the Church blesses and sanctifies the marital union for life. Just as secret mental reservations would impair the unity achieved between the communicant and our Lord in the Sacrament of Holy Communion (even though Christ's presence in His Body and Blood is real), so in like manner, a less than total and full commitment of bride and groom makes their union less than complete. Just as their loyalty to God is to be permanent and total, so their unity to each other, which in the Sacrament is sanctified and incorporated into that divine relationship ought to be permanent and total.

In the Orthodox Church, the purposes of marriage are numerous. High on the list is the procreation of children. The couple is understood to be co-workers with God not only in the perpetuation of human life through the conception, birth and physical care of children, but also in the more profound sense of the spiritual nurture of new members of God's Kingdom. That is why birth control methods which would frustrate this purpose of marriage deliberately are not approved by the Orthodox Church. But there are other purposes to marriage besides this. The emphasis on mutual support, and aid assistance and mutual fulfillment is strongly made by the Orthodox. The marriage ceremony provides for the triple exchange of the marriage rings and the triple exchange of the marriage crown emphasizing the mutuality and shared equality of the couple. Yet it is always in the context of the presence of God and membership in the whole people of God, the Church. That mutual caring, support, concern and assistance is at the basis of the love relationship of husband and wife. That is why the Bible finds it appropriate to compare marital love with the love of Christ for the Church. His self-sacrificing, caring, supporting, protective and saving love for us is the example for all people, but in a unique way it is a perfect pattern for the love of husband and wife. That love takes time, effort and patience to develop. It is expressed in many different ways. Marital sexual relations are not only means for procreation but also express the total union of the couple in all things of their lives. That is why many Orthodox theologians believe that Birth Control methods may be used by Orthodox Christian couples when the other purposes of marriage are also respected. In whatever the Orthodox Christian married couple does in their life together, it maintains the sacramental character when it is done in unity with Christ and His Church. . . .

From the preceding, it is understandable why the Orthodox Church thinks of Marriage first in reference to its own members. Membership in the Church does not require marriage. It is optional in the sense that an Orthodox Christian has the choice - as a Christian - to select a chaste celibate life or to marry. Sexual relations outside of marriage are not appropriate to the life in Christ. Those who are not able or do not desire to live the celibate life in the Orthodox Christian community are expected to marry.

Notes: *Father Stanley Harakas wrote this statement for a booklet published by an ecumenical group in Massachusetts devoted to helping churches and pastors interpret the meaning of marriage to those seeking mixed marriages. While Father Harakas is a member of the Greek Orthodox Church, his statement reflects the conservative sacramental view of marriage held in common by all corporate members of the Eastern Orthodox branch of Christianity.*

GREEK ORTHODOX ARCHDIOCESE OF NORTH AND SOUTH AMERICA

STATEMENT ON THE FAMILY (UNDATED)

Family

The Orthodox Church affirms the duty of the procreation of the human race, as our Creator commanded that man "Be fruitful and multiply and fill the earth" (Gen. 1:28). She is also aware of the added responsibility given to man in the second charge of managing his own reproductive behavior, to "subdue" the earth and "have dominion over every living thing" (Gen. 1:28-29). Herein can be found the answers to such modern issues as "maintaining the balance of nature" and "guarding against overpopulation".

The Church also stresses the sacramental character of Christian marriage; in the Sacrament of Matrimony, natural marriage enters the realm of God's eternal Kingdom. Within its bounds, husband and wife are called to perfect their love for one another into a life long communion and to grow in oneness towards Christ. And out of this mutual love of husband and wife for one another, all other purposes of marriage flow. Husband and wife pledge their mutual support to one another not only in the joy of life but also in trials and tribulations. They exclusively provide for one another's sexual fulfillment in an all embracing love.

Notes: *The Greek Orthodox Archdiocese of North and South America is the largest of its kind in the United States; its first parish was founded in 1767. This statement emphasizes the sacramental, procreative, personal and social dimensions of sexuality and marriage from a conservative theological perspective.*

INDEPENDENT FUNDAMENTAL CHURCHES OF AMERICA

RESOLUTION ON THE FAMILY AND DIVORCE (1978)

WHEREAS, God has set forth the family as the basic unit of society to preserve and maintain the social order, and to propagate the race; and

WHEREAS, the marriage relationship pictures the eternal union of Christ and His church, and that such a union between man and woman is ordained by God to endure for life; and

WHEREAS, we are experiencing in our society Satanic forces fracturing and destroying our family structure through easy divorces and through forming unscriptural relationships of family living;

THEREFORE BE IT RESOLVED, that we, the members and delegates of the 49th Annual Convention of the Independent Fundamental Churches of America, meeting at Estes Park, Colorado, June 24-30, 1978, go on record as being opposed to the unholy substitutes for marriage presently being practiced in our society, such as "trial marriages", "no-fault divorces", and living together in no-marriage; and

BE IT FURTHER RESOLVED, that we of the Independent Fundamental Churches of America encourage all pastors of our movement to teach and instruct their constituencies concerning the biblical order and sanctity of marriage and the evils of divorce, and that in all these matters we may seek by God's grace to be scripturally correct.

Notes: *The Independent Fundamental Churches of America is one of the oldest and largest of the fundamental church groups dating back to 1922. Its commitment to a literal interpretation of the Bible leads it to reaffirm a conservative interpretation of sexuality, marriage, and the family.*

LUTHERAN CHURCH-MISSOURI SYNOD

EXCERPT FROM "HUMAN SEXUALITY: A THEOLOGICAL PERSPECTIVE" (1981)

II. Marriage and Its Purposes

The earthly estate of marriage is a divine institution. It is therefore subject to certain divine requirements which remain in effect until the close of this age regardless of the social customs, civil laws, or ecclesiastical rites which may come to surround it. That God Himself established marriage and pronounced it good also means that He created it *for* the good of humanity. He is at work in marriage to accomplish His purposes. In marriage God intends to provide for (1) the relation of man and woman in mutual love (Gen. 2:18); (2) the procreation of children (Gen. 1:28); and (3) the partial remedy for sinful lust (1 Cor. 7:2).

Both the fourth and sixth commandments presume and support these purposes of marriage in human life.

A. Marriage

Marriage is the lifelong union of one man and one woman entered into by mutual consent. It is ordinarily expected that this consent and commitment will be public, that marriage is not a merely personal decision but one which concerns all those who are now to treat this man and woman as husband and wife. Although marriage derives its validity from the commitment of a man and woman to a permanent sharing of their lives, the institution of marriage will normally be circumscribed by various civil laws imposed by society. Even though the legal restrictions with which our society surrounds marriage do not belong to the essence of marriage,[8] there is good reason to believe that they will ordinarily serve human well-being—a purpose for which God has established civil authority (Rom. 13:4a). Such restrictions serve the important social function of safeguarding rights of the spouse and children. More important still, they may encourage thoughtful, reflective commitment and thus protect the interest not only of society but also of those who think they are in love. Unjustified disregard for the legal requirements which have been established by the state concerning marriage violates God's command for obedience to the authorities He has placed over us.

The essence of marriage does not consist in legal requirements nor in ecclesiastical ceremonies. To say otherwise would be to retract the Biblical emphasis on marriage as a worldly or earthly institution. Not the pronouncement of a minister but the consent of the partners belongs to the essence of marriage. Indeed, not until the fourth century A.D. is there even evidence of priestly prayer and blessing in connection with the marriage of Christians. It was felt to be entirely a secular act, though, of course, one carried out—like all acts—"in the Lord."[9] To say that marriage is not primarily an ecclesiastical matter is not to say that it is autonomous, however. Marriage remains a divine institution given by God to His creatures to nourish their common life together and to preserve human life toward the final goal of all creation.

While recognizing that marriage as a divinely ordained earthly estate can be legitimately contracted in the civil realm, Christian couples will ordinarily desire to make their vows in a public worship service. In such a context they are able to hear what the Word of God teaches concerning the sanctity of the marriage bond and to permit fellow Christians to join them and their families in asking God's blessings on their life together. For such couples the ecclesiastical marriage rite is not the church's way of making sacred something otherwise profane. Rather, the church's act of consecration signifies that marriage is holy because it is God-ordained and that it can be received with thanksgiving (1 Tim. 4:5).

Sexual intercourse engaged in outside of the marriage relationship is forbidden by the Scriptures and must be condemned by the church (Gen. 2:24; 1 Thess. 4:2-5; cf. Gal. 5:19; Eph 5:3; Col. 3:5; 1 Cor. 6:16-20).[10] This, of course, includes all casual sexual relations, which are accepted practice in our society, and arrangements whereby couples live together without being married. Even when the partners feel themselves united by a deep bond of love and intend to be married at some point in the future ("engagement"), the same judgment must be made.[11] Where there is no commitment to a complete, lifelong sharing of life in marriage, sexual relations are contrary to God's will.

Because marriage is not essentially a legal or ecclesiastical matter, it is possible, however, for a man and woman to give themselves physically to each other, affirming to each other and to the public their consent to share their future lives in a permanent union, recognizing that their union might be fruitful and to do this without a public ceremony. Such a relationship in reality constitutes marriage (common-law marriage)[12] and cannot be called fornication. While not a violation of the Sixth Commandment, such a way of proceeding may involve an element of deceit in that it implies that the individuals involved are living in a single state, a condition which does not in fact exist and which may cause offense to some.

Moreover, this relationship sets aside the regular societal safeguards which have been established for the protection of the rights and interests of all the parties involved, and in some states it is a violation of the legal requirements for marriage.[13]

Christians hold to the principle that the Fourth Commandment ("Thou shalt honor thy father and thy mother, that it may be well with thee, and thou mayest live long on the earth") must also be applied to the estate of marriage. Accordingly, the blessing of parents will ordinarily be sought. Christian couples, in keeping with the Fourth Commandment's injunction that parents in all things be honored and held in high esteem by their children, will already have sought the blessing of their parents on their union prior to the marriage ceremony. Such couples will therefore recognize the appropriateness of inviting parents to declare their blessings upon their union. Christians recognize that God's blessings follow when those desiring to enter marriage seek the advice and consent of parents on decisions of importance to a wider circle of persons than themselves alone. God's order of things concerning the family and civil order should not be disparaged or ignored. "Be subject for the Lord's sake to every human institution . . ." (1 Peter 2:13a)

B. The Purposes of Marriage

1. Mutual Love: The Relational Purpose of Marriage

The Bible, despite its quite natural preoccupation with other concerns, is not oblivious to the awesome human significance of the encounter between a man and a woman who give themselves fully to each other in a "one flesh" union of love.[14] The relation between husband and wife has a significance and meaning in and of itself, distinct from any other purposes (such as procreation) which their union may serve.

This relational aspect of marriage is emphasized in Genesis 2. The beasts of the field, the birds of the air, every living creature has been called forth by the creative Word of God. And then, as the pinnacle of this creation, the man has been formed from the dust of the ground. Obedient to his Creator, he names the animals, placing each in its appropriate role beneath himself. But, we read, "For the man there was not found a helper fit for him" (Gen. 2:20). No answer to the loneliness of the man had yet been given. God himself had not yet announced His good pleasure. Against the background of all the stately cadences in chapter 1 which had pronounced the various aspects of creation "very good," we hear now a different divine utterance. It is "not good"—not good that the man should be alone.

God therefore provides the woman as helpmate. This means not primarily one who will help the man as an assistant in his work. Rather, the woman is "a helping being, in which, as soon as he sees it, he may recognize himself."[15] She is the mirror in which the man will come to know himself as man. The man and woman have been created toward fellowship, and neither can come to know the self rightly apart from the other. The woman is given to the man in order that neither of them may be alone, that together they may know themselves in relation to one who is other than self.[16]

Having created the woman, God brings her to the man, and he in turn responds with those words which we have read rather too solemnly: "At last!" At last, here is one who is "bone of my bone and flesh of my flesh." This is an expression of "joyous astonishment."[17] It is Romeo's "O, she doth teach the torches to burn bright!"—uttered when he catches sight of Juliet.[18] The predicament of the man's loneliness—his "aloneness"—has been discerned and overcome by God's creative Word. A relation has been established in which one may come to know oneself and the other in a fellowship of love.

The union of husband and wife extends to the most intimate sharing in the act of sexual intercourse. The complete physical sharing of husband and wife is characterized by relaxation, enjoyment, and freedom from guilt. Decisions relative to this physical sharing should be made by husband and wife after prayerful discussion, as they keep in mind always that mutual enjoyment of God's beautiful gift is the goal they both seek (1 Thess. 4:4-5; 1 Cor. 7:5). Couples need to remember that their physical commitments are *personal* commitments. The act of intercourse is described in the Bible as an act of knowing: ''Adam knew Eve his wife'' (Gen. 4:1). This is no mere euphemism; or, if it is, it has an uncanny aptness. In the intimate sharing of the sexual act, a union in which the self is naked before the other, a unique knowing takes place. This is not knowledge *about* sex. It is knowledge of the self and the other as sexual beings united with one another in this most intimate union of giving and receiving.[19] The man and the woman, two different beings, while retaining (even accenting) their differences, nevertheless become one. The knowledge of that fellowship—like the knowledge of that fellowship in which God ''knows'' those who are His—can never be fully communicated apart from the experience of the union itself. It can only be said that in this union the partners come to know themselves even as they know the other. They know themselves only ''in relation'' to each other.

It is, of course, possible to forget that we are here talking of mutual *love* and to imagine that nothing more than a satisfaction of sexual appetite is involved. Clearly, however, though we might settle for no more than that, to do so would be to fall short of the personal relationship for which God has created us. The satisfaction of appetite alone, apart from any commitment of love, has not yet risen from the animal to the human, personal sphere.[20]

> *To view our sexuality in the context of a personal relationship of mutual love and commitment in marriage helps us to evaluate the practice of masturbation. Quite clearly, chronic masturbation falls short of the Creator's intention for our use of the gift of sexuality, namely, that our sexual drives should be oriented toward communion with another person in the mutual love and commitment of marriage. By its very nature masturbation separates sexual satisfaction from the giving and receiving of sexual intercourse in the marital union and is symptomatic of the tendency of human beings to turn in upon **themselves** for the satisfaction of **their** desires.*
>
> *In childhood, masturbation may often be a form of temporary experimentation. However, children of God are warned against the voluntary indulgence of sexual fantasies as endangering faith and spiritual life. Such inordinate desires are clearly called sin by our Lord (Matt. 5:28). As the child grows and matures, youthful lusts and fantasies (2 Tim. 2:22) are left behind.*
>
> *For those who are troubled by guilt and who seek God's help in overcoming problems in this area, pastors and Christian counselors need to stand ready to offer Christ's forgiveness, remind them of the power of the Holy Spirit to help them lead ''a chaste and decent life in word and deed,'' and hold before them the joys of remaining faithful to what God's Word teaches about His intention for the good gift of sexuality.*

The satisfaction of sexual appetite does not necessarily involve a personal relationship at all. At that level the man, for example, need not be concerned with woman as woman, as a personal being who calls him to fellowship, but simply with her physiological functions and capacities. And at that level it is quite understandable that people should regard their partners as essentially interchangeable. C.S. Lewis has described the situation quite well:

> **We use a most unfortunate idiom when we say, of a lustful man prowling the streets, that he ''wants a woman.'' Strictly speaking, a woman is just what he does not want. He wants a pleasure for which a woman happens to be the necessary piece of apparatus.**[21]

When the church condemns such a casual approach to sexual encounters as contrary to the will of God, it does more than take recourse in some special ''religious'' insight. It calls people back to a realization of the human, personal significance of the sexual act. A society in which casual sexual encounters and divorce prevail is on its way to viewing sexual partners as interchangeable. Its tendency is to dehumanize people and treat them solely in terms of their sexual functions, abstracting such functions from any content of personal significance.

The relationship of mutual love, one of the purposes for the fulfillment of which the Creator ordains marriage, is something very different. "Eros makes a man really want, not a woman, but one particular woman. In some mysterious but quite indisputable fashion the lover desires the Beloved herself, not the pleasure she can give."[22] And, indeed, lovers— however fickle they may prove to be at some future moment—are genuinely captivated by one another. They will quite naturally swear fidelity to each other. They rightly recognize the immense human and personal significance of the encounter with the beloved. It is this mutual love, implanted by the Creator in His creatures, with its original tendency toward permanent commitment, which marriage institutionalizes and seeks to make permanent.[23] Thus does the Creator continue today to deal with the predicament of "aloneness" within the human creation. He continues to give men and women to each other in the one-flesh union of marriage.

2. Children: The Procreative Purpose of Marriage

Men and women are called out of their loneliness into the fellowship of marriage. Yet, their union might now turn wholly inward and become a purely self-serving one. This is not to be. The union of the man and woman who in their embrace have excluded all third parties is to be a fruitful union. They are privileged to give life to future generations.

The Biblical injunction to "be fruitful and multiply" is to be understood as a blessing as well as a command. It is one of God's good gifts to His people, for procreation is an actual sharing in God's ongoing creative activity. We may even speak of the blessing as a kind of natural promise embedded within the creation: a sign and manifestation of the truth that genuine love is lifegiving and fruitful. Hence, in the Christian tradition the child has been regarded as a blessing from God (Ps. 127:3-5; 128:3). A willingness to give birth involves a willingness to align ourselves—in wonder, humility, and hope—with that blessing embedded in the order of creation itself.

The child reveals to the parents "the depth of their carnal unity. He partakes of both. He is both one and the other, and he is this at the same time."[24] In marriage two different and separate individuals are united without having their individuality obliterated. As a result of God's creative power at work through their union the child incarnates—makes physical and represents in the flesh—the mystery of this union. With the birth of a child, husband and wife come to share a common work. The birth of their child is the public manifestation that this union of husband and wife is not one which turns inward, concentrating solely upon itself. Theirs is the task of raising the child up to become a mature and responsible member of the human family. Moreover, Christian parents have reason to look upon the birth of a child from their union as an occasion to have this child brought into the divine family and to nourish it as it grows to spiritual maturity. They have God's promise that He desires to have their child become an heir of eternal life and a member of His household through Holy Baptism. Theirs is the high privilege of joining in the common work of raising a child up in the knowledge of Jesus Christ, whose forgiveness enables us to live together in unselfish love toward each other.

Couples may, of course, remain childless either voluntarily or involuntarily. From the Christian perspective, *involuntary* childlessness need stand under no special stigma. While couples who are involuntarily childless can find great comfort knowing that the Child Jesus has come among us and that all Christians are members of the one family He has created, nevertheless it is still true that a childless couple may sorrow greatly at their inability to bear children. This is perfectly understandable, since one of the natural purposes of marriage has failed to come to fruition in their union. We need not gloss over that fact. Indeed, we do well to share their sorrow where we can.

However, we ought not characterize their union as "incomplete." To do so would be to take back all that was said concerning the relational purposes of marriage. It would be to forget the profound significance of the one-flesh union. That union of husband and wife has a full and sufficient meaning in itself, and the joining of a man and woman in marriage should not be envisaged merely as a means of reproduction. Furthermore, husband and wife, even when childless, can still engage in a common work. Their union need not turn inward solely upon itself. They can permit the absence of children itself to be creative and fruitful in new ways in their shared life. To be sure, it will take greater thought for them to find some other work in which their oneness may incarnate itself, but it is possible for them to do so. And, of course, they may seek to adopt children. It would be hard to find anywhere in our lives a more exact paradigm of *agape* (self-giving love) than the love which will move people to become parents or to provide foster care for those children who for a variety of reasons are without a family to provide for them. To offer such love is a special blessing and opportunity available to the childless couple.

In view of the Biblical command and the blessing to ''be fruitful and multiply,'' it is to be expected that marriage will not ordinarily be *voluntarily* childless. But, in the absence of Scriptural prohibition, there need be no objection to contraception within a marital union which is, as a whole, fruitful.[25] Moreover, once we grant the appropriateness of contraception, we will also recognize that sterilization may under some circumstances be an acceptable form of contraception. Because of its relatively permanent nature, sterilization is perhaps less desirable than less-far-reaching forms of contraception. However, there should be no moral objection to it, especially for couples who already have children and who now seek to devote themselves to the rearing of those children, for those who have been advised by a physician that the birth of another child would be hazardous to the health of the mother, or for those who for reasons of age, physical disability, or illness are not able to care for additional children. Indeed, there may be special circumstances which would persuade a Christian husband and wife that it would be more responsible and helpful to all concerned, under God, not to have children. Whatever the particular circumstances, Christians dare not take lightly decisions in this area of their life together. They should examine their motives thoroughly and honestly and take care lest their decisions be informed by a desire merely to satisfy selfish interests.

With respect to voluntary childlessness in general, we should say that while there may be special reasons which would persuade a Christian husband and wife to limit the size of their family, they should remember at all times how easy it is for them simply to permit their union to turn inward and refuse to take up the task of sharing in God's creative activity. Certainly Christians will not give as a reason for childlessness the sorry state of the world and the fear of bringing a child into such a world. We are not to forget the natural promise embedded in the fruitfulness of marriage. To bear and rear children can be done, finally, as an act of faith and hope in the God who has promised to supply us with all that we ''need to support this body and life.''

3. Restraint of Sin: The Healing Purpose of Marriage

Marriage as we experience it is not an idyllic order set in an unfallen world. There is nothing sinful about our sexuality *per se,* but our sexuality, like all aspects of our lives, has been disordered as a result of sin. Appetite uncontrolled by mutual love constantly threatens to break out in disruptive ways in our lives. Love itself can become a god to be pursued at all costs, even at the cost of broken promises and unfaithfulness to those to whom we have committed ourselves. Because sin permeates the whole of our lives, it threatens to distort our sexual experience.

Christian teaching has therefore stressed that the Creator graciously uses marriage as an order by which He preserves human life and disciplines human beings as He works out His plan to make them part of that redeemed community which He is preparing in His Son. This point has crystallized itself in many people's minds in the words of St. Paul's injunction that ''it is better to marry than to be aflame with passion'' (1 Cor. 7:9). Or, as Paul writes a few verses earlier in that same chapter, ''because of the temptation to immorality, each man should have his own wife and each woman her own husband'' (v.2).

Sexual appetites need to be controlled and disciplined. Marriage functions under God's ordinance to domesticate our passion and channel it in ways which, to some extent, bring it back into accord with the Creator's order. Within marriage sexual passion is committed to fidelity even if conditions should change for the worse and fidelity seem less attractive than it once did. Marriage becomes then, under God's goodness, a place of remedy. Our untameable appetites and romantic impulses are here brought down from their lofty pretensions to earth and bound to the good of one other person. Lovers are quick to promise faithfulness, and, as we have said, they are right to do so. To keep those promises is more difficult. Marriage as an institution is used by God to foster and enrich our commitment to the needs of others, to teach us the extent to which love must be committed if it is truly to be love. There may be, it is true, marriages in which such contented commitment never fully develops. Even then, however, a kind of healing can take place when there is steadfast determination to honor the Creator and the partner He has given.

Precisely because marriage is intended to help us control our sexual desires, there can be no such thing as a trial marriage. Continued commitment to a marital union is not to depend on what our desires and wishes may be at any given time. Instead, the institution of marriage and the commitment to which it binds us should serve to discipline and shape our desires. These desires, permeated by sin, need to be controlled. Marriage is not simply to be evaluated by our wishes. These wishes must also be shaped by marriage.

It is all too easy to misunderstand the teaching that "it is better to marry than to be aflame with passion." This can come to sound like a recommendation to do with one man or woman what we would really like to do with many—and to think that in so doing we act correctly. With such a view marriage becomes an essential self-serving device. But those who can find no more than this in Paul's advice have not yet begun to penetrate to this deeper concern. Marriage is not a restraint of sin merely in the sense that it permits each person to satisfy his instincts in a socially approved context. It is a restraint of sin—a place of remedy—in that it provides the possibility for husband and wife to serve the needs of each other. In their sinful condition the husband and wife are able to serve each other's passionate needs and to offer their loving support to one another. By so complementing one another, husband and wife join in the task of bringing their lives into accord with the divine intention for human desire.[26]

Within marriage passion is also ordered toward the procreation and rearing of children. We should not overlook the sense in which not only the marital union itself but also the family is a place designed to help us in our weakness. Gabriel Marcel has written that "a family is not created or maintained as an entity without the exercise of a fundamental generosity. . . ."[27] To give birth, jointly to nourish and sustain that life to which they have given birth—all this is the common work of husband and wife. And it is an act of self-spending which can only be compared to a gift. It implies a certain fundamental generosity, a willingness to spend one's time and energy, one's person, in nourishing and sustaining a new life. Thus the family is not only an institution in which parents raise their children to maturity. It is also a place in which God is at work shaping and molding the parents themselves. The family as an institution will not flourish unless the self-interested impulses of the parents are controlled and, sometimes, broken. In this way, too, marriage is a place of healing, shaping its participants for a life in common and providing them with a place where they can delight in the acts of self-giving which all genuine community requires.

Real healing takes place in marriage not merely when sin is restrained, but when husband and wife love each other as Christ loved them and "gave himself up for us, a fragrant offering and sacrifice to God" (Eph. 5:2). That is to say, sin is not only curbed, but it is *forgiven* in the name of Christ and so is daily removed as the destructive force which separates people from each other. Christian couples need to remember that the controlling principle of the new life in God's redeemed community works genuine healing also in the marital union and in the family circle: ". . . and be kind to one another, tenderhearted, forgiving one another, as God in Christ forgave you" (Eph. 4:32).

III. Some Problems

Against the background of this discussion of marriage and its purposes we may proceed to comment briefly on a few issues connected with marriage and sexuality. Our intention here is not to discuss fully all relevant issues, such as, for example, the problems of pornography or abortion, but instead to deal with some of the problems most frequently mentioned in requests to the Synod.[28] It should be noted that we have chosen to concentrate first on a positive development of the order of marriage and its purposes. No discussion of particular problems, however urgent they may appear to be, is likely to be helpful if carried out in isolation from a developed theological understanding of sexuality. Furthermore, it ought to be obvious that no brief discussion of the problems taken up can be exhaustive or fully adequate. It will be enough to point out the direction in which the analysis above leads with respect to certain issues.

A. Divorce and Remarriage

In response to the questioning of some Pharisees, Jesus was Himself prompted to discuss the issue of divorce (Matt. 19:3-9; cf. Matt. 5:31 f.). In so doing He appeals to the primal will of the Creator that a man and woman who have become one flesh are not to be "put asunder." Although the law of Moses had allowed divorce, this was due to the hardness of the sinful human heart (Deut. 24:1-4). But "from the beginning it was not so," and Jesus appeals to that primal ordinance in order to demonstrate what marriage ought to be and to convict those who fall short of what it is meant to be.

It is for our purposes most important to recognize the seriousness with which all traditional Christian teaching has regarded divorce. C.S. Lewis has made use of the "one flesh" imagery to provide a simple explanation of this common Christian teaching.

> **All [Christian churches] regard divorce as something like cutting up a living body, as a kind of surgical operation. Some of them think the operation so violent that it cannot be done at all [Catholic teaching on indissolubility]; others admit it as a desperate remedy in extreme cases. They are all agreed that it is more like having both your legs cut off than it is like dissolving a business partnership or even deserting a regiment. What they all disagree with is the modern view that it is a simple readjustment of partners. . . .[29]**

We can see that the retention of this traditional view is no mere traditionalism but, on the contrary, takes seriously the will of God for marriage, as well as the needs of our human nature. We remind ourselves of some of the implications of the three purposes of marriage developed above. Consider first marriage as a union in mutual love. The promises lovers make are not foolhardy. They answer to some of the deepest needs of human beings: the need never to be left entirely alone, whatever the future may bring; the need to be sure that, whatever uncertainties the future may hold, these two people can at least say that theirs will be a future together; the need to be able to give themselves entirely and completely to another—to be naked before the other, and to be so in complete trust and confidence; the need to know that their person, not just their functions, is valued, and that they are not interchangeable with any other partner. The order of marriage instituted by God answers to these deep human needs. It gives rise to a set of hopes and expectations which ought not be disappointed, not only because we have a commandment to the contrary, but because to disappoint them is to fail in a fundamental human commitment answering to an equally fundamental human need.

When we consider the child who is the fruit of marriage, we may also come to realize the enormous seriousness of divorce. It is fairly common to hear people say in connection with divorce that they fear especially for the children. This statement, though it may ordinarily refer only to the disruption and uncertainty which divorce brings to the life of the child, may also point to an even deeper reality. If the child is the sign of the unity—indeed more, the incarnation of the unity—of this man and woman who now propose to rupture their oneness, then of course we must fear for the child. What event could be more calculated to disturb the child at the very center of his personal identity? Parents are not merely a cause and children an effect which can easily be separated. Here again we must remember that our commitments in the flesh are personal commitments. The child's personhood, his sense of identity is involved. To tear the marriage asunder is in some sense to do the same to the child.

Moreover, Christian parents need to remember their commitments to their children are also spiritual commitments. Husband and wife who have joined themselves in the one-flesh union of marriage (Eph. 5:31) are committed to fulfill their parental duty by bringing up their children ''in the nurture and admonition of the Lord'' (Eph. 6:4 KJV). It goes without saying that the task of bearing a credible witness to the Lord's instruction regarding the permanency of marriage and the meaning of the self-giving love which makes marriage work (Eph. 5:21 ff.) is made more difficult for divorced parents.

Thirdly, marriage can scarcely function as a place of remedy or healing if we refuse its constraints and reject its disciplines. In marriage God would have us learn what commitment to another person involves. He offers no guarantees that such commitment will always be easy or pleasant. There is only one sure way to protect ourselves against the cost of commitment to others, and that—to make no such commitment at all, whether in marriage or in other ways—is to tread the destructive path of disobedience and rebellion against the Creator (Rom. 1:24-32). Marriage cannot function in accord with its God-ordained purpose if it is given up whenever our desires and wishes encourage us to do so or if we merely resign ourselves fatalistically to a deteriorating relationship. There is another alternative. If, in prayer and hope, we recommit ourselves to what we have promised, those desires and wishes may be transformed and marriage will fulfill its task of healing.

God is at work in history gathering a faithful community. In marriage we are given some taste of what such fidelity involves and requires. We are given an opportunity to be faithful to one person as God has been faithful to us all. This is the principle articulated in the passage which perhaps more than any other has shaped Christian thinking about marriage, Eph. 5:31-32: '''For this reason a man shall leave his father and mother and be joined to his wife, and the two shall become one flesh.' This mystery is a profound one, and I am saying that it refers to Christ and the church. . . .'' This is the pattern of love which ought to permeate marriage. It is the only kind of love which can answer to our deepest needs. It must be a love which is willing to go as far as Christ did in His commitment to His people, a love which so commits itself to the good of the beloved that nothing short of death can break the bond of its commitment.

It remains true, of course, that ours is a world distorted by sin. Marriages are broken daily, and our personal relationships are often characterized by something less than a Christlike fidelity. In response to this the church in its public teaching must hold up and bear witness to the need for fidelity in marriage. Yet the church must face the fact that divorce has become a prevalent practice in our society. According to the Scriptures, fornication is the only ground for divorce (Matt. 5:32; 19:9).[30] The act of fornication by a partner in marriage breaks the unity of the marriage. In this situation the individual offended may have the right to secure a divorce. However, this does not mean that he or she must or should exercise this right. In some cases forgiveness can save the marriage.

> *The divorce of Christian pastors must be taken with utmost seriousness. It is difficult to see how the church can maintain the integrity of its witness—especially in an age where divorce is prevalent—if it permits pastors who have divorced their wives for less than Biblical reasons to continue in the office of the public ministry. Generally a pastor who has been divorced, except in cases of unchastity or desertion on the part of his wife, ought not to remain in office nor be reinstated in the office of pastor. However, it is possible that under very exceptional circumstances a former pastor may by the grace of God come to the point of being in a position to be reconsidered as a person qualified to be entrusted once more with the powers of the pastoral office.*[31]

It is equally true that in the application of this teaching to individual cases pastors may confront marriages which cannot be preserved, even after long and serious attempts to do so. The conflict between the Creator's primal ordinance and the brokenness of human life in a world characterized by our "hardness of heart" will continue until the end of the age. In such circumstances the pastor is called on to deal with the brokenness of human life in a sinful world while at the same time seeking ways to affirm the Creator's will for marriage. These can only be occasions for sorrow, repentance, and reaffirmation of God's never-failing commitment to us.

A person who has obtained a divorce for unscriptural reasons may under certain circumstances, with repentance as the primary prerequisite, remarry. The absence of hope for a reconciliation is also a consideration, and there may be other pastoral concerns as well.

> *Those who are seeking a divorce for a reason other than that allowed by the Scriptures need to be warned against the danger of "planned repentance." Since genuine sorrow over one's sin against God and faith in the forgiveness of Christ belong to the essence of repentance, it goes without saying that to proceed premeditatively in doing that which one knows to be contrary to God's will, with the intention of becoming contrite later, makes it impossible for faith and the Holy Spirit to remain in the heart (2 Sam. 11; 1 John 1:8; 3:9; 5:18). To proceed in securing a divorce with the full knowledge that such an action is contrary to God's will **with the intention of becoming repentant** at some point in the future is, therefore, to enter into great spiritual peril.[32]*

B. Headship Within Marriage

The principle which determines how husbands and wives are to conduct themselves toward each other within the order of marriage is that of mutual service (Eph. 5:21). Their attitude toward each other's assigned role is to be shaped by their recollection of the self-giving love of Christ for the church (Eph. 5:2). "For the Son of man also came not to be served but to serve, and to give his life as a ransom for many" (Mark 10:45). As the church's Head devoted Himself totally to the needs of His church, so the husband is to devote himself to the needs of his wife. And as the church yields itself completely to the love, care, and direction of the Lord, so the wife is to yield herself to her husband.

The apostle's exhortation that husbands and wives "be subject to one another out of reverence for Christ" (Eph. 5:21) must not be interpreted to mean that there ceases to be hierarchy within marriage. The call to mutual service presupposes that an ordered relationship between husband and wife exists. Under the principle of mutual service, however, hierarchy within marriage is viewed not as a political relationship of the ruler over the ruled but as an arrangement whereby the welfare of the other may be served.

The Christian husband will therefore understand that the position of headship has been entrusted to him for the exercise of sacrificial love toward his wife. Mindful of Christ's willingness to suffer death for His beloved, the church, the husband will seek to bind his wife to himself by love and gentleness. The Christian wife will understand that, in requiring that she be subject to her husband, God has put her in a position of supporting her husband in his responsibility to care for those who belong to his household. Such a relationship, which cannot be equated simply with obedience, carries with it the honor of accepting a role which the Son of God Himself assumed before His Father (1 Cor. 15:28).[33]

Where mutual service of the kind we find in the life and work of Christ prevails within the hierarchy of marriage, permanence of the marriage bond is assured.

> *To understand something of the sense in which hierarchy in marriage is to be recommended we should distinguish two sorts of hierarchies: of function and of merit.[34] Hierarchies of function occur when those who are different are nevertheless united in an organic unity which is more than a contractual association. Thus, for example, we might consider the relation of parent and child. The parent's legitimate*

authority over the child is not based simply on the fact that the parent knows more and has more experience than the child. If these were the only considerations, we could equally well assign children to other adults (or to some kind of state-run organization) for their rearing. But the family is a fellowship, a community. And the members of such an organic unity have different roles to play in the life of the whole (Eph. 6:1-4; 1 Peter 3:1-7). (We may think of Paul's reference to the church as Christ's body having many members.) Hence, in a hierarchy of function a kind of inequality of authority exists. Yet, we would scarcely conclude from this that one member of the union (the parent) was of greater value or "worth more" than another (the child). In referring to this hierarchy of function we are saying nothing more than that in their common life together some must lead and others follow if the character of the union is to be maintained and their common life sustained.

A different example may make clear what a hierarchy of merit would involve. If we grant that within the classroom teachers have a legitimate authority, this is no doubt because of the knowledge the teachers have acquired and are able to impart. If, however, after class a teacher with no mechanical ability should walk into the parking lot and find that his car will not start, any one of his students with mechanical aptitude immediately becomes his superior in a new role relationship. Hierarchy here depends on some superiority.

*We may note important differences between hierarchies of the two sorts. Hierarchies of function are stable. The roles of super and subordination do not change. In hierarchies of merit, however, the roles are constantly changing. Hierarchies of merit are fluid and in a constant state of change precisely because no one **merits** superordination in all aspects of life. We can even say that a sort of equality is built into hierarchies of merit in the sense that they involve a constant set of changes. At any given moment not equality but super-and subordination pertain. However, these roles are constantly shifting, and no one is always in authority. Consequently, distinctions which rest upon merit never make one person head of another **per se.** They do so only with respect to certain activities.*

*It will never be difficult for people to deny the existence of hierarchies of function, for it will always be a little mysterious that they should exist at all. It is difficult to give reasons of the normal sort to justify their existence. We are accustomed to accept as reasons explanations why—on the basis of some superior attribute or ability—one person **merits** headship. Yet just these sorts of reasons are ruled out in discussing hierarchies of function.*

*The Christian claim that a hierarchy of **function**—with wife subordinate to husband—is appropriate in marriage proceeds from the Christian view of male **and** female. Husband and wife are not interchangeable members of a contractual association. They are members of a body, a union. Their personhood is protected not by stressing that both are persons but by emphasizing the difference which is fundamental to the fellowship in which they come to know themselves as man and woman, in which, that is, they realize their identity. Such a union in love cannot come to fruition unless the different roles of husband and wife are recognized. Without a willingness to complement each other in this way, a power struggle must ensue whenever disputed matters arise. Without, that is, a recognition by both husband and wife of legitimate authority within their union, the permanence of that union is endangered. The insight of Ephesians 5 goes deepest after all: Permanence and hierarchy imply each other.*

A few qualifications are still in order. It will be helpful to note that several standard objections to hierarchy within marriage fail to touch the position outlined above. It will always be inappropriate to ask for some special reason why the man ought to exercise headship over the woman, other than the reason that God ordained the hierarchy which exists in marriage. Any other such reason would almost certainly imply some superior ability or merit on the part of the husband, but that is not the sort of hierarchy involved. Similarly, advocates of the subordination of wives who try to point to some traits in justification of the husband's headship also miss the point. And finally, it is improper to object that the wife is considered on this account to be of less worth than the husband. Considerations of merit and value are specifically excluded in hierarchies of function. Instead, they proceed solely from the requirements of an organic union in love committed to permanence. Such a union is not dominated by considerations of either authority or merit but rather by mutual service of the kind we find in the ministry of Jesus Christ in our behalf.

The connection between permanence and hierarchy has been looked at in this section largely from the side of the wife. That is, if the permanence of the union is to be certain, she must be willing to recognize the superordinate role of the husband. However, as we have begun to set forth in this section, the implications for the husband's understanding of his role are not less important. In cases of disagreement, how shall he exercise headship? Must he "wield authority as a domestic tyrant"?[35] If he is really committed to mutual service and the permanence of this union, his first question ought certainly to be, what are *her* desires, *her* wishes, *her* needs? The distortion which sin brings to human relationships all too often enters in here as well, for this is certainly not the first question husbands always ask themselves. Because the authority which has been entrusted to them can be misused, it is not out of place in Christian teaching to stress that love will seek to treat the other as partner. This should not be misunderstood to mean that marriage is, therefore, a mere contractual association. Rather it is a necessary emphasis in the face of misuse of the concept of hierarchy. Our marriages are lived out in a fallen creation, a fact which must enter into our understanding of what is possible and desirable in marriage. . . .

IV. Some Affirmations

We may summarize the chief points of our discussion of human sexuality articulated in this report in the following propositions. We honor God and the neighbor rightly when we

—delight in our creation as male and female and affirm our identity as male or female;

—see in our creation as sexual beings an intimation of our creation for fellowship and give thanks for the healing which God offers in marriage;

—regard marriage as a divine, lifelong institution, ordained by God for the good of man and woman;

—respect marriage as the typical, though not necessary, expression of our creation as male and female;

—affirm God's will that sexual intercourse be engaged in only between a man and woman committed to a complete and lifelong sharing of their lives with one another in a marriage covenant not to be broken;

—affirm that the mutual love of husband and wife, while possessing God-given meaning in and of itself, is by divine blessing ordered toward the birth of a child; and

—affirm that this union of mutual love is the only proper context for human procreation.

Endnotes

[8] While "mutual consent" constitutes the essence of marriage, there are certain conditions set forth in the Scriptures under which proper consent cannot be given—e.g., *married persons* cannot give consent. Martin Chemnitz dealt with this question in the following way: "What God has joined together, let not man put asunder." But in order that it should be such an indissoluble bond and inseparable union, it is necessary that it be a divine union, that is, that it not be in conflict with the teaching of the Word of God about the essence of marriage. . . . For instance, if there is an impediment in the degrees either of consanguinity or of affinity which God in His own Word strictly prohibited; if a person

had another lawful wife beforehand; if the consent was not freely and expressly given; if the kind of error with respect to the person entered in which happened to Jacob with Leah; if a person's nature is simply not fit for marriage, etc. . . . Moreover, they do not separate a marriage that has been divinely joined, *but show that it is not a lawful or divine union''* (*Examination of the Council of Trent,* Part II, trans. Fred Kramer [St. Louis: Concordia Publishing House, 1979], pp. 738 f.; italics ours).

[9] For a discussion of the beginning of ecclesiastical participation in marriage ef. E. Schillebeeckx, O.P., *Marriage: Human Reality and Saving Mystery,* trans. N.D. Smith (New York: Sheed and Ward; 1965), pp. 244 ff. As a human institution a wedding rite will normally provide (1) a reverent context for announcement of the consent which is of the essence of marriage, (2) for the giving of thanks and praise to God for the institution of marriage, and (3) for the prayers of the congregation that the marriage will be a God-pleasing and fruitful one.

[10] The Greek term *porneia* is used in the Scriptures (Septuagint and the New Testament) to include the whole range of sexual immorality, i.e. fornication (Matt. 15:19; Acts 15:20, 29; 1 Cor. 5:1; 6:18; Gen. 38:24; Lev. 18). *Porneia* is sometimes used in the narrower sense of marital infidelity or adultery (Matt. 5:32; 15:19; 19:9; Lev. 20:10-11). The Scriptures categorically condemn every form of fornication as sin against God (Lev. 18; 20:10-11; 1 Cor. 6:9-10, 18; Eph 5:3; Col. 3:5).

[11] The nature of commitment in the sequence of engagement and marriage is a twofold one: The promises involved in engagement (betrothal) are made with a view to the pledges given as part of the marriage ceremony, where the promise to live together as one flesh is given in public.

[12] The usual requirements for a valid common-law marriage recognized as legally binding in some states are: (1) an agreement presently to be husband and wife; (2) living together as husband and wife; and (3) holding each other out as husband and wife.

[13] At the present time approximately a third of the U.S.A. states legally recognize common-law marriages.

[14] The frankly erotic quality of the Song of Songs is not a frequently mentioned topic within the church. Yet it could and should be. Consider the following comment of Stephen Sapp: "Although God neither appears nor is mentioned in it (which makes it 'secular' for us), for the sages he is not absent from the Song, nor are his love and concern for his creatures unmanifested in it. Rather they are clearly shown in the enjoyment and pleasure (given by God to man in the creation) which the lovers find in each other and in their surroundings" (*Sexuality, the Bible, and Science,* p. 26).

[15] C.F. Keil and F. Delitzsch, *Biblical Commentary on the Old Testament,* vol. 1, trans. James Martin (Edinburgh: T. & T. Clark, n. d., reprinted by Eerdmans Publishing Co., 1971), p. 86.

[16] It is clear that Gen. 2:18-25 has reference not only to marriage but to the broader male-female duality. Here, however, we use it primarily to refer to marriage itself as the center of the male-female relation. That this is justified, v. 24 makes evident.

[17] Keil-Delitzsch, p. 90.

[18] William Shakespeare, *Romeo and Juliet,* I. v. 45.

[19] Cf. Helmut Thielicke's fine discussion (*The Ethics of Sex,* trans. John W. Doberstein [New York: Harper and Row, 1964], pp. 66 ff.) of the distinction between sexual knowledge and knowledge about sex.

[20] Thielicke, pp. 20-26.

[21] C.S. Lewis, *The Four Loves* (New York: Harcourt Brace and Company, 1960), pp. 134 f.

[22] Ibid., p. 135.

[23] We have, of course, described marriage as we in our culture ordinarily experience it. It is equally possible that it might not be preceded by mutual love (e.g., marriages might be arranged by parents), but the institution of marriage would still be ordered toward such a relationship of mutual love, and we would expect it to give rise to this love.

[24] Robert Mehl, *Society and Love: Ethical Problems of Family Life,* trans. James H. Farley (Philadelphia: The Westminster Press, 1964), p. 46.

[25] The case of contraception has been the cause of considerable disagreement within Christendom. The position and the problems of the Roman Catholic Church with respect to this matter have been well publicized, though perhaps not well understood. The teaching of Pope Paul VI in *Humanae vitae* itself largely a rearticulation of the traditional Catholic position, is that "each and every marriage act must remain open to the transmission of life" (*Humanae vitae* [New York: Paulist Press, 1968, par. 11]). (We might note that, technically, an encyclical is *not* held to be infallible teaching. From the Catholic perspective the pope here speaks, of course, with great authority, but he does not utter infallible teaching.) Catholic teaching recognizes both the relational and the procreative purposes of marriage and affirms that both are to be fulfilled within marriage. Its position on birth control derives from its insistence that no single *act* of sexual intercourse can seek to enhance one of these purposes (the relational) while deliberately frustrating the realization of the other (the procreative). It is not enough, according to this teaching, for the marital union of husband and wife as a whole to be fruitful. Rather, every act of intercourse must place no artificial impediment in the way of fruitfulness. From what the Scriptures say about the threefold purpose of marriage, we could judge that such a viewpoint isolates the sexual act from its human, personal context and focuses too narrowly on the procreative function apart from the personal context. This is, in fact, a judgment shared by many contemporary Roman Catholic moral theologians.

[26] We must, in this connection, add the observation that many marital unions offer healing in quite another, almost paradoxical, sense. Serious illness may afflict one of the partners, or professional responsibilities may make it necessary for one of the spouses to be absent from home for longer periods of time. Such situations call for the discipline of continence. That is to say, personal fulfillment is found at a moral and spiritual level quite apart from the opportunity of partners in marriage giving themselves to each other in sexual intercourse. Experiences of this kind fall under the category of bearing one's cross of discipleship. No less than the power of the Holy Spirit is available to married partners under circumstances of this kind. In fact, they have been given the specific promise: "God is faithful, and he will not let you be tempted beyond your strength, but with the temptation will also provide the way of escape, that you may be able to endure it" (1 Cor. 10:13).

[27] Gabriel Marcel, *Homo Viator: Introduction to a Metaphysic of Hope,* trans. Emma Crauford (New York: Harper Torchbooks, 1962), p. 87.

[28] With respect to abortion, the official position of The Lutheran Church—Missouri Synod is that "since abortion takes a human life, abortion is not a moral option, except as a tragically unavoidable byproduct of medical procedures necessary to prevent the death of another human being, viz., the mother . . ." (1979 Resolution 3-02A, "To State Position on Abortion"). This issue is not treated in this study, since the CTCR and its Social Concerns Committee are in the process of preparing a new report on abortion. When completed, it will be made available to the members of the Synod for study and guidance.

[29] C.S. Lewis, *Mere Christianity* (New York: The Macmillan Company, 1960), p. 82

[30] Traditionally theologians in our Synod have noted that, while there is only one Scriptural ground for divorce, viz., fornication, there are cases in which Christians may suffer

"malicious desertion." Dr. John H.C. Fritz, in his *Pastoral Theology*, states on the basis of 1 Cor. 7:15 that malicious desertion occurs when a spouse deserts the other party "with the manifest intention of not returning to the abandoned spouse, and will not by any means be persuaded to return." Such desertion, rather than a cause for divorce, Fritz says, "is in itself divorce" and constitutes the dissolution of the marriage (p. 181). In a forthcoming report on "Divorce and Remarriage" the Commission will give this matter more detailed attention as it seeks to offer guidance to pastors and congregations as they deal with problems such as this in their ministry of pastoral care.

[31] Cf. the article by Martin H. Scharlemann, "The Pastoral Office and Divorce, Remarriage, Moral Deviation," *Concordia Journal* 6 (July 1980): 141-150.

[32] In his discussion of penitence in the Smalcald Articles Luther writes: "It is therefore necessary to know and to teach that when holy people, aside from the fact that they still possess and feel original sin and daily repent and strive against it, fall into open sin (as David fell into adultery, murder, and blasphemy), faith and the Spirit have departed from them. This is so because the Holy Spirit does not permit sin to rule and gain the upper hand in such a way that sin is committed, but the Holy Spirit represses and restrains it so that it does not do what it wishes. If sin does what it wishes, the Holy Spirit and faith are not present, for St. John says, 'No one born of God commits sin; he cannot sin.' Yet it is also true, as the same St. John writes, 'If we say we have no sin, we deceive ourselves, and the truth is not in us'" (Smalcald Articles III, iii, 43-45).

[33] In the New Testament the term *hypotassó* ("to be subject") is not a condescending term. Luke chooses *hypotassó* to describe Jesus' loving subordination of Himself to His parents (Luke 2:51). In this verse the word carries with it a twofold nuance. On the one hand, it presupposes that a hierarchy of relationships exists within the created order (e.g., Col. 3:18-4:1). The term also denotes a readiness to surrender one's own will in service to others.

[34] It should be noted that this discussion deals only with subordination of wives to husbands, not of women to men in general. It is far less clear, in fact, whether the Bible anywhere really enjoins the latter. The distinction between the two kinds of hierarchy is taken from Charles Williams, "A Dialogue on Hierarchy," *The Image of the City and Other Essays*, ed. Anne Ridler (London: Oxford University Press, 1958), pp. 127 f.

[35] Francis W. Beare, "Ephesians," in *Interpreter's Bible*, vol. 10 (New York: Abingdon, 1953), p. 718.

Notes: *The Lutheran Church-Missouri Synod, often called simply the Missouri Synod, traces its origins to a group of Saxon Lutherans who left Germany in 1839 to flee the rationalism which they claimed had captured the Lutheran Church in Germany. It is by far the most conservative Lutheran group in the United States. While recognizing that marriage was ordained by God, it maintains in the Lutheran tradition that marriage can be legitimately contracted in the civil realm. This statement reserves sexual intercourse for the monogamous marriage relationship and holds that the purposes of marriage are procreation and the fulfillment of the marriage partners.*

NATIONAL ASSOCIATION OF EVANGELICALS

CHRISTIAN LEADERS AND FAMILY LIFE RESOLUTION (1988)

In the decade of the 70s, the National Association of Evangelicals (NAE) made the observation that Christian homes often did not stand in significant contrast to those of the world. Many Christian families were torn by the same conflicts experienced by those who were not united in Christian faith.

Studies done since 1984 by the NAE Task Force on the Family indicate that this situation has not improved but worsened. It is clear that Christian families are being touched by the same destructive forces as families outside the church. This is a condition that calls for action by the Christian community. Family life must be given a renewed priority. Resources needed to heal and strengthen family relationships must be provided.

The NAE Task Force on the Family believes the place to start in the recovery of the Christian family is with Christian leaders and their families. Christian leaders live in highly stressful situations which make it very difficult to meet the emotional needs of their families, including those of their spouses. These stresses are created by unreasonable expectations, the perception of being objects of unsuitable veneration, the feelings of being trapped on a treadmill, relegated to the sidelines or isolated. Often these leaders and their spouses have not developed close friends in whom they can confide and through whom God's love and grace can be mediated when needs arise.

A number of factors contribute to the reluctance of some Christian leaders to address family concerns or take the lead in initiating strong family life programs in their churches or places of leadership.

Some obvious factors are:

1. A sense of inadequacy as they view their own families;

2. The difficulty of making their own families' legitimate needs primary over the needs of other families;

3. The expectation that they be models of an ideal elite instead of seeing themselves as fellow-strugglers in dealing with family pressures.

NAE, therefore, calls on those in Christian leadership to make their own families a matter of priority in ministry. We urge them to become part of a mutual support system. We encourage them, under the Lordship of Christ, to lead their families to emotional health through God's unconditional love.

We call on churches and Christian organizations to provide adequate resources to enable leaders and their spouses to meet the physical, economic, emotional and spiritual needs of their families; to protect their leadership from unreasonable demands on their time, energy and privacy; to be alert to what would thwart an effective ministry to church families and, in turn, weaken their ministries to the families of others.

We call all within the evangelical community to pray and work for the recovery of Christian family life, with its spiritual and moral distinctives, as a public witness to the grace of Jesus Christ.

Feelings on what is appropriate for the Christian family run deep and there is no one position that prevails within the evangelical community. The National Association of Evangelicals (NAE), therefore, calls upon Christian families to carefully consider all relevant factors touching the education and schooling of their children.

NAE affirms that education is not simply pouring facts into a mind. It is a lifelong endeavor which involves building understandings, perspectives, values and life skills through direct experience, personal processing of information, social interaction and inner struggle. The success of these learning processes depends on the readiness of the student to grow, as well as the quality of the education offered.

The home, church and school all play important educational roles. Clearly both the church and family are responsible for communicating Christ and Christian values, the foundation on which all learning will build. Furthermore, the positive witness of Christian families and the broader family of the church ideally will complement what is learned in school. However, we live in a world where the "ideal" and the "reality of life" are rarely synonymous.

Schools, whether public or private, are not all of equal quality. Before enrolling a child in any school, parents must explore the school's educational philosophy and environment and decide, under the guidance of the Holy Spirit, how to best fulfill their responsibility to raise their children in the nurture of the Lord. We urge honest consideration of the following:

1. The quality of the education offered;

2. The perspective of world view expressed in that education;

3. The specific needs of each child—the ways the home, church and school can work together to help the child mature in faith;

4. The best methods for Christian teachers, parents and students to serve as salt and light in a needy world;

5. Whether the decision reflects the practice of good stewardship of time and financial resources.

NAE recognizes that parents have the primary responsibility for the education of their children.

In support of all parents seeking to make good decisions regarding the schooling of their children, NAE affirms the responsibility and right of parents to choose the educational options most consistent with their religious conscience and best suited for their children. We further affirm the importance of mutual respect between parents whose views on schooling may differ and NAE encourages all Christian parents to develop a Christian world view and life style and to disciple their children in that view.

Notes: *The National Association of Evangelicals was formed in 1942 by a group of Fundamentalist Christians interested in limiting their ecumenical activities to those with whom they were in essential doctrinal agreement. It is less conservative than the American Council of Christian Churches, a similar group that was founded in 1941. This resolution, like other NAE documents, links the recovery of family life to the example set by the families of Christian leaders and educational institutions.*

NATIONAL ASSOCIATION OF EVANGELICALS

RESOLUTION ON FAMILY VIOLENCE (1988)

In a society under stress, the family is impacted. Domestic violence has escalated into an urgent national problem with spiritual as well as physical, legal, psychological and social implications that cannot be ignored.

We must be alert to the facts:

—Domestic violence is evident in one out of ten families throughout the nation;

—Domestic violence ranges from physical brutality and sexual abuse to mental cruelty and neglect;

—Domestic violence is a pattern often perpetuated in the family from generation to generation;

—Domestic violence is no respecter of social class, economic status, educational achievement, age, sex, race or ethnic origin.

More alarming, pastors and other clergy are reporting increasing numbers of parishioners— both perpetrators and victims of domestic violence—coming to them for counsel. It is evident Christian families are under stress and vulnerable to violence.

Therefore, in keeping with our long-standing commitment to the family as an institution ordained by God, the National Association of Evangelicals affirms that the Bible:

1. Provides the principles for the prevention of family violence (Eph. 4:31-32).

2. Forbids all forms of violence or abuse in human and family relationships while still upholding proper parental discipline (Eph. 4:25-29; Heb. 12:7-11).

3. Instructs us on family relationships between husbands and wives; and children and parents (Eph. 5:21-6:4 and I Peter 3:7). To repudiate the mutuality of responsibility between family generations is to "deny the faith" (I Tim. 5:8 NIV).

Furthermore, NAE calls upon local churches to develop a biblically-based philosophy of discipline; oppose violence in the media which contributes to family violence; urge all segments of our society to cooperate with the church and civil government to put an end to family violence in its various forms; call upon society to promote justice and support laws against family violence which can help provide an orderly framework for our lives together, recognizing the rights and responsibilities of families to promise/exercise appropriate discipline; seek training in the prevention, treatment and follow-up of family violence; and minister to the needs of both perpetrators and victims of family violence.

Notes: *This resolution demonstrates how the NAE, along with many other religious bodies, is recognizing the need to deal with growing incidents of family violence within and outside the churches.*

OLD GERMAN BAPTIST BRETHREN

DOCTRINAL TREATISE ON MARRIAGE AND DIVORCE (1954)

Marriage is the first and oldest institution in the world, and dates from the Garden of Eden. God, seeing that it was not good for man to be alone, made for him a woman and thus sanctified and set His approval on the marriage relation. No institution in nature can be more holy, and none should be more highly respected.

In the beginning God intended that there should be one woman for each man, and that a union between the two should be for life. The idea of divorce, or separation, never entered into the primary arrangement. Divorce became an after consideration, and was brought about by sin, and the hardness of the hearts of the people. When the Pharisees tempted Jesus concerning divorce, He answered them in these words: "Have ye not read, that He which made them at the beginning made them male and female, and said, "For this cause shall a man leave father and mother, and shall cleave to his wife: and they twain, shall be one flesh? Wherefore they are no more twain, but one flesh. What therefore God hath joined together let not man put asunder." Matt. 19:4-6.

Here, in this Scripture, the Savior plainly forbids man to terminate the marriage relationship, and warns them that to do so would be contrary to the direct act of God. The irrevocable character of the marriage covenant is the burden of the Savior's words. It is the first and primary lesson to be learned about the institution of marriage, and if it had been heeded, would have saved much sin and sorrow from entering the world.

Jesus further instructs the Pharisees, saying, "Moses because of the hardness of your hearts suffered you to put away your wives: but from the beginning it was not so. And I say unto you, 'Whosoever shall put away his wife except it be for fornication, and shall marry another, committeth adultery.; and whoso marrieth her which is put away doth commit adultery.'" Mat. 19:8-9. This permits the putting away of the unfaithful companion, but does in no way annul or set aside the marriage contract. The guilty wife is not permitted to remarry giving clear proof that she is still bound to her husband. That this is true is shown by the fact that anyone afterward marrying her would be guilty of adultery. Where one is bound, the other is bound also and that for life.

Putting away the wife for fornication was just and right in the sight of God. This we

113

understand from the language of Paul in 1 Cor. 6:13-16, ''The body is not for fornication, but for the Lord; and the Lord for the body. . . . Know ye not that your bodies are the members of Christ? shall I then take the members of Christ and make them the members of an harlot? God forbid. What? know ye not that which is joined to an harlot is one body? for two, saith He, shall be one flesh.'' Thus in putting away his guilty companion, the husband was withdrawing himself from a continuation in an unholy triple alliance. And, of course, the wife would have the same recourse to this Scripture should the husband be the guilty party.

Consider marriage further, we can not too thoroughly emphasize the importance of the parties in the marriage contract being suited to each other in race, temperament, sentiment, training and religion. A union for life ought to be entered into with the utmost care, and with as little haste as practicable. Nor should any religious convictions of the parties be overlooked. In II Cor. 6:14 we have this subject under consideration, and are told, ''Be ye not unequally yoked together with unbelievers.'' There is no closer union than that existing between husband and wife, and in view of this relationship, in which both are considered one flesh, the importance of a oneness in Christ Jesus can not be too often and too forcibly emphasized. Only when two are agreed in the one faith can they walk together in perfect harmony, and bring up their children in the nurture and admonition of the Lord.

It is a great mystery, second to none in nature, that two individuals—a man and woman— two composite characters and personalities—can so blend their lives that God is pleased to call them one flesh. Yet it is God's decree, and when God joins them together, they are blended in *love,* (God is love): and whenever *love* is the joining link, then the mystery of becoming one flesh quickly loses its impossibilities. As time goes on that love grows stronger and stronger: each one labors unselfishly in that growing love, for the welfare and happiness of the other until soon their thoughts are blended in one pattern; their desires are one, their views are one, their aims in life are one, they walk and labor heart in heart, and hand in hand as one body and one flesh and one mind; ever respecting each other and permitting love and reason to rule their lives. Such a marriage, where the first love is never allowed to end, because love guides them, is of God—joined of God—from such an home will flow all that God intended when He created and joined the first man and woman together; and instituted the first marriage state and home.

It is homes of this sort which are a blessing to both church and nation, and from them emanate our great leaders and outstanding citizens. But a home that is invaded with discord and infidelity can be equally a curse as well. These conditions together with divorce are the breeding grounds of crime and corrupt morals. Delinquent parents often produce delinquent children and all because the sanctity of the marriage vow is broken. No church that has any regard whatever for the standing of her members, or her influence for good in the world, can afford to tolerate any looseness along this line. Churches that maintain their members in good standing in direct violation of the Savior's teaching on marriage and divorce, can take their full measure of blame for the moral corruption which has overtaken this country. They can be sure that God will require it of them in the day of judgment. No amount of legislation can make up for the deficit caused by a delinquent home and a delinquent church. Without a standard here that is wholly above reproach, there is no possibility of maintaining a high spiritual standing in the sight of God or men.

Notes: *The Old German Baptist Brethren represent the conservative wing in the Brethren movement. They continue to wear plain garb and are committed to nonparticipation in war, government, secret societies, and worldly amusements. Believing that marriage is the first and oldest institution in the world, the Old German Baptist Brethren teach that monogamous marriage was ordained by God to overcome loneliness and allow two different individuals to meld mysteriously into one. Because marriage is a lifetime commitment, divorce is allowed only on the grounds of adultery.*

PACIFIC YEARLY MEETING OF THE RELIGIOUS SOCIETY OF FRIENDS

STATEMENT ON MARRIAGE (1973)

Friends from their beginning have believed in the social institutions of marriage and the family; in fact, it never occurred to early Friends to question them. However, marriage has always been considered not a contract, but a uniting of a man and a woman in the presence of God and by God, not by priest or magistrate.

In earlier years there was a struggle, not against the legalizing of marriage, but for recognition of their marriages without words from the two authorities recognized by the English government. In 1661, in a case of an inheritance for Quaker children, they appealed to an English court for recognition of the marriage and won the case.

Marriage as commitment of man and woman to each other is the basis of the family, needed not only to give children a human shelter and a place of trust but to give shelter and trust to the partners. A man and woman offer each other support in many and subtle ways. In a confused and shifting world each has a close partner with whom understanding can be shared, a companion in the joy and grief and struggle of life.

The effect of a marriage may extend far beyond the couple themselves. A happy marriage will provide a loving atmosphere not only for the couple's children but for the Meeting and the wider community. A broken marriage can bring distress to all involved and may eventually impose a burden on the Meeting and the community. Therefore the civic community provides for the legal formalization of marriage, while the religious community provides for the celebration of marriage as a ''sacrament'' - a divine gift entrusted to both partners for safekeeping and nurturing. The Meeting is not a casual witness, but expresses its loving concern through the ''marriage committee'' and calls for the exchange of vows ''in the presence of God.''

It is to be expected that all marriages pass through many phases: of joy, of stress, of boredom, and of lack of fulfillment. Through all these phases the quality of a marriage is tested. Partners will find that the quality of their marriage is deepened and the level of fulfillment is raised if they are willing to try patiently to work things through.

At the same time, we recognize that personalities and circumstances beyond either partner's control may change as the years go by and that incompatibilities may develop that surpass their endurance. If a marriage is continually harmful, and professional help has been of no avail, a divorce may be advisable. Recognition of such a situation requires self-knowledge and clear thinking; care for the other's good must still be present. Just as the Meeting offers its loving support to those contemplating marriage, so it should give its loving care to those whose marriage is in trouble.

Some Friends are experiencing other forms of intimate relationship. We hold these Friends in loving concern and remain open to the light which their experiences may shed on our understanding of the traditional monogamous marriage. Friends trust that all intimate relationships will be conducted with dignity, mutual care, and a deep sense of responsibility.

To learn to love the other person as he or she actually is, steadily, and wishing only that his potentialities be realized - that may take a lifetime. Love trusts and endures, protects and cherishes.

Our marriage promises invoke divine assistance. If we know God in our lives as love beyond self-love, we find the needed help in a relationship which is not easy and which requires all the maturity of spirit we can bring to it. And, having tried over the years to the best of our ability, we may find that such a depth of trust and caring has become ours - such a union of lives - that we can only say, ''This is the grace of God.''

Notes: *The Pacific Yearly Meeting of the Religious Society of Friends was established in 1947 within the Pacific Coast Association of Friends. Later, a committee recommendation led to the formation of the North Pacific Yearly meeting (1972) and the Intermountain Yearly Meeting (1973). This statement affirms the personal and social dimensions of marriage and holds up as an ideal the lifelong monogamous relationship. However, it does recognize that there are causes other than adultery that justify the granting of divorce.*

PRESBYTERIAN CHURCH (U.S.A.)

EXCERPT FROM THE REPORT "SEXUALITY AND THE HUMAN COMMUNITY" (1970)

To the Churches—Foreword

In November of 1966 the Council on Church and Society. The United Presbyterian Church in the United States of America, took an action to launch a study on "sexuality and the human community." Subsequently, the Council named a Task Force to do the study under the direction of the Rev. J. C. Wynn, Ed.D. At the conclusion of its work, which was begun October 13, 1967, the Task Force Report was prepared by the Rev. Richard S. Unsworth. . . .

The Task Force report on the study of sexuality and the human community was received and studied by the Council on Church and Society in November of 1969. In 1970, the Council concluded its study and took appropriate action to direct that the report of the Task Force be transmitted to the 182d General Assembly (1970) with a request that the General Assembly receive the report, direct that it be published, and recommend it to the churches for study and appropriate action. After adding the phrase "this action is not to be construed as an endorsement of the report," the 182d General Assembly (1970) approved the request by a vote of 485 affirmative, 259 negative.

Additionally, a motion made from the floor, approved by a vote of 356 affirmative, 347 negative, directed that a statement of belief incorporated in the motion be included in any publication of the report of the Task Force; and, that an Appendix to the Paper, which had been added by a minority group of the Council on Church and Society, should likewise be included in any publication of the Task Force report.

Also, the General Assembly requested the Department of Church and Society to provide further Biblical rationale to assist in the study of the report.

Furthermore, the 182d General Assembly (1970) considered and approved statements and recommendations in related areas of education, research, and legislation.

This book, therefore, includes materials authorized for publication by the 182d General Assembly (1970). In addition, in the Appendix there is a guide for studying and using the material prepared by the General Division of Church Educational Services of the Board of Christian Education.

A Task Force Study Document

Introduction

In 1966, the Council on Church and Society of The United Presbyterian Church in the United States of America, formed a community to study the Christian concept of sexuality in the human community and to provide the church with a report of its endeavors. Sexuality as we understand the term refers to our entire experience as persons who are created male and female and not exclusively to coital behavior. The report that follows is a brief résumé of the reflections and conclusions of that committee after more than a year of meetings, discussions, and papers.

The assignment given was this:

To explore the mystery of sexuality in a broad range of human experience; to identify and analyze the forces that enhance or inhibit the realization of sexual values; and to evaluate the church's role and responsibility in interpreting the meaning of sexuality and in bringing a Christian ethical view to bear upon its expression in human relationships.

Our task is to speak *to* rather than *for* the church in fulfilling this mandate. Speaking to the church is no guarantee of immunity however, from the mounting pressures in our society both for and against discussion of changing patterns of sexual behavior. We proceed in this task, not because our answers are final; but because we believe God is Lord of the present and its changes, the past and its values, and the future and its hope. Indeed, the redemptive possibilities of the present age may possibly be found more readily in the changes that unnerve us than in the continuities that comfort us.

Ours is a modest proposal, and one that we recognize may be obsolete almost before the ink is dry. Both sexual attitudes and patterns of sexual conduct are changing in our culture at an accelerating rate, so our report can only be a comment on a rapidly passing scene. The knowledge explosion affects the discipline which underlie our report and its conclusions, and that fact also serves to underscore the *pro tempore* character of our report.

The work of our committee encompassed a wide range of problems and considerations about human sexuality. The popular media and the presence of new contraceptive techniques have given the impression that the single issue is that of coital behavior. We do not think that is the case, and we have tried to reflect a broader appropriation of the concept of human sexuality both in the work we did and in the report we now submit. We dealt with questions of sexuality in family relationships, male and female sexuality, masturbation, dating, homosexuality, contraception, abortion, artificial insemination, as well as with questions which involved coital behavior more directly: *viz,* premarital, marital, and extramarital sexual activity and the sexual behavior of single adult persons.

In dealing with these many questions, we frequently surprised ourselves by discovering the degree of restlessness we shared with what we understood to be the conventional morality of the church. In certain areas of our consideration, such as homosexuality, abortion, and the sexual behavior of single adult persons, we concluded that taboos and prohibitions often play a larger role in the thinking of Christians than does careful ethical reflection in the light of the gospel. As one of our number asked, ''Has not Protestantism fostered false impressions and false information about sexuality? We should resolve to correct those errors of which we are aware.''

Our abiding concern has been with the development (1) of ethical considerations which can refine and strengthen the teaching of the church on matters of sex, and (2) of ethical guidelines which help Christians make responsible decisions about their own sexual behavior and about the attitudes of the community on sexual matters.

In the course of these developments, we turned repeatedly to the theological issues and questions of Biblical tradition which have informed the church's view of human sexuality through the ages.

We also found ourselves relying heavily on the social and behavioral sciences. Insights from psychology and psychiatry about the workings of sex influenced us to think often with criteria of psychological health in mind. The vocation of the church has always included the ''cure of souls.'' It is to the benefit of that vocation that psychology, ''the science of souls,'' has been so productive in recent decades. The accumulation of empirical data about sexual conduct, pioneered in the Kinsey report, has contributed measurably to our perception of the meaning of sexual expression to various groups of persons in the society. Studies of psychosexual development have made possible far greater understanding of the different meanings that one's own sexuality and sexual conduct may have at different stages in the life cycle. And psychiatry has now accumulated a great deal of helpful insight about the pathology of guilt and its relation to sexual experience.

This scientific probing of the mystery of sexuality has had, on the whole, the beneficial effect of attacking the myths and taboos which have surrounded some aspects of sex, and lifting the shroud of guilt and shame which has inhibited the proper realization of our sexual nature. These developments in psychology and psychiatry are to be received with gratitude by a church committed to the realization of the "responsible freedom of the new life in Christ."[1]

The insights of sociologists, anthropologists and demographers have also had a bearing on our discussions. We frequently found ourselves challenging the conventional wisdom of the Christian community concerning sexuality, only to find that those conventions were too often the culture-bound wisdom of a part of the community: to wit, the white, Protestant, and middle-class part. But the Christian community encompasses a wide diversity of racial, ethnic, and cultural groups, and therefore a wide variety of assessments of sexuality and sexual behavior. The polygamy that is permitted among some African Christians would be unthinkable among the Protestants of Geneva; and the cloistering restrictions upon women in some Latin countries would be altogether unacceptable to most American teenagers. This sobering fact of social and cultural pluralism within the church made it difficult to achieve many generalizations about the appropriateness of specific forms of sexual behavior.

Biblical and Theological Foundations

Our theological procedure has been Biblical, and has relied heavily on covenantal thinking. We have taken serious account of the current debates in ethics within the Protestant and Roman Catholic communions of the church. Three approaches to ethical thinking appeared recurrently in our discussions. They might be designated by the terms, "orders of creation," "convenental ethics," and "situation ethics." While we tried as far as possible to benefit from the insights and criticisms derivative of each of these methods, we found the covenantal framework the most congenial and, in our estimation, the most adequate to the Biblical heritage, the experience of the church, and the insights of contemporary secular thought.

The theme of the Confession of 1967, "In Jesus Christ, God was reconciling the world to himself," is the theme which pervaded our discussions about human sexuality and which, we hope, has most directly influenced our conclusions. While acknowledging the many ways that sexual behavior can be abusive and alienating, we tried to express its proper role in human experience in terms of growth and reconciliation. This emphasis also seemed most adequately expressed in the language of the covenant, where love, faithfulness, healing, and hope dominate.

Particularly in view of the explosively growing population, and of the radical improvement in contraceptive technology, we stressed the relational and celebrational aspects of sexual activity at least as much as the procreative. The purpose of our Lord in coming that we might "have life and have it abundantly" (John 10:10) surely must include an appreciation of our sexual nature as one avenue for realizing that promise, whether or not a procreative purpose is served at the same time. It is through human relationships, including their sexual dimensions, that God often speaks his redemptive word to this world. We have been very wary of secular or religious statements which ascribe saving significance to sexual engagements. Yet we are deeply sensitive to the fact that sexual activity has its role in the saving activity of God.

One widely accepted theological approach to the realm of human sexuality is to treat it in terms of the orders of creation. While we do not think that sexuality can be understood apart from its place in the ordering of creation, we have encountered two reservations about theological reflection which lean too exclusively on this approach. One is the fact that the church, when reflecting on God's work of ordering creation has often been tempted to see its task in reflecting on sexuality as one of ordering, too. The emphasis then becomes one of restraint, prohibition, legalism, and the definition of limits.[2] All of that may be necessary, but it does not attend to the equally Christian calling to glorify God by the joyful celebration of and delight in our sexuality. The attempts by some theologians to encourage Christians to appreciate the fact that our sexuality can be fun as well as functional has thrown some of our fellow faithful into paroxysms of fear and guilt.

A second reservation about the "orders of creation" approach to understanding sexuality concerns the emphasis we have found on marriage and the family as the exclusive model for ordering all sexual activity. By understanding sexuality primarily in terms of its place in the orders of creation, we emphasize its procreative function still, admitting the relational functions of sexual expression but subordinating them to those concerned with child-bearing and nurture. We feel that Roman Catholicism may have suffered in its understanding of sexuality by emphasizing the religious superiority of the virginal estate. But Protestantism has, in reaction, suffered from an equally single-minded preoccupation with marriage and the family. Our theologians have given first place to the moral norms which function well in support of marriage and the family, and by their silence have left the impression that the single estate is a deficient one, requiring more explanation and apology than guidance. So, less by intent than by omission, Protestantism has left the unmarried in the shadow of an ethical structure designed to serve another manner of life than theirs.

This has meant that the church has made less pertinent ethical statements than it might have to the not yet married, to those who are single by vocational choice or statistical accident, to the homosexual, to the widowed, the divorced, and the many others who do not live in the "normal" estate of marriage.

We have tried, as befits Presbyterians, to articulate a position which is consistent with the view of man and his destiny found in the Bible. Recognizing that the worldly circumstance in which our ancestors found themselves may have called for a sexual ethic appropriate and adequate to that circumstance, we have not found in that fact alone a warrant for duplicating their ethic in the often different circumstance of our own life. We are obligated to ask in our day, as Biblical man asked in his, how God is speaking to our time about sexual relationship. Theology is a dynamic science capable of new insight and interpretation relative to changing cultures.

We can find no systematic ethical guidance for our time from a method of Biblical interpretation which relies solely on the laws or stories of the Bible.[3] Understood in their historical context, however, these laws and stories provide us with useful insight into the pattern of God's redemptive and reconciling activity in all ages, whose design it is to enable us to "grow up in every way into him who is the head, into Christ." (Eph. 4:15).

Our task, in speaking to particular problems as well as in addressing the total phenomenon of sexuality, has been one of understanding God's revelation in the person of Jesus Christ, in whose maturity as man we are to find a model for our own. In him we find one who has overcome alienation from God, is open to the world, is accepting of himself, and establishes communion with his fellowmen through responses of tenderness and strength, of love and service. The church has always attested his full humanity. Therefore, one cannot imagine that he was unaware of his own sexuality, and there is no evidence that he denied this aspect of his humanity in the manner of some of his later followers. The morality of his relationship with others was enviably positive, rooted as it was in concern for their well-being rather than in anxiety about his own purity.[4] He kept faith with his brothers and sisters, and in so doing deepened the roots of hope for all of us. He lived in the integrity of God's covenant with Israel to be their God, and he became the messenger of a new covenant which has bound us into the destiny of the people God loves and chooses and frees.

One of the important conclusions we draw from God's revelation in Christ is that our sexuality is an instrument of God's reconciling activity. The God who would overcome our alienation from himself and from each other has invested human sexuality with far more than procreative significance. It is truly a vehicle of the spirit and a means of communion. It is also true that our sexual endowments can be, and often are, turned to self-serving and uncharitable purposes. Thus, sexual gestures are not intrinsically moral or immoral. They derive their moral significance from the reconciling or the alienating purposes they serve.

The New Testament contains no record of Jesus' teachings concerning most matters of sexual behavior. It would be proper to assume that his concern for particular expressions of human sexuality would have been based on the way they might serve or injure human communion, whether with God or with other persons. Indeed, our Lord condemned more strongly those who misused each other, grinding down the poor, climbing over others' rights and the like, than he did the sexually miscreant.[5]

To emphasize the purpose of sexual activity in serving human relationships well or poorly is to throw the weight of concern on the motives and consequences of that activity. It is not, however, to say that our sexuality is morally neutral. Sexuality is one of the definitions of the power of our being as persons. Like all powers, it has some moral significance even when it is not used. Power withheld may be a most ethically meaningful form of power. We suppose that is the case with the assumed celibacy of Jesus, whom one can easily imagine foregoing marriage in deference to the claims of his vocation as the bearer of a new covenant.

As the messenger of the new covenant, Jesus threw open to all mankind the promise of God's creating, forgiving, and healing love. The promise of God to bestow the power of his spirit on all who are in the covenant with him becomes a universal promise in Jesus. Knowing that, we have been constrained to interpret the meaning of sexual behavior in the light of that covenant promise. Such a covenant has had the effect of keeping hope alive among us as well as establishing our confidence in God's provident care in our present-day affairs. We have had great concern, therefore, to keep alert to the fact of the covenant when dealing with the ethical significance of various forms of sexual behavior.

We regard as contrary to the covenant all those actions which destroy community and cause persons to lose hope, to erode their practical confidence in the providence of God, and to lose respect for their own integrity as persons. Clearly, such actions are not susceptible of being catalogued, for sexual gestures which may in one instance cause deep guilt and shame, whether warranted or not, may in another context be vehicles of celebrating a joyous and creative communion between two persons.

By the same token, those sexual expressions which build up communion between persons, establish a hopeful outlook on the future, minister in a healing way to the fears, hurts and anxieties of persons and confirm to them the fact that they are truly loved, are actions which can confirm the covenant Jesus announced.

A true understanding of this covenant, which is both described and promised in the Scriptures, gives rise to productive insights into the ethical concerns of human sexuality. The covenant is a link between our spiritual past and our future. Understanding and participating in the covenant helps us evolve a style of life which is consistent with our past and appropriate both to the times in which God is now speaking to us and to the future which he is opening before us. By calling to mind the loving intent of God toward his creatures, ''I will be your God and you shall be by people,'' it frees us from a faithless captivity to the cultural patterns of the past while at the same time encouraging us to preserve the human values which informed those patterns. We are thus left to examine the new patterns of sexual behavior which emerge in each new era with spiritual clarity and cultural detachment, and to affirm or criticize those patterns on the basis of the way they serve or deny the reconciling work of the Holy Spirit among us.

Christian Goals of Interpersonal Relationship

We believe that the revelation in Jesus Christ and the covenant into which he has drawn us both offer some definition of the goals of interpersonal relationships. While no list of phrases or adjectives could be exhaustive, those goals are at least the following:

Interpersonal relationships should enhance rather than limit the spiritual freedom of the individuals involved.

They should be vehicles for expressing that love which is commended in the New Testament—a compassionate and consistent concern for the well-being of the other.

They should provide for the upbuilding of the creative potential of persons who are called to the task of stewardship of God's world.

They should occasion that joy in his situation which is one of man's chief means of glorifying his Creator.

They should open to persons that flow of grace which will enable them to bear their burdens without despair.

These are some of the goals which should inform any judgments we make about the specifics of sexual relationship. A glance can be adulterous and alienating; or it can be tender and reassuring. A physical intimacy can be charged with hostility; or it can affirm and liberate those who share it. The goals of interpersonal relationship we have described can be pursued or frustrated across the whole range of ways that men and women relate to each other. Our hope is to see the thinking and the teaching of Christian community rest more on goals such as these, and less on the attempt to describe sexual acts as intrinsically good or bad. . . .

7. *Courtship and Marriage*

    a. *Courtship before marriage.* Protestant Christianity has traditionally placed great emphasis on the sanctity of the family, and therefore on the permanence of the marriage bond. It has recognized the need of just divorce laws and has urged a compassionate attitude toward those whose marriages are broken by divorce, in the hope of making them better able to succeed in a subsequent marriage, should one be undertaken.[17]

Behind this emphasis is the conviction that sexual behavior is to be confined to non-coital contact before marriage and to coital exclusively during marriage. Again, Christian theology has urged compassion toward those who have not met such standards, in the hope that they may be helped to understand and abide by them.

These premarital expectations are an outgrowth of the value that has been attached to virginity in the Christian tradition; although Protestantism largely discarded the Roman Catholic attitude toward clerical celibacy it has maintained the norm of virginity before marriage. This reflects at least three factors: (1) the primacy of procreation in the Christian tradition's view of marriage; (2) the influence of Biblical references to fornication;[18] and (3) the value attached to self-restraint as a rehearsal for and a sign of a person's capacity to be faithful in the marriage and family relationship. It must be added that these expectations were applied in principle to men but in practice to young women. In fact, in some western cultures young men who remained virginal were looked on askance, as having failed to demonstrate their manhood.

Increasingly, the expectation of premarital virginity is not being met either by men or women. This change is not necessarily to be regarded as a sign of the lowering of standards of young people. It follows from a variety of influences. As the pattern of our society changes from the larger family unit and relies more and more exclusively on the immediate family, there is a tendency for courtship patterns to take the form of sequential and increasingly intense monogamous relationships. This pattern has developed along with a steady postponement of the age of the onset of puberty. Thus, the standard of premarital virginity, which once was expected to be maintained during a relatively short period of two to five years, is now more difficult to maintain during the ten or more years that commonly elapse between puberty and marriage in our time.

While we are not competent to comment on the efficacy of any particular form of contraception, the fact remains that inexpensive and efficient means of contraception are increasingly and readily available. Thus, the function of virginity as the main protection against out-of-wedlock pregnancy is in decline.

It is also in decline as a testimony to one's capacity for faithfulness to the marriage bond. To increasingly large numbers of young people, within and without the church, being a virgin at marriage proves nothing by itself. More significant is one's personal maturity and readiness to accept joyously the responsibilities of life together. To put it plainly, fewer and fewer young people are willing to think of a non-virgin as a "fallen" person. That designation, if used at all, would more likely describe a weak or neurotic or promiscuous person whose sexual activity, whether coital or non-coital, is in the service of self rather than in the creation and celebration of meaningful communion with another person.

In our time, a pattern of many intense but short-lived relationships may be a more ominous portent of unfaithfulness than the simple failure to come virginal to the marriage relationship. In fact, our culture could unwittingly erode the capacity for faithfulness in its young by disregarding the emotional and spiritual significance of various forms of sexual behavior, while simplistically maintaining the arbitrary standards of technical virginity. The church's understandable preoccupation up to now with coital activity has led to stresses at both extremes that call for correction. On the one hand, there is little medical or psychological evidence that premarital coital experience between persons who subsequently marry is necessarily damaging either to their emotional health or to the personal adjustment, including the sexual adjustment, that they make to each other. On the other hand, there is little evidence that sexual restraints and coital abstinence can be demonstrated as harmful to the person. The pressure for premarital coitus may be rationalized by an appeal that it assures a healthy adjustment in marriage; but a healthy adjustment in marriage depends on much more than this. And the fact that premarital restraint may sometimes be associated with fears or neuroses is a comment on the deficiencies of personal growth rather than proof of the harmfulness of sexual restraint.

In place of the simple, but ineffective and widely disregarded standard of premarital virginity, we would prefer to hear our church speak in favor of the more significant standard of responsibly appropriate behavior. Responsibly appropriate behavior might be defined as sexual expression which is proportional to the depth and maturity of the relationship and to the degree to which it approaches the permanence of the marriage covenant. Such a definition clearly means that sexual promiscuity is neither responsible nor appropriate.

Admittedly such an approach makes difficult the detailed definition of which acts are fitting and which are not. Yet, that difficulty is measurably less than the difficulty of attaching intrinsic definitions to certain acts as "appropriate" and "inappropriate" without regard to the context in which they take place.

The real aim of developing such a Christian ethical sensibility ought to be such realistic awareness of oneself and open sensitivity toward another that it would be possible to understand and admit when a sexual expression is appropriate and when it is not. To be well practiced in the effort to "grow up in every way into Christ" will involve, among other things, candor with oneself when any kind of sexual relationship becomes casual, or exploitive, or manipulative, or an acting out of conflict, or abusive. It is these and similar motives which define a sexual gesture as

inappropriate. For the same gesture may be altogether appropriate when it expresses the friendship and delight, the trust and the hope that two people have in each
other and their relationship.

To shift attention from our preoccupation with premarital virginity to a concern for
responsibly appropriate behavior is not to give either tacit or explicit approval to
premarital sexual intercourse. It is rather to stress the need for Christian persons to
be aware, in their courtship experience, of the need for responsible understanding
and regulation of their sexual expression at all stages of a relationship. This seems
to our committee both a viable and a desirable shift from the present implicit
assumption in our society that, in courtship, anything is permitted as long as
intromission is avoided.

A concern for the development of a sense of the appropriate in courtship would also
provide good preparation for an understanding of sexual conduct in marriage. Since
a chief goal of marriage is the perfection of interpersonal relationship, a courtship
which has helped a couple develop profound sensitivities to each other, and
tenderness in response to each other's needs and desires, can prepare them for a
healthy adjustment of their sexual energies in the marriage that follows.

If in the course of such a courtship, a couple has taken a responsible decision to
engage in premarital intercourse, the church should not convey to them the
impression that their decision is in conflict with their status as members of the body
of Christ. If they are Christians, whatever joys and sorrows, doubts and delights,
attend the development of their relationship are part of their experience as Christian
persons, moving toward marriage, and are elements of human experience as
susceptible as any others to that reconciling ministry to which the church is called.

b. *Courtship within marriage.* Courtship is a form of honoring and delighting the
other person, with the hope of winning a loving, accepting response in return. A
man and a woman may show their care and concern for each other in many ways; by
dutifulness, by faithfulness, by offering comfort. Courtship is simply finding
words, gestures, and tokens to make explicit what those other forms of caring
imply.

Thus, courtship often leads to marriage. The tragedy is that it too often ends there.
If one chief purpose of marriage is to "build up communion between persons . . .
and confirm to them the fact that they are truly loved,"[19] then clearly courtship has
as much place within marriage as before it.

The forms that courtship takes, like the forms of sexual expression which are
regarded as permissible, will vary according to their cultural setting. But Christians
are more concerned with the love that is conveyed than with the forms of expression
which convey it.

The question of what constitutes appropriate sexual behavior between married
persons, like the form of courtship, is conditioned by cultural expectations more
than by abstract ethical considerations. Feelings tend to run high about various
modes of sexual expression in marriage. But a variety of attitude studies concerning
different sexual practices would suggest that these feelings correlate more readily
with class or ethnic or other cultural factors than with the religious factor. Matters
of taste and feeling are of ethical significance to the degree that they are the material
of a caring relationship. But it is these sensitivities, rather than any certain forms of
sexual gesture, which should occupy the ethical concern of Christians. The church
ought to be able to support an understanding of sex in marriage which asserts that
nothing is forbidden except that which offends the sensibilities of one's partner.
Sexual intimacy is not a privilege to be claimed, but a gift to be given. It should be
seen as an avenue not to power over but to friendship with one's partner.

The Christian affirmation of fidelity in marriage includes more than sexual fidelity. The confinement of sexual activity to the marriage relationship represents a discipline of eroticism's restlessness, the purpose of which is not simply the preservation of one's own moral purity, but the nurture of a truly reciprocal and caring relationship between husband and wife which supports each one's unique worth as a child of God. Such a relationship is one form of the expression of *agape,* that Christian love which seeks the peace and well-being of the other. The caring that characterizes such a relationship extends to every facet of the relationship; the economic, the psychological, the vocational, and many other facets, including the sexual. For marriage partners to confine their sexual activities to their relationship with one another, therefore, is normal to and supportive of the total web of concerns they will have for each other's well-being. Sexual fidelity is important because it both symbolizes and supports the total fidelity of the marriage relationship, which in turn has always been suggestive to Christians of the fidelity of God to his people and of Christ to his church.

We recognize that there may be exceptional circumstances where extramarital sexual activity may not be contrary to the interests of a faithful concern for the well-being of the marriage partner, as might be the case when one partner suffers permanent mental or physical incapacity. But an exception is an exception and not a new rule, so it is difficult to make general judgments about such exceptions. Such judgments finally have to be made by and on the responsibility of the person who takes the exception. Our concern for the church is that it might see the question of marital fidelity in broad enough terms to understand that faithfulness in marriage and coital exclusivity are not synonymous. It is quite possible to be coitally monogamous yet maritally unfaithful. In any case, the church must not leave the Christian who finds himself in an exceptional circumstance with nothing more reliable than his own rationalizations to fall back upon as an ethical resource.

In our attempt to understand sexual activity in premarital and marital relationships, we have dealt with coital union as one point along a continuum of sexual expression, and in that we have departed from the tendency of the past to focus entire attention on coitus and disregard the ethical significance of many other forms of sexual relationship. We believe that many of our difficulties in evolving a useful and effective Christian ethical reflection on sexual responsibility for our time are rooted in an overestimation of, and an overemphasis upon, coital union.

Indeed, many marriages survive with either minimal or no coital relations. If married persons face circumstances which prevent normal sexual sharing with their partners, there is nothing to suggest that they will incur physical or psychological harm by mutually deciding to practice sexual restraint, even abstinence, in the face of those circumstances.

As with celibacy, the decision for sexual restraint is not in itself an unhealthy decision. If it comes as the consequence of an unhealthy state of mind, it is the state of mind, rather than the restraint that should be given attention. We feel this is an important observation to make in an era when arbitrary culture pressures to prove one's worth by sexual performance are very great.

c. *Courtship and race.* Since this is also an era when racial consciousness is running excessively high, and since sexual fears and feelings of guilt seem to play an important part in exacerbating interracial tensions, we feel it is important to underscore the fact that any restrictions, legal or conventional, against marriage by persons of different races are without standing in Christian ethical discussion. On the contrary, they represent an arbitrary and alien prohibition against the free association of Christian persons and ought to be opposed on religious grounds. By extension, the same opposition ought to be offered by Christians to those customs and social pressures which discourage interracial dating and courtship. The argument that interracial marriages face especially strong social disapprobation is a reflection on the immaturity of the society, rather than a comment on the ethical status of such relationships.

8. *Sterilization*

Sterilization involves the permanent and usually irreversible termination of the power to reproduce.[20] It is therefore a procedure which must rest on the most serious moral reflection, and the right of all the individuals involved must be fully explored before it is undertaken.

Therapeutic sterilization, undertaken when pregnancy would seriously endanger the life of the mother, is a matter for decision by hospital committees on sterilization, the woman involved and her family and physician. The moral right of the woman to care for her own life by insuring against any potential offspring is clear.

Sterilization of convenience involves the voluntary decision of a man or a woman to submit to surgical sterilization as a means of efficient contraception. Hospital committees have the obligation to review such decisions, and attending physicians have the conscientious responsibility of pointing out to the persons involved, the permanence, the medical seriousness and the possible psychological effects of this procedure. With current advances in contraceptive technique, it is probable that this means of contraception will be elected with diminishing frequency. However, in the event of serious hereditary physical or mental deficiencies which could be passed on to future children, or in the circumstance where another pregnancy could clearly endanger the mental or physical health of the mother, a couple might still elect this means of birth control, and do so to their advantage.

Eugenic sterilization is the sterilization of a mentally disordered person, whose disorder is either hereditary (and so would affect future offsprings) or debilitating in such degree that the person could not care for and rear any future offspring. Since eugenic sterilization involves a decision about an individual taken on his or her behalf by the community, it constitutes a heavy moral burden on those who must make the decision. Although the responsibility to the community must be exercised, such decisions should be taken with a certain prejudice in favor of the rights of the individual affected. As with many other decisions which society takes on behalf of the mentally ill, this one puts before the decision-maker the temptation to play God and to prefer unduly the rights of the community.

In the foreseeable future, sterilization for population control may become a more widespread practice. India, faced with explosive population growth and the constant danger of famine, has adopted a program with monetary incentives as well as penalties to encourage the sterilization of men. The object is to limit family size to not more than three children. The decision to sterilize men is made primarily because of the relatively simpler and less dangerous surgical procedure involved.

India's program presumes voluntary sterilization, and to that we see no moral objection. Should the population problem become so severe as to tempt governments to impose compulsory sterilization, however, a serious bodily right would be infringed upon. It would seem to us more morally acceptable, although still problematical, for public policy to be expressed in the adoption of one or another of the mass contraceptive techniques, now under study, which are reversible, and which regulate rather than destroy the power to reproduce.

Since it can be predicted, without exaggeration, that safe and widespread means of population control may have to be adopted by governments as a means of insuring survival of our human race, there seems to be positive moral warrant for pressing forward the development of mass contraceptive techniques, so that these can be relied upon rather than the more permanent tactic of required sterilization.

9. *Artificial insemination*

Artificial insemination is another means of conception control, designed to overcome barriers to natural conception which may be provided by special and peculiar chemical conditions in one partner or the other, or to provide healthy sperm from a donor male, to take the place of the infertile sperm of the husband.

Legal and moral questions have been raised about this process, especially in the case where the sperm of a donor male are used in place of or in addition to those of the husband. The question of eugenic and selective application of the procedure has also been raised, with alarm by some.

It is our opinion that no challenge can properly be lodged against the legal rights, including the right of inheritance, of offspring conceived by means of artificial insemination. When a couple decide to use artificial insemination to establish a pregnancy, the child is bound to its parents by spiritual, psychological, and physical bonds which clearly weigh more heavily in any moral calculation than could the technical fact that artificial means might have been used to introduce the husband's sperm, or the chemical fact that a sperm other than the husband's fertilized the wife's ovum.

We do not therefore see any moral barrier to the process of artificial insemination, either in the instance where artificial means are used to enable the husband's sperm to fertilize the wife's ovum, or in the case where the sperm of a donor male is added. In the latter instance, the physician and the pastor or counselor should explore with both partners the effect of this process on the husband's feelings about himself and about his contemplated offspring. But where there is a maturity of perspective and a thoughtful decision involving both partners, there should be no moral hindrance.

10. *Single adult persons*[21]

Early in this report, we observed that the style of Christian reflection on the ethics of sex which relies for its method on an understanding of the "orders of creation" has resulted in marriage and the family becoming the model for ordering all sexual activity. Nowhere is this more obvious than in the paucity of ethical guidance the church has to offer the single adult person. Our standards and teachings about premarital sexual conduct assume that the practices and restraints which are being recommended are justifiable in terms of their value in preparing the couple for successful adjustment to marriage. But what of the person who never marries, or who having been married, is once again single? The conventions of society and those of the church both suggest that such a person must continue in or revert to the standards of conduct appropriate to those who are preparing for marriage.

The inadequacy of this approach as a source of positive guidance and mature understanding of sexual behavior for the single adult should be obvious. And that single adult portion of the population is increasing, counting together the never married and formerly married. Some of those who never marry are homosexual, some have made vocational decisions which preclude marriage, some have hung back from the permanence of the marriage relationship for reasons of fear or lack of self-confidence in heterosexual relationships, but many are simply the victims of circumstance.

Add to the never-married adults all those whose marriages have terminated through divorce, separation, or death, and a significantly large minority of persons are the victims of a "conspiracy of silence" in the church concerning any positive and realistic ethical guidance for their sexual lives.

The number of single persons is growing in our society, primarily as a reflection of the higher survival rate among women past sixty-five years of age. Present demographic projections suggest that the ratio of women over sixty-five to men of comparable age may be as high 1,403 to 1,000 by the year 1980. Current medical research has produced readily accessible forms of hormone therapy which are designed to offset some of the disabilities and discomforts of the aging process, and which have the effect as well, of preserving the capacity for full sexual functioning by men and women well into the sixties and seventies. Is abstinence or sublimation the only advice the church will have to give to single persons? Or, will it be able to explore new forms of male-female relationships and, while affirming the primacy of marriage and the nuclear family as the pattern for heterosexual relationship, be able to condone a plurality of patterns which will make a better place for the unmarried?

Our committee has found itself possessed of more questions than answers in this area of its inquiry. Yet it is persuaded of at least the following:

Sexual expression with the goal of developing a caring relationship is an important aspect of personal existence and cannot be confined to the married and the about-to-be-married.

Interpersonal relationships between men and women can be altogether celibate and still be spiritually and psychologically rewarding. Thus, celibacy is a valid option for those who adopt it voluntarily. Yet we question whether society has the right to impose celibacy or celibate standards on those who do not choose them.

The church has at least the obligation to explore the possibilities of both celibate and non-celibate communal living arrangements as ethically acceptable and personally fulfilling alternatives for unmarried persons. The past experience of the church with spiritual and utopian communes of various sorts ought to provide some help in thinking through the comparable possibilities for our time. It may well be that an increased ratio of women to men, particularly among older persons, calls for such new exploration in our own culture.

The church should take the lead in re-examining and, where appropriate, calling for the revocation of laws governing sexual behavior. Many of them serve no purpose of protecting the welfare of the community and, indeed, seriously infringe upon the rights of persons in their private lives and their intimate personal relationships.

In another part of the legal realm, the church should press serious discussion of those welfare laws which discourage open and responsible marriage relationships and thus contribute to the instability and uncertainty of the life patterns of some single persons. Provisions of the Aid to Dependent Children plan which call for the withdrawal of funds if there is a man in the home, and Social Security provisions which cut off the retirement funds of widows who remarry are both examples of the injustices that now prevail, and that frustrate the possibility of productive relationships for some single persons. Current proposals of government, such as those outlined by President Nixon in 1969, seek to redress these injustices and should be given an attentive hearing in the churches.

Conclusion

Throughout our deliberations, the committee was aware that more was at stake than restating classic Christian concerns and values about sex and sexual behavior. We have been keenly aware that new technological and cultural dimensions of modern life have provided a radically new spiritual environment in which men and women must understand and use their sexuality. We have been equally impressed with the fact that, as the churches' reflection on these matters has lagged farther and farther behind the new developments, a generation is growing up which takes little notice of what the churches may have said in the past, and looks elsewhere for its understanding of what constitutes mature and healthy perspectives on sex. We think it imperative that the church apply much more flexible and imaginative thought to these problems, since they are so close to the center of one's personal experience and thus to the sources of one's ethical sensitivities.

We have attempted to open the questions that have occurred to us as fully as possible, without standing off from questions because they are puzzling or disturbing. We have developed a point of view on some issues which we are ready to regard as thoroughly responsible Christian thinking. In other instances, we recognize that our suggestions must stand much criticism and examination, and perhaps alteration.

We commend these suggestions to the church, however, as the consequence of sober thought and a serious attempt to be obedient to the gospel. The Confession of 1967 speaks of "man's perennial confusion about the meaning of sex" as one of the sources of his alienation from himself, his neighbor, and God. Our effort, on which this paper reports, has been to overcome some of this confusion and to give some particular suggestions of what might be the meaning of "the responsible freedom of the new life in Christ" as it bears on our nature as male and female children of God. . . .

Sexuality and the Human Community:

1. Appendices to the Task Force Document

The General Assembly, on motion from the floor with a vote of 356 affirmative, 347 negative, directed that a paragraph be attached to the paper and that the minority report of the Council on Church and Society also be appended to it.

A. An Attachment to the Paper

1. "We, the 182nd General Assembly (1970), reaffirm our adherence to the moral law of God as revealed in the Old and New Testaments, that adultery, prostitution, fornication, and/or the practice of homosexuality is sin. We further affirm our belief in the extension Jesus gave to the law, that the attitude of lust in a man's heart is likewise sin. Also we affirm that any self-righteous attitude of others who would condemn persons who have so sinned is also sin. The widespread presence of the practice of these sins gives credence to the Biblical view that men have a fallen nature and are in need of the reconciling work of Jesus Christ which is adequate for all the sins of men."

B. Appendix to the Paper

The following minority of the members of the Council on Church and Society wish to register their view that this document does not deal to their satisfaction with the following questions, among others:

1. Who precisely are "the covenant community" referred to in this paper?

2. In what way is the sexual behavior of Christians supposed to be different from that of non-Christians?

3. How are the New Testament passages, which deal explicitly with sexual behavior, relevant to this difference?

4. Does not the paper disregard the tension between the demands of the gospel regarding sexual behavior and prevailing sexual mores?

5. Does the paper distinguish clearly enough between acceptance of persons and rejection of immoral behavior?

JOHN R. BODO, Pastor, Old First Church, San Francisco, California

HARRY R. DAVIS, Professor of Government and Chairman, Department of Government, Beloit College, Beloit, Wisconsin

THEODORE M. GREENHOE, Pastor, Memorial Presbyterian Church, Midland, Michigan. . . .

3. A Statement of the 182nd General Assembly (1970)

The Council on Church and Society in 1966 provided for the appointment of a Task Force to study the Christian concept of sexuality in the human community. The committee was authorized: "To explore the mystery of sexuality in a broad range of human experience; to identify and analyze the forces that enhance or inhibit the realization of sexual values; and to evaluate the church's role and responsibility in interpreting the meaning of sexuality in human relationships."

The findings of the Task Force are incorporated in a report entitled "Sexuality and the Human Community."

The 182nd General Assembly (1970):

Receives the report "Sexuality and the Human Community," for study: this action is not to be construed as an endorsement of the report.

Directs that it be published.

Recommends it to the church for study and appropriate action.

Further: believing that Christian faith affirms sexual being as a God-given dimension of life to be used for the creative intent and purposes of God; and recognizing that the church has a responsibility to speak and act in regard to a wide-spread concern about the state of sexual morality today, the 182nd General Assembly (1970) addresses the church and the society in these areas: (1) education, (2) research, (3) legislation.

Education

Believing that sound wholesome education about human sexuality is an essential part of general education for all persons; knowing that sexuality involves the whole person with particular needs at each level of human development for understanding the meaning of sexuality in human relationships; and noting that education about sexuality, including biological, psychological, social, and moral aspects, is a proper and necessary concern of the home, school, church, and community:

The 182nd General Assembly (1970):

1. Urges: (a) increased attention to these concerns in the development of Christian education materials for children, young people, and adults; (b) that these materials be free of the double standard of a morality which oppresses and stereotypes both men and women; and (c) greater attention to the attitudes toward sex which are conveyed implicitly and explicitly in all other church publications.

2. Calls upon churches to provide opportunities for the discussion of matters of human sexuality especially in settings which engage Christians in discussion across sexual and generational lines. Toward this end, we further recommend the exploration by church groups of the techniques of human relationship training.

3. Commends the efforts of such agencies as the Sex Information and Education Council of the United States, the National Council on Family Relations and other groups which work at the development of responsible and thoughtful programs of sex education for private and public schools.

4. Encourages United Presbyterians to be informed about and participate in the development of sex education programs in the schools, to help establish a healthy, responsible, and affirmative view of human sexuality.

5. Calls for increased opportunities for specialized education for clergymen in all areas of human sexuality.

Research

Noting the extraordinary development and accumulation of new knowledge about rapidly developing events in today's world; and recognizing an essential need to interpret and assess such knowledge for ethical reflection on moral responses in sexual matters; the 182nd General Assembly (1970):

1. Calls special attention to the need for research in sexual ethics.

2. Expresses its special interest in and support of research projects concerning homosexuality such as that now in progress under the aegis of the National Institute of Mental Health.

3. Encourages further research into the means of contraception in the awareness of the radical need for readily available safe, inexpensive, and efficient means of birth control.

4. Encourages further study of abortion.

5. Encourages dialogue with other religious groups on aspects of human sexuality.

6. Calls for a new inquiry into the nature of marriage in the light of the gospel.

7. Requests the Department of Church and Society to provide further Biblical rationale for the report entitled ''Sexuality in the Human Community,'' to be appended to the report when it is distributed in the Church.

Legislation

Believing that the law should provide for the optimal condition of physical and mental health, and should allow for the optimal exercise of private moral judgment and choices in matters related to the sexual sphere of life; and recognizing that religious convictions held by individuals should not be imposed by law on the secular society; the 182nd General Assembly (1970):

1. Calls for repeal of laws hampering access to contraceptive help and equipment recognizing the need to maintain proper professional control over the prescription and use of dangerous substances.

2. Declares the artificial or induced termination of pregnancy is a matter of the careful ethical decision of the patient, her physician, and her pastor or other counselor and therefore should not be restricted by law, except that it be performed under the direction and control of a properly licensed physician.

3. Urges the establishment of medically sound, easily available, and low cost abortion services; the support and expansion of responsible counseling services on problem pregnancies; and the support for groups working responsibly for repeal of abortion laws which are not in harmony with Section 2 above.

4. Calls upon judicatories and churches to support and give leadership in movements toward the elimination of laws governing the private sexual behavior of consenting adults.

5. Calls for changes of those Social Security regulations which penalize older persons who marry by the reduction of their pension payments.

6. Calls for changes in those Aid to Dependent Children provisions which withdraw funds if there is a man in the house.

Endnotes

[1] Confession of 1967, 11, 4, d.

[2] It need not work out this way, to be sure. In Karl Barth's *Church Dogmatics,* Vol. 3, Part IV., for example, the orders of creation become limits in a positive sense. The task of special ethics, then, is one of disciplining man's freedom within these limits. The limitation of being divided into two sexes becomes for humankind one sphere of God's affirmation of his creatures. The boundary lines of creation function as a definition of human possibility, rather than a defense against it.

[3] We would find it intolerable, for example, to base our treatment of fornication on the death penalties imposed in Deuteronomy 22, or to exclude eunuchs and bastards from ''the assembly of the Lord,'' as prescribed in Deuteronomy 23.

[4] A notable example is Jesus' response to the woman who anointed him while he was at table with one of the Pharisees. (Luke 7:36 *et seq.*)

[5] Helmut Thielicke observes that, "Jesus dealt with the sensual sinners incomparably more leniently than with the sinners who committed the sins of the spirit and cupidity." *The Ethic of Sex,* Harper and Row, New York, 1964, p. 278-279. . . .

[17] A report "The Marriage of Divorced Persons" was adopted by the 179th General Assembly (1967), *General Assembly Journal,* Part 1, 1967, p. 158-183; Action on Proposed Constitutional Changes. *General Assembly Journal,* Part 1, 1968, pp. 82-84.

[18] Passages translated from the New Testament as fornication are based on the Greek work *porneia.* Their context, for the most part, is concerned with pagan practices of cultic and commercialized prostitution. Passages translated as adultery are based on the term *maicheia,* and usually referred to sexual intercourse between a man and another man's wife. (See *Theological Dictionary of the New Testament,* Gerhard Kittel, Wm. B. Eardmans, 1967/68, Vols. V and VI.

[19] *cf. supra,* page 11

[20] Dr. P. S. Jhaver, an Indian surgeon, has invented a device known as the "Jhaver clip," which promises easily reversible male sterilization if extensive experiments on men in India are successful.

[21] *cf. supra* P. 6

Notes: *The Presbyterian Church (U.S.A.) was formed through the 1983 merger of the United Presbyterian Church in the U.S.A. (UPCUSA) and the Presbyterian Church in the U.S. (PCUS). The "Task Force Report on Sexuality and the Human Community," after considerable debate and a relatively close vote (485 affirmative, 259 negative), was received without endorsement by the 182nd General Assembly of the United Presbyterian Church (U.S.A.) in 1970. Some of the report's more radical recommendations (such as sanctioning certain forms of pre- and post-marital intercourse and the acceptance of homosexual relationships), prompted the 182nd General Assembly, after a heated debate and very close vote (356 affirmative, 347 negative), to mandate that a statement of traditional belief and an appendix to the paper issued by a minority group be included in any publication of the task force's report. Like similar reports received by church bodies in the 1970s, "Sexuality and the Human Community" is based on a positive and wholistic understanding of sexuality and affirms nonnuclear family patterns and the single life.*

REFORMED CHURCH IN AMERICA

EXCERPT FROM "GENERAL SYNOD REPORT ON BIBLICAL PERSPECTIVES ON MARRIAGE, DIVORCE AND REMARRIAGE" (1975)

Introduction

Our age is characterized by many conflicting philosophies and value systems. Some advocate a variety of marriage forms (e.g., contractual, communal, "living together," etc.), easy divorces, and experimental sexual relationships. There is growing evidence that such lifestyles produce tragic results: growing numbers of disillusioned persons and many deprived, disturbed children. What is to be the church's response? Only the leading of God's Word and Spirit can provide the needed perspective. Each biblical concept offers positive guidance and combats numerous misconceptions. When taught with sensitivity by elders and pastors, teachers and parents, God's design for married life and human sexuality can prevent many pained lives and offer therapy to others. Surely the Word calls us to repentance and deeper maturity in these matters.

Biblical Goals for Marriage

The biblical understanding of marriage is related to the nature and purpose of God. Biblical views of man, marriage, sex, and family refuse to explain life in terms of man's self-chosen aims. The Bible insists that attempts to understand life apart from the divine purpose are ultimately folly. The Creator's design establishes the dignity of the divine gift of marriage. Within the Word three goals for marriage emerge.

1. Marriage Is for Fellowship

Men and women were created for fellowship with God and for his glory. Their dignity rests in their relational capacity. Men and women were designed for fellowship with each other and for fellowship in human community (Gen. 2; Exod. 20:2-17; Isa. 11:6ff.; 54:1-3; Matt. 19:4-11; John 15:1-17; 17:6-26; Acts 2:42-47; Eph. 1:9-10; 2:13-21). Marriage and human sexuality cannot be understood simply as the result of physical drives, rational formulations, social imposition, or religious moralism. While marital union is not in the realm of things commanded (as are fellowship with God and his people), it is a divine gift not to be profaned. The intimacy of marriage gives expression to the human desire for relatedness. The relationship of husband and wife is often compared to the reciprocal relationship of God and his people and its described in the language of the covenant (Isa. 5:1ff.; 61:10; Hos.; John 3:29; Eph. 5:21-33). Marriage is a covenant bond designed by the Creator, is redeemed in Jesus Christ, and is best realized amidst the covenant people.

2. Marriage Is for Human Fulfillment

It is designed to bring persons into their God-intended human fullness. Humanity in its wholeness involves both male and female. The interdependence so essential to human completeness can be expressed in marital union and also in larger community. In marital union husband and wife become "one flesh" (Gen. 2:24). This unity involves far more than sexual encounter; it is a joining of lives at many levels. With it come mutual love, knowledge (Gen. 4:1; 1 Cor. 13:12; 1 John; etc.), and joy prompting persons to celebrate it in poetic refrain like Adam (Gen. 2:23). Marriage provides opportunity for mature love so vital to the wholeness of persons (Gen. 24:67; Prov. 5:15-19; Song of Sol. 1:1ff; 2:16; 8:6f.; Eph. 5:21-33; 1 and 2 John). Marriage is a covenant commitment which protects the mutuality of sex and the meaning of personhood. It acknowledges responsibility for the continued well-being of the other. God is concerned about marriage because he is concerned for persons (Mal. 2:13-16). Christ healed those broken by marital and sexual sins that they might again become whole persons.

3. Marriage Is for Family and the Community of Faith

No better means has been devised for the rearing of each new generation and for the nurture of persons than the family. Concern for the family is found in the Old Testament (Deut. 6:7, 20ff.; Hos; Prov.; etc), in Jesus' ministry (Matt. 19:13-15), and in the life of the early church (Acts 2:39; 16:15, 31-33; 18:8; 1 Cor. 1:16; 7:12-14). Much of the responsibility for a child's instruction in the faith and for his incorporation into the covenant community rests with the parents. Husband and wife are often the means for each other's consecration (1 Cor. 7:14ff.). In covenant theology, marriage and family are regularly linked to God's saving work. Through godly households, the promise of salvation is transmitted to future generations. Although marriage and family are repeatedly threatened by sin, we are convinced they will remain as channels of God's grace.

Old Testament Light on Marriage and Divorce

1. Marriage in Light of Creation

Men and women are created in God's image with a capacity and a need to communicate and to relate (Gen. 1:26). They need to relate to each other as well as to their transcendent Maker. It was because man was alone that God created a helper for him. The institution of marriage results from the Creator's action (Gen. 2:18-25). Marriage gives expression to man's capacity for relating, for knowing and loving, for choosing and covenanting. "Therefore a man leaves his father and his mother and cleaves to his wife, and they become one flesh" (Gen. 2:24). Marriage expresses the Creator's love for mankind. God's love is reflected in the mutual love of husband and wife. Male and female, each with uniqueness, come together to produce a special oneness. Such was the divine intent.

2. Marriage as Affected by the Fall

Approaches to marriage which neglect the impact of the Fall often naively suggest that education and sexual experience can produce marital bliss. Unfortunately the consequences of sin remain clearly evident in most marriages. Many unions are ruined not so much by ignorance as by selfish willfulness. Violation of God's design still exchanges beauty and ecstasy for chaos and judgment. Immediately after their revolt, the first couple experienced distortion of their self-image (Gen. 3:10) and sensed evil at work (Gen. 3:14f.). They also experienced other disruptions. For woman, sin married the joy of childbearing and rearing, and her relationship with her husband. She feared lest he lord it over her and use her (Gen. 3:16). Man became aware of the tendency to deify his wife's wish, of his twisted relation to nature, of his warped estimate of labor, and of his mortality (Gen. 3:17-19). Only because of God's providential grace were they able to face these complications together.

Alienation from God brought about other distortions of marriage and sex. Fornication, incest, homosexuality, and adultery ("to pollute, Heb. *naaph,* Gr. *moicheia*) violate covenant life and mar the riches of humanity. Inasmuch as persons and families were destroyed by adultery, it was considered the equivalent of murder and deserving the death penalty. Even in the earliest stages of human history, a breach of the marriage relationship was regarded with disfavor.

Divorce is the result of our sinful condition and an expression of our sinfulness. The Hebrew term for divorce (*garash*) means to cast out a mate as one drives out cattle or an enemy. Such rejection, alienation, and covenant breaking are also conveyed by the Greek terms (*kerithuth; apoluo*). The bill of divorce legislated in many ancient societies was intended to protect the rights and continued existence of deserted women. That such a need existed in Israel indicated the presence of sin, of "hardness of heart." The famous passage, Deuteronomy 24:1-4, recognizes divorce on grounds of indecency or infidelity, but is no wholehearted approval of the practice. It aimed to curtail any returning to a former mate following divorce and remarriage. Such switching of mates was considered a defiling abomination polluting the land (Jer. 3:1) and inviting judgment (Ezek. 16:38). Divorce was tolerated in the community of faith only because it was sometimes the lesser of two evils. Nevertheless divorced persons were not excluded from the covenant community.

3. Marriage in the Light of Grace

Marriages are redeemable because of God's gracious activity in history. As persons experience God's liberation, they discover that his transforming power affects every aspect of life including marriage. The Old Testament law abounds with instruction concerning marriage and family. The law moreover was an expression of grace, a gift of God to his redeemed people for their welfare. The law must not be separated from the cradle of the covenant of grace. Only as persons experience God's saving power and share in the new life of his covenant people can they begin to appreciate the Old Testament estimate of marriage and family (Deut. 5:16, 18, 21), warnings against sexual impurity (Lev. 18:6-30), protection for wives, widows, and other women (Exod. 21:9-11; Num. 30:1-16; Deut. 22:13-27). Here clothed in the language of the times is concern for marriages within the covenant community (Num. 5:11ff.; Josh. 23:12f.). The people of God realized that the influence of these marital unions would continue to the third and fourth generations (Exod. 20:5; 34:6f.; Deut. 5:9). There was an effort to keep all accountable in their marital and familial relations regardless of rank (2 Sam. 11-12). The family was indeed both the object and the agent of God's redemptive work.

The prophets often recount how God's grace works in marriage. They find a prototype for marriage in the divine marriage, in God's persisting love for his people (Isa. 5:1ff.; 54:8; 61:4f.; Jer. 3:8ff.; 5:7; 9:2; 13:27; 23:10; 29:23; Ezek. 16). The covenant union between God and his people involves mutual obligations intended to foster fellowship and growth. Even when God's people are apostate or adulterous, his husband-like love will not let them go (Hosea). God's relationship to his people can provide an analogy for marriage among the faithful in that one should love the other in spite of difficult circumstances. In some sense the prophets suggest that marriage can serve as a channel of God's grace. Marriage is a covenant intended to sustain and renew the lives of persons and their children. God "hates divorce" and infidelity because of the violence it does to persons and to covenant life (Mal. 2:13-16).

Poet and sage likewise magnify the joy of marriage and desire to safeguard it (Song of Sol.; Prov. 2:16ff.; 6:24ff.; 7:5, 27; 9:13ff.). Pure marital relations are extolled: "Drink water from your own cistern . . . rejoice in the wife of your youth . . . be infatuated always with her love" (Prov. 5:15ff.). Aware of the conflicting views of marriage and human sexuality, the sages offer models for wives as well as husbands (Prov. 18:22; 31:10-31). Blessed are those households which fear the Lord (Ps. 128).

Jesus' Teaching on Marriage

Jesus established norms for his followers both by what he said and did. In the Gospels, discussion of marriage, adultery, divorce, and remarriage is concentrated in several chapters (Matt. 5; 19; Mark 10; 12; Luke 16:18; 20:27ff.; John 2; 4; 8).

1. Marriage in the Kingdom Perspective

Jesus set marriage in proper perspective by emphasizing the primary importance of God's rule: "Seek first his kingdom and his righteousness, and all these things shall be yours as well" (Matt. 6:33). Love within the family must be subordinated to the king's claim (Luke 14:26). To deify marriage is to destroy all chances that it might be Christian. "I have married a wife" (Luke 14:20) is no excuse for neglecting Christ's call. Believers may suffer loss of mates and homes for his sake (Matt. 19:29). Nevertheless, Christ enriches the marriages of his followers. They discover that the kingdom's values fill and enrich every dimension of wedded life.

2. Jesus on the Nature of Marriage

One cannot understand the divorce issues until he understands human nature and the Creator's plan for marriage. Thus when questioned about the grounds for divorce, Jesus replied, "Have you not read that he who made them from the beginning made them male and female" (Matt. 19:4; also Mark 10:6). The differentiation and mutuality of the sexes are part of man's makeup. Male and female were created to complement and complete each other in marriage and in community. Marriage gives expression to this original intent. "For this reason a man shall leave his father and mother and be joined to his wife, and the two shall become one. So they are no longer two but one" (Matt. 19:5-6a; Mark 10:7f.). Affirming truths long accepted in the covenant community, Jesus indicates that marriage requires the maturity to leave one household to risk founding another. It means to assume the responsibilities of husband and wife, to covenant with each other before God, to embark upon a lifetime of self-giving (*agape*). In Hebraic parallelism, Jesus stresses the unity of two who consummate their marriage. The one flesh concept central to his thought may be seen as both real and ideal. It suggests a reality which couples experience, yet something toward which they strive as long as they live.

3. Jesus on Divorce

On the basis of God's design, Jesus opposed the practice of divorce. "What therefore God has joined together, let no man put asunder'' (Matt. 19:6b; Mark 10:9). For Christians, marriage is never simply a social institution or a civil contract. It is a sacred union formed by God. The two are one before God. Divorce may occur but it is not in God's intent. Conscious of the Judaic debate on divorce, Jesus' listeners queried: ''Why then did Moses command one to give a certificate of divorce, and to put her away?'' (Matt. 19:7; also Mark 10:3f.). Jesus insisted that while Moses permitted divorce, he had not advocated it. Moses was curbing the practice of depriving a wife of her rights through desertion and of switching back to a former wife after her remarriage to someone else. He sought a remedy where sin had worked havoc. Of this Jesus says, ''For your hardness of heart Moses allowed you to divorce your wives, but from the beginning it was not so'' (Matt. 19:8; Mark 10:5). It is one thing to recognize the existence of human failure; it is another to sanction it. Jesus insisted that the design of creation had precedence over the Mosaic concession.

Most significant is Jesus' declaration, ''And I say to you: whoever divorces his wife, except for unchastity, and marries another, commits adultery'' (Matt. 19:9; compare to Mark 10:11ff.; Luke 16:18. The exceptive clause is found in variant form in Matt. 5:31f.). Only in Matthew 19:9 do we have the exceptive clause and the remarriage clause coordinated. The primary thrust of the verse is Jesus' ruling on divorce. Here Jesus abolishes every other ground for divorce permitted in Mosaic provisions and Jewish practice *except* adultery (*porneia*—unchastity, fornication, illicit sexual intercourse). Jesus is especially hard on the man or woman (Mark 10:12) who divorces the partner in order to marry another. This is labeled adultery, a sin against one's spouse and God. This enlarged understanding of adultery bids us not to define it simply as sexual infidelity.

Jesus recognizes then but one basis for divorce. Note that while divorce is permissible, it is *not* obligatory. A strict interpretation of Jesus' words might tolerate divorce only where there has been sexual infidelity. However, a broader understanding of adultery would include other expressions of unfaithfulness and covenant breaking that pollute and destroy a marital union (see ''Basic Policy on Divorce and Remarriage,'' MGS, 1962:205-218). Adulterous attitudes (Matt. 5:27f.) and certain acts on non-sexual infidelity can also violate and kill a union (thus Paul's reference to desertion in 2 Cor. 7:15 is included under Jesus' exception). Yet one must beware of missing the intent of Jesus' words. He does not allow for an open-ended list of reasons for divorce as one's culture or times may dictate. He calls for determined, covenantal fidelity even where adultery has occurred. Jesus' words might have appeared harsh had we no further indication of his ministry of forgiveness, but such is not the case.

4. Jesus' Ministry of Forgiveness

The sin of adultery must not be magnified so as to obscure our common need for grace. Knowing the reality of their own sins, all Christians should be humbled by Jesus' words (Matt. 5:21-30). Nowhere is the compassion of Jesus more evident than when he deals with those broken by sexual sin. Noteworthy is his attitude toward the woman of Sychar, whose marital failures and adulterous situation had left her empty. By restoring her relation to the Father, Jesus laid the basis for renewing all of her relationships (John 4). Confronted by a woman taken in adultery, Jesus ruled out the death penalty and offered God's grace. He forgave and urged her to sin no more (John 8:1-11). His actions disclose understanding of the widespread problems men and women face. His forgiveness provides the basis for a fresh start. Where sin and guilt are confessed, healing can begin. Every person caught in the snares of adultery, marital discord, or divorce is redeemable. No sinner stands beyond Christ's reach. Disciples are called to seek forgiveness for their own failures and to minister the gospel of forgiveness and reconciliation to others (Luke 7:36-50; Matt. 18:15-22). Jesus nowhere suggests that forgiveness should be denied to divorced persons nor that remarriage should be denied to those who have experienced his forgiveness.

5. Marriage as Vocation

While marriage will continue throughout history (Matt. 24:38; Luke 17:27), it remains a temporal, not eternal, institution (Matt. 22:23-30; Mark 12:18-25; Luke 20:27-36). Like the Sabbath, marriage was made for the benefit of mankind and not the reverse. To exaggerate its merit to the point of making it imperative for the full development of persons is a mistake. Although marriage is a holy calling, it is not for all. Jesus spoke of marriage as a vocation, stressing the disciples' choice in the matter. Christians may prefer to remain single for legitimate reasons (Matt. 19:10-12). Such persons may find fulfillment and completeness in the family of faith, the church, and in their respective callings. To the suggestion that celibacy might be preferred, Jesus responded, "Not all men can receive this precept, but only those to whom it is given" (Matt. 19:11). In other words, most disciples will choose to marry. With Christ, either married or single life can be a beautiful venture.

Discussion of marriage, divorce, and remarriage is closely related to questions about family and children (Matt. 19:13-15; 18:1-6). Woe to those who lead a child into a life of sin, who restrict entrance into the kingdom. Those who choose to marry should be prepared to be responsible parents who will nurture their children in the Christian life. Even where a marriage is broken, this duty remains. This high obligation should condition any discussion of divorce and remarriage.

Marriage and Family in the Early Church

1. An Apostolic Voice in the World

The first-century world abounded with proponents of new ethics, marital experimentation, and sexual freedom. Yet the Christian view of marriage caught on at Antioch, Ephesus, Corinth, and Rome. The greatness of the early church lies in that it offered an uncompromising model rather than an ethic of accommodation. Its prophetic voice in a pagan world provided a new ideal of marriage and family. The church insisted that marriage was a holy estate in which partners were accountable to God and to each other so long as they lived (Rom 7:1-4). Christians exhibited a quality of love in marriage as well as in congregational life. Theirs was a lofty ideal. "Let marriage be held in honor among all, and let the marriage bed be undefiled; for God will judge the immoral and adulterous" (Heb. 13:4). Congregations worked for these goals and called members to be accountable. Immorality was identified for what it was. Those afflicted by sin were called to repent and to reshape their lives after Christ's Word. Where this was not forthcoming, disciplinary action was exercised for the sake of the parties concerned, and for the sake of the church's life and witness (1 Cor. 5:1f.). Apostolic exhortation was anything but permissive (1 Cor. 6:9-11)! Persistence in sexual deviation or in marital discord was viewed as incompatible with life in the kingdom. Yet the church was not recriminatory in spirit. Grace abounded as believers acknowledged Christ's forgiveness. Sin-broken persons were transformed and so were their marriages (1 Cor. 6:9ff.; Eph. 2:1ff.).

2. Application of the Gospel to New Situations

Under the leading of the Holy Spirit, the early church found itself with the exciting task of working out the implications of Jesus' teaching in new situations. It engaged both in proclaiming its view of marriage to a troubled world and in problem solving in behalf of those troubled with marital discord. The challenge was to apply the gospel without surrender to the spirit of the times. Paul's letter to Corinth provides many examples of this type of activity (especially 1 Cor. 7).

a. Paul counters those forbidding marriage and advocating celibacy. Marriage and its sexual dimensions are to be acknowledged as God's gifts. Marital love involves responsible caring for each other, self-control (not prolonged continence), and self-giving (1 Cor. 7:1-7; also cf., 1 Tim. 4:1-3).

b. Single persons and widows may remain single (which Paul prefers), marry, or remarry. Whatever be the case, love not lust must prevail (1 Cor. 7:6f.). Elsewhere he advises young widows to remarry (1 Tim. 5:11-14).

c. Acknowledging Christ's command, Paul advises against divorce where both are Christians (1 Cor. 7:10 and 11b). Paul also discusses what should be done if separation or divorce does occur. He personally thinks that reconciliation should be attempted and where that fails, members should remain single (1 Cor. 7:11a).

d. In a mixed marriage (one between believer and unbeliever), the union should continue as long as the unbeliever consents. The believer should not initiate separation. If the unbeliever leaves, the believer "is not bound" to the marriage vow. Paul apparently held that desertion is comparable to the unfaithfulness of adultery. Desertion by the unbeliever can thus end a union. Yet as long as the union endures the believing mate can be used of God to reach the other and to consecrate the children (1 Cor. 7:12-16).

The above illustrations reveal God at work in and through the early church. The church operated on the basis of the apostolic Word. When the Word spoke to a given situation, it was applied with firmness. Where the particular problem was not expressly covered, the church prayerfully sought the Spirit's guidance. This precedent remains valid. The stewardship of divine gifts always involves deliberation and decision.

3. Instruction Regarding Marriage and the Family

The early church apparently felt it necessary to embark upon a program of instruction concerning sex, marriage, and family. The New Testament letters contain such a body of catechetical materials: 1 Corinthians 11-14; Ephesians 5:21-33; 6:1-4; Colossians 3:18-25; 1 Timothy 3:1-13; 5:1-16; Titus 2:1-8; 1 Peter 3:1-9. This was to be taught by elders, teachers, pastors, and parents. Church leaders were also expected to exemplify these standards in their households (1 Tim. 3:2-5). A brief survey will disclose the substance of these teachings.

a. There is order and beauty in God's creative plan which includes family and congregational life (1 Cor. 11-14; 1 Pet. 3). Paul and Peter saw this order in creation as providing sense and stability for life. Differentiation of the roles of husbands and wives (1 Cor. 11:3; 1 Pet. 3:1) in no way diminishes the equality of male and female before god (Gal. 3:28). Each person has unique gifts. Interdependence of members is desirable in both church and home.

b. The most excellent way of love (*agape*) transforms Christian marriage as well as the rest of life (1 Cor. 13). Love is the key to right-relatedness, the end for which men and women were created. The capacity to love is a gift of God and not inherent in man. Deep in the human heart is a longing which will not be satisfied until the love of God is expressed in all relationships.

c. Explicit instruction is offered regarding the relationships of husbands and wives, parents and children, single members, orphans, and widows so that all members might understand their responsibilities and privileges in family living (Eph. 5:21-6:4; Col. 3:18-25; 1 Tim. 3:1-13; 5:1-16; Titus 2:1-8; Heb. 13:4; James 1:27; 1 Pet. 3:1-9). It is understood that love for Christ and for each other is the determinative force in Christian marriage and family life. The overriding emphases are mutuality, reciprocity, and love which seeks the development of the other's potentiality. Members of Christian families are "joint heirs of the grace of life" (1 Pet. 3:7).

These instructions are valid still. Love and fidelity are to be learned of Christ through the Word. Respect for persons, appreciation for one's sexuality, the beauty of chastity before and in marriage, and how to deal with human failure are to be learned within the context of the covenant people. There is little doubt that the quality and hope of life for future generations are dependent on the continuation of the Christian family. A positive educational approach must exist in every congregation and home if great ill is to be avoided, true human maturity to be attained.

Guidelines for Today

The Christian community should provide the best environment for dealing with the concerns of marriage, divorce, remarriage, and human sexuality. The church knows the One who is able to transform all human life and as a redeemed fellowship has the capacity to reach those afflicted by loneliness, divorce, or marital discord because it realizes their true potentiality in Christ. It can also provide for its members a distinctive foundation for marriage in God's Word. Where the members are concerned for and accountable to each other, there will be concern for each union. There will be corporate concern for each marriage, each divorce, and each remarriage because the church is aware of the impact on the children, on her common life, and on her witness in the world. In each case, the church can acknowledge Christ as Redeemer and Lord. In these crucial moments of life, she is called to proclaim his grace and to declare his claims. If the church is to be a redeemed fellowship, she must offer acceptance and establish expectations in accord with Christ's Word. There are several things which the church has a right to expect of and must be willing to demonstrate to those considering marriage. These include the following

1. Covenantal Fidelity

Christian marriage involves making a covenant before God and his people in accord with his Word. The church's liturgy embraces this covenant concept. A covenant calls for mutual responsibility and faithfulness. This fidelity, a kind of loyalty or stubborn commitment to the marriage and to the partner, is a necessary part of marriage. Each marriage relationship has its own ebb and flow with varying degrees of happiness and tension. In light of these changes in every marital relationship, fidelity is absolutely essential to the growth of individuals and to the growth of their marriage. Too often people enter marriage without understanding that God requires fidelity, an act of the will, not the emotion of "being in love." In a society where a lack of commitment seems to characterize so many marriages, this dimension of fidelity must be reviewed regularly.

2. Forgiveness

Marital disruption is one of the most severe tests of the Christian idea of grace. The church is called to be a fellowship where those who falter and fail can rebuild and where the divorced can find love and patient support. Some congregations (including elders and ministers) have not developed their ability to exercise the forgiveness of Christ toward repentant adulterers and divorced persons. Yet the Bible indicates that failures or sins in this area are no more grievous than other sins nor any less forgivable. Paul rightly admonishes, "Let grace abound," not that there might be more sin, but that there may be new life (Rom. 5:20-6:2). Christian realism includes acknowledging the new possibilities included in God's forgiveness. Where the once flesh relationship has been irreconciliably shattered, there one has divorce (*de facto*) and it must be recognized. In fact, where a marriage has been destroyed, the Christian community may even counsel severance to prevent further damage to persons involved. Likewise, in counseling divorced persons considering remarriage, a minister and the elders are often compelled to decide which is the better of two difficult alternatives. Each case must be examined on its own merits. Should the minister either agree to officiate at the remarriage or not, he should share his reasons with the couple. The Word and Spirit, the mind of the church, and one's own conscience must be considered in making the decision. The action of the Reformed Church in America ("Basic Policy on Divorce and Remarriage," MGS, 1962:215) remains valid:

> A pastor can in good conscience officiate in the remarriage of divorced persons if in his judgment, and the judgment of the congregation's board of elders the persons have met the following requirements: Recognition of personal responsibility for the failure of the former marriage, penitence and an effort to overcome limitations and failures, forgiveness of the former partner, fulfillment of obligations involved in the

former marriage, and a willingness to make the new marriage a Christian one by dependence on Christ and participation in his church.

Those who have undergone the trauma of divorce need time to reflect upon their experience and time to rebuild. *First,* persons should take time for reflection on the causes of the previous failure. Repentance is necessary. It involves not only penitence for one's own part, but a change in one's attitude and actions. Harmful personality traits and behavioral patterns should be modified before any remarriage. *Second,* personal realization of God's forgiveness is a vital part of one's readiness for remarriage. This includes forgiving the former partner and seeking forgiveness. Otherwise a residue of bitterness can cloud future interpersonal relations. Continuing obligations to the former mate or children, financial and otherwise, should be met. *Third,* there must be a vision of what the new marriage can mean and the determination to make it Christian. Recognition of human limitations at this point rightly leads one to a reliance on Christ and on the supportive family of faith. Willingness to be a full participant in the people of God is prerequisite to proceeding with remarriage. Where the forgiveness of God has been accepted and life redirected to obedient service, the prospects for a sound marriage exist.

3. Growth

Growth within a marriage relationship is vital if joy and gratitude for God's gift are to continue. Where only individual development, personal pleasure, and professional advancement are stressed, the result is generally a moving apart. Such priorities dominate many social circles with corrosive effect. In contrast the church offers three goals which call for mutual growth and service. First, marriage as designed by God calls for couples to strive for a heightened sensitivity to each other and a deepening relationship in the Spirit. Second, God intends that each may uphold and complement the other over the years that there may be mutual fulfillment. Finally, God desires both that couples guide their own children in the Christian life and that they as a family be Christ's witnesses in their community.

Much can be accomplished in a congregation when couples join together to support each other in Christ. Local congregations can provide the atmosphere and activities which promote growth by focusing on goal setting in marriage, problem solving, child rearing, and husband-wife communication. Continuing education on how to handle stress, conflict, and crises is needed in every marriage. Conflicts and difficulties can be viewed not as the start of disintegration of a marriage, but as a reminder of the couple's need for God's grace and healing power. In such a Christian context, second and third marriages also have potential for achieving God's design. Couples do need to work at reaffirming their vows and at enriching their marriages. Continual reaffirmation can occur not only at anniversaries, but at meals, in family prayer, and in sexual intimacy. Congregations can also provide opportunities at the Lord's Table and on designated Lord's Days for couples to renew their commitment to each other and their mutual commitment to Christ and to his work.

Marriage remains a beautiful but fragile gift because, like the gospel, "we have this treasure in earthen vessels." Nevertheless, we rejoice in this gift because God's transcendent power works in and through it (2 Cor. 4:7). Therefore, in marriage our goal is always that "the life of Jesus may be manifested in our mortal flesh" (2 Cor. 4:11).

Notes: *The Reformed Church in America traces its origins to the first Dutch settlers in America, members of the Reformed Church in the Netherlands. It has remained conservative and accepted the Belgic Confession, the Heidelberg Catechism, and the Canons of the Synod of Dort. This statement reaffirms a traditional approach to marriage while allowing for divorce for reasons other than adultery and the remarriage of divorced individuals. There is a recognition of the fragility of the marriage relationship and the need for the church to cultivate compassion in marriage relationships and in church members for those whose marriages fail.*

REFORMED CHURCH IN AMERICA

EXCERPT FROM "CHRISTIAN ACTION COMMISSION REPORT ON HUMAN SEXUALITY" (1978)

Human Sexuality: Biblical Perspectives

In the beginning was the Covenant! In the mystery of God's own choosing, he spoke these words to his people, "You shall be my people, and I shall be your God." With this a People of Covenant was born and from that time to this we have been struggling to discern the full implications of what it means to be a Covenant People both in our common life together and in our life lived before God.

As Reformed Christians, we have always been known as "People of the Book", and it is to our biblical sources we turn when we have sought for exits from our moral dilemmas. On the surface, this appears to be a proper point of departure, but upon a more thorough examination it becomes apparent that the verdict of Scripture is uneven and evolving and does not yield to ready systematization. What we begin to discover is layer upon layer of developing theologies and ethical co-existing in a dynamic conversation as the Covenant People are confronted by the ethical imperatives of a God who declares, "You shall therefore be holy, for I am holy." (Leviticus 12:45). From the earliest times the response of the Covenant People is to mirror the nature of God himself. The necessity for holiness publicly and privately stands unamended for the People of the Covenant, yet the strategies used to accomplish this directive have reflected the shifting cultural climate in which we are given to live out our obedience. Thus, the truth remains intact, while the working out of the implications has adjusted itself as the People of the Covenant continue to live before their Holy God.

This is not to suggest that Holy Scripture does not provide us with fertile beginnings, but it does imply that Holy Scripture does not commit us to completed endings. In the long march that makes up the biblical trek, we find an unfolding story laced with a rich variety of interpretations and understandings, but if one seeks within the pages of the Bible in Testaments Old or New for a systematic ethic, which would be everywhere applicable in all times and in all places, he will turn away frustrated.

The source of that frustration will center on the lack of specific rules and regulations set down by Holy Scripture. Particularly did the Old Testament seek to codify their holiness, but even in this area of sexuality, there are great gaps and many silences which drive us inevitably to the conclusion that as far as specific sexual acts are concerned the Bible is neither as prescribed as the puritans would prefer, or as boundaryless as the "situationists" would suppose.

Thus, from the pages of Holy Scripture, we are given the principles which must govern our acts and motives in human sexuality, and these are to reflect, not the fashion and fad of the passing scene, but are to reflect the very nature of God himself. The precise formularies by which we determine the working out of our holiness have varied and do vary as the Covenant People maintain their lively interfacing with a Holy God.

A. The Beginnings of the Tradition: (Genesis)

As the people of the Covenant ruminated over what sexuality meant for them in the light of God's creative intention, we find quite different traditions operating in the Book of Genesis. They are not contradictory, but their focus is different and both are quite useful as the Covenant People continue to make sense out of the mystery of their election.

The oldest tradition, which probably dates from approximately 950 B.C. sets the intention of God within the context of community versus isolation. God made man and woman for mutuality and life-fulfilling companionship. God's assessment was, "It is not good that man should be alone." I will make a helper fit for him." (Genesis 2:18)

140

The human personality was not created for solitude but for community. The sexual relationship is given as a gift in relationship. Man, alone, is incomplete. Woman, alone, is incomplete. God completes their partiality by gifting to them the sacrament of sexuality which graciously signals God's intention that the "two should become one." God created humankind for companionship with himself; God, too, desired companionship and now his man also needs companionship in that grand creative scheme of things.

The second tradition in Genesis points us in the direction of seeing our human sexuality as being the profound hook-up with that mysterious phrase "imago dei". "So God created man in his own image; male and female created he them." (Genesis 1:27) Probably, in the beginning, being made in the image of God suggested humankind as collaborators with God's creativity as stewards of the earth, and as co-creators with God as we subdue as well as replenish the earth. Time narrowed the focus until procreation came to be the physical parable of the mysterious life force which God built into creation itself, and through that very sexuality we're closing in on the life of God himself in whose likeness we were fashioned, but have shown persistently that we lack the ability to fulfill that image.

B. The Externalizing of the Tradition (The Law)

First a Zig and then a Zag, the covenant People begin to legislate the corporate life of the people in order to publicly reflect the holiness of God lived out in human life. It was a noble experiment but in the "fullness of time" that approach was rendered secondary and it was judged as defective. To examine the codes detailed in Leviticus and Deuteronomy is to be struck by the desire for ritual purity irrespective of volitional concerns. These regulations have almost no bearing upon the morality or immorality of sexuality in itself, but mostly speak to ceremonial transgressions and how to remedy these stains on their ritual holiness. Christians reading this culturally conditioned set of laws and codes have instinctively relegated it to "ceremonial law", which after the Incarnation was no longer binding. This actually becomes an example of the way we begin to see the process of interpretation working as the Covenant People reflect ever more deeply on the nature of their response to the holiness of God. It is easy to dismiss this as a theocratic attempt to impose external conformity at the expense of interior conviction. While this is what happens, the intention was laudable even if the working out of the principles was inadequate. Yet, as Covenant People we note that this was another landmark of awareness in that living conversation between God and his Beloved. Obsolete now, certainly, but a serious attempt to reflect the holiness of God outwardly in the body politic. (Examples: Leviticus 15, 18, 20)

C. Internalizing the Tradition (The Prophets)

Even when the Covenant People seemed immersed in meeting the cultic requirements of the Law, there was that niggling remembrance that there was more to it than outer conformity. Often obscured or seemingly buried, yet, finally its wisdom, too was perceived: ". . . and you shall love the Lord your God with all your heart, with all your soul and with all your might." (Deuteronomy 6:5) With the emergence of the great prophets of reform in the fifth century B.C., came a deeper insight. Without abandoning the requirements of the Law, they began to see the need for a change of heart, as well as the need for ritual purity. What had before been cultic rites were more searchingly viewed as a dynamic, personal, moral concepts and now both the public nature of society and the private nature of the individual were being faced by the Covenant People in their conversation with a Holy God. (Examples: Wisdom literature, Malachi; Hosea; Isaiah)

D. The Humanizing of the Covenant (The Christ)

In the person and work of Jesus of Nazareth the Covenant takes human shape. Both the message and the messenger blend into an intricate weave as regards human sexuality. For those born and bred within the Reformed tradition, we have been trained to think not only biblically but also Christologically. When we turn to the pages of the Gospel we discover a celibate Jesus, who enthusiastically enters into the prophetic tradition of an Isaiah or a

141

Jeremiah, who promulgates no new sexual ethic, who does not abrogate the requirements of the Law, yet who goes for the jugular of morality in that he centers the real issue of purity in that which proceeds from within a person, not that which is performed from without. (St. Mark 7:1-23)

The same frustration which greets us in the Old Testament awaits us in the New. Jesus lays down few eternal verities as far as the specific areas of sexuality are concerned, but does enunciate principles by which we may profitably evaluate our own sexuality. The concrete data surrounding the life of Jesus is not sufficient to build a solid case for Our Lord's views of many of the issues associated with sexuality. Jesus does speak strongly on the issue of marriage and divorce, and by both word and deed he endorses the concept of full participation of women in the Covenant community, not simply as being a male after-thought, but as full participants in their own right. Apart from these areas there is little else that would help us as far as the particularia of our human sexuality is concerned.

We are left with a Jesus who did give us an impressive array of principles, but who does not easily answer all the attendant problems associated with our human sexuality in specific areas. Jesus, as the bearer of the Covenant has always been viewed as the model of the Covenant's requirements and in this we are helped. Jesus is portrayed for us as the epitome of *unselfish love* (John 13:34), *service* (Mark 10:44-45). and *forgiveness* (Matthew 6:12; Luke 17:34). The emphasis which Jesus gave on the primacy of the law of love (Mk 12:28-34) has had profound implications for our understanding of human sexuality. (Luke 7:36-50)

In the teachings of Jesus, sexuality is neither deified nor demeaned; it is regarded as part of the created order with inherent possibilities for either the demonic or the beatific. The United Presbyterian Church in the U.S.A. in a study paper entitled HUMAN SEXUALITY AND THE HUMAN COMMUNITY makes the following statement:

> . . .those sexual expressions which build up communion between persons, establish a hopeful outlook on the future, ministering in a healing way to the fear, the hurts, the anxieties of persons, and confirm that fact to them that they are truly loved, are actions which can confirm the Covenant Jesus announced. . . .

Just as in the latter part of the Old Testament, the basic morality or immorality of the sexual side of human nature is not to be located so much in the deed done as much as in the motive and intention of an individual. The real criteria then becomes, not only the physical act, but the possibilities for alienation and reconciliation built into any given moral situation.

The object of biblical ethics is that man and woman should come to more closely resemble the Holy God who sovereignly and freely chooses to live in Covenant with his people and this must be reflected in the quality of relationships as the human family seeks to order its varied relationships. This is the ethical yardstick supremely mediated to us through the word and deed of Jesus of Nazareth.

E. The Tradition Interpreted (St. Paul)

In the mission and expansion of the Church after the resurrection and ascension of Jesus, we find that St. Paul becomes the principal interpreter for the universalized requirements of the Covenant. That Covenant is no longer to be seen in terms exclusively of Israel, but now in a broader sweep of the "New Israel" which is open to any who are desirous of entering into the Covenant obligations.

It is frequently asserted that Paul is to be seen as a crotchety old misogynist and that this accounts for his rather grim outlook on things sexual. This view is too superficial to do justice to the teachings of the Apostle. Being a pious Jew by birthright, Paul accepts both the fact and the essential goodness of sexuality. (1 Corinthians 7) As far as women, in his masterful treatise in Galatians, Paul espouses human equality (chapter 3) and human freedom (chapter 4) which extends to men and women. The highest statement in the New Testament concerning the position of womanhood is written by Paul ". . . there is neither male nor female, for all are one in Christ Jesus''. (Galatians 3:28) When Paul strains to find the highest parallel between the love which exists between Christ and his Church, Paul finds it in the relationship between a loving husband and a faithful wife. (Ephesians).

The reservations which are expressed by Paul center around very pragmatic ethical concerns, and this continues to illustrate the way in which the Covenant community expresses its response to the holiness of its sovereign Lord. The two issues which tended to color Paul's reactions were first of all the Church's expectation of the immediate return to Christ, which would tend to make their sexual situations very tentative; and secondly the prominence of sexual immorality which seemed to be everywhere prevalent and threatened to rival the worship of God as far as the allegiance of men and women were concerned.

To a fervent Jew, reborn, to be sure, but still a Jew, worship could be ascribed to God alone. The ancient Covenant brooked no rivals, for idolatry was the ultimate evil when it sought to usurp the place granted only to God, and it must be resisted and dethroned whether it be the idolatry of exhibitionism of the body, or temple prostitution or other forms of promiscuity. For in the institutionalized forms of immorality so rampant in Paul's day, he deplored the depersonalized and depersonalizing attitude toward human sexuality and greatly opposed the Greek insistence that sexual pleasure should be divorced from human love and care. St. Paul saw many of the forms of contemporary immorality in terms of its idolatrous competition for the hearts and lives of God's people, and in this it must be resolutely rejected. The obligations of the Covenant unswervingly insists that: ''Thou shalt have no other Gods before me.'' St. Paul the apostle, makes universal that experience which had previously been particularized in Israel. Even in this universal mission the insistent requirement is that the Holy God be served in the holiness of his people. Though it is couched in the language and conditions of the day, it still reveals that stubborn truth that God must be served concretely in the ordinariness of living, be they Jew or gentile, male or female, bondsmen or freeman.

F. The Tradition Continuing (Church and Spirit)

In the beginning looms the Covenant. In the end we meet the Covenant. We are living ''between the times'', and part of what it means for us to be faithful is the willingness to become part of the process of discovery as much as the ability to produce a full, final and authoritative definition of the ethical requirements of being a People of the Covenant. We have many clues, as a pilgrim people, but few dogmas, ''for there is no permanent city for us here on earth; for we are looking for a city which is to come.'' (Hebrews 13:14)

The Bible itself was content to have it so, for in its strata and substrata, it yields varying answers to specifics at varying times. Still, having said that, the thread running the length and breadth of the biblical journey has never ceased to be the incessant wrestling with the mystery of how a not so holy people can more obediently reflect the nature of a holy God.

In the sphere of our human sexuality some biblical themes emerge which give content to our decisions as we seek to resonate with that great tradition in which we stand.

Notes: *In this report, the Reformed Church in America reaffirms its "covenantal" theology of sexuality derived from the Bible and asserts that the morality of sexual acts should be determined by motive and deed rather than the deeds themselves.*

SALVATION ARMY

POSITION STATEMENT ON MARRIAGE (1983)

The Salvation Army affirms the New Testament standard of marriage, that is, the voluntary and loving union for life of one man and one woman to the exclusion of all others, this union being established by an authorized ceremony.

"Voluntary" indicates that the parties freely choose or, in some cultures, agree to enter into the marriage. "For life" indicates there can be no such thing as a trial or temporary marriage. "One man and one woman" means that marriage is possible only between members of the opposite sex, and "to the exclusion of all others" stresses the fidelity inherent in the marriage bond.

By its nature, marriage rests on a relationship of love, a reflection of God's love for the human race. The permanence of the marriage bond provides for security and developing mutual trust, referred to in Scripture as a "one flesh" relationship (Genesis 2:24, Ephesians 5:31), which Jesus affirmed: "What God hath joined together let no man put asunder" (Matthew 19:6).

The exclusive nature of marriage leaves no room for sexual infidelity. In sexual intercourse spouses express to one another profound feelings of love, mutual respect, interdependence and belonging. Sexual relations outside marriage will always fall short of this. Only assurance of each other's total loyalty leads to the proper growth of the marriage relationship.

The Salvation Army asserts that God's standard concerning marriage, revealed in Scripture, pertains to all people everywhere. Jesus taught that divorce is failure (Mark 10:2-12; Matthew 19:3-12). Salvationists believe, however, that His attitude to those caught up in marital strife would never be anything but loving and compassionate.

Therefore, The Salvation Army, while defending vigorously the ongoing relevance of God's will for men and women in relation to marriage, recognizes the reality that some marriages fail and is willing, under God, to offer counsel and succor to couples so affected. Where remarriage could lead to the healing of emotional wounds, the Army will permit its officers to perform a marriage ceremony for a divorced person. Sound doctrine with practical mercy are the hallmarks of the Salvationist's approach to marital and emotional strife.

The Salvation Army reasserts that the strengthening and encouragement of the institution of marriage remains an essential precondition for sound family life which is, in turn, crucial to a stable society.

Notes: *The Salvation Army began in Great Britain in 1865. It is an international religious and charitable movement dedicated to preaching the Christian gospel and disseminating its teaching while actively supplying basic human necessities. This statement on marriage, which reaffirms traditional biblical teachings on monogamy and fidelity, was approved by the Salvation Army Commissioners' Conference of February 1983.*

SALVATION ARMY

POSITION STATEMENT ON THE FAMILY (1983)

In spite of changing life-styles and values, the family unit—father, mother and children— is still the primary social institution in contemporary American life.

The American family, while smaller than a generation or more ago, remains the basic source of nurture, of love, of economic and other life supports, of fundamental education and socialization and of spiritual and moral development. Other social institutions serve best as supportive resources.

In the face of emerging alternative life-styles and modes of living, which in recent years have grown in incidence and open acceptance, The Salvation Army affirms its absolute conviction that the marriage of one man with one woman is a sacred institution ordained by God and that a traditional good-faith commitment to an indissoluble union is one of the most rewarding of life's decisions for any man or woman, providing the optimal conditions for both personal fulfillment and the bearing and rearing of children. Thus The Salvation Army, through all its programs and services, seeks to strengthen marriage and enrich family life, while extending the appropriate ministrations of a caring Christian community to all persons in need.

Notes: *Like the previous statement, this was approved by the Salvation Army Commissioners' Conference of October 1983. It reaffirms monogamous marriage as ordained by God and upholds fidelity in marriage.*

SEVENTH-DAY ADVENTIST CHURCH

EXCERPT FROM "CHURCH MANUAL" (1986)

Social Relationships

The social instinct is given us of God, for our pleasure and benefit. "By mutual contact minds receive polish and refinement; by social intercourse, acquaintances are formed and friendships contracted which result in a unity of heart and an atmosphere of love which is pleasing in the sight of heaven."—*Testimonies,* vol. 6, p. 172. Proper association of the sexes is beneficial to both. Such associations should be conducted upon a high plane and with due regard to the conventions and restrictions which, for the protection of society and the individual, have been prescribed. It is the purpose of Satan, of course, to pervert every good thing; and the perversion of the best often leads to that which is worst. So it is highly important that Christians should adhere to very definite standards of social life.

Today the ideals that make these social relationships safe and happy are breaking down to an alarming degree. Under the influence of passion unrestrained by moral and religious principle, the association of the sexes has to an alarming extent degenerated into freedom and license. Sexual perversions, incest, and sexual abuse of children prevail to an alarming degree. Millions have abandoned Christian standards of conduct and are bartering the sweet and sacred experiences of marriage and parenthood for the bitter, remorseful fruits of lust. Not only are these evils damaging the familial structure of society, but the breakdown of the family in turn fosters and breeds these and other evils. The results in distorted lives of children and youth are distressing and evoke our pity, while the effects on society are not only disastrous but cumulative.

These evils have become more open and threatening to the ideals and purposes of the Christian home. Adultery, sexual abuse of spouses, incest, sexual abuse of children, homosexual practices, and lesbian practices are among the obvious perversions of God's original plan. As the intent of clear passages of Scripture (see Ex. 20:14; Lev. 18:22, 29 and 20:13; 1 Cor. 6:9; 1 Tim. 1:10; Rom. 1:20-32) is denied and as their warnings are rejected in exchange for human opinions, much uncertainty and confusion prevail. This is what Satan desires. It has always been his plan to cause people to forget that God is their Creator and that when He "created man in His own image" He created them "male and female" (Gen. 1:27). The world is witnessing today a resurgence of the perversions of ancient civilizations.

The degrading results of the world's obsession with sex and the love and pursuit of sensual pleasure are clearly delineated in the Word of God. But Christ came to destroy the works of the devil and reestablish the relationship of human beings with their Creator. Thus, though fallen in Adam and captive to sin, those who are in Christ receive full pardon and the right to choose anew the better way, the way to complete renewal. By means of the cross and the power of the Holy Spirit, all may be freed from the grip of sinful practices as they are restored to the image of their Creator.

It is incumbent upon the parents and the spiritual guides of the youth to face with no false modesty the facts of social conditions, to gain more fully a sympathetic understanding of the problems of this generation of young people, to seek most earnestly to provide for them the best environment, and to draw so near to them in spirit as to be able to impart the ideals of life and the inspiration and power of Christian religion, that they may be saved from the evil that is in the world through lust.

But to our young men and young women we say, The responsibility is yours. Whatever may be the mistakes of parents, it is your privilege to know and to hold the highest ideals of Christian manhood and womanhood. Reverent Bible study, a deep acquaintance with the works of nature, stern guarding of the sacred powers of the body, earnest purpose, constancy in prayer, and sincere, unselfish ministry to others' needs will build a character that is proof against evil and that will make you an uplifting influence in society.

Social gatherings for old and young should be made occasions, not for light and trifling amusement, but for happy fellowship and improvement of the powers of mind and soul. Good music, elevating conversation, good recitations, suitable still or motion pictures, games carefully selected for their educational value, and, above all, the making and using of plans for missionary effort can provide programs for social gatherings that will bless and strengthen the lives of all. The Youth Department of the General Conference has published helpful information and practical suggestions for the conduct of social gatherings and for guidance in other social relations.

The homes of the church are by far the best places for social gatherings. In large centers where it is impossible to hold them there, and where there is no social center of our own, a proper place free from influences destructive to Christian standards should be secured rather than a place that is ordinarily used for commercial amusements and sports, such as social halls and skating rinks, which suggest an atmosphere contrary to Christian standards.

Chaperonage

The happy and cordial association of those older in years with the young people is one of the most wholesome influences in the lives of children and youth. "There is danger that both parents and teachers . . . fail to come sufficiently into social relation with their children or scholars."—*Counsels to Parents, Teachers, and Students*, p. 76. It is the duty of our schools and other institutions to care for the morals and reputation of those placed in their charge. Chaperonage is an obligatory duty with them. It is equally the duty of the home. Parents should strongly sustain the regulations of the institutions in which their youth and children are placed, and should institute in their homes equal safeguards. To make this possible, it is their duty to learn how to be welcome companions of their children; but it rests chiefly upon the young people themselves to make of chaperonage not an irksome and repugnant association but an honored and happy relationship.

Courtship and Marriage

Courtship is recognized as a preparatory period during which a man and a woman, already mutually attracted, become more thoroughly acquainted with each other in preparation for intended marriage. Christian marriage is a divinely sanctioned union between a believing man and a believing woman for the fulfillment of their mutual love, for mutual support, for shared happiness, and for the procreation and rearing of children who will in turn become Christians. According to God's design, this union lasts until dissolved by the death of one of the partners.

Marriage is the foundation of human society, and true affection between man and woman is ordained of God. "Let those who are contemplating marriage weigh every sentiment and watch every development of character in the one with whom they think to unite their life destiny. Let every step toward a marriage alliance be characterized by modesty, simplicity, sincerity, and an earnest purpose to please and honor God. Marriage affects the after life both in this world and in the world to come. A sincere Christian will make no plans that God cannot approve."—*The Ministry of Healing*, p. 359.

The failure to follow these principles in Christian courtship may lead to tragedy. Unity of husband and wife in ideals and purposes is a requisite to a happy and successful home. The Scriptures counsel, "Be ye not unequally yoked together with unbelievers" (2 Cor. 6:14). Differences regarding religion are likely to mar the happiness of a home where partners hold different beliefs and lead to confusion, perplexity, and failure in the rearing of children.

Differences concerning the worship of God, Sabbathkeeping, recreation, association, and training of children often lead to discouragement and finally to complete loss of Christian experience. Let us take heed to the following admonition: "Unless you would have a home where the shadows are never lifted, do not unite yourself with one who is an enemy of God."—*Messages to Young People*, p. 440.

Marriage "was designed to be a blessing to mankind. And it is a blessing wherever the marriage covenant is entered into intelligently, in the fear of God, and with due consideration for its responsibilities" (ibid., p. 434).

Conclusion

Standing amid the perils of the last days, bearing the responsibility of speedily carrying the last offer of salvation to the world, and facing a judgment that will culminate in the establishment of universal righteousness, let us with true heart consecrate ourselves to God, body, soul, and spirit, determining to maintain the high standards of living that must characterize those who wait for the return of their Lord.

Notes: *The Seventh-day Adventist Church is an evangelical sabbatarian church whose teachings have been supplemented by insights drawn from the prophecies and visions of its founder, Ellen G. White. Like other conservative groups, the Seventh-day Adventists reserve coitus for the monogamous marriage relationship, emphasize the importance of strong family ties, and reaffirm the need for strong parental authority and guidance.*

SOUTHERN BAPTIST CONVENTION

RESOLUTION ON STRENGTHENING FAMILIES (1981)

WHEREAS, The family has been clearly divined in God's Word and accepted by the Jewish and Christian society of America for over two hundred years; and

WHEREAS, Traditional Judeo-Christian family values are being threatened; and

WHEREAS, American families need to have affirmation by the Christian community; and

WHEREAS, Our churches have increasing opportunities to minister to singles and single parent families; and

WHEREAS, The Southern Baptist Convention has voted to launch in 1982 a three-year emphasis on *Strengthening Families;*

Be it therefore *Resolved,* That we urge all Southern Baptist churches and families to engage in activities and instruction to further the *Strengthening Families* emphasis; and

Be it further *Resolved,* That we urge families to establish and maintain vital relationships with God and each other through prayer and the study of God's Word; and

Be it finally *Resolved,* That we express our determination to share the love, wholesomeness, and strength of the family of God with all the families of man.

130.   John Meador (Ut.) moved the adoption of Resolution No. 4. R. H. Patterson (S.C.) spoke to the resolution. The motion passed.

Notes: *The Southern Baptist Convention was formed in 1845 by the Baptist congregations in the southern United States. During the twentieth century, the denomination has been* *embroiled in serious conflict between those who champion innovative perspectives and approaches and the more conservative elements of the convention, who think the innovations deviate from traditional Baptist teachings and standards. Currently, the convention is governed by a group of very conservative leaders who seek to exercise absolute control over the denomination. This resolution demonstrates its commitment to a conservative biblical approach to the family.*

SOUTHERN BAPTIST CONVENTION

RESOLUTION ON FAMILY PLANNING (1981)

We reaffirm Resolution No. 20—On Permissiveness and Family Planning made by the Southern Baptist Convention meeting in St. Louis, June 12, 1980:

"WHEREAS, The Southern Baptist Convention in annual session in 1977 spoke clearly and forthrightly to the issue of permissiveness as follows:

WHEREAS, The permissiveness of the so-called new morality has permeated our society and has affected even our churches, and

WHEREAS, We believe that the rights of the family are being infringed upon when information, medication, and supplies are being furnished the unmarried minor-aged children without parental consent.

Therefore be it *Resolved,* That we call upon elected and employed government officials to work towards the return of parental or guardian control of minors in the matter of sexual information and devices, and we oppose any governmental agency withholding or threatening to withhold funds from public-funded agencies that require parental consent or parental knowledge before dispensing medication or devices, and

Be it further *Resolved,* That we oppose the distribution of birth control devices to minors except with parental or guardian consent.

Furthermore, be it *Resolved,* That we ask our churches to speak out against this permissiveness of the new morality and, under the leadership of pastors and parents, supplement and reinforce the sex education taught in the home in order to strengthen the biblical teachings of chastity before marriage and fidelity to marriage vows.

Be it further *Resolved,* That the Baptist Joint Committee and the Christian Life Commission be requested to communicate this action to Congress and the President."

178.   Secretary Porter reported ballot results on an amendment to Resolution No. 10 (see Item 169). Of the 13,551 messengers registered at the time, 5,298 voted: yes, 3,048 (57.53%): no, 2,179 (41.13%); and unusable ballots, 71 (1.34%). Resolution No. 10, as amended, was declared adopted.

Notes: *This resolution on family planning considers the family the sole and proper institution for educating children about sexuality and birth control devices. This resolution was adopted in 1981 with 5,298 individuals casting affirmative ballots and 2,179 casting negative votes (71 ballots were unusable).*

SOUTHERN BAPTIST CONVENTION

RESOLUTION ON THE FAMILY (1988)

WHEREAS, The family was ordained by God to be the basic institution of society; and

WHEREAS, the family and biblical values are under constant attack from materialism, secular humanism, substance abuse, and rebellion against authority; and

WHEREAS, Traditional Christian values of home and family are often attacked and ignored in the media and secular education;

Be it therefore RESOLVED, That the Southern Baptist Convention meeting in annual session June 14-16, 1988, go on record as affirming the importance of the home as the center for Christian nurture, training, and instruction (Proverbs 22:6) and

Be it further RESOLVED, That Christian education in the church regarding biblical standards and moral values be supported by teaching and example in the home;

Be it further RESOLVED, That Southern Baptists express our appreciation for those organizations and ministries which uphold the standards of God concerning proper moral and family values; and

Be it finally RESOLVED, That we believe that devotion to God, respect for authority, obedience to divine commands, self-discipline, self-control, and love should be both modeled and taught (1 Timothy 1:5) in the home.

Notes: *This resolution, very similar to ones adopted in 1981 and 1982, reaffirms the Southern Baptist Convention's commitment to a literal interpretation of the Bible on matters pertaining to the family.*

UNITED CHURCH OF CANADA

EXCERPT FROM "GIFT, DILEMMA AND PROMISE" (1984)

Sexuality and Selfhood

Acknowledgments and Affirmations

a. WE AFFIRM that our sexuality is a gift of God. In its life-enhancing, non-exploitive forms it is a primary way of relating to ourselves and to one another, and is the way God has chosen to continue the human race.

   We acknowledge that human sexuality, like all other aspects of human nature is affected and distorted by human sinfulness. We recognize the ambiguity of human nature and therefore of human sexuality. "All have sinned and fallen short of the glory of God." (Romans 3:23)

b. WE AFFIRM that God works in Christ through the Spirit to redeem human nature and, with it, human sexuality. (Romans 8:21)

c. WE AFFIRM that the giving and receiving of affection, whether physical or emotional or both, is a basic need. The forms which this may take are many and varied. Because the hunger for intimacy is ultimately a hunger for God, this is a profoundly spiritual experience. It may lead to a more profound humanness or to manipulation, distortion, control.

   We acknowledge that the roles and expectations that accompany gender are largely cultural in origin and arbitrary in nature.

d. WE AFFIRM that even in the midst of ambiguity, we are called upon to make responsible decisions with regard to the expression of our sexuality and to cope with the consequences.

   We need to, "hear the pluralism and diversity of moral decision-making within the church as a possible way in which God is engaging us," says one of the responses to the Human Sexuality Study.

e. WE AFFIRM the church's call to proclaim the worth of human sexuality and to speak out concerning the abuses of human sexuality in individual lives, in the community and in the structures of society. In this respect, we understand that our responsibility is more to challenge and support than to condemn, more prophetic and pastoral than imperial.

We acknowledge that the way we experience and express our sexuality is shaped largely by the ways in which we are socialized, by our unique journeys through the stages of human development, and by our personal journey of faith.

f. WE AFFIRM the role of the church as a community of faith, offering support, challenge and guidance in sexual decision-making.

g. WE AFFIRM that the church is called to a ministry of prophetic witness in the face of evil, pastoral care in the face of pain and confusion, education in the face of conflicting values and ignorance. This includes the ethical dimensions of: birth control and family planning; family life education; marriage preparation and enrichment; counselling in situations of marriage breakdown; separation and divorce; unfulfilling relationships; sexual exploitation in the family; sexism (personal and social discrimination against others on the basis of gender); concerns of singles; of unmarried couples; homosexual persons and single-parent families.

h. WE AFFIRM that the church is called to initiate and support research and educational programs to increase our understanding of the causes of exploitive sexual behaviour and other destructive expressions; to reduce the incidence of such destructive expressions, and to improve our ministry to all who are harmed by such behaviour.

Marriage

Acknowledgments and Affirmations

a. WE AFFIRM that marriage is a gift of God through which Christians make a covenant with one another and with God.

In marriage we offer one another the promise of lifelong companionship, rich expression of human affections and sexuality, and nurture for the children. Marriage as an institution can undergird each relationship and provide stability for society.

We affirm the value of marriage and that the church must work both to redeem and care for the institution and to support those entering into a covenant relationship with each other.

We acknowledge that marriage can also be destructive. Marriage as an institution is shaped by cultural attitudes that are patriarchal and oppressive.

As an institution at the present time it more readily supports male supremacy than human equality, reflecting current values in society. It can degenerate into exploitation, abuse and violence, including rape.

Marriage is an instrument which shares in human sin and which may be redeemed by grace to become the vehicle God intended. It is not to be idealized or idolized as an end in itself.

b. WE AFFIRM that in Christian marriage a man and woman give themselves to each other in the full intention of a lifelong commitment.

Nothing less can measure its totality, even though they may fail in their best intentions and efforts.

In self-giving they become one, a new unity. Yet they do not own each other, as no human being may so possess another. They own the gifts of love and commitment and grace that each has freely offered.

This self-giving love over the years may lead into the most mature and complete joy in each other.

c. WE AFFIRM that this unity is a creation of God and is greater than the two individuals.

It creates holy ground on which the two, and all others, must walk carefully and gently, yet forthrightly and with courage. It has boundaries, between them, and with others, that may not be trespassed. It takes precedence over other relationships. It calls for that caring which heals hurt and tends growth.

d. WE AFFIRM that sexual intercourse in marriage is intended to be:

- a profound expression of the whole person;
- a yearning for total union with the other;
- a creative and holy expression of fulfillment in the other person.

We acknowledge that:

- sexual intercourse may be exploitive, using the other for one's gratification;
- it is possible to be genitally exclusive while not being genuinely faithful. Faithfulness cannot be contained in or reduced to sexual exclusivity, any more than covenant can be contained in or reduced to law.

e. WE AFFIRM that marriage from a Christian perspective is based on faithfulness expressed through:

—choosing each other above all others;

This choosing has its greatest meaning when it is given and maintained gladly rather than as a grudging legalism.

—risking and being vulnerable in the relationship;

The alternative is, in the long run, to retreat into alienation or two solitudes;

—willingness to put into the relationship the patience, understanding and the work required to help it grow;

—accepting and nurturing the other for his or her unique gifts; putting each other before one's own interests in a lifelong commitment which is spiritual, emotional and physical;

—and that these intentions are most fully achieved and symbolized when sexual intercourse in marriage is exclusive.

Faithfulness of this kind is a spiritual gift to be received in the grace of God. It recognizes that when we fail, God is faithful still, and we may discover forgiveness and renewal.

f. WE RECOGNIZE the commitment that is present in many relationships other than Christian marriage; and that the church is called to minister to people in these relationships as in others.

g. WE AFFIRM that the church is called to emphasize and work for the essential values in marriage and family that contribute to the wholeness of persons and to challenge those forms and attitudes that limit and degrade personal worth, even when the culture supports them.

These include the unjust social structures of patriarchy and sexism, as well as distorted attitudes such as rigid role-stereotyping.

Intimacy

Acknowledgments and Affirmations

a. WE AFFIRM that God has made us with a longing to belong, to reach out to one another, to touch each other's lives as members one of another.

Though we think and act as if we were individuals, in fact we are social beings, needing one another.

b. WE AFFIRM that all people experience a hunger for intimacy that is a profoundly spiritual matter, a hunger for God. It is in our experience of the intimate God that we find the grace and possibility of intimacy with one another.

God leads us:

- to treat the other as a person of equal value to oneself;

- to respect the other's relationships with other people;

- to be vulnerable to the changes, even the hurt, that may come from openness to another;

- to commitment and patience as the relationship grows;

- to take the discovery of self more fully through experiencing the other;

- to take seriously the dangers in intimacy and be careful to limit or prevent them;

- to recognize our failures of intimacy and be willing to accept forgiveness.

God is a God of loving kindness, patience, forgiveness.

In risking intimacy we may glimpse God's grace.

In being forgiven, we learn to forgive.

We acknowledge that there are many forms of intimacy; some are enriching; others are exploitive. The Bible offers many models to help us understand and express these. Ultimately, God is the most intimate and yet transcendent companion in life's journey of intimacy, and so the source and energy of all our seeking for each other.

c. WE AFFIRM the importance in intimate relationships of respecting the integrity of others, of setting limits on our actions.

The Bible expresses this both in terms of responsible love and of guidelines or rules for behaviour.

d. WE AFFIRM singleness as a state in which people may find intimacy and fulfillment.

We acknowledge that the church has too readily accepted marriage as the norm for society and so has not valued single persons for themselves or given them the place that is rightfully theirs, nor allowed them the opportunity of sexual fulfillment. Each person needs to struggle faithfully with these decisions.

e. WE AFFIRM that celibacy, freely chosen, can be an expression of God's will and can include emotional intimacy. We acknowledge that the church has not taken celibacy as a vocation with sufficient seriousness, and so has neither benefitted fully from its riches nor provided the support it requires. Its value as a temporary or as a lifelong commitment needs further study.

f. WE AFFIRM that learning to express our longing for intimacy both lovingly and responsibly is a lifelong task as God calls us into full humanity.

Sexism, Society, Self

Acknowledgments and Affirmations

a. WE AFFIRM that the intention of God for all persons is full equality in both our personal and social lives, including acceptance of our sexual differences and similarities.

b. WE AFFIRM that the essence of equality is the acceptance and appreciation of the gifts of all persons female and male.

   We acknowledge that all sexism in language, in social and economic structures, in the conventions of our society and in the attitudes of individuals, is destructive to human dignity and opposed to the will of God.

c. WE AFFIRM that God calls us as a church to eliminate all forms of sexism (personal and social discrimination against others on the basis of gender) in the life and worship of the congregations, presbyteries, conferences and national structures of The United Church of Canada, in keeping with guidelines established by the General Council of The United Church of Canada.

d. WE AFFIRM the need for ongoing research and action in relation to those aspects of life in which sexism (personal and social discrimination against others on the basis of gender) is commonly found.

e. WE AFFIRM that the traditional patriarchal structuring of society can be redeemed and eventually transformed through the grace of God and the struggles of those willing to face the contradictions of sexism. We affirm that Christians are called to work towards an inclusive society.

Sexual Orientation

Acknowledgments and Affirmations

a. WE AFFIRM our acceptance of all human beings as persons made in the image of God, regardless of their sexual orientation.

   Accumulated social science research and the articulated experience of the vast majority of both heterosexual and homosexual men and women affirm that sexual orientation is not so much a matter of choice as a ''given'' aspect of one's identity, resulting probably from a complex interaction of genetic and environmental factors.

b. WE AFFIRM salvation for all people is by grace through faith and that all believers in Christ are accepted as full members of the Christian church, regardless of their sexual orientation.

   We acknowledge that the church has encouraged, condoned and tolerated the rejection and persecution of homosexual persons in society and in the church, and call it to repent.

c. WE AFFIRM that the church is called to initiate and encourage communication and discussion with homosexual believers about sexuality in order that fellowship may be increased and misunderstanding, fears and hostilities lessened.

   In learning more about sexual orientation the church can benefit from the input of the homosexual community which is working to articulate its own history, understanding of sexuality and its relationship to the broader church and society.

d. WE AFFIRM that members of the church, individually and corporately, are responsible for becoming more aware of discrimination against homosexual persons, taking action to ensure that they enjoy their full civil and human rights in society, working to end all forms of discrimination against them, and for personally supporting the victims of such discrimination.

In March 1977, the Department of Church in Society of the Division of Mission in Canada, passed the following resolution:

". . . We affirm the right of persons regardless of their sexual orientation to employment, accommodation and access to the services and facilities that they need and desire.

Recommendation: That in all areas covered by The Canadian Human Rights Act, provision should be made for prohibiting discrimination on the basis of 'sexual orientation'."

e. WE AFFIRM the need, as the church engages its heterosexual and homosexual members in dialogue, to recognize the personal and professional risks to which homosexual persons open themselves as they respond to this invitation.

f. WE AFFIRM the need for all church members, both heterosexual and homosexual, to study and understand sexuality and lifestyles in the light of the gospel.

Notes: *The United Church of Canada was formed in 1925 by the union of the Methodist Church, Canada, the Congregational Union of Canada, the Council of Local Union Churches, and the majority of the Presbyterian Church of Canada. This statement was adopted by the 30th General Council of the United Church of Canada in 1984. It reaffirms traditional Christian sexual morality while introducing a wholistic vision of human sexuality and affirming the virtue of the single life.*

UNITED CHURCH OF CHRIST

EXCERPT FROM "HUMAN SEXUALITY: A PRELIMINARY STUDY" (1977)

Preface

The United Church Board for Homeland Ministries was commissioned to do this study to fulfill the following vote of the 1975 General Synod of the United Church of Christ:

The United Church of Christ has not faced in depth the issue of human sexuality. Changing morality and ethics within American society present both problems and challenges to the church.

Therefore, the Tenth General Synod requests the Executive Council to commission a study concerning the dynamics of human sexuality and to recommend postures for the church.

One might ask, "What's a nice church like yours doing in an area like this?" Our history, our present concerns, and the pains and joys of people all direct us to see sexuality as a vital area of ministry.

The United Church of Christ traces its roots to

—the Reformation earthiness of Martin Luther;

—the concern for the common life of John Calvin;

—the authority-defying dissent and imprisonment of British Separatists in the sixteenth and seventeenth centuries;

—Pilgrims who sought a holy commonwealth in a new world;

—Anne Hutchinson who defended a woman's right to know and speak;

—Pennsylvania German men and women who covenanted to marry and to farm in mutuality;

—men and women who fought slavery and created schools for women and ministries where there were none, who fought for just laws, sexual equality, and the right of the young to know.

It is consistent with this denomination to see sexuality as part of the total human experience and to insist that questions of sexual justice are as important for Christians as matters of sexual expression. The United Church of Christ has a long history of concern for civil rights. It was the first denomination to ordain women. The Antoinette Brown Award is given in honor of the woman who, in 1853, broke the sex barrier in ministry.

This book is the product of a wide inquiry into the issues of human sexuality. In the early stages of the sexuality study, major efforts were given to definitional work. A variety of church groups offered their input. Minority caucuses, the Gay Caucus, and the Advisory Commission on Women in Church and Society of the United Church of Christ were invaluable.

A staff team worked in season and out to shape the study's directions and then its conclusions. They are a superb body of persons—insightful, dedicated, resourceful. . . .

The study team made some choices about where to put energies. These choices are reflected in the continuity and contents of this book. Our definition of sexuality is foundational. We begin with some of the contextual contours of sexuality today. Major concentration is given to biblical interpretation and some specific texts that provide guidance for an understanding of sexuality. . . .

We rejoice in the excellent response of the 1977 General Synod and hope this book will have wide use. We consider it a preliminary report and invite response to it through use of the feedback form in the study guide. We rejoice in our sexuality and in yours. A gracious, holy God has made that a special gift to the human community. We rejoice in our creation and in our Creator!

Edward A. Powers
Sexuality Study Administrator

Toward a Definition of Sexuality

One's sexuality involves the total sense of self as male and female, man and woman, as well as perceptions of what it is for others to be female and male. It includes attitudes about one's body and others' bodies. It expresses one's definition of gender identity. Sexuality is emotional, physical, cognitive, value-laden, and spiritual. Its dimensions are both personal and social.

A distinction should be made at the outset between sex and sexuality. Sex refers to the physical act of making love, to genital expression. "Sex is, in fact, only a small part of sexuality. . . . Sexuality is then, an integrated, individualized, unique expression of self."[1]

Sexuality is *emotional*. The infant person experiences what is later understood to be sexuality as it is fed and cuddled, in the sense of warmth or distance between bodies, in comfort or discomfort at wetness or dryness of body, in pleasurable sensations of one's own body. In the early years the child experiences bodily pleasure and discovers sensuality. With the coming of puberty boys and girls experience new awareness of their bodies, other persons, and related emotions. Throughout all of life sexuality deals with one's feelings about self and others, pain and pleasure, distance and closeness, love and hate, physical touching or restraint.

Sexuality is *physical*. It involves touching, physical closeness, and genital sexual expression. It is expressive of the desire for human contact and satisfaction of the need for closeness, intimacy, and physical pleasure. All five senses are involved in one's sexuality.

Sexuality is *cognitive*. Mental attitudes, self-understanding, analyses of human experience and relationships help express who and what persons are as sexual beings. One's understandings of genitalia, coitus, nakedness, other- and same-sex roles affect the body and its sexual expressions. Language is a key part of our sexuality both in naming bodily parts, physical acts, and our own experiences, and in communication with other persons.

Sexuality is *value-laden*. One's sense of the ought, the fitting, the possible, and the communal reflect value systems and ethical structures. Words and concepts such as justice, love, norm, should, and should not are ethical in character and central to a full understanding of sexuality. Values relate both to self-understanding and to expectations of others and of social structures. Values shape how and what persons communicate to one another. One's values determine approaches to honesty, fidelity, promise-keeping, truth-telling, and the purposes of sexual expression.

Sexuality is *spiritual*. The sexual act involves mutual self-giving. The spirit of one person relates deeply to the spirit of another. One chooses to relate to another and to oneself. There is a voluntary surrender of self to another through which a larger unity is achieved without the abridgement of freedom. Elements of transcendence, commitment, being in touch with another and with oneself are involved in one's sexuality and relationships to others as sexual beings. For Christians, sexuality is understood as the gift of God and as a dimension through which the love of God and neighbor is expressed.

Sexuality is *personal*. Each person is a sexual being on her or his own terms. In that sense one's sexuality is unique, one of a kind. "Our sexuality belongs first and foremost to us. It is pleasure we want to give and get. It is vital physical expression of attachments to other human beings. It is communication that is fun and playful, serious and passionate."[2]

Sexuality is *social*. It involves couples or partners. It has familial and community of caring contexts. Our sexuality has a bearing on the approach of such issues as war, economics, politics, or national priorities. It relates to such social policy questions as rape laws, equality of women and men in matters of employment, guidelines for genetic research, and abortion. It affects cultural understandings of socialization as male and female, the role of pornography, the meanings of marriage and community.

Sexuality is a central dimension of each person's selfhood, but it is not the whole of that selfhood. It is a critical component of each person's self-understanding and of how each relates to the world. . . .

Chapter 3: Faith, Ethics, and Sexuality

Psychologist Carl Jung said that when sexual questions were brought to him, they invariably turned out to be religious questions: religious questions that were brought to him always turned out to be sexual. The religious and sexual dimensions of our lives are deeply intertwined, whether we are conscious of that or not.

This chapter addresses five basic questions from a Christian perspective:

—What is the meaning of our sexuality?

—How and why do we experience alienation from our sexuality?

—How can we experience reconciliation with our sexuality?

—What goes into a decision about a sex-related issue?

—What are some principles for sexual morality?

What is the Meaning of our Sexuality?

Sexuality, while not the whole of our personhood, is very basic and permeates and affects our feelings, thoughts, and actions. Sexuality is our self-understanding and our way of being in the world as female and male. It includes attitudes about our own bodies and those of others. Because we are body-selves, sexuality constantly reminds us of our uniqueness and particularly: we look different and feel differently from any other person. Sexuality also is a sign and a symbol of our call to communication and communion with others. The mystery of our sexuality is the mystery of our need to reach out and embrace others, physically and spiritually. Sexuality expresses God's intention that we find our authentic humanness in relatedness to others.

Sexuality, then, involves much more than what we *do* with our genital organs. It is *who we are* as body-persons who experience the emotional, cognitive, and physical need for intimate communion with others. All persons are sexual beings. No matter if we happen to be children or aged, divorced or widowed, unmarried and/or celibate, physically handicapped or mentally retarded, we are still sexual (even if others find that fact difficult to understand).

Our religious beliefs are interwoven with the ways we experience ourselves and others sexually. What we as particular Christians believe about such basic religious beliefs as God's purpose in creating us as sexual beings, what we believe about human nature and destiny, about sin and salvation, about love and community will condition our sexual self-understanding. How we experience ourselves and others sexually will also affect what we believe in our Christian faith.

A summary of three basic themes from the Bible concerning sexuality is important at the beginning of our theological reflection. First, the Bible expresses the unity of the person and the goodness of our sexuality. God creates us as whole beings, not as divided beings or spirits to whom bodies are accidentally or temporarily attached. God creates us sexual and deems this an important dimension of the goodness of creation. ("Male and female [God] created them. . . . And God saw everything that [had been] made, and behold, it was very good [Gen. 1:27, 31].")

Second, sexual expression is intended to be both personal and social in its effects. Although they are that, sex acts are more than biological functions or release from tension. When biblical writers used the verb to know as a synonym for sexual intercourse ("Adam knew Eve his wife, and she conceived and bore Cain [Gen. 4:1]"), they understood that coitus can be a deeply personal way of knowing and communicating with another person. And if sexual expression can be deeply personal, by that very fact it also has social implications. Like all others, both early Hebrew and Christian communities found it necessary to regulate the forms of approved sexual expression, knowing that sexual acts have results for the wider community whether for good or ill.

Third, in our own lives we experience profound ambiguity and the Bible knows this. We know alienation as well as communion, bondage as well as freedom, death in the midst of life as well as unbounded life, brokenness as well as health. As an intrinsic dimension of personhood, sexuality participates in such ambiguity. The Bible reflects this ambiguity of human sexual experience. Its pages describe sexual oppression, rape, impersonal sex, and infidelity as well as accounts of joyous human fulfillment in wholesome sex.

The following statements could summarize the divinely intended *purposes* of human sexuality:

First, sexuality is a basic dimension of every human life and is intrinsic to who we are and who we are becoming. At times it may distort one's personality in profound ways, and yet sexuality is intended for our fulfillment and joyous human wholeness.

Second, sexuality expresses the human need and desire for communion. We are destined for communion with God and with one another. As an important form of communication, giving and receiving, sexuality is intended to enhance that communion.

Third, this communion can be described through Christian understandings of love. The basic moral issue surrounding any form of sexual expression, then, is to what degree and in what manner this act nurtures and sustains love-communion or in what way such expression inhibits or destroys it.

Our experience as sexual beings is mixed. Thus, we must look more closely at the experience of our sexuality in terms of Christian understandings of sin, judgment, and salvation.

How and Why do We Experience Alienation from our Sexuality?

Associations of sexuality with "sin" reflect common experience. Indeed, the very notion of sin has a distinctly sexual suggestion in the popular mind. The phrase "living in sin," for example, more quickly suggests one who has an improper sexual relationship than one who exploits the powerless or the poor. To be sure, there are numerous forms of sexual sin, such as the denial of women's full equality, impersonal and irresponsible genital sex, selfish and cruel sex acts. The sex-drenched appearance of our present culture is not so much an affirmation of full human sexuality as a flight from it through the quest for sexual sensation or performance technique. However, the basic form of sexual sin lies precisely in our alienation from our sexuality. Every dehumanizing sex act is linked with this more fundamental alienation.

At its root, sin always involves alienation in three directions: *separation from self, from neighbor* (meaning all creaturely companions), and *from God.* All three forms of separation are interwoven, but for the sake of understanding they will be considered one by one.

First, we experience alienation from the sexual dimension of our own selfhood. In such alienation we feel separated from our bodies. The body is experienced as "something I *have*" rather than as "something I *am.*" Sexuality is experienced as focused on the genitals more than diffused throughout selfhood and relationships. Sexuality becomes depersonalized, losing its character as the will-to-communion and becoming instead the anxious quest for pleasurable reassurance of worth as embodied self.

The experience of the alien body, however, takes its toll on the emotions and on the mind's patterns. The loss of being in touch (quite literally) with the body produces loss of touch with emotions. The results are fear of bodily feelings and inability to recognize many of them, the sense of shame about emotional expression, and perhaps the gnawing sense that in some deep but little understood way "I" am unacceptable.

Even conscious thought patterns are not immune from the influences of sexual self-alienation. Particularly for men in our society, this is often evidenced in competitive styles of thinking and communication that make hearing one another difficult, in the overemphasis upon rationality at the expense of feeling, in discomfort with cognitive ambiguity, which presses us to over-simplify things in terms of rigid categories.

Second, sexual alienation finds expression in our relationships with other people. We distance ourselves from others, fearful of letting in too much emotional and physical expression. Centuries of male sexism infect the interpersonal relations of both sexes. Men and women struggle with one another, often unconsciously in patterns of dominance and submission. Women frequently relate to other women with a competitiveness for male attention, which society has taught them is essential for their self-worth. Fear of sexual violence controls women's lives. Men find emotional intimacy and tenderness with other men a threat to the vigorous masculine, heterosexual self-image. Spouses find it difficult to talk honestly with each other about sexual needs and anxieties, and performance fears invade their love-making. Spouses become jealous and possessive of each other's bodies and selves, making affirmation difficult.

Sin is experienced as the betrayal of a covenant, the rupture of a vital relationship, the violation of an intimate bond. This brokenness brings with it a deep sense of guilt, which focuses upon the misuse of freedom, the freely chosen separation of persons from patterns of fidelity. Our alienation from others often results from the misuse of power that dehumanizes.

Sexual alienation is also expressed in the larger patterns of society and in the way humans relate to nature. We cannot adequately understand much of the world's organized violence without seeing its links to machismo, that hypermasculine image of power and toughness. We fail to understand white racism unless we recognize the history of the sexual exploitation of minority persons. We cannot fathom our ecological crisis unless we see how our alienated bodies are cut off from the organic sense of connectedness with nature and all that is earthy in God's creation.

Third, and most fundamentally, sinful alienation is separation from God. Some of our distorted religious and cultural influences have, sadly enough, convinced us that sexuality is a regrettable necessity in God's eyes and that our sexuality is an obstacle to our relationship with the divine. Believing this, we experience guilt for being sexual and having sexual desires. Moreover, we experience hostility toward God (then possibly guilt over the hostility) for God's alleged rejection of what is so much part of us. In our sexual alienation we fail to experience the divine immanence—God's presence infusing our embodied, creaturely world. Without a sense of God's presence in the flesh, we seek God only where it is "proper"—in transcendence, in aboveness and beyondness. Without immanence we lose touch with divine transcendence. (One wonders to what degree the accelerated flight of youth from our churches is linked to all of this. The God for whom our bodies are either evil or unreal is experienced as alienating and out of reach from our own intimate reality.)

How and why has all this happened? The individual histories of our alienation are as complex and varied as each person is unique. Nevertheless, there are some important and common threads within our experience. One thread goes back to the body-spirit dualism expressed in Greek philosophy and culture at the beginning of the Christian era. This dualism infected Christian understandings of the human self in ways that distorted the more wholistic view of the Old Testament (the body-spirit unity, the psychosomatic oneness of each person). For many Greeks, the immortal spirit was the temporary prisoner of a corruptible, mortal body. The good life consisted of escape from "the flesh" into the larger life of the spirit. Such a view was tempting for the early church, which was trying to cope with its surrounding culture—absorbing elements of Greek thought in order to interpret the new Christian message to the non-Jew, but also resisting the sexual distortions found among many non-Christians. Furthermore, the early church was waiting expectantly for the sudden coming of the new age. In this atmosphere the embodied and fleshly life of earth seemed insignificant or an impediment. Thus, the body-spirit dualism impacted Christian life and thought in lasting ways throughout the intervening centuries.

A second impetus to dualism was at least as important as the Greek influence. This was present within the Old Testament communities and in the early Christian church. The *subordination of women* was systematically present in the institutions, interpersonal relations, and religious life of patriarchal cultures. The alienation of mind from body, of reason from emotions, of nature from history, of the sacred from the secular, of higher life from fleshly life found cause and expression in the subordination of women to men. Men assumed their superiority in reason and spirit; hence, they assumed they were destined to lead the civil and the religious community. Women were identified with the traits of emotion, body, and sensuality. Their menstruation was labeled religiously unclean and a source of emotional instability. While men retained undisputed control, the life of the body, the emotions, and human sensuality became suspect (except for times of pleasurable escape), relegated to a lower order of existence and suppressed by those who aspired to the spiritual life.

The writings of the early church leaders were saturated with this dualism. The Greek type was there (Origen believed that original creation was entirely spiritual and sexless) as was the dualism inspired by male dominance (Tertullian called woman "the gate of perdition"). For a variety of reasons the greatest theologian of the early centuries, Augustine, was suspicious of human sexuality. He linked original sin causally with the lustful sex act that conceived the child. The development of the monastic movement in the medieval church fostered the cult of virginity, with its conviction that celibacy was a higher form of spiritual life than marriage. The Protestant Reformation and the subsequent puritan movement denied the special virtue of celibacy and brought new dignity to marriage. Yet, even there the deeply rooted suspicion of sexuality lingered. There was little recognition of the male sexism which sustained that suspicion and treated women unjustly, while depriving both sexes of their fullest personal development.

Since our histories are part of us, both for good and for ill, these influences of past centuries are far more than quaint relics of the past. They have become part of who we are.

How Can We Experience Reconciliation with Our Sexuality?

At the root of our alienation is *fear*. Thus, a simple intellectual understanding of the problem and its history cannot release us into fuller life. But the Christian gospel does not announce "salvation by correct understanding." Rather, it announces reconciliation by the gracious power of God, experienced through Jesus Christ and received by human openness and trust. Life's renewal is given many different Christian terms: salvation, redemption, reconciliation, and resurrection. But by whatever name it is called, this renewal experience, like that of estrangement, separation, and sin, is three-dimensional. *God, neighbor,* and *self* are all experienced in mysterious interdependency and harmony.

Resurrection of the body-self is always a miracle, although it is usually experienced through the common and everyday stuff of human relationship and event. We recognize that the source of power is beyond ours. It is the mysterious creativity of life itself. God's power in our midst. We experience the miracle that in God's incarnation in Jesus Christ our own bodies are affirmed. The miracle of recognition occurs in the midst of our disunity. In the midst of our sexual self-rejection we are totally accepted. We are accepted in all dimensions of our sexuality—in our masculinity and in our femininity, in our heterosexuality and in our homosexuality.

Frequently, we are conscious that this experience of bodily acceptance is God's gift through human relationships. With the assistance of modern psychology in the psychosexual development of the child, we are aware of the importance of physical holding, breast feeding, sensitive toilet training, comfortable and appropriate sex education. The child who is given a sense of the trustworthiness and goodness of her or his own body, rather than a legacy of shame and bodily rejection, receives a gift of grace. The same gift can be received by adults when one person is loved into a new self-acceptance by another. And we can experience grace through human agency in the pain of struggle and judgment. In our own time the women's movement has made it possible for many women to experience a new life of self-respect and intellect and a sense of power born of openness to their own pain and possibilities. Likewise, the movement has been a gift of grace to many men, who, through women's judgment upon their stereotyped masculinity and through their own self-awareness, have experienced new depths of self-acceptance in body and emotion.

So the self experiences resurrection of the body in the realization of unity. The "I" really is one person. Body and mind are more united. My body is me, just as my mind is me. At the same time I discover that I belong intimately to others and to the world.

To be sure, the experience of such acceptance is never once-and-for-all. Nor is it experienced completely. Yet, it is real, and such moments of grace are often followed by periods of growth in this newness. Four terms might illustrate such growth: *freedom, sensuousness, love,* and *androgyny.*

Psychologists studying the sexual lives of persons who display healthy self-acceptance and who know they are loved, point to a variety of ways these persons experience *freedom.* Such persons enjoy genital acts with greater intensity than the average person, and yet specific sex acts are not central to their philosophies of life. They can experience sex acts with a freer and broader range of emotions—from sheer playfulness and eroticism to mystical ecstasy. There is a freer acceptance of their own sexuality and that of others, and yet there is greater faithfulness and integrity in marriage. There is an unusual degree of affirmation of the partner's individuality, an eagerness for the freeing growth of the other.

Two important Christian insights concerning the nature of freedom in Christ are suggested by these descriptions. One is the freedom from works righteousness—freedom from the belief that our basic worth is in what we do and is our release into the freedom of being what we *are*. Indeed, the sexual relationship is always trivialized when it becomes a performance or an expression of technique devised to prove the expertise of the lover. Furthermore, true freedom is experienced in the paradox of commitment, which means that genuine sexual freedom is found in the creative tensions between spontaneity and discipline, between responsiveness and responsibility.

Sensuousness, another mark of growth, should be distinguished from sensuality. Sensuality, in fact, is a rejection of the body, for here the body is understood as an object, a tool, driven by ego needs to seek pleasures. Ironically, the libertine, who is driven to an increasingly varied diet of sex experiences, is similar to the ascetic, who renounces sexuality: both are alienated from the body, which they treat as an object. In authentic sensuousness we experience the rhythms of the body. We are in full tune with it. We are open to its joys and pains, its stresses and delights. In short, the body mediates the spirit.

The possibility of increased sensuousness seems to lie in the possibility of "letting go," and the capacity to let go, to relax, and to trust seems, in turn, to be linked to the experience of grace. Our bodies are, in some sense, the temple of God. If I really sense that I am totally accepted, then I can let go and trust my body-self in a new way. Just as the highest states of physical pleasure and emotional delight are possible only when we can let go, so also sensuousness, in general, is the experience of those who can trust—in grace, acceptance, and mutuality. And in this experience our sexuality seems to expand beyond a narrow genital focus, infusing the entire body with feeling and pleasure and thus giving a new warmth to all our relationships. Such might be the experience of new sensuousness.

The integration of *love* with sex is another indication of growth in the resurrection of the body. Such integration is never automatic. Some persons still see sexual intercourse primarily as the means of procreation. Others see it primarily as a means of pleasure. Both procreation and pleasure are important considerations but should not be seen in isolation. Personal communication and intimate communion result from the fullest self-giving of one to another as sex becomes a dimension of love.

This possibility is not simply a matter of romance, of being in love—grand as this is. It is more basically a capacity of self-giving that rests upon one's security in having been and being loved. One who is fundamentally unsure of his or her own worth and thus is anxious about receiving the partner's approval can never be free enough to really love in and through sexual activity. But once again, such security, such assurance of self-worth is a gift of grace, bringing the real possibility of that psychic intimacy, which is loving sex.

Androgyny is the fourth theme that illustrates the resurrection of our body-selves. Literally, the word means the union of the male (*andro*) and the female (*gyne*) in one human personality. More accurately, however, the term means the blending of those personality characteristics that traditionally have been thought of as masculine with those traditionally labeled feminine. Characteristics such as autonomous and dependent, rational and emotional, initiating and nurturing, cognitive and intuitive, assertive and receptive are thought to be gender-related. While contemporary research has cast immense doubt on the notion that such traits are biologically determined or are only appropriate to one gender, and while such qualities seem to a large extent to be culturally shaped, stereotypes like these persist. But for each individual's personality to achieve full development requires both sets of traits.

In addition to the possibility of fuller development of our own unique personalities beyond the confines of gender stereotypes, there are numerous benefits that can occur as a fuller humanity is more widely experienced. Greater justice for women certainly is one. Another is the release of men from their harmfully exaggerated masculine stereotypes for social relationships, resulting in less violence and exploitation in institutional life. Interpersonally, androgyny offers the promise of closer friendships with persons of the same sex, since women's competing with one another for masculine approval and men's shielding their deepest needs from one another are both diminished. And, surprisingly enough, the capacity for heterosexual love seems richer between androgynous women and men. When dominance and submission are removed from a couple's relationship, when aggression subsides, each partner is able to discover in the other an intimate friend. (Isn't it surprising and saddening how many husbands and wives do not know each other as genuine friends?) Beyond stereotyped sex roles, each partner is able to identify more fully with the other and thus is able to discover the other as a sexual person.

An increase in androgyny depends in considerable measure upon institutional change: changes in sex-role images conveyed by the mass media, changes in the ways major institutions treat the two sexes, changes in laws and public policies. Yet, change within the self is not totally dependent upon what happens "out there." Basically, we do not have to *become* androgynous, for we already *are*. We simply need to accept the power to be what we essentially are—unique individuals, female and male, each with the capacity to be firm and tender, receiving and giving, rational and intuitive, like a skillful duet in which two instruments blend into a harmonious oneness. In Christian faith the power of God's grace frees us to be what we essentially are. And this makes sense in daily experience: the capacity to be an authentic individual and to move beyond conventional gender stereotypes is the capacity only of those who truly know their own self-worth, who accept their acceptance. . . .

What Are Some Principles for Sexual Morality?

If sexuality is intrinsic to every human being, if sexuality expresses our desire for communion, and if the name of that communion is love, what, then, is love?

Three ancient Greek words for love can point us to its several dimensions: *Eros* (sensual attraction and desire for fulfillment). *Philia* (friendship and mutual affection), and *Agápe* (self-giving and other-regarding love). Authentic sexual love is multidimensional and involves all of these. It is attraction to another and the desire for sexual and personal fulfillment in and through the other. It is friendship and mutuality based upon an affectionate community of concern and shared interests. It is the desire to give to another out of the fullness of one's own personality and the willingness to receive from the depths of the other to whom one is committed in a close, trusting, faithful relationship. Love cannot be fully understood apart from its dimension of justice. Love without justice is only shallow sentimentality. Justice divorced from love cannot accurately be called justice. It is, rather, a balance of power relationships. Love, in expressing its dimension of justice, becomes concerned for power, but it is the empowerment of those who are in any way oppressed so that they have rightful access to the means for human fulfillment. Love with its justice dimension becomes our ongoing struggle for love's fullest possible expression in human relationships. This concern applies to ourselves and to our loved one, to the smallest communities and to the larger groups and institutions of our common life.

An attempt to express love's principles for guidance in specific questions of physical-emotional sexual expression would at least include these:

1. *Love's justice requires a single standard* rather than a double standard. This should mean that there is not one ethic for males and another for females, one for the unmarried and another for the married, one for the young and another for the old, nor one for those who are heterosexually oriented and another for those oriented toward their same sex. The same basic considerations of love ought to apply to all.

2. *The physical expression* of one's sexuality in relation to another ought to be *appropriate to the level of loving commitment* in the relationship. Human relationships exist on a continuum—from the fleeting and casual to the lasting and intense, from the relatively impersonal to the deeply personal. Physical expressions also exist on a continuum—from varied types of eye contact and casual touches to varied forms of embraces and kisses, to bodily caresses and genital petting, to foreplay and genital intercourse. In some way or another we inevitably express our sexuality in every relationship. The

morality of that expression, particularly its more physical expression, will depend upon its appropriateness to the shared level of commitment and the nature of the relationship.

3. *Genital sexual expression* ought to be evaluated in terms of the basic elements of a moral decision, informed by love:

Motive (why should I, or why shouldn't I, do this?): Each genital act should be motivated by love. This means love for one's partner. It also means a healthy love of oneself. Infusing both of those loves is love for God, whose good gift of sexuality is an invitation to communion.

Intention (*what* am I aiming at in this act?) Each genital act should aim at human fulfillment and wholeness, God's loving intentions for all persons. In marriage the procreation of children may at certain times be the intent of intercourse, but statistically those times will be in a small minority, and even then the desire for children is part of our quest for wholeness, for wholeness is known in relationships. Fulfillment also requires sexual pleasure. Good genital sex is highly erotic, warm, intimate, playful, and immensely pleasurable. At times it can also be almost mystical in its possibilities of communication and communion. In each of these ways it can contribute to wholeness— a deep sense of being at one with oneself, with the other, and with God.

The Act (are certain sexual acts intrinsically right and good and certain others inherently wrong and bad?): It is difficult to label whole classes of acts as inherently right or wrong, since the moral quality of any act hinges so heavily upon what is being communicated by it in the particular context. What are our intentions and what are their effects? We can surely say that sexual acts that are characterized by loving motives and intentions will exclude all acts that are coercive, debasing, harmful, or cruel to another.

Consequences (what will most likely result from this act, and in what ways will I be willingly accountable?): Responsibility for the results of a sexual act is a mark of love. This involves responsibility to the ongoing relationship, its commitments, and its promises. It means responsibility to the partner's emotional health insofar as that is linked with a given sexual act. If a child is conceived and born, it means responsibility for nurture. Responsibility also means that this particular act must be weighed in terms of its effect on the well-being of the wider human community. Will it endanger the love and justice by which communities must exist?

The above principles of sexual love or principles like them may well be sufficient moral guidance for some Christians. Others will find it important to elaborate more specific rules of sexual love. For example, many would insist that one crucial rule for genital intercourse is that it be confined to the permanently intended covenantal union. Others would agree with the rule but would permit exceptions. Whatever option is chosen, we need to remember that rules by themselves can never create love. They can protect persons at those boundaries of our experience where we express the still alienated dimensions of selfhood in exploitive and hurtful ways. However rules are used, they should nurture and strengthen our growth and that of others into Christian maturity and responsible freedom, not inhibit it.

Because we are not utterly whole persons, at times we will express our unhealed lives in sexual ways that hurt others and ourselves. And because our sexual socialization has been so surrounded by misinformation, fear, and guilt, these will mar our sexual expression. In our sexuality the final word of the gospel is always the word of gracious love: forgiveness, acceptance, empowerment for new life. The Word was made flesh and our flesh is confirmed. God is present and at work in all sexual loving. And God's promise is that we might yet become more joyously at one with our sexuality and thus more fully at one with life itself. . . .

The Family and Human Sexuality

Toward the end of our study, it became clear that major reforms in marriage, divorce, and child custody laws would be needed if we were to move toward a more just and humane society. We also became aware that many of society's institutions work against the stability of the nuclear family and against any acceptance of the validity of long-term living arrangements not formalized as legal marriage. We did not feel prepared to suggest very specific alterations in family law, but we do propose that the following two areas need to be closely examined.

The De Facto Family

For most practical purposes the only legally protected form of family is that consisting of parents (preferably two) and the children they have borne or adopted since their marriage. Obviously, there are many persons today who live together under relatively stable, but informal, conditions. Some of these individuals live communally; others in situations that closely resemble a marital arrangement. Historically, persons who lived together for lengthy periods were considered to be involved in common law marriages, which, in theory, created the same kind of contractual obligations as a more formal marriage. This concept and a number of other judicial fictions are practiced somewhat today, but generally only when they are required to prevent gross injustice to women and/or children who have been part of a stable relationship but who find themselves needing some ''proof'' of that relationship. This can occur when a woman wishes to bring suit for the wrongful death of the man she has been living with, when she seeks workman's compensation, or when she seeks social security benefits. There is, therefore, in many states a way to ''create'' a marriage when it is expeditious to do so.

Insofar as the state has legitimate interests in the regulation of marriage (health, protection of young children and dependent spouses, and inheritance, for example), it should pursue these in the regulation of nontraditional living arrangements. However, we feel the need for the church to explore more critically the policies that limit or preclude the existence of nontraditional, yet relatively stable, living arrangements. For example, local communities can restrict, through zoning, the number of persons unrelated by blood or marriage who can live in the same house. Similarly, the multiple parenting of children (as in Israel's kibbutzim) and the idea of having children ''exchanged'' between sets of parents so that they can gain a variety of life experiences are hampered by present social and legal restrictions.

Pressures on the Family

The fact that over a third of the marriages end in divorce is itself a comment on the growing instability in traditional ideas about marital commitments. The statistics, however, do not begin to measure the trauma that divorces present to the parties directly involved and to their children. Family counselors, frequently visited by the more affluent who are considering divorce, no longer try to keep marriages together at any cost but recognize that sometimes the best counseling for all the people involved is to work to make the separation hurt as little as possible. Regrettably, such counseling is not presently accessible to all who could benefit by it.

In most states specific grounds for divorce are still required: one party must become vilified as mentally cruel, adulterous, or a host of other labels, while the other is exonerated. As early as 1967 the National Conference of Commissioners on Uniform State Laws urged a movement toward a ''breakdown of marriage'' perspective, where the proof of a ''breakdown'' is no more than the fact of a separation for a specific length of time. No one has to prove something terrible about the other party, not even incompatibility, and one partner can initiate the separation simply by moving out. To the argument that this makes marital dissolution too easy, sociologist Jessie Bernard says, ''But if one party is adamant in his or her insistence on divorce, the marriage has actually broken down; living together under legal duress does not reconstitute the marriage. The no-fault divorce recognizes this bitter reality.'' When these no-fault cases are heard in court, they are a motion ''in the interest of the Jones family'' and not as ''Mary Jones versus John Jones.''[96]

This approach leaves major questions open concerning the protection of the children and the nonworking spouse. There are several possibilities. A task force of the Citizens' Advisory Council on the Status of Women looked at property distribution systems in other countries. In West Germany, for example, after certain kinds of property were removed from the total (that owned before the marriage, gifts, and inheritances), the remaining estate was divided equally. Another system, which also replaces the combination of alimony and child support payments now in existence, would be a monthly cash payment to the parent who is keeping the children by the other party (assuming that he/she is working steadily) in recognition that raising children means that they must be supported and that the newly single parent-guardian must be maintained properly as well.

Under these newer schemes, child custody is viewed in a new way. In close to 90 percent of the cases the child is now given to the woman, under the presumption that she will be a better parent. The reality that follows is that the father ends up seeing less and less of the child. Reform systems recognize that neither parent should be presumed, merely by sex, to be the best for the child, but that a nonadversary method should be designed that will, among other things, take into serious account the wishes of the child. As with no-fault divorce, this system would not require that a father prove that his wife is unfit before he could realistically have a chance to gain custody, which is now the case in many states.

Toward Humane Public Policy

The analyses of selected public policy issues presented in this chapter rest upon the conviction that sexuality has to do with the quality of life of the whole community and that this is the serious business of Christians. Many present public policies came into being in an earlier time under church influence or religious values (including some of the most repressive and dehumanizing ones).

On the one hand, the efforts of individuals and of church bodies in the public arena are directed toward healing the brokenness in human relationships and being the advocate for the defenseless, the uninformed, and the victimized.

On the other hand, our approach is toward affirmative action—creating a humane social order, strengthening relationships of fidelity and caring, establishing structures of sexual justice.

The Christian's mandate in the search for justice is given in Jesus' reading of Isiah as he entered the synagogue in Nazareth:

> The Spirit of the Lord is upon me,
> because [God] has anointed me to preach good news to the poor.
> [God] has sent me to proclaim release to the captives
> and recovering of sight to the blind.

—Luke 4:18

Endnotes

1. Eleanor S. Morrison and Vera Borosage, eds., *Hamar Sexuality: Contemporary Perspectives* (Palo Alto, CA: Mayfield Publishing Co., 1973), pp. lx.f.

2. The Boston Women's Health Collective, *Our Bodies, Ourselves* (Rev. ed., New York: Simon & Schuster, 1976), p. 38.

Notes: *The United Church of Christ was formed in 1957 by the merger of the Congregational-Christian Churches and the Evangelical and Reformed Church. The two uniting bodies were themselves products of mergers in the early twentieth century. This preliminary study, which calls for a positive and wholistic approach to sexuality and also for radical changes in the United Church of Christ's traditional approach to sexuality (e.g. allowing pre-and post-marital coitus and the acceptance of homosexual couples), was received and* *remanded to the local congregations for further study and discussion by the Eleventh General Synod of the United Church of Christ in 1977.*

UNITED CHURCH OF CHRIST

RESOLUTION ON "HUMAN SEXUALITY: A PRELIMINARY STUDY" (1977)

Recommendations in Regard to the Human Sexuality Study

Adopted by the Eleventh General Synod, United Church of Christ
Washington, D.C., July 1 - 5, 1977
VOTE: 409 Yes; 210 No (66% - 34%)

RESOLVED that the Eleventh General Synod of the United Church of Christ:

1. Receives the report, "Human Sexuality: A Preliminary Study" with appreciation, and commends it to the congregations, Associations, Conferences, and Instrumentalities of the United Church of Christ for study and response.

2. Reaffirms the present important ministries throughout the United Church of Christ and recommends the development of new liturgies, theology, and counseling services which enable the full participation and sharing of gifts of all persons: children, youth, older persons, nuclear families, those who live alone, or choose other lifestyles.

3. Calls upon the United Church Board for Homeland Ministries to continue to provide leadership in developing resources concerning human sexuality for appropriate use by various age groups in local churches and to provide consultative services and training for Conferences, Associations, and congregations who wish to sponsor programs concerned with human sexuality and family life.

4. Requests the UCC-related seminaries, Conferences, and Instrumentalities to continue developing courses and resources through which clergy, seminary students, and laity may be prepared to minister in the area of human sexuality and to address related public policy issues.

5. Urges pastors, members, congregations, Conferences and Instrumentalities to support programs in which information about human sexuality can be made available through such major American institutions as elementary and secondary education, adult education, social welfare agencies, medical services, and the communication media.

6. Encourages the congregations of the United Church of Christ, assisted by Conferences and Instrumentalities, to study and experiment with liturgical rites to celebrate important events and passages in human experience (transitions, anniversaries, separations, and reunions) and relationships of commitment between persons. The Office for Church Life and Leadership and the Board for Homeland Ministries are asked to facilitate the sharing of such liturgical experience.

7. Calls upon the Board for Homeland Ministries, the Commission for Racial Justice, the Office of Communication, and the Conferences to develop and share model programs that can help local churches minister to and educate their communities about the components of sexual violence, including rape, marital violence, child abuse, abusive medical practices and domination and submission images in the media of relationships between women and men portrayed as exclusive expressions of human interaction.

8. Calls upon pastors, congregations, Conferences and Instrumentalities to address, in their own programs and in those of public and private agencies, the concerns for sexuality and lifestyle of persons who have physical or emotional handicaps, or who are retarded, elderly, or terminally ill. Because of its faithful ministry through care of

the young, handicapped, retarded and aged, we urge the Council for Health and Welfare Services to encourage administrators and staff of members institutions to respect the needs for intimacy of adult persons served, and protect their rights of sexual expression as important to self-worth, affirmation of life, and avoidance of isolation.

9. Urges the Board for Homeland Ministries, the Commission for Racial Justice and the Office for Church in Society to work for the protection of persons threatened by coercive use of sterilization, medical treatment, experimental research, or the withholding of medical information, and to fully inform these persons of their rights under the law.

10. Calls upon pastors, members, congregations, Conferences and Instrumentalities to encourage the extension of contraceptive information and services by both public and private agencies for all youth and adults as instrumental in preventing undesirable pregnancies and fostering responsible family planning.

11. Affirms the right of women to freedom of choice with regard to pregnancy expressed by the Eighth General Synod and interpreted as a Constitutional right in the January 22, 1973 decisions of the Supreme Court which remove the legal restrictions on medical termination of pregnancy through the second trimester. Pastors, members, congregations, Conferences, Instrumentalities and agencies are urged to resist in local communities or in legislative halls attempts to erode or negate the 1973 decisions of the court and to respect and protect the First Amendment rights to differences of opinion and freedom from intimidation concerning the issue of abortion.

Deplores the June 20, 1977 decision of the U.S. Supreme Court and recent actions of the U.S. Congress that effectually deprive the poor of their Constitutional rights of choice to end or complete a pregnancy, while leaving the well-to-do in the full employment of such rights.

Calls upon UCC members, congregations, Associations, Conferences and Instrumentalities to assure that publicly supported hospitals provide medical services to women within their usual service area to exercise their Constitutional right to end or complete pregnancies; and to petition their State legislatures and the U.S. Congress to assure that the poor will be provided with medical services to exercise their Constitutional rights to end or complete pregnancies.

12. Calls upon Instrumentalities to address the economic structures which victimize women (and men) and explore such strategies as compensation for housework and child care, Social Security for homemakers, programs for displaced homemakers, insurance benefits for pregnancies, and quality day care.

13. Affirms the wide public attention being given to issues related to sexuality and sex roles, particularly as they affect women, but expresses concern regarding the need to explore such issues as they affect men. The Eleventh General Synod urges the Board for Homeland Ministries, the Office for Church Life and Leadership, Conferences, Associations, and congregations to develop programs which take into account the needs, experiences and viewpoints of both males and females, and which encourage further understanding of sexual identity; the effects of sex role stereotyping and present economic, legal, political, and other societal conditions based upon gender.

14. Recommends to all Instrumentalities, agencies, Conferences, Associations, and congregations that language they use reflect both feminine and masculine metaphor about God, and draw upon the diverse metaphor of God represented in the Bible, in the Christian tradition and in contemporary experience.

15. Recognizes that diversity exists within the UCC about the meaning of ordination, the criteria for effective ministry, and the relevance of marital status, affectional or sexual preference or lifestyle to ordination and performance of ministry. It requests the congregations, Associations, and Conferences to address these issues seeking more

full and common understanding of their implications. It requests that Office for Church Life and Leadership to develop resources to facilitate such understanding.

16. Urges congregations, Associations, Conferences, and Instrumentalities to work for the decriminalization of private sexual acts between consenting adults.

17. Urges that States legislatively recognize that traditional marriage is not the only stable living unit which is entitled to legal protection in regards to socio-economic rights and responsibilities.

18. Deplores and condemns the dehumanizing portrayals of women and men, the abuse of children, and the exploitation of sex in printed and electronic media of communication, recognizes the rights of adults to access to sexually explicit materials, and affirms that efforts toward change must recognize First Amendment principles.

Notes: *This resolution was adopted by the Eleventh General Synod of the United Church of Christ in 1977 after a prolonged and heated debate. It accepts and remands the controversial "Human Sexuality: A Preliminary Study" to its congregations, associations, and state, regional, and national agencies for further study and reporting. It also calls upon the congregations, leaders, and agencies of the United Church of Christ to institute education programs on sexuality, to develop experimental liturgical rites to celebrate the life cycle, and to address such issues as sex education in the schools, family and sexual violence, the exploitation of sex in the mass media, equal rights for women, and other topics.*

UNITED CHURCH OF CHRIST

MINORITY RESOLUTION ON "HUMAN SEXUALITY: A PRELIMINARY STUDY" (1977)

The Minority Resolution Recognized by the Eleventh General Synod

Whereas 34% of the delegates to the Eleventh General Synod voted negatively on "Recommendations in Regard to Human Sexuality Study"; and

Whereas "Human Sexuality: A Preliminary Study," the foundation for these Recommendations, was preliminary in nature; and

Whereas the Executive Council sent the Study to the Eleventh General Synod without recommendation, and sent it to delegates too late for sufficient time for study; and

Whereas we feel it is important that local churches have opportunity to examine, discuss, and respond to the Study; and

Whereas it appears there is a limited theological, biblical, and ethical viewpoint reflected in the Study which does not characterize the diverse perspectives of the United Church of Christ; and

Whereas there is a diversity of sociological and psychological perspectives not reflected in the Study; and

Whereas we appreciate the opportunity to engage in significant theological and ethical discussion; and appreciate the work done by those involved in preparing the Study to open this dialogue;

Therefore be it resolved:

1. We call upon the local churches, Associations, and Conferences of the United Church of Christ to examine and discuss the Study and, prior to the Twelfth General Synod, respond to the Study through their Conference structures;

2. We call upon the local churches, Associations, and Conferences to seek study materials on the subject reflecting biblical, theological, and ethical perspectives not reflected in the Study;

3. The minority resolution be included in the study guide prepared by the United Church Board For Homeland Ministries and wherever the eighteen recommendations of the Eleventh General Synod are reported.

Notes: *This minority resolution on "Human Sexuality: A Preliminary Study" was recognized but not adopted by the Eleventh General Synod of the United Church of Christ in 1977. It calls for the members and agencies of the United Church to examine, discuss and respond to the study from the more traditional biblical, theological, and ethical perspectives not represented in the report. Those who proposed the resolution took an active role in the formation of United Church People for Biblical Witness (see index), an organization dedicated to maintaining a conservative theological and ethical approach to sexuality within the United Church of Christ.*

UNITED CHURCH OF CHRIST

RESOLUTION ON SEXUAL HARASSMENT IN THE CHURCH—NO LONGER NAMELESS (1989)

Sexual Harassment in the Church—No Longer Nameless

Background

Sexual harassment has long been considered a hidden problem - one with no name - in all of society and in the church. Particularly in the church, there has been a pattern of denial of the existence of such a problem. That has begun to change somewhat in the past two decades. What was once ignored, denied, tolerated or trivialized as mere flirtation or harmless attention is now illegal as well as unacceptable under federal gender discrimination regulations in many business, industry, education and other public sector settings. In 1986 the Supreme Court declared sexual harassment a form of sex discrimination, and increased public awareness of the issue.

Sexual harassment can and does occur in every setting of the church; a startling and disappointing fact in the institution that is based on values of equality and respect for all persons. The Coordinating Center for Women (CCW) in its 1986 research project on the status of women in church and society learned that sexual harassment is a problem in the church. In response to the question "What is your experience with sexual harassment in the work place?" 25% of lay women reported sexual harassment in the workplace; 45% of clergywomen reported having had that experience. No men responded to the survey, clergy or lay, recorded having experienced such discrimination.

Even if women are unable or unwilling to name a behavior as sexual harassment, their sharing of experiences inside and outside the church describes and documents the experience. The clergywomen's network, women in seminary settings, women employed by the church and women who participate in the volunteer life of the church report a variety of experiences of sexual harassment in the church. There are two types of sexual harassment:

The first is characterized by the imposition of unwelcome sexual activity, suggestion, or behavior in a relationship of unequal power, i.e. pastor/parishioner; counselor/client; doctor/patient; instructor/student; senior minister/associate; manager/support staff; etc.

The second type of harassment is that which creates a hostile, intimidating or offensive atmosphere in the workplace, even in the absence of direct damage to victims.

Some examples of actions which may constitute either type of sexual harassment:

- unnecessary or unwanted touching, patting or contact with a person's body;
- deliberate assaults, molestation;
- demanding or suggesting sexual favors as a condition for favorable treatment or for employment;
- behavior patterns which include frequent and unwanted comments, jokes or suggestions of a sexual nature, particularly out of context, or when accompanied by the other behaviors described.

Both clergy and laity may be victims of this unprofessional behavior from clergy as well as victims of inappropriate behavior directed toward them by lay persons. The UCC must deal with this issue as one for both the church as workplace and the church as faith community and pastoral support systems.

WHEREAS, all sexual relationships which breach Christian ethics are particularly troubling in the church as they profoundly affect pastor/parish relationships, educational and employment issues, as well as questions of morality and ethics; and

WHEREAS, the church as employer has a responsibility to its employees to maintain a workplace free from the degrading and dehumanizing effects of sexual harassment;

THEREFORE, BE IT RESOLVED, the 17th General Synod of the UCC requests the CCW, in cooperation with the Network for United Church of Christ Clergywomen, United Church Board for Homeland Ministries, Office for Church In Society, Office for Church Life and Leadership and United Church Board for World Ministries to develop for consideration by General Synod Eighteen a pronouncement and proposal for action including an educational program to focus the attention of the whole church on the issue of Christian ethics dealing with sexual harassment and abuse within pastoral, professional and personal relationships in the church. Problems which must be addressed include misconduct of clergy and other church professionals vis-a-vis parishioners, clients, staff colleagues, interns or students involving sexual harassment and abuse;

BE IT FURTHER RESOLVED, the 17th General Synod calls on the whole church to learn to recognize sexual harassment and its implications;

BE IT FURTHER RESOLVED, the 17th General Synod calls upon all local churches, Church and Ministry committees of Associations and Conferences, national agencies and Instrumentalities, seminaries and other institutions to become aware of sexual harassment within their jurisdictions and to develop ways to put it to an end.

Notes: *This resolution adopted by the Seventeenth General Synod of the United Church of Christ is one illustration of how the church has assumed a leading role in detecting, uncovering, and correcting the serious but usually unnoticed and unattended problem of sexual harassment within the church.*

UNITED CHURCH OF CHRIST

RESOLUTION ON INCLUSIVE LANGUAGE (1989)

WHEREAS, the use of inclusive language for God is a theological issue, important to the wholeness and well-being of the entire Church; and

WHEREAS, prayerful and discerning study of God's Word is essential to the mission and integrity of the United Church of Christ; and

WHEREAS, the UCC seeks an approach to the scriptures that is faithful to the original texts, responsive to our traditions, to contemporary needs and to the diversity present in our life together; and

WHEREAS, the rich variety of images of God in the Scriptures is a gift to the Church, entrusted to us for the articulation of our faith under the guidance of the Holy Spirit; and

WHEREAS, past General Synods have affirmed the significance of inclusive language and the importance of genuine dialogue in which members of the Church are sensitive to one another's burdens and share a common hope; and

WHEREAS, nevertheless, the way in which inclusive language is sometimes employed or ignored in the Church gives birth to pain or a sense of loss among us;

THEREFORE, BE IT RESOLVED, the 17th General Synod of the UCC affirms the importance of continuing study of inclusive language and updating of the "Inclusive Language Guidelines," marked by careful scholarship, theological vitality and an openness to Biblical interpretation and faith language that may include new and renewed understandings of ancient texts;

BE IT FURTHER RESOLVED, the 17th General Synod invites the Office for Church Life and Leadership (OCLL) to guide this theological endeavor and to accept responsibility for it (in such a way that the seminaries, Conferences, local congregations and Instrumentalities of the UCC be asked to engage together in this vital task during the biennium 1989-91), offering a progress report to General Synod 18, and that OCLL disseminate during the next biennium, in conversation with the seminaries, Conferences, local churches and Instrumentalities, educational resources and materials that address the hopes and promise, as well as the questions and reservations present in the midst of discussions of inclusive language and the nature of authoritative texts;

BE IT FURTHER RESOLVED the 17th General Synod urges that, in this interim period (1989-91), all who publicly use the Bible and other selected Biblical resources identify the version of Scripture or source of quotation, and that the recognized and established Instrumentalities continue to identify the version of Scripture or source of re-written or paraphrased material used in all resources and written materials;

BE IT FURTHER RESOLVED, the 17th General Synod recognizes that the responsibility for the use of inclusive language in worship, in the writing of material for publication or other public use of the Bible continues to rest with the person in leadership.

Such responsibility includes: 1) Choosing from among existing or emerging translations by scholars from credible Greek, Hebrew and Aramaic texts, and 2) choosing from among Biblical paraphrases, lectionaries and other selected Biblical resources that identify the grace of God in relation to the realities and concerns of contemporary life;

BE IT FURTHER RESOLVED, the 17th General Synod recognizes that genuine, open and honest discussion on important issues such as inclusive language and the Trinitarian formula involves the gift of trust and represents not a burden but an opportunity and a challenge for the Church. The 17th General Synod also urges that this task be undertaken in faith, hope and love, with a sense of gratitude for the unity we share as companions of our Savior Jesus Christ, who breaks down the dividing wall of hostility and summons us to a costly and joyful discipleship. The Word of God remains a lamp to our feet and a light to our path!

Notes: *This resolution adopted by the Seventeenth General Synod of the United Church of Christ in 1989 illustrates how the United Church of Christ has taken a leading role in extending the call for equal rights for women to the arena of language, including scriptural and liturgical language. It recognizes the variety of male and female metaphors and images used to describe God in the Bible and calls upon churches to follow the Bible's practice.*

UNITED CHURCH PEOPLE FOR BIBLICAL WITNESS

POLICY STATEMENT (1978)

United Church People for Biblical Witness, formed out of the minority caucus of GS 11 in response to the United Church of Christ Preliminary Human Sexuality Study, intends:

1. to promote renewal of the church, faithfulness to our reformation heritage, and obedience to the authority of "the Scriptures of the Old and New Testaments . . . as the rule of Christian faith and practice" (Service of Ordination);

2. to provide study materials on human sexuality issues reflecting biblical, theological, ethical, psychological, and sociological perspectives not reflected in the UCC preliminary study;

3. to encourage genuine dialogue and debate within the United Church of Christ on the issues of the Human Sexuality Study with fairess to all points of view;

4. to lift up the family as the fundamental unit of human society while affirming the special contributions that single persons can make in our church and society;

5. to remind the church that the eighteen Recommendations in Regard to Human Sexuality adopted by the Eleventh General Synod, July, 1977, created the basis for implementation and action and that the intent of these recommendations needs to be clarified before the church takes further action upon them;

6. to uphold a faithful biblical standard of ethical morality in all areas for clergy and lay people in the church;

7. to deal specifically with issues of homosexuality:

   a. to advocate the rejection of proposals for ordaining practicing homosexual persons and for church recognition of homosexual unions;

   b. to encourage ministries of compassion, healing and justice for homosexual persons (and all sexually disordered persons);

   c. to affirm the civil rights of homosexual persons as human beings, balanced by considerations of the welfare of society, public morality, and respect for the rights of others as stated in Article 29 of the United Nations Declaration of Human Rights in 1949.

Notes: *This Policy Statement was adopted by the National Steering Committee of the United Church People for Biblical Witness, meeting in St. Louis, Missouri, July 12-14, 1978. It seeks to reverse several of the radical recommendations contained in "Human Sexuality: A Preliminary Study" received by the Eleventh General Synod of the United Church of Christ in 1977. United Church People for Biblical Witness published* Issues in Sexual Ethics, *edited by Martin Duffy, to provide members of the United Church of Christ with biblical, theological, and ethical perspectives not included in "Human Sexuality: A Preliminary Study."*

UNITED METHODIST CHURCH

EXCERPT FROM "BOOK OF RESOLUTIONS" (1988)

A. The Family.—We believe the family to be the basic human community through which persons are nurtured and sustained in mutual love, responsibility, respect, and fidelity. We understand the family as encompassing a wider range of options than that of the two-generational unit of parents and children (the nuclear family), including the extended family, families with adopted children, single parents, stepfamilies, couples without children. We affirm shared responsibility for parenting by men and women and encourage social, economic, and religious efforts to maintain and strengthen relationships within families in order that every member may be assisted toward complete personhood.

B. *Other Christian Communities.*—We further recognize the movement to find new patterns of Christian nurturing communities such as Koinonia Farms, certain monastic and other religious orders, and some types of corporate church life. We urge the Church to seek ways of understanding the needs and concerns of such Christian groups and to find ways of ministering to them and through them.

C. *Marriage.*—We affirm the sanctity of the marriage covenant which is expressed in love, mutual support, personal commitment, and shared fidelity between a man and a woman. We believe that God's blessing rests upon such marriage, whether or not there are children of the union. We reject social norms that assume different standards for women than for men in marriage.

D. *Divorce.*—Where marriage partners, even after thoughtful consideration and counsel, are estranged beyond reconciliation, we recognize divorce as regrettable but recognize the right of divorced persons to remarry. We express our deep concern for the care and nurture of the children of divorced and/or remarried persons. We encourage that either or both of the divorced parents be considered for custody of the minor children of the marriage. We encourage an active, accepting, and enabling commitment of the church and our society to minister to the members of divorced and remarried families.

E. *Single Persons.*—We affirm the integrity of single persons, and we reject all social practices that discriminate or social attitudes that are prejudicial against persons because they are unmarried.

F. *Human Sexuality.*—We recognize that sexuality is God's good gift to all persons. We believe persons may be fully human only when that gift is acknowledged and affirmed by themselves, the church, and society. We call all persons to the disciplined, responsible fulfillment of themselves, others, and society in the stewardship of this gift. We also recognize our limited understanding of this complex gift and encourage the medical, theological, and social science disciplines to combine in a determined effort to understand human sexuality more completely. We call the church to take the leadership role in bringing together these disciplines to address this most complex issue. Further, within the context of our understanding of this gift of God, we recognize that God challenges us to find responsible, committed, and loving forms of expression.

Although all persons are sexual beings whether or not they are married, sexual relations are only clearly affirmed in the marriage bond. Sex may become exploitative within as well as outside marriage. We reject all sexual expressions which damage or destroy the humanity God has given us as birthright, and we affirm only that sexual expression which enhances that same humanity, in the midst of diverse opinion as to what constitutes that enhancement.

We deplore all forms of the commercialization and exploitation of sex with their consequent cheapening and degradation of human personality. We call for strict enforcement of laws prohibiting the sexual exploitation or use of children by adults. We call for the establishment of adequate protective services, guidance, and counseling opportunities for children thus abused. We insist that all persons, regardless of age, gender, marital status, or sexual orientation are entitled to have their human and civil rights ensured.

We recognize the continuing need for full, positive, and factual sex education opportunities for children, youth, and adults. The church offers a unique opportunity to give quality guidance/education in this area.

Homosexual persons no less than heterosexual persons are individuals of sacred worth. All persons need the ministry and guidance of the Church in their struggles for human fulfillment, as well as the spiritual and emotional care of a fellowship which enables reconciling relationships with God, with others, and with self. Although we do not condone the practice of homosexuality and consider this practice incompatible with Christian teaching, we affirm that God's grace is available to all. We commit ourselves to be in ministry for and with all persons.

Notes: *The 1968 formation of the United Methodist Church brought together in one body a majority of those Americans in John Wesley's lineage. According to the church's Council of Bishops, "Traditionally United Methodists have not only been happy to be guided by* [The Book of] Discipline *as a book of church law, but they have also usually regarded it with a certain degree of reverence of the church across the passage of almost two centuries of time." (p. v* Book of Discipline*). This excerpt from the* Discipline, *while reaffirming traditional Christian sexual morality and views of the family, makes accomodations for changes in contemporary social practices, such as nonnuclear family patterns, single parenting, step-families, childless families, the single life, and monastic movements.*

WESLEYAN CHURCH

STATEMENT ON MARRIAGE AND FAMILY (1985)

We believe that the family is the primary unit of society and is ordained of God.

Family Living

Marriage is the act that unites as one a man and a woman. Within this union children should be born and reared. Stable homes are essential for a stable society. The wholesome relationship of individual to group as it should be learned in the family affects favorably in all other institutions of society. Conversely, disturbing forces in society make an impact on the home. The growing acceptance of some modern family concepts, the mobility of people, and the development of stress are some factors that have an erosive effect, frequently resulting in the breakdown of the traditional family.

Providing encouragement and direction for a Christian marriage and family are vital ministries of the church. These ministries represent the best hope for counteracting destructive trends in modern society. Our homes are to be maintained as centers of moral and spiritual renewal. To achieve this, each Christian family should establish a family altar, have mutual love and respect, take time for companionship, show respect for God and His church, and consecrate itself to Christian witnessing.

(Public Morals and Social Concerns)

Marriage

In 1984 the General Conference of the Wesleyan Church adopted an Article of Religion entitles ''Marriage and the Family.'' The article sets forth the following principles.

1. The Scriptures are the authority concerning marriage and divorce.

2. Monogamy (the union of one man with one woman) is God's plan for marriage.

3. Marriage is a lifelong relationship and a covenant union made in the sight of God, taking priority over all other human relationships.

4. Human sexuality is to be expressed only within the framework of marriage.

5. Marriage is divinely designated for the birth and rearing of children.

6. Man is created in the image of God and human sexuality reflects that image in terms of intimate love, communication, fellowship, subordination of the self to the larger whole, and fulfillment.

(*Discipline* 109)

Divorce

Wesleyans are committed in their membership vows to observe the teachings of Scripture concerning divorce:

1. The only scriptural grounds for considering divorce is the sexual sin of the spouse such as adultery, homosexual behavior, bestiality, or incest.

2. Appropriate counseling to restore the relationship must always precede a consideration of divorce.

3. To obtain a divorce on other than scriptural grounds is a sin against God and man. Such putting asunder of what God has joined is a direct and deliberate act of disobedience against both the Law and the Gospel. It separates one from God and subjects a member to Church discipline (1631; 1634).

(*Discipline* 131:10; 187:6)

Remarriage

Wesleyans believe that the Scriptures teach the following in regard to remarriage after divorce:

1. Recognizing the fallen state of man, divorce has been recognized in the Scriptures as a valid and permanent dissolution of marriage with all its rights and responsibilities. Divorce is not reversible. There is no way to ''restore'' a dissolved marriage. The divorced (unmarried) status can be changed only by a new marriage to the same person or another person. No divorced and remarried person has two spouses - only a former spouse and a present spouse, as in Deuteronomy 24 and 1 Corinthians 7.

2. Divorce, however sinful the act and however serious the consequences, is not unpardonable. A redeemed sinner or reclaimed backslider is ''free'' to marry ''in the Lord'' or to remain unmarried - a eunuch for the kingdom of God's sake. The one exception to this freedom of choice is mentioned by the Apostle Paul. It is a believer who disobeys the commandment of God and puts away a believing spouse. That person must remain unmarried to leave room for reconciliation to the spouse (1 Cor. 7).

3. The right to remarry in no way excuses the sin of divorce. It only implies that the Church must forgive and restore those whom the Lord forgives and restores. Neither penance nor penalty remain to the truly penitent and restored sinner - or backslider - whatever the traumatic consequences of the sin may be.

(*Discipline* 187:6)

Divorce and the Minister

The Wesleyan Church applies these same principles regarding divorce and remarriage to its ministers:

1. **Eligibility.** Any person sustaining a marriage relation contrary to the Scriptures and the Membership Commitments (131:10; cf. 187:6) is ineligible for license, commission, or ordination in The Wesleyan Church (*Discipline* 1104).

2. **Dismissal.** Any minister who enters into a marriage relation contrary to the Scriptures, and to those expositions of Scripture in the Membership Commitments (131:10), after having been ordained, commissioned, or licensed, shall be dismissed from his ministerial standing, provided that guilt shall be established in accord with judicial process (*Discipline* 1129; 1576-1580).

3. **Restoration.** A minister who has been disqualified for the ministry through a marriage contrary to the Scriptures and the Membership Commitments (131:10; 1129) shall not be restored to the office and work of a minister as long as both his former and latter spouse are living, and then only if he has manifested repentance and has been approved. (Refer to *Discipline* 1138 and 1141 for further details.)

4. **Performance.** In performing marriages, Wesleyan ministers shall not unite in marriage any person who is divorced, unless such divorce and remarriage is in keeping with the Scriptures and the Membership Commitments (131:10). In carrying out this duty the minister shall be guided by the principles set forth in 187:6 (*Discipline* 1130).

Church Membership

The statements in *The Discipline* are not intended to restrict from membership in The Wesleyan Church a person who has been previously involved in divorce and remarriage even though it did not qualify as permissible under the exception clause of Matthew 5:32. Such a person who has sought and found God's forgiveness for sins occasioned by marriage, divorce, or remarriage, and who is at present living in harmony with the principles of Christ as taught in the Scriptures is eligible for membership in The Wesleyan Church.

If a lay member has been dismissed from the Church for a violation of the scriptural teachings concerning divorce, he may be reinstated by the local church when he evidences repentance and amendment of life and meets the requirements of Church membership.

(Ruling of the Board of General Superintendents.)

Notes: *The Wesleyan Methodist Church was formed in 1968 by the merger of the Wesleyan Methodist Church and Pilgrim Holiness Church. Two diverse streams of holiness tradition—one pre-Civil War and the other from the late nineteenth century—united. This statement adopted by the 1984 General Conference of the Wesleyan Church affirms monogamous marriage as God's plan for humanity and teaches that coitus is reserved for marriage. Divorce is allowed only on the grounds of adultery and remarriage is permissible.*

Jewish Groups

The organized Jewish religious communities in the United States involve approximately half of the six million Jewish citizens in the U.S. They are generally divided into three main branches—Orthodox, Conservative and Reform—each of which has approximately one million adherents. The selected statements printed below illustrate how Jewish groups depends upon the Torah, Mishnah, *and* Talmud *for their basic understanding of sexuality and marriage and how similar the statements read even though there are major differences separating Reform Jews from Orthodox and Conservative Jews.*

CONSERVATIVE JUDAISM—ISAAC KLEIN

EXCERPT FROM "A GUIDE TO JEWISH RELIGIOUS PRACTICE" (1979)

XXXVI.

Family Purity (I)

1. Introduction

"Do not come near a woman during her period of uncleanness to uncover her nakedness" (Lev. 18:19).

"If a man lies with a woman in her infirmity and uncovers her nakedness, he has laid bare her flow and she has exposed her blood flow; both of them shall be cut off from among their people" (Lev. 20:18).

"Rabbi Akiba said: 'Happy are you, Israel! Before whom do you make yourselves pure? Before your Father in Heaven. As it is written: "The miqweh [hope] of Israel is the Lord" [Jer. 17:13]. Just as the miqweh makes clean those who are unclean, so the Holy One makes Israel clean'" (M. *Yoma* 8:9).

"All things die and are reborn continually. The plant which bows its head to the earth leaves its life capsulized in the dormant seed. In our own bodies, death and regeneration proceed cell by cell. Our fingernails grow, die, and are discarded; our hair also. Our skins slough off dead cells, while a tender new layer forms below the surface. Within us our organs repair and renew themselves repeatedly. Throughout each teeming and dying body, moreover, flows an undying spirit. It is confined to no single area, but, as the sages taught, it 'fills the body as the ocean fills its bed.' That spirit is the soul. Only a conscious being has a soul. Of what is such a being conscious? He is aware of himself. He is aware also of his own growth processes and of his history. Our consciousness tells us that we are created beings and so are mortal. Our soul tells us that we are the image of the Creator and so cannot be mortal. Our knowledge of ourselves, then, is paradoxical. How do we reconcile it and make ourselves whole? Jews solve the paradox with the ritual cycle of *tumah* and *taharah*, in which we act out our death and resurrection'' (Adler, in *Jewish Catalog*, p. 167).

Of the laws of *tum'ah* and *tohorah*, to which so much space is devoted in the Torah and the Talmud, only the laws governing . . . (family purity) are still relevant. This is not by accident. A prominent Jewish scholar writes: ''The preservation of the menstrual laws alone, with their restrictive regulations entirely unimpaired, is not to be explained as being due to their having become ingrained into the sexual habits of the Jewish people, still less on grounds of their supposed hygienic justification. It is rather a conscious emphasis on, and an attempt at the inculcation in a particularly significant area of human interest, of that self-discipline which must be—in all aspects of life—an integral element in the Jewish ideal of cultivating 'holiness' (Kedushah)'' (Loewe, *Position of Women in Judaism*, p. 48).

Hence, we must treat these laws from the aspect of holiness and wholesome family relationships.

The much heralded ''sexual revolution,'' which our generation sees as espousing a ''new'' philosophy of sex, is in reality old-fashioned libertinism with an academic degree attached to it. The ''new morality'' is neither new nor morality, but rather the old immorality that reappears from time to time and seeks legitimation. It creates more problems than it solves. In many cases it leads to the undermining of the fabric of the family and the vulgarization of sex, or at best its trivialization. Hence, there is the urgency of reaffirming the traditional Jewish sexual morality.

Modern man is heir to two conflicting traditions neither of which is Jewish: on the one hand, the rebirth of the old paganism with its absolute-pleasure principle, which found its extreme expression in the sacred prostitutes of Canaan and the debaucheries of ancient Rome; and on the other, the Christian reaction to the excesses of paganism and its unbridled sexual laxity—sex became identified with original sin, and celibacy was regarded as the ideal form of life.

Modern man, while opting for pagan libertinism, also suffers a guilty conscience because of his Christian heritage. The children of Israel identify with contemporary civilization and are thus beneficiaries of its triumphs and victims of its aberrations. In the sexual area they are innocent sufferers, because Judaism is free of both extremes. It rejects the espousal of uncontrolled sexual expression that paganism preaches, and also Christianity's claim that all sexual activity is inherently evil (see Gordis, *Sex and the Family in the Jewish Tradition;* Lamm, *A Hedge of Roses;* also *Our Bodies, Ourselves*, p. 24).

Jewish marriage is based on a healthy sexual viewpoint that rejects the two extremist principles, and so are the regulations governing the conjugal relationship between husband and wife, *tohorat hamishpahah*, the purity of family life. . . .

Notes: *The author of this statement is distinguished Conservative scholar Rabbi Isaac Klein, who is Rabbi Emeritus of Congregation Shaarey Zedek, Buffalo, New York, former president of The Rabbinical Assembly, and the author of* Responsa and Halakhic Studies. *In this selection, he reaffirms the goodness of sexuality and the sanctity of the family while rejecting contemporary changes in traditional sexual morality.*

UNION OF AMERICAN HEBREW CONGREGATIONS

RESOLUTION, ADVOCATING UNIFORM MARRIAGE, DIVORCE AND DESERTION LAWS (1923)

WHEREAS the safety and preservation of humanity's ideals are dependent upon the sanctity of the home which is created through marriage, and

WHEREAS the laws of the several states are at wide variance in their provisions for marriage, and

WHEREAS the divorce laws of the several states are at equally wide variance, and

WHEREAS the desertion laws of each state are limited in their jurisdiction, be it

RESOLVED that the Union of American Hebrew Congregations advocate the enactment of uniform marriage, divorce and desertion laws, and that proper steps be taken by the Union in aid of their enactment.

Notes: *The Union of American Hebrew Congregations was founded in 1875 in Cincinnati, Ohio, by Rabbi Isaac Mayer Wise, the leader around whom the various reform efforts coalesced. This resolution adopted in 1923 calls for uniform marriage, divorce, and desertion laws to protect the sanctity of the family.*

UNITED SYNAGOGUE OF AMERICA

RESOLUTION ON MARRYING WITHIN THE FAITH (1989)

WHEREAS, current statistics on intermarriage indicate that Jews are marrying out of the faith in ever increasing numbers; and

WHEREAS, the future of Judaism is primarily dependent upon marriage between Jews;

NOW, THEREFORE, BE IT RESOLVED that the UNITED SYNAGOGUE OF AMERICA through its various departments:

a. establish and enhance ongoing programs to encourage Jews to marry within the faith, and establish programs within synagogue communities to facilitate the meeting of Jewish couples with the goal of encouraging Jewish marriages, such programs to represent a priority concern; and

b. prepare appropriate materials to be incorporated into the curriculum of all educational institutions on this subject; and

c. prepare appropriate program materials for informal educational enterprises, most notably youth groups; and

d. provide Family Education programs, with a major portion thereof devoted to advising parents on how to avoid interdating and intermarriage by their children; and

e. utilize the pulpit and the public relations media of the synagogue to stress the importance of marriage within the faith and problems attendant to marriage outside the faith.

Notes: *The United Synagogue of America founded in 1913 by Rabbi Solomon Schechter serves conservative synagogues. This resolution adopted in 1989 calls for a concerted effort and educational program to discourage marriage with non-Jewish partners.*

UNITED SYNAGOGUE OF AMERICA

RESOLUTION ON MIXED-MARRIAGE FAMILIES (1989)

WHEREAS, it is a Mitzvah to do everything possible to encourage the maintenance and preservation of the Jewish home and family; and

WHEREAS, the non-Jewish spouse of a mixed marriage could benefit from a further and better understanding of the teachings and precepts of Judaism; and

WHEREAS, there are children of mixed marriages who are not halachically Jewish, who may be deprived of a Jewish education which may cause them to be forever lost to the Jewish community;

NOW, THEREFORE, BE IT RESOLVED that the UNITED SYNAGOGUE OF AMERICA, with the assistance of its affiliated congregations and subject to the rules of the Committee on Congregational Standards, develop and implement out-reach programs of an educational and social nature which will enable and encourage such non-Jewish persons to learn more about Judaism and the Jewish family, with the hope of their converting to Judaism and to full participation in Jewish life and congregational activities; and

BE IT FURTHER RESOLVED that the UNITED SYNAGOGUE OF AMERICA, with the assistance of its affiliated congregations and subject to the rules of the Committee on Congregational Standards, develop and implement specifically designed out-reach programs which will enable and encourage such children of mixed marriages who are not halachically Jewish to become familiar with the precepts and teachings of Judaism, with the hope of their converting to Judaism by the time they reach Bar or Bat Mitzvah age.

Notes: *Although conservative Judaism does not allow mixed marriages and seeks to prevent them through educational programs, the United Synagogue of America recognizes, in this 1989 resolution, their growing presence in contemporary society and seeks to maintain a Jewish presence and influence in these families.*

Other Religious Bodies

America is now home to hundreds of groups which are neither Christian (i.e., Catholic, Protestant, or Eastern Orthodox) nor Jewish. There is Hinduism and Buddhism from Asia; Islam from the Middle East, the Far East and elsewhere; the Latter-day Saint tradition native to the United States; the New Age Movement; and other traditions, both ancient and modern. Most of these groups have not issued formal statements on sexuality and marriage. Presented here are selected statements, some formal and others informal, which may be representative and suggestive of alternative approaches to sexuality and marriage.

AMERICAN HUMANIST ASSOCIATION

EXCERPT FROM "HUMANIST MANIFESTO I AND II" (1973)

Sixth: In the area of sexuality, we believe that intolerant attitudes, often cultivated by orthodox religions and puritanical cultures, unduly repress sexual conduct. The right to birth control, abortion, and divorce should be recognized. While we do not approve of exploitive, denigrating forms of sexual expression, neither do we wish to prohibit, by law or social sanction, sexual behavior between consenting adults. The many varieties of sexual exploration should not in themselves be considered "evil." Without countenancing mindless permissiveness or unbridled promiscuity, a civilized society should be a *tolerant* one. Short of harming others or compelling them to do likewise, individuals should be permitted to express their sexual proclivities and pursue their life-styles as they desire. We wish to cultivate the development of a responsible attitude toward sexuality, in which humans are not exploited as sexual objects, and in which intimacy, sensitivity, respect, and honesty in interpersonal relations are encouraged. Moral education for children and adults is an important way of developing awareness and sexual maturity.

Notes: Humanist Manifesto I and II *serves as a definitive statement for the humanist movement, which traces its origins to the 1920s. The American Humanist Association (which was founded in 1941), accepts the basic perspective of the* Manifesto *that emphasizes human responsibility toward humanity as a whole, supports responsible use of human freedom, and decries the exploitation of individuals within and outside genital sexual relationships.*

CHURCH OF JESUS CHRIST OF LATTER-DAY SAINTS

STATEMENT ON CHASTITY AND FIDELITY (1986)

The Savior showed love and compassion toward the sinner but he always condemned the sin. Along with his love came the firm admonition, "Go, and sin no more" (John 8:11).

God's standard for sexual morality has always been clear. "Thou shalt not commit adultery" (Exo. 20:14). In modern and in ancient times God has commanded that all his children lead strictly moral lives before and after marriage—intimate relations being permissible only between a man and a woman joined in marriage. Accordingly, all such relations outside of marriage are out of harmony with God's eternal plan for his children.

Unnatural affections, including those toward persons of the same gender, run counter to that plan. Individuals are responsible to make right choices. Lustful feelings and desires, which may lead to more serious sins, are sinful, whether directed toward those of the same or the opposite gender.

Priesthood leaders should encourage all to conform their lives to God's standard of morality.

Notes: *In 1988, the Church of Jesus Christ of Latter-day Saints reported a membership of 4.3 million people and 9,500 congregations in the United States and 115,000 people and 350 congregations in Canada. There were more than 6.4 million members worldwide. This 1986 statement on chastity and fidelity that reserves sexual intercourse to heterosexual marriage relationships reaffirms a long-standing moral teaching of the Church of Jesus Christ of Latter-day Saints.*

CHURCH OF JESUS CHRIST OF LATTER-DAY SAINTS

STATEMENT ON MARRIAGE AND THE CHURCH OF JESUS CHRIST OF LATTER-DAY SAINTS (1990)

The Church of Jesus Christ of Latter-day Saints teaches that the marriage covenant is divinely ordained and sacred. Under the authority of the priesthood exercised exclusively in the temples of the Church, a man and a woman are legally married for this life and for eternity as well.

At this time, and for many years past, individuals and groups engaged in the practice of plural marriage or polygamy have no affiliation with The Church of Jesus Christ of Latter-day Saints. Any member who practices or teaches polygamy is subject to excommunication from the Church.

In the 1870s and 1880s, the Congress of the United States passed various laws prohibiting polygamy and restricting the freedoms of individual Church members (including their right to vote) and withdrawing legal rights from the Church (including the right to hold property). After seeking the will of the Lord and upon receiving a revelation, President Wilford Woodruff in 1890 issued the "Manifesto," declaring that the Latter-day Saints were no longer authorizing plural marriages and that it was their wish to conform to federal laws.

Notes: *The First Presidency of the Church of Jesus Christ of Latter-day Saints, comprising three men (the president and two counselors) who are assisted by the Council of Twelve Apostles, regulates the affairs of the church. This 1990 statement reaffirms the church's teaching that marriage is divinely ordained and sacred. It is to be monogamous, not polygamous, and, when consecrated in the church's temple, is for this life and for eternity.*

ISLAM

EXCERPT FROM "THE LAWFUL AND THE PROHIBITED IN ISLAM" (UNDATED)

1. The Physical Appetites

Allah Subhanahu wa Ta'ala created man as His vicegerent on earth in order that he might populate and rule it. Obviously this purpose cannot be realized unless the human species perpetuates itself, living, thriving, cultivating, manufacturing, building, and worshipping its Creator. Accordingly, the Creator has placed certain appetites and impulses in man so that he is impelled toward the various activities which guarantee the survival of the species.

Among the appetites which an individual must satisfy for his personal survival is that of food and drink. The sexual appetite, however, is for the purpose of the survival of the species. Sex is a strong driving force in the human being which demands satisfaction and fulfillment. Human beings have responded to the demands of the sexual appetite in three different ways:

1. One way is to satisfy ones sexual need freely with whomever is available and whenever one pleases, without any restraints of religion, morality, or custom. This is the position of the advocates of free sex, for they do not believe in any religion. This philosophy reduces the human being to the status of an animal, and, if practiced universally, would result in the destruction of the family structure and of all society as we know it.

2. The second approach is to suppress, and try to annihilate, the sexual drive; this approach is advocated by ascetic religions and other-worldly philosophies, approaches which lead toward monasticism and an escape from the world. Such advocacy of suppression of a natural appetite, or rather annihilation of its functioning, is contrary to Allah's plan and purpose, and is in conflict with the course of the natural order which requires the use of this appetite for the continuity of life.

3. The third approach is to regulate the satisfaction of this urge, allowing it to operate within certain limits, neither suppressing nor giving it free rein. This is the stand of the revealed religions, which have instituted marriage and have prohibited fornication and adultery. In particular, Islam duly recognizes the role of the sexual drive, facilitates its satisfaction through lawful marriage, and just as it strictly prohibits sex outside of marriage and even what is conducive to it, it also prohibits celibacy and the shunning of women.

   This is the just and intermediate position. If marriage were not permitted, the sexual instinct would not play its role in the continuation of the human species; while if fornication and adultery were not prohibited, the foundation of the family would be eroded. Unquestionably, it is only in the shade of a stable family that mercy, love, affection, and the capacity to sacrifice for others develop in a human being, emotions without which a cohesive society cannot come into being. Thus, if there had been no family system, there would have been no society through which mankind would be able to progress toward perfection. . . .

2. Marriage

No Monasticism in Islam

The stand of Islam is, on the one hand, against sexual license; consequently, it prohibits fornication and adultery, and blocks all ways leading to them. On the other hand, Islam is also against suppressing the sexual urge; accordingly, it calls people toward marriage, prohibiting renunciation and castration.[1]

As long as he possesses the means to marry, the Muslim is not permitted to refrain from

183

marriage on the grounds that he has dedicated himself to the service or the worship of Allah and to a life of monasticism and renunciation of the world. . . .

Marrying More than One Woman

Islam is a way of life consonant with nature, providing human solutions to complex situations and avoiding extremes. This characteristic of Islam can be observed most clearly in its stand concerning the taking of more than one wife. Islam permits the Muslim to marry more than one woman in order to resolve some very pressing human problems, individual as well as social. . . .

Justice Among Wives - A Condition

The condition which Islam lays down for permitting a man to have more than one wife is confidence on his part that he will be able to deal equitably with his two or more wives in the matter of food, drink, housing, clothing and expenses, as well as in the division of his time between them. Anyone who lacks the assurance that he will be able to fulfill all these obligations with justice and equality is prohibited by Allah Ta'ala from marrying more than one woman, for Allah Ta'la says:

> . . .But if you fear that you will not be able to do justice (among them), then (marry) only one. . . .(4:3)

And the Prophet (peace be on him) said,

> Anyone who has two wives and does not treat them equally will come on the Day of Resurrection dragging one part of his body which will be hanging down.[2]

The equal treatment mentioned here pertains to the *rights* of the wives, not to the love the husband feels toward them, for equality in the division of love is beyond human capacity and any imbalance in this regard is forgiven by Allah Ta'ala who says:

> And you will not be able to do justice among (your) wives, however much you may wish to. But do not turn away (from one of them) altogether. . . .(4:139)

This is why the Prophet (peace be on him) used to divide his time among his wives equally, saying,

> O Allah, this is my division in regard to what I can control. Then do not take me to task regarding what Thou controllest and I do not control,[3]

referring to the attachment and affection which he felt for one particular wife. And when he planned to go on a journey, Allah's Messenger (peace be on him) would cast lots among his wives, and the one who was chosen by lot would accompany him.[4]

Why Marriage to More than One Woman Is Permitted in Islam

Islam is the last and final word of Allah Subhanahu wa Ta'ala, ending the series of His messages to mankind. It therefore came with a general law suitable for all times and places, and for the whole of humanity. It did not legislate for the city dweller only, while neglecting the nomad, nor for the cold regions while ignoring the hot ones, nor for one particular period of time, forgetting later times and the generations to come.

Islam recognizes the needs and interests of all people, of individuals as well as groups. And among human beings one finds that individual who has a strong desire for children but whose wife is barren, chronically ill, or has some other problem. Would it not be more considerate on her part and better for him that he marry a second wife who can bear him children, while retaining the first wife with all her rights guaranteed?

Then there may also be the case of a man whose desire for sex is strong, while his wife has little desire for it, or who is chronically ill, has long menstrual periods, or the like, while her husband is unable to restrain his sexual urge. Should it not be permitted to him to marry a second wife instead of his hunting around for girlfriends?

There are also times when women outnumber men, as for example after wars which often decimate the ranks of men. In such a situation, it is in the interests of the society and of women themselves that they become co-wives to a man instead of spending their entire lives without marriage, deprived of the peace, affection, and protection of marital life and the joy of motherhood for which they naturally yearn with all their hearts.

Only three possible alternatives exist for such surplus women who are not married as first wives:

1. to pass their whole lives in bitter deprivation,

2. to become sex objects and playthings for lecherous men; or

3. to become co-wives to men who are able to support more than one wife and who will treat them kindly.

Unquestionably, the last alternative is the correct solution, a healing remedy for this problem, and that is the judgement of Islam:

> And Who is better than Allah in judgement, for a people who have certain faith? (5:53(50))

For this is the Islamic "polygamy" which people in the West consider so abhorrent and to which they react with such hostility, while their own men are free to have any number of girlfriends, without restriction and without any legal or moral accountability, either in respect to the woman or to the children she may bear as a result of this irreligious and immoral plurality of extra-marital relationships. Let the two alternatives - plurality of wives or plurality of illicit affairs - be compared, and let people ask themselves which is the proper course of action, and which of the two groups is correctly guided!

3. The Relationship Between Husband and Wife

The Qur'an emphasizes the spiritual objectives of marriage, making them the foundations of marital life. These objectives are realized in the peace of mind which comes through wholesome sexual experience with the spouse whom one loves, in the enlargement of the circle of love and affection between the two families united through marriage, and in the nurturing of affection and tenderness among the children under the loving care of their parents. These are the objectives mentioned by Allah Ta'ala:

> And among His signs is that He created for you mates from among yourselves, that you may dwell with them in tranquility, and He has put love and mercy between you. Indeed, in this are signs for those who reflect.(30:21)

The Sexual Relationship

At the same time, the Qur'an does not neglect the sensual aspect and the physical relationship between husband and wife. It guides human beings to the best path, fulfilling the demands of the sexual urge while avoiding harmful or deviant practices.

It is reported that the Jews and Zoroastrians used to go to extremes in avoiding any physical contact with menstruating women, while the Christians continue to have sexual relations with them without regard to the flow of blood. The Arabs of the period of *jahiliyyah* would not eat, drink, or sit with women who were menstruating and would send them to separate dwelling just as the Jews and Zoroastrians did.

Accordingly, some Muslims asked the Prophet (peace be on him) about what is permitted and what is forbidden in relation to menstruating women. The following verse was then revealed:

> And they ask thee about menstruation. Say: It is a hurt, so refrain from women during their menstruation and do not approach them until they are cleansed. And when they have cleansed themselves you may go in to them in the manner ordained by Allah; indeed, Allah loves those who turn to Him and He loves those who are clean. (2:222)

Some people understood the phrase, "Refrain from women," as meaning that they should not live together in the same house during the menstrual periods. The Prophet (peace be on him) then explained the correct meaning of this verse, saying,

> I ordered you only to refrain from having intercourse with menstruating women and did not tell you to send them out of the house as the foreigners do. . . .

5. Divorce

Marriage as stated previously, is a strong bond by means of which Allah joins a man and a woman. While they are "single" as individual human beings, after marriage they are termed a "couple." Marriage makes of them a pair, and thus the sorrow and joy of the one are equally the sorrow and joy of the other. The Qur'an describes this bond in beautiful and vivid language:

> . . .They (wives) are your garments and you are their garments. . . .(2:187)

meaning that each is the protection, the covering, the support, and the adornment of the other.[5]

Each of the two spouses has rights in regard to the other which must be recognized and which are not to be diminished. These mutual rights are equivalent except in relation to what is particular to men by virtue of their natural position, as Allah says:

> . . .And they (women) have (rights) similar to those (of men) over them in an honorable fashion, but men have a degree over them. (2:228). . . .

Mutual Tolerance Between Husband and Wife

A husband must be patient with his wife if he sees something in her which he disapproves and dislikes. He should recognize that he is dealing with a human being with natural imperfections, and he should balance her good qualities with her failings. . . .

While on the one hand Islam requires the men to be tolerant and patient with what he dislikes in his wife, on the other it commands the wife to try to please her husband as far as her ability and charm allow, and warns her not to let a night pass during which her husband remains angry with her.

When Divorce Becomes Permissible

If all these efforts fail and every course tried proves to be of no avail, the husband may resort to the final solution permitted by the *Shari'ah* of Islam. In response to the bitter realities of life, when difficulties cannot be resolved except through the separation of the two parties in an honorable fashion, Islam has made the provision of divorce. Islam has permitted divorce reluctantly, neither liking nor commending it. Said the Prophet (peace be on him),

> "Among lawful things, divorce is most hated by Allah."[6]

That a thing is lawful yet detested by Allah means that it is permissible under unavoidable circumstances, when living together becomes a torture, mutual hatred is deep-seated, and it becomes difficult for the two parties to observe the limits of Allah and to fulfill their marital responsibilities. In such a situation separation is better, and Allah Ta'ala says,

> But if they separate, Allah will provide for each of them out of His abundance. . . . (4:130). . . .

The Divorced Woman's Freedom to Remarry

After the expiration of the divorced woman's *'iddah*, neither her ex-husband, guardian, nor anyone else can prevent her from marrying anyone she chooses. As long as she and the man who proposes to her follow the procedure required by the *Shari'ah*, no one has the right to interfere. What some men of today do in attempting to prevent their ex-wives from remarrying, intimidating them and their families, is in fact something pertaining to *jahiliyyah;* likewise, what some families or guardians of divorced women do to prevent them from returning to their husbands when they want to be reconciled, as indeed "Peace is better," (4:128) is also of *jahiliyyah* Allah Ta'ala says:

> And when you divorce women and they complete their term (*'iddah*), do not prevent them from marrying their (former) husbands if they agree among themselves in an honorable manner. This is to instruct those among you who believe in Allah and the Last Day. That is more virtuous and pure for you; and Allah knows and you do not know. (2:232)

The Woman's Right to Demand Divorce

The woman who cannot bear to live with her husband has the right to free herself from the marriage bond by returning to her husband the *mahr* (required marriage gift) and gifts he has given her, or more or less than that according to their mutual agreement. It is, however, preferable that he should not ask for more than he has given her. Allah Ta'ala says:

> . . .And if you (the judges) fear that the two may not be able to keep to the limits ordained by Allah, there is no blame on either of them if she redeems herself (from the marriage tie by returning all or part of the *mahr*). . . .(2:229)

The wife of Thabit bin Qais came to the Prophet (peace be on him) and said, "O Messenger of Allah, I do not approach Thabit bin Qais in respect of character and religion, but I do not want to be guilty of showing anger to him."[7] The Prophet (peace be on him) asked her about what she had received from him. She replied, "A garden." He asked, "Will you give him back his garden?" "Yes," she said. The Prophet (peace be on him) then told Thabit,

> "Accept the garden and make one declaration of divorce."[8]

It is not permissible for woman to seek divorce from her husband unless she has borne ill-treatment from him or unless she has an acceptable reason which requires their separation. Said the Prophet (peace be on him),

> If any woman asks her husband for a divorce without some strong reason, the fragrance of the Garden will be forbidden to her.[9]

Endnotes

[1] Renunciation means remaining celibate and renouncing worldly activity for the sake of devoting oneself to the worship of God. Castration denotes suppressing sexual desires by removing the testicles.

[2] Reported by the compilers of *Sunan* and by Ibn Hibban and al-Hakim.

[3] Reported by the compilers of *Sunan.*

[4] Reported by al-Bukhari and Muslim.

[5] Al-Tirmidhi transmitted that Abu Hurairah reported Allah's Messenger (peace be on him) as saying, "The Believers who show the most perfect faith are those who have the best disposition, and the best of you are those who are best to their wives." In a *hadith* narrated by 'Aishah, the last words are "and are kindest to their families," as transmitted by al-Tirmidhi. (Trans.)

[6] Reported by Abu Daoud.

[7] Her meaning was that although Thabit was a good man, she was unable to get along with him and thus might not be able to show him the respect due to a husband. (Trans.)

[8] Reported by al-Bukhari and al-Nisai.

[9] Reported by Abu Daoud.

Notes: *This statement illustrates how Islamic scholars derive their views from the Quran,*

Hadith, and Shariah. It reaffirms marriage as a divine gift, reserves sexual intercourse for the marriage relationship, and explains the Muslim views on polygamy and divorce.

NEW VRINDABAN COMMUNITY

EXCERPT FROM "JOY OF NO SEX" (1981)

CHAPTER TWO—The Case for No Sex

Orgasm: The Great Cheater

In a limited, specific sense, celibacy means controlling the sense of touch in relation to the genital organ. The sense of touch applied to the genitals produces pleasure. In this way, the pleasure principle assures the continuation of the species. People are eager to reproduce and take on the responsibility of children because the sex act is pleasurable.

All sexual attraction and stimulation lead to orgasm, the release of semen. If a man engaged in sex does not experience orgasm, he does not feel satisfied. After orgasm, however, he often feels cheated because orgasmic pleasure lasts only a few seconds. Moreover, he often feels guilty because he yielded to the allurements of the flesh. And he feels drained of strength because he has wasted his vital fluid.

During orgasm, both mental and physical energy are lost, much more than in other forms of sense indulgence. Indeed, all the senses—touch, smell, sound, taste, and sight—are brought into play in the most intense manner. "Sexual excitement is furnished from all the sense organs of the body," Freud observed. It is therefore said that the greatest pleasure, however, is a high one, for at orgasm the entire system is drained.

The Transformation of Sexual Energy

> In the degree in which a man's mind is nearer to freedom from all passion, in that degree also it is nearer to strength. (Marcus Aurelius)

When properly used, sexual energy enables us to enjoy good memory, artistic imagination, and spiritual perception. Great works of art, literature, music, architecture, and philosophy were produced by men who channelled their sexual energy into creative endeavor. If sexual energy is allowed to flow upward, it feeds and enlivens the nerves and brain, opening the door to heightened intellectual and spiritual power. If allowed to flow downward, it weakens us spiritually and physically.

> The energy created by sexual restraint is the motive power which makes it possible for us to conceive desirable ends, and to think out the means for realizing them. (Aldous Huxley)

When celibacy is strictly observed, sexual energy is converted into immense spiritual powers, called *ojas shakti* by yogis. A sharp intelligence, photographic memory, an iron determination, and a steady desire for self-realization arise from *ojas shakti*. "If the senses are restrained, intelligence increases." (Mahabharata) The power of celibacy brings success in all endeavors. "The masters of all the more intensely emotional arts have frequently cultivated a high degree of chastity. . . . Men of great genius have apparently been completely continent throughout life." (Havelock Ellis) By celibacy, one becomes a better poet, artist, religious man, athlete, musician, mathematician, or scientist. Even politicians benefit. Mahatma Gandhi attributed his political power to celibacy.

Regardless of our field of endeavor, our powers of concentration and retention are adversely affected by seminal loss. Celibacy, on the other hand, sharpens the ability to concentrate and helps us retain what we have learned. Success in any field requires concentration. A close relationship exists between the quality of mind and *ojas shakti*.

"Energy is gained by the establishment of continence." (Patanjali) Athletes transform sexual energy into physical prowess; scientists transform it into intellectual insight; yogis transform it into spiritual realization in the quest for the Absolute Truth, God. If an athlete cannot remain celibate during training, he cannot perform his best. Similarly, a student or scientist cannot concentrate on his studies if the mind is always dwelling on sex. "The abstinent scientist can devote more of his energy to study," Freud observed. And if a religious man cannot control his sexual desires, he is called a hypocrite. "Celibacy is indispensible for self-realization," said Gandhi. All maximum endeavors require the discipline of celibacy.

In his "Exhortation to Chastity," Tertullian pointed out that if an athlete is willing to practice celibacy for the sake of a game, how much more should we be willing to be celibate for spiritual purposes:

> What is profitable for a time should always be practiced. Then it will always be profitable. Shall one be willing only to abstain from what is ordinarily deemed a pleasure for the sake of a victory in wrestling and the like and be incapable of a similar abstinence for the sake of the noblest of victories? There are enough sexual stoics in the world to prove by experience that continence is not only possible but also practical.

During the crucial years between ten and thirty, the background for our careers is formed. Whatever mental and physical habits we follow at this time are usually retained to the end of life. Unfortunately, during this important formative period, many young people are degraded by bad association, either with their peers or teachers.

Before teachers can help their students, however, they must first be established in knowledge themselves. "Know thyself" is the starting point for complete and perfect knowledge. When we know ourselves, we see the need to control ourselves. Self-knowledge and self-control go hand in hand, for one is the practical application of the other. Celibacy is the epitome of self-control.

Self-Control: Gateway to Real Pleasure

> To control the sexual impulse efficiently has always been and ever will be regarded as the highest test of human wisdom. (Auguste Comte)

Sense Gratification

We are pleasure-seeking creatures. Everyone shuns pain and pursues pleasure. Pleasure in this world means gratifying the senses by contact with sense objects. To gratify the sense of smell, I smell a redolent flower. To gratify hearing, I listen to music. To gratify sight, I look at something beautiful. To gratify taste, I eat and drink. To gratify touch, I feel an object with my hands. Because sex brings all these senses into play, it is the most intense form of sense indulgence. During sexual intercourse, all the senses are being excited and gratified.

The objects that give us pleasure are varied and apparently limitless. Although there's a kind of general agreement among people about what is pleasurable, it's often said that one man's pleasure is another's pain. In the animal kingdom, pigs like stool, and cows like grass. Swans like nectar; crows like garbage. Of all creatures, man experiences pleasure in the greatest variety of ways: sensual, intellectual, and spiritual.

Types of Pleasure

> Due to defective knowledge, men err in their choice of pleasures. (Plato)

On the sensual level, people take pleasure in sex, eating, sleeping, and intoxication. On the intellectual level, pleasure is found in ideas, books, theater, music, architecture, etc. And on the spiritual level, pleasure is taken in devotion to God and renouncing sense gratification.

Freud saw the life instinct propelled by the need to gratify hunger, thirst, and sex. It is commonly said that a man first thinks of satisfying his stomach, then his genitals. When a man is hungry and thirsty, he eats and drinks, and thereby satisfies his needs and reduces pain and tension. On this gross level, pleasure is simply the relief of pain.

The Need for Self-Control

> An intelligent person does not take part in the sources of misery, which are due to contact with the material senses. Such pleasures have a beginning and an end, and so the wise man does not delight in them. (Bhagavad Gita)

> Self-restraint is indispensable for individual as well as universal progress. (Gandhi)

There is no victory more glorious than mastery over our own mind and senses. When we are self-controlled, we sleep peacefully and awake enthusiastically. We know happiness and contentment. Self-mastery means conquering the body and subduing the restless mind. Until we control the body and mind, we are subject to the slavery of cruel taskmasters, such as lust and ignorance.

He who rules his own mind and senses has no need for crown and scepter. He is already the lord of himself and is a real superman. It is harder to control oneself than to rule the world. Indeed, he who has conquered himself has already conquered the world.

To be self-controlled, we must be well established in renunciation. This means renouncing the mind's endless and insatiable desire to know and experience new things. Temptations must be resisted, evil thoughts subdued, and base desires rejected. Only then will we have lasting peace and joy.

Self-control is discipline. It is restraint by oneself over oneself. It is the power to keep the mind and senses submissive to the direction of the intelligence and eternal soul. Self-control yields all knowledge. It increases energy and purifies. A wonderful entourage follows in its path: charity, compassion, knowledge, forgiveness, patience, nonviolence, sincerity, mildness, modesty, determination, liberality, contentment, truthfulness, benevolence, and freedom from anger and malice. Self-control gives us the fortitude to withstand tribulation and endure great suffering in defense of what is right. By it, the mind becomes clear and discriminating. In short, self-control opens wide the doors to material and spiritual peace and joy.

The Endless Itch

> No attained object of desire can give lasting satisfaction; it can produce merely a fleeting gratification. Desires last long; the demands are infinite; the satisfaction is short. The satisfied passion leads more often to unhappiness than to happiness. As long as we are given up to a throng of desires, we can never have lasting happiness or peace. (Schopenhauer)

When under the control of the sex drive, people tend to believe that genital contact is the only way to fulfill the need for pleasure. Still, they are never fulfilled. Fire is never extinguished by pouring fuel on it. Material pleasure never satisfies; it must constantly be renewed. After today's sexual partner is lost, people start looking for tomorrow's. They lament for what they have lost or consumed, and they hanker for what they don't have.

The sex urge is like an itching sensation, and sexual intercourse is like scratching that itch. Even if a person has a limitless supply of sense objects, he can never remove the sexual itch. It is insatiable. The more the itch is scratched, the worse it becomes.

For animals, sex is a biological call and nothing more. But for man, a great deal more is involved than genital manipulation. Man possesses a mind capable of creating sexual fantasies. Man is often motivated by aesthetics, romance, intimacy, fear of loneliness, the desire to give pleasure, and the desire to enjoy pleasure in the company of another. This is not merely a biological response or hormonal reaction like an animal's rutting. Though sex has its biological basis, it is secondary to the desire to enjoy pleasure by giving and receiving in an intimate relationship. But alas! In this world, such relationships, even at best, are temporary.

The Turbulent Senses

The senses are very turbulent. Compared to controlling the senses, it is easy to tame a tiger or an elephant, walk on burning coals, conquer a great empire, or move mountains. Compared to eradicating lust within the heart, it is easy to travel to the moon. Not without reason have the unruly senses been compared to wild horses and the raging wind. All the more reason they must be controlled! We must learn to harness wild horses and use the wind. This is possible by devotion, faith, determination, and constant practice. Just as a doctor treats a disease by various methods, the yogi controls the unruly senses by certain practices, including fasting, chanting, meditation, exercise, worship, and knowledge. What is that knowledge? Is it esoteric? No. It's the most common, basic fact of all.

"I Am Not This Body."

> Our body fills us with desires and passions and vain imaginings and a host of frivolities. But once having got rid of the foolishness of the body, we shall be pure, and know the clear light of truth. (Plato)

> Sex is a thing of bodies, not of souls. (Hermes)

Sex makes people think, "I am this body." This is the greatest mistake of all, the mistake underlying all other mistakes. We are not these bodies. This perception is the first step in self-realization and is the basis of all yoga.

It is impossible to be free of the bodily conception as long as we are enslaved by the body's demands to gratify the senses. Illicit sex would never take place if people did not identify with the body. It is this false identification that brings about the miseries of birth, old age, disease, and death.

"You are not that body," yogis have taught their students since time immemorial. "You are Brahman, pure spirit soul—eternal, full of knowledge and bliss," This is our identity, and on this platform we can begin to relish the joy of no sex. Thus, to get rid of the Myth of the Need for Sex, we *must* understand "I am not this body." This is the beginning.

Unfortunately, at birth we forget our true identity. And we are not taught the truth by parents or teachers because they are also illusioned. Indeed, as soon as we emerge from the womb we are being conditioned to think "I am this body." Then, through the body's senses, we attempt to enjoy material life.

But why is this so? Have we actually willed ourselves into this miserable situation? Or has someone else willed it? What have we done to deserve this? Why are we slaves of habit and ignorance?

Often, to shun responsibility, people say, "Well, God made me this way. This is the way I am." But this cannot be so. We should not blame God. We hold the key to our destiny. Everything is situated on desire, and if we so desire it, our goals and lifestyles can be changed. It is all a question of knowing and then desiring to act on that knowledge. After all, knowledge without action is only theoretical. It won't help us. And action without knowledge is downright dangerous and can quickly destroy us.

Knowledge: Guide for the Intelligence

> A man's pure consciousness is covered by his eternal enemy in the form of lust, which is never satisfied and which burns like fire. The senses, the mind, and the intelligence are the sitting places of this lust, which veils man's real knowledge and bewilders him. (Bhagavad Gita)

Real knowledge is self-knowledge. "Know thyself," the Delphic Oracle advised. Only when we know our true identity can we act properly. Who am I? What am I? First, I must understand what I am not. If my arms and legs are severed, I'm still here. If I analyze the body in this way, I discover that I'm not the body at all. Then, what am I? *Aham brahmasmi.* I am an eternal soul.

What is the soul?

The soul is the subject of many great discourses. Philosophers from Socrates to the present have discussed the soul. It is also discussed in the great religious scriptures of the world: Christian, Hindu, Islamic, Judaic, and Buddhist. The discourse on the soul found in Bhagavad Gita is among the best and explains the subject to my personal satisfaction:

> The individual soul is unbreakable and insoluable, and can be neither burned nor dried. He is everlasting, all-pervading, unchangeable, immovable, and eternally the same. Some look on the soul as amazing, some describe him as amazing, and some hear of him as amazing, while others, even after hearing about him, cannot understand him at all. (Bhagavad Gita)

This is the foundation of knowledge. When the intelligence is properly fixed in knowledge of the soul, it can guide the mind properly.

How does this work?

One technique to allay sexual agitation is to reflect on the true nature of the material body. The body is a bag of blood, pus, urine, bile, and stool. Some gurus suggest that when we are sexually disturbed, we should think of embracing a dead body. Who lusts after a corpse? The person himself is not even there. We even say, "Oh, he's gone." It is not the material body that attracts, but the infinitesimal spiritual spark of life within—that is, the soul.

By thinking of the true nature of the body and the soul, we can slowly gain strength to subdue passion. This is the proper use of intelligence. The intelligence *must* be used to control the mind.

The Mind: Taskmaster of the Senses

> The working senses are superior to dull matter; mind is higher than the senses; intelligence is still higher than the mind; and the soul is even higher than the intelligence.

> Thus knowing oneself to be transcendental to material senses, mind, and intelligence, one should control the lower self by the higher Self and thus—by spiritual strength—conquer this insatiable enemy known as lust. (Bhagavad Gita)

The senses are like five spirited horses pulling a chariot. The chariot is the material body; the mind, the reins. The person seated within the chariot is the soul. Intelligence pulls the reins.

> From whatever and wherever the mind wanders due to its flickering and unsteady nature, one must certainly withdraw it and bring it back under the control of the Self. (Bhagavad Gita)

Accepting and rejecting, accepting and rejecting. This is the mind's business. The mind depends on the intelligence to interpret information fed to it by the senses. Then the mind tells the senses to act in a certain way, or to refrain from acting. The mind is a friend when it acts in real knowledge for one's welfare, but an enemy when it doesn't. As an enemy, it makes one think, "I am this body," and thus causes suffering through repeated birth and death.

The mind is a friend when it is under the control of the intelligence. Then it is serene, grave, self-controlled, and pure. It looks at life simply and directly. When the mind is an enemy, it is controlled from within by desire and from without by sense objects. Then it is restless, frivolous, and impure. Lust makes its abode in the mind and orders it to act for sense gratification. If unchecked, the mind can go mad and lead one to a most hellish place.

Engaging the Senses

> All men are forced to act helplessly according to the impulses born of the modes of material nature; therefore no one can refrain from doing something, not even for a moment. (Bhagavad Gita)

The modes of nature are goodness, passion, and ignorance. All activities fit into one or more of these modes. For instance, out of goodness, people engage in some humanitarian activity. Out of passion, they engage in sex and war. Out of ignorance, they engage in sleep and intoxication. Even sitting in a corner "doing nothing" is doing something. A yogi seated with all his senses drawn inward is doing something: sitting in meditation. A prisoner sitting idly in jail is "doing time." Whether we like it or not, we cannot *do nothing*.

It is said that an idle mind is the devil's workshop. If the mind is not engaging the senses in positive activities, then the senses will engage the mind in sense gratification. For one whose mind is not controlled, the runaway senses tell the mind what to think. Then the hierarchy of soul-intelligence-mind-and-senses is overturned, and one lies exposed and vulnerable to whatever sense objects come his way. If we at all desire the self-control necessary to relish the joy of no sex, we *must* control the mind. Then the mind will control the senses by engaging them intelligently in accordance with spiritual knowledge.

Notes: *This statement is an excerpt from the book* Joy of No Sex *by Kirtananda Swami Bhaktipada. He is the founder of the New Vrindaban Community, which follows the same pattern of belief and worship of the International Society of Krishna Consciousness. This selection outlines his belief that sublimated genital sexuality is a means to true pleasure, higher intelligence, and true knowledge.*

UNIFICATION CHURCH

EXCERPT FROM "THE IDEAL SPOUSE" (1969)

"You women of the Unification Church should not let just some man off the street grab your heart, which you have been cultivating so carefully. Don't be misled. Truly speaking, if your faith has deepened, and if you have had some spiritual experiences, you cannot act carelessly. Love comes from God, and to build unprincipled relationships without God's approval is satanic. To push God aside and to love each other—this is the satanic world.

"If there are some who have been longing for each other, they must repent from the time they hear this speech. Our ancestors sinned and brought terrible consequences upon the world. Therefore, if you marry someone of your own choice, apart from God, you will, far from begin regarded as good ancestors later on, bring about further damage. It is never permissible to love each other in such a situation. You must put everything into God's hands. If you enter a marriage, you must be able to make love with God at the center and seeing His smiling face. Such a relationship is truly the joy of God. Originally, the act of love would not have been a shameful thing at all, but the most precious and sacred experience. But man violated God's Principle, and history has viewed this relationship as an evil and sinful act that we should be ashamed of.

"We must welcome True Parents on the earth in order to create a new history and become new ancestors; the original standard must start from True Parents."

Notes: *In a December 31, 1990 letter to the editors of this volume, Dr. Tyler Hendricks, Vice-President of the United States Headquarters of the Unification Church, explained the significance of this statement:*

"This statement presents concisely the Unification view of 1. the centrality of the family in the order of creation; 2. the centrality of the family, specifically the husband/wife relationship, in salvation history; 3. the absolute goodness of husband/wife love, both

spiritual and physical, in the original (unfallen) creation; 4. the correspondingly crucial function of corrupted husband/wife love as constitutive of the fallen condition of the human race; and 5. the involvement of marriage and family in the ultimate creation of the Kingdom of Heaven on earth at the second coming.''

UNIFICATION CHURCH

EXCERPT FROM "DIVINE PRINCIPLE" (1973)

"Originally, God's purpose of creating Adam and Eve was to form a trinity by uniting them into one body in love as the True Parents of mankind, thus establishing the four position foundation centered on God. If they had perfected themselves without the fall, forming a trinity as the True Parents centered on God, and had multiplied children of goodness, all their descendants would have grown to become married couples of goodness centered on God, each pair forming a trinity with God. Natually, the Kingdom of Heaven on earth would have been realized centering on the first human couple, in accordance with the realization of God's three great blessings to them [cf. Gen. 1:28]. However, due to the fall, Adam and Eve established the four position foundation centered on Satan, thus resulting in a trinity centered on Satan. Therefore, their descendants have also formed trinities centered on Satan, and have brought about a human society of corruption.

"Therefore, God must work to have all fallen men born anew through the True Parents of mankind, Jesus and the Holy Spirit—one as the second Adam and the other as the second Eve—and then having all form respectively a trinity centered on God. But because of the undue death of Jesus, he and the Holy Spirit have fulfilled only the mission of spiritual True Parents, by forming the spiritual Trinity centered on God. Since Jesus and the Holy Spirit have undertaken the mission of spiritual rebirth only, the saints still remain in the position of their spiritual children, having been restored through the spiritual Trinity only.

"Christ must come again in flesh in order that he may become the True Parent both spiritually and physically, by forming the substantial Trinity centered on God. He will then, by giving them rebirth both spiritually and physically, have all fallen men form (by couples) substantial trinities centered on God, after having liquidated the original sin. When fallen men have established the four position foundation in the original form centered on God, then the Kingdom of Heaven on earth will be restored through the realization of God's three great blessings to man.''

Notes: *In a February 5, 1991 letter to the editors of this volume, Dr. Tyler Hendricks, Vice President of the United States Headquarters of the Unification Church, stated that this selection is from a speech that Rev. Moon delivered in Japan in 1969. While it is on "sexual ethics, [it] is not complete at all. In fact there is no systematic treatment of that subject* per se. . . . *[It] expresses the spirit and 'prolegonemna,' if you will, for a Unification treatise on sexual ethics.*

UNIFICATION CHURCH

EXCERPT FROM "CHRISTIANITY IN CRISIS: NEW HOPE" (1974)

"The Lord will not appear miraculously in the clouds of heaven. Why? Because God is sending His Son to restore the things that once were lost. The first ancestors lost the kingdom of God on earth. Satan invaded the world and took Eve to his side, and then Eve took Adam away, leaving God alone and separated from man. All mankind has therefore suffered under the bondage of evil. God must send a new ancestor for humanity, to begin a new history.

''The work of God is restoration, always in the opposite direction from His original loss. This means that God first needs to find His perfected Adam, an Adam who instead of betraying God will become one with God. And then Adam must restore his bride in the position of Eve. Perfected Adam must restore his bride in the position of Eve. Perfected Adam and perfected Eve, united together, will be able to overcome Satan and expel him from the world. In this way, the first righteous ancestors of mankind will begin a new history.

''God's first beginning was alpha. This was invaded by evil, so He will restore the world in omega. Jesus is referred to as the last Adam in 1 Cor. 15:45. God wanted to bless Adam and Eve in marriage when they were perfected. As a heavenly couple, they could bear children of God. This life was not realized in the garden of Eden. That is why Jesus came in the position of Adam. God intended to find the true bride and have Jesus marry. The True Parents of mankind would have begun in the time of Jesus, and they could have overcome and changed the evil history of the world. Since that hope was not fulfilled by Jesus, after 2,000 years he is returning to earth as a man to complete in full the mission he only partially accomplished. The kingdom of heaven on earth will be established at that time.

''The new history of goodness will thus begin. With the truth of God and True Parents for mankind, a new alpha in God's history will begin and continue for eternity. The ideal of God is to restore the first God-centered family on earth. With this one model as a center, all the rest of mankind can be adopted into this family. We will become like them, and the first heavenly family will be expanded, multiplying into the tribal, national, and worldwide kingdom of God on earth.

''Ladies and gentlemen, I believe my message is absolutely clear and simple. God intended to begin the history of goodness in Adam. But Adam fell. God worked to restore history and begin anew in Jesus Christ. But the people of his time lacked faith and did not give him a chance. Therefore, the promise of the Lord of the Second Advent will be fulfilled. He is destined to come to earth as the Son of man in the flesh. He comes as the third Adam. He will take a bride and thereby bring about this most joyful day of heavenly matrimony, referred to as 'the marriage supper of the Lamb' in the book of Revelation. He will fulfill the role of True Parents. True ancestry from God will be established and heaven on earth can then be literally achieved.''

Notes: *This statement by Rev. Moon is from a speech he delivered in the United States in 1974. It explains how the marriages he consecrates are the beginning of the formation of the new Kingdom on Earth.*

Acknowledgments

"Excerpt from 'The Lawful and the Prohibited in Islam.'" Reprinted with permission of American Trust Publications.

Index to Organizations, Statements, and Subjects

Citations in this index refer to page numbers; page numbers rendered in boldface after an organization name indicate the location of that organization's statement(s) within the main text.

Index to Organizations, Statements, and Subjects

Index to Organizations, Statements, and Subjects